FINTECH REGULATION IN CHINA

This is the first book-length treatment of the regulation of financial technology (Fintech) in China. Fintech brings about paradigm changes to the traditional financial system, presenting both challenges and opportunities. At the international level, there has been a fierce competition for the coveted title of global Fintech hub. One of the key enablers of success in this race is regulation. As the world's leader in Fintech, China's regulatory experience is of both academic and practical significance. This book presents a systematic and contextualized account of China's Fintech regulation and, in doing so, identifies and analyzes relevant institutional factors contributing to the development of the Chinese law. It also takes a comparative approach to critically evaluating the Chinese experience. The book illustrates why and how China's Fintech regulation has been developed, if and how it differs from the rest of the world, and what can be learned from the Chinese experience.

ROBIN HUI HUANG is Professor (senior level) at the Faculty of Law, Chinese University of Hong Kong. He is a leading expert in corporate and financial law with a focus on Chinese and comparative issues. He is also Adjunct Professor of Law at the University of New South Wales, Li Ka Shing Visiting Professor of Law at McGill University, Honorary Professor at East China University of Political Science and Law, and Guest Professor at China University of Political Science and Law. He is Specially-Invited Research Fellow of the Supreme People's Court of PRC and Expert Advisor of Shanghai Financial Court. He has had about 120 publications, including 10 books and many papers in premier publishing houses and top journals in the United States, United Kingdom, Australia, Canada, Germany, Israel, Hong Kong, Mainland China and elsewhere. He acts as a Chinese law expert in international litigations and serves as an arbitrator in China and overseas.

FINTECH REGULATION IN CHINA

Principles, Policies and Practices

ROBIN HUI HUANG
The Chinese University of Hong Kong

CAMBRIDGE
UNIVERSITY PRESS

University Printing House, Cambridge CB2 8BS, United Kingdom

One Liberty Plaza, 20th Floor, New York, NY 10006, USA

477 Williamstown Road, Port Melbourne, VIC 3207, Australia

314–321, 3rd Floor, Plot 3, Splendor Forum, Jasola District Centre,
New Delhi – 110025, India

79 Anson Road, #06–04/06, Singapore 079906

Cambridge University Press is part of the University of Cambridge.

It furthers the University's mission by disseminating knowledge in the pursuit of
education, learning, and research at the highest international levels of excellence.

www.cambridge.org
Information on this title: www.cambridge.org/9781108488112
DOI: 10.1017/9781108768962

© Robin Hui Huang 2021

This publication is in copyright. Subject to statutory exception
and to the provisions of relevant collective licensing agreements,
no reproduction of any part may take place without the written
permission of Cambridge University Press.

First published 2021

A catalogue record for this publication is available from the British Library.

Library of Congress Cataloging-in-Publication Data
Names: Huang, Robin Hui, 1976– author.
Title: Fintech regulation in China : principles, policies and practices / Robin Hui Huang, The
Chinese University of Hong Kong.
Description: Cambridge, United Kingdom ; New York, NY : Cambridge University Press,
2021. | Includes bibliographical references and index.
Identifiers: LCCN 2020052361 (print) | LCCN 2020052362 (ebook) | ISBN 9781108488112
(hardback) | ISBN 9781108738446 (paperback) | ISBN 9781108768962 (ebook)
Subjects: LCSH: Financial institutions – Law and legislation – China. | Technological
innovations – Law and legislation – China. | Financial institutions – Technological
innovations on – China. | Financial institutions – Effect of technological innovations on –
China.
Classification: LCC KNQ940 .H828 2021 (print) | LCC KNQ940 (ebook) | DDC 346.51/08–
dc23
LC record available at https://lccn.loc.gov/2020052361
LC ebook record available at https://lccn.loc.gov/2020052362

ISBN 978-1-108-48811-2 Hardback
ISBN 978-1-108-73844-6 Paperback

Cambridge University Press has no responsibility for the persistence or accuracy of
URLs for external or third-party internet websites referred to in this publication
and does not guarantee that any content on such websites is, or will remain,
accurate or appropriate.

To my wife, son and daughter

CONTENTS

List of Figures and Tables   *page* viii
Foreword by Laurence Li SC   ix
Preface   xi
Acknowledgements   xiii
List of Abbreviations   xiv

1 Introduction   1

2 Online P2P Lending   14

3 Initial Coin Offerings   52

4 Cryptoassets   97

5 Mobile Payment   137

6 Data Privacy in Mobile Payment   178

7 Robo-Advisors   222

8 Equity Crowdfunding and Central Bank Digital
   Currency   257

9 Conclusion   286

   Index   291

FIGURES AND TABLES

Figure 3.1 ICO life cycle process   *page* 55
Table 2.1 Geographical distribution of online P2P platforms   21
Table 7.1 A comparison of robo-advisory services between China and the United States   227

FOREWORD BY LAURENCE LI SC

This is a timely book. Professor Huang provides an expert analysis of the Fintech scene in China. It is possibly the most comprehensive review of the topic to date. Practitioners and policymakers will find this book informative and useful reading.

Fintech is the single fastest and largest growth theme in finance and financial services today. And China is leading the world in Fintech development as well as application.

Part of the reason may be the relative 'green field' nature of financial services in China. I once heard a story by a US banker: some years ago, a Chinese official visited the United States and was shown a computerized cheque-reading system. He was dazzled by both the idea that a small piece of paper could in effect represent money and that a machine can clear and execute thousands of instructed transfers per minute.

The same Chinese official later saw the US banker again. This time, he took out his smartphone. China skipped over the whole cheque system – saved expensive investments, avoided dated methodologies and leaped to a way of operating things which runs faster and unlocks more potential.

This book is timely not only because of the positives which Fintech has brought. It is timely also because new things can unlock benefits and risks in equal measure.

I remember when, as a student, I could not get a credit card, and the only credit available to youngsters was student loans. Banks offered debit cards, which could be used at the front end like credit cards. But you must have the money before you can spend it. In retrospect, that was a very effective way of curtailing credit and instilling discipline.

Now, an app can make an assessment of anyone's credit risk and lend, and does so instantly. This is surely smart credit; it's also wide credit. It changes individual behaviour; it changes social capacity; it changes systemic risk level and profile.

P2P lending, crowdfunding, ICOs, crypto assets, robo-advice, mobile payment ... these are many of the new possibilities which Fintech has brought us – and which responsible authorities the world over need to find ways to monitor and regulate with as little stifling as possible.

This book is ambitious in discussing these Fintech possibilities as well as certain attempts at monitoring and regulating them. There are no perfect or universal solutions. That makes this book all the more useful. Its analysis will be of interest to readers on both sides of the aisle.

Regulation must adapt to the market. Fortunately, Fintech itself may offer a large part of the solution. Regtech can help to keep Fintech on its straight and narrow path. Authorities must master the same powerful tools which tech firms and financial service practitioners are deploying. Perhaps that can be the topic of Professor Huang's next book.

I warmly congratulate Professor Huang on this book.

Laurence Li SC
Chairman
Hong Kong Financial Services Development Council
7 December 2020

PREFACE

Financial technology (Fintech) brings about paradigmatic or revolutionary changes to the traditional financial system, presenting both challenges and opportunities. In 2020, when this book was largely written, unlike many traditional businesses, Fintech seemed to be accelerated rather than hampered by the outbreak of the COVID-19 pandemic. Due to the various restrictions and even lockdowns imposed during the pandemic, more people and institutions have embraced Fintech, doing shopping, payment and investment through online platforms. In any event, Fintech looks set to reshape the financial landscape, producing significant impacts on the business community and society at large.

At the international level, therefore, major advancements in Fintech in the past decade have created fierce competition between nations to be the next regional or global Fintech hub. One of the main enablers of success in the development of a robust Fintech market is regulation. Indeed, Fintech has both benefits and risks. Regulation is key to ensuring that we fully enjoy the benefits of Fintech while adequately managing its risks, as well as setting the right direction of development for Fintech in the future.

As the world's leader in Fintech, China's experience is of both academic and practical significance. In fact, China has both stories of success and lessons of failure. The Chinese experience can have important implications for the international discourse and debate on the regulation of Fintech. Fintech is an evolving concept with new products or services emerging constantly. Hence, it seems neither desirable nor feasible to discuss all Fintech sectors in this book, and it would be necessary to be selective about the topics to be covered. I thus choose to focus on the following topics: online P2P lending, cryptoassets, initial coin offerings, mobile payments, data protection, robo-advisory, equity crowdfunding and central bank digital currency.

To the best of my knowledge, this is the first English-language book-length treatment of the development and regulation of Fintech in China.

It has several features which I hope will benefit readers. The first is that it presents a systematic and contextualized account of China's Fintech regulation, so that readers can have a holistic view of the regulatory approach and regulatory perimeter in China. Second, it tries to identify and analyze factors the interaction of which has contributed to the constitution of the institutional environment in which China's regulation of Fintech has been made and enforced. This will help readers understand not only what the law is but also why the law is the way that it is. Third, it takes a comparative approach to critically evaluating the Fintech regulation in China. The comparative analysis covers some major Fintech jurisdictions in the region and internationally, such as in the United States, the United Kingdom, Singapore and Hong Kong. Hence, readers can broaden their horizons and gain a deeper understanding of the strengths and weaknesses of the Chinese experience.

Fintech regulation is a cutting-edge and largely uncharted territory, and the right key can be found only after lots of trial and error. I would appreciate all comments which may help me improve the book in a future edition.

ACKNOWLEDGEMENTS

This book is a product of the research that I have conducted under a project (no. 14613219) funded by the Hong Kong Research Grants Council's General Research Fund, titled 'The Regulation of Fintech in China'. Portions of this book spring from articles that I have published previously, and I am grateful for the use permissions granted by the relevant journals (for Chapters 2–4, European Business Organization Law Review and Banking & Finance Law Review; for Chapters 5–6, Washington University Global Studies Law Review and Chicago-Kent Journal of Intellectual Property).

I thank my editors at Cambridge University Press for editing the manuscript intelligently and efficiently and in the process making it better. I would like to acknowledge the anonymous reviewers who provided extensive comments on my proposal for this book, which proved invaluable in outlining and writing the text.

Thanks also go to the participants in various conferences and workshops held in the United States, Singapore, Mainland China and Hong Kong, including but not limited to Rainer Kulms, Douglas Arner, David Donald, Nicholas Howson, Junhai Liu, Lin Lin, Dong Yang, for their valuable comments on the earlier version of some parts of the book. Dr Charles Chao Wang, Ms Christine Menglu Wang, Mr Xiyuan Li Mr Warwick Wang Lik Chan, Ms Ivana Zhirong Gu, Mr Warwick Wang Lik Chan and Ms Vivian Zhiwei Zhu provided excellent research assistance for this book.

Furthermore, I am indebted to Mr Laurence Li SC, Chairman of Hong Kong Financial Services Development Council; Professor Howell E. Jackson of Harvard Law School; Professor Michael Klausner of Stanford Law School, Professor Omri Ben Shahar of Chicago Law School; Professor Luca Enriques of Oxford Law School; and Professor Simon Deakin of Cambridge Law School for taking the time to review the book and offer very kind and encouraging words in the foreword and endorsements.

Last, but not least, I thank my family members, who have been generous with their support during the development of this project. I dedicate this book to my wife, son and daughter.

xiii

ABBREVIATIONS

AI	artificial intelligence
AML	anti–money laundering
AMLD	Anti–Money Laundering Directive
AMLO	Anti–Money Laundering and Counter Terrorist Financing (Financial Institutions) Ordinance Chapter 615
ASIC	Australian Securities and Investment Commission
ATS	automated trading service
AUD	Australian dollar
BIS	Bank for International Settlements
CBIRC	China Banking and Insurance Regulatory Commission
CBRC	China Banking Regulatory Commission
CFPB	Consumer Financial Protection Bureau
CFT	combating the financing of terrorism
CFTC	Commodity Futures Trading Commission
CII	critical information infrastructure
CIRC	China Insurance Regulatory Commission
CIS	collective investment scheme
CPC	Communist Party of China
CSA	Canadian Securities Administrators
CSRC	China Securities Regulatory Commission
C(WUMP)O	Companies (Winding Up and Miscellaneous Provisions) Ordinance (Chapter 32)
DC/EP	Digital Currency Electronic Payment project
DLT	distributed ledger technology
DNCR	Do Not Call Registry
EC	equity crowdfunding
EFTA	Electronic Funds Transaction Act
EMI	Electronic Money Intuition
EMR	Electronic Money Regulations 2011
ESMA	European Securities and Markets Authority
EU	European Union
FATF	Financial Action Task Force
FCA	UK Financial Conduct Authority

xiv

FDIC	Federal Deposit Insurance Corporation
FinCEN	Financial Crimes Enforcement Network
FIPs	Fair Information Practices
FSB	Financial Stability Board
FSS	Fintech Supervisory Sandbox
FTC	Federal Trade Commission
G7	Group of Seven
GAV	Global Accelerated Ventures
GBP	British pound sterling
GDP	gross domestic product
GDPR	General Data Protection Regulation
GP	general partner
GPS	Global Positioning System
HKMA	Hong Kong Monetary Authority
ICO	initial coin offerings
IMF	International Monetary Fund
INPEF	Internet non-public equity financing
IOSCO	International Organization of Securities Commissions
IP	Internet protocol
IPO	initial public offerings
IRS	Internal Revenue Service
JMLSG	Joint Money Laundering Steering Group
KYC	know-your-client
LHoFT	Luxembourg House of Financial Technology
LP	limited partner
MAS	Monetary Authority of Singapore
MiFID	Markets in Financial Instruments Directive
MIIT	Ministry of Industry and Information Technology
MLO	Money Lenders Ordinance Chapter 163
MMS	multimedia message service
NFC	near-field communications
NIFAC	National Internet Finance Association of China
NPCSC	Standing Committee of the National People's Congress
OECD	Organisation for Economic Co-operation and Development
P2P	peer-to-peer
PBOC	People's Bank of China
PD	Prospectus Directive
PDPA	Personal Data Protection Act
PDPO	Personal Data (Privacy) Ordinance
PSA	Payment Services Act 2019
PSD2	Payment Service Directive 2
PSR	Payment Systems Regulator

PSR 2017	Payment Services Regulations 2017
QR code	quick response code
RGFS	risk guaranty fund scheme
RMB	Chinese renminbi
SAC	Securities Association of China
SAFE	State Administration of Foreign Exchange
SDF	Stellar Development Foundation
SEC	Securities and Exchange Commission
SFC	Hong Kong Securities and Futures Commission
SFO	Securities and Futures Ordinance (Chapter 571)
SGQR	Singapore quick response code
SME	small and medium-sized enterprises
S-PSA	Singaporean Payment Services Act
SOE	state-owned enterprises
SVF	stored value facility
SVF Ordinance	Payment Systems and Stored Value Facilities Ordinance
TLA	Federal Truth in Lending Act
UK	United Kingdom
UMSA	Uniform Money Service Act
US	United States
VATP	virtual asset trading platform
WAP	wireless application protocol

1

Introduction

1.1 Overview

With the rapid expansion of the internet market and the booming of start-ups and small and medium-sized enterprises (SMEs), China has, over the past decade, seen explosive growth of so-called internet finance, a joint product of internet and the financial sector, which is more commonly referred to as Fintech in other jurisdictions. The term 'Fintech', a portmanteau word made of 'finance' and 'technology', is often used to describe the intersection of finance and technology. As the technology is mainly related to the internet, it has come to be known as internet finance in China. In fact, there is no precise and widely accepted definition of internet finance or Fintech. While Fintech is basically understood as technologies which are used to change and improve the existing business mode of finance,[1] internet finance is defined as 'a new type of financial mode that integrates the functions of financing, payment and information media via internet and mobile communications technology'.[2]

Although the two terms may have some subtle difference in terms of their focus, they essentially cover the same subject matter and thus will be used interchangeably in this chapter. For instance, as the Hong Kong Steering Group on Financial Technologies (Steering Group) suggested, Fintech 'may refer to the application of information and communication technology in the field of financial services',[3] mainly including digital payment and remittance, financial product investment and distribution platforms, peer-to-peer (P2P) financing platforms, cybersecurity and data security technology, big data and data analytics, as well as distributed ledgers.[4]

---

[1] Daniel McAuley, 'What Is FinTech', 23 October 2015, https://medium.com/wharton-fintech/what-is-fintech-77d3d5a3e677#.k5c6aipyy.

[2] Financial Stability Analysis Group of the People's Bank of China, *China Financial Stability Report 2014* (China Financial Publishing House, July 2014), p 171.

[3] Steering Group, *The Report of the Steering Group on Financial Technologies*, 26 February 2016, p 13, www.fstb.gov.hk/fsb/ppr/report/doc/Fintech_Report_for%20publication_e.pdf.

[4] Ibid, pp 15–16.

At the international level, major advancements in Fintech in the past few years have created a race among nations to be the next big Fintech hub. One of the main enablers of success in the development of a successful Fintech ecosystem is regulations. Laws and regulations set the direction for Fintech development. If such regulations are too stringent, they may dissuade start-ups, whose lean business models cannot afford to comply with the costly regulations in the traditional manner. But one should not throw caution to the wind, because Fintech is still subject to issues of fraud or loss of investment, and extremely relaxed regulations can put participants in Fintech at risk. Hence, there is a great need to strike a proper balance between fostering innovation and protecting consumers.

1.2 China's Fintech Markets and Regulatory Responses

As noted above, despite the widespread use of the term, Fintech does not have a settled definition. One reason is that the Fintech market is in a constant state of flux, with the rapid emergence of new products and the ongoing evolution of technologies. Furthermore, the Fintech industry appears to vary from country to country because, as a disruptive form of financial innovation, Fintech is closely related to and deeply shaped by the local financial system. Indeed, it is neither desirable nor feasible to come up with a universal and static definition of Fintech. Hence, instead of covering a little bit of everything that might be broadly seen as Fintech, this book will focus on several representative sectors of Fintech in the specific context of China.

1.2.1 Online P2P Lending

As noted earlier, the P2P financing platform is a key Fintech player, which refers to an online platform that matches capital providers and capital users, where the operator of the platform manages and facilitates the financing process. When the financing mode takes the form of a loan, it is usually known as online P2P lending, also called online or P2P lending.

As an important form of the Fintech industry, China's online P2P lending has undergone a roller-coaster period in the past decade.[5] There was an explosive growth in the first several years to become the largest in the world, with online lending platforms having mushroomed across the

---

[5] This topic will be discussed in more detail in Chapter 2.

country. Then, it was followed by a free fall in the past couple of years and hence the market shrank drastically, with the closure or transformation of most of the platforms. There are good reasons behind each of the two phases. The initial rapid development is a consequence of the simultaneous emergence of three key factors, namely deep penetration of the internet, large supply of funds and unmet financial needs. The early market exhibited several distinctive features in terms of the size of platforms, the level of market concentration and business models. As online lending gathers momentum in China, many problems have come to light. In 2016, China issued an important regulation for online lending, introducing a number of significant measures, such as the restriction on the business model that can be adopted by platforms, registration requirements, custodian requirements, information disclosure requirements and lending limits. The regulation has far-reaching implications, including a reshuffling of the market and more collaboration between online lending platforms and traditional banks. However, now it appears that the regulation has failed to achieve its purposes due to the problems with both substantive rules and enforcement mechanisms.

1.2.2 *Offering and Trading of Cryptoassets*

Cryptoassets, or virtual assets, which is another name some would call it, have emerged as a very hot topic of Fintech in recent years, attracting a great deal of attention from market participants and regulators. Bitcoin is probably the most well-known cryptoasset and has frequently popped up in the headlines of newspapers over the years. The number of cryptocurrencies has grown substantially since January 2009 when Bitcoin was created, and other popular cryptoassets include Ethereum, DASH and Ripple, to name but a few. Nowadays even traditional investors would no longer ignore the impact of such cryptoassets. As cryptoassets are still in their early stage of development as compared to other more traditional and regulated trading markets, there are ongoing debates on their nature, usages and risks. It thus becomes very important to find a proper way to regulate cryptoassets, and the regulation of cryptoassets has two distinct but related aspects: one is about its offerings, namely initial coin offerings (ICO) and the other about its trading or use as a medium of exchange and value storing.

The ICOs, or 'token sales', refer to a new fundraising tool which allows organizations, mainly entrepreneurs or start-ups, to launch a business based on distributed ledger or blockchain technology to raise operating

4   INTRODUCTION

funds. The development trajectory of the ICOs in China is broadly similar to that of online P2P lending, or more accurately, the former presages the latter. Specifically, the ICOs underwent a period of explosive growth in China since the second half of 2016 but were then banned in September 2017. The outright ban on ICOs may hamper revolutionary technological developments and dampen the growth of this potentially beneficial market in China. Hence, by completely stifling technology innovation and market development, the Chinese regulatory approach needs to be reconsidered in light of international experiences. Indeed, ICOs can be broadly divided into five categories, namely pre-sales of products or services, offering of shares, issuing of debentures, issuing of derivatives, collective investment schemes and crowdfunding. Instead of a blanket ban, China should adopt a flexible and targeted regulatory approach according to the particular category of the ICOs.[6]

As a result of the broad ban on ICOs, cryptoassets cannot be created nor traded in China. Furthermore, as some scholars have insightfully pointed out, statutory intervention is required for the commodification of cryptoassets, particularly in civil law jurisdictions.[7] This is certainly true for China. As there is not much to be discussed about the Chinese law on cryptoassets, this book will instead look at the relevant law in Hong Kong, which is a special administration region in China and has considerable influence on Mainland China in relation to the financial markets and the relevant regulation. Due to the difficulties in regulating cryptoassets under the traditional framework, Hong Kong has set up its first comprehensive regulatory regime on cryptoassets in November 2018, imposing new standards on cryptoasset fund managers, distributors and platform operators. In November 2019, Hong Kong further clarified its position on the regulation of cryptoasset exchanges. Indeed, while the characteristics of cryptoassets, such as anonymity and disintermediation in transactions, bring significant benefits, they come with a range of significant risks concerning investor protection and market integrity. Overall, the new regulatory regime for cryptoassets in Hong Kong is a significant development, addressing the issues of regulatory gaps and regulatory arbitrage that existed under the previous framework as well as introducing enhanced regulatory standards. This has the effect of improving investor protection, but there are some remaining concerns. Chief amongst them are the

---

[6] This topic will be discussed in more detail in Chapter 3.

[7] See e.g. Rainer Kulms, 'Blockchains: Private Law Matters' (2020) *Singapore Journal of Legal Studies* 63.

problems with regulatory scope, the application of traditional regulatory standards to cryptoassets that do not fall within the definition of securities or futures, problems with the sandbox mechanism, and ultimately as a matter of regulatory philosophy, the need for a better balance between investor protection and market development.[8]

1.2.3 Mobile Payment and Data Protection

China has become one of the leaders in the global mobile payment market in terms of market volume, growth rate and innovation capability. This can be attributed to a number of enabling factors, including technological advancement in China, mobile payment's competitive advantages and its wide acceptance by Chinese people. Mobile payment brings about significant benefits as well as various risks, and thus should be regulated in a way that reaps its benefits while containing the risks as well. Over the past decade, China has gradually established a regulatory regime which is composed of various rules issued by different regulators in a piecemeal manner. China's regulatory regime for mobile payment has several key elements, such as the entry and exit mechanism, management of customer reserves, anti–money laundering measures and consumer protection. The Chinese regulation has strengths and shortcomings, particularly in relation to the overall structure and approach of the regulation. There is also a need to address the negative effects on competition in the mobile payment market that may be brought about by the high entry threshold and the centralized clearing mechanism.[9]

While mobile payment brings great benefits such as convenience, flexibility and efficiency, they are not without risks. Among the risks that consumers face, the data privacy risk is probably one of the most serious, which is in large part caused and exacerbated by the involvement of multiple players and the extensive collection of personal information.[10] China has been trying to consolidate and modernize its regulatory regime for data privacy to suit the need of the new digital era. Over the past few years, China has made great efforts to enact new laws and regulations to delineate the scope of personal information, introduce obligations for data controllers and processors, and incorporate the principles of the Fair Information Practices. However, there are some

---

[8] This topic will be discussed in more detail in Chapter 4.
[9] This topic will be discussed in more detail in Chapter 5.
[10] This topic will be discussed in more detail in Chapter 6.

remaining concerns, including, among others, the ineffective requirements of consent and disclosure, the ambiguous principle of purpose limitation, and the limited applicability of the principle of data minimization. There is a need for China to enact a specific law for data protection, establish a unified law enforcement agency, and enhance private and public enforcement. To be sure, the issue of data privacy is not unique or limited to mobile payment, and this area of discussion may apply to other sectors of Fintech and even beyond.

1.2.4 Robo-Advisor

As a form of artificial intelligence in the financial markets, robo-advisory has grown rapidly to provide automated investment services alongside human advisors. Automated investment advice firms have brought significant benefits by improving the delivery of high-quality and less-biased financial advice. However, robo-advisors also bring risks due to their high dependence on technology. To boost market development, the Chinese government has taken the development of intelligent finance as one of its key tasks. In the area of robo-advisory services, China has several advantages, such as strong consumer demand and a rapidly rising middle class, as well as disadvantages such as regulatory risks and low-level service quality. The overhigh and inconsistent entry threshold, insufficient asset management powers of robo-advisors, weak fiduciary duties and inadequate information disclosure duties have hindered the development of robo-advisory services in China.

Major Fintech jurisdictions such as the United States and Hong Kong have established sophisticated regulatory systems for robo-advisors in crucial aspects such as information disclosure and fiduciary duties. By analysing overseas experiences and local conditions, this research argues that Chinese law should allow robo-advisors to provide limited discretionary asset management services as well as consulting services. It recommends establishing a uniform piece of legislation for both human and artificial intelligence (AI) investment advisors, which contains consistent standards as well as additional requirements for robo-advisors. A streamlined and relaxed regulatory system for the entry threshold of the advisory service market should be established to regulate financial and non-financial companies. The robo-advisors should be subject to more detailed rules on information disclosure duties and fiduciary duties. The service provider and the algorism designer should be jointly and severally liable according to their roles in the investment decision-making processes.

1.2.5 Other Sectors

Equity crowdfunding was once a popular idea in China and almost gained formal recognition of the regulator. However, due to various reasons, particularly the later crisis of its sibling, namely debt crowdfunding or online P2P lending, equity crowdfunding failed to be written into the 2019 Securities Law. This means that in the foreseeable future, equity crowdfunding is unlikely to be legally permitted as a special Fintech sector in China. The situation may change, however, as the Chinese economy is facing increasingly serious downward pressure, and also because there are unique advantages to equity crowdfunding, particularly when it comes to the financing needs of small and medium-sized enterprises.

A very recent major development of Fintech in China is the Digital Currency Electronic Payment project (DC/EP) initiated by the People's Bank of China (PBOC), which is the Chinese central bank. Unlike Bitcoin and other types of cryptoassets, DC/EP has the backing of the credit of a state and is based on a more complicated system of operation. China is at the international forefront of developing central bank digital currency (sovereign digital currency), which has attracted a lot of attention. However, the development is still at its early stage and only time will tell as to how the DC/EP will operate in practice and what effects it will bring to the people in China and beyond.

1.3 Regulatory Framework

As discussed earlier, there is no clear definition of Fintech, and there are a growing number of businesses which could potentially be included under the rubric of Fintech. Indeed, apart from the general feature that they are enabled by the use of new technologies, these businesses are in fact so different from each other, in terms of the nature and type of business or the technologies applied. For instance, online P2P is considered a banking business while equity crowdfunding is one type of securities activity; mobile payment is a banking business while robo-advisor is a service of securities business. Hence, it may be more appropriate to treat Fintech as a new format of business rather than a new industry.

8 INTRODUCTION

1.3.1 Governmental Regulators

As Fintech is not an industry, there is no unified law for the Fintech market as a whole, nor is there a unified industry regulator. This is particularly so in China, which adopts the traditional sectors-based regulatory structure for its financial markets.[11] As the central bank, the PBOC assumes responsibility for monetary policies and the stability of the financial system generally. The China Banking and Insurance Regulatory Commission (CBIRC) and the China Securities Regulatory Commission (CSRC) are the authorities responsible for regulating the banking and insurance sectors and the securities sector, respectively. Before April 2018, the banking and insurance sectors were regulated separately by the China Banking Regulatory Commission (CBRC) and the China Insurance Regulatory Commission (CIRC). The CBRC and the CIRC merged to form the CBIRC in April 2018.[12] For convenience, however, this book still refers to the CBRC as the banking regulator as many relevant rules on Fintech were actually issued by it, unless there is a special need to distinguish between the CBRC and the CBIRC.

On 14 July 2015, the PBOC led a total of ten governmental agencies and ministries to jointly issue 'Guiding Opinions on Promoting the Healthy Development of Internet Finance' (Guiding Opinions),[13] setting out the policy goals and division of regulatory responsibilities for the Fintech businesses in China. The Guiding Opinions consist of three parts. The first part indicates the overall policy of the Chinese government to encourage innovations and support the development of internet finance. In particular, it notes that internet finance can usefully supplement existing financial institutions and play an important role in promoting the growth of SMEs and creating jobs.

---

[11] Robin Hui Huang, *Securities and Capital Markets Law in China* (Oxford University Press, 2014), section 2.2. For a broader discussion of the institutional structure of financial regulation, see Robin Hui Huang and Dirk Schoenmaker (eds), *Institutional Structure of Financial Regulation: Fundamental Theories and International Experiences* (Routledge, 2015).

[12] For a detailed discussion of the reform and its implications, see Robin Hui Huang, 'zhongguo Jinrong Jianguan Tizhi Gaige de Luoji yu Luojing: Guoji Jingyan yu Bentu Xuanze'(中国金融监管体制改革的逻辑与路径：国际经验与本土选择) ['The Logics and Path of the Reform of China's Financial Regulatory Structure: International Experiences and Local Choice'] (2019) 3 *Faxue Jia* 法学家*[Jurist]* 124–137.

[13] Guanyu Cujin Wulianwang Jinrong Jiankang Fazhan de Zhidao Yijian 关于促进互联网金融健康发展的指导意见[Guiding Opinions on Promoting the Healthy Development of Internet Finance] (issued on 17 July 2015 by ten governmental agencies and ministries).

The second part attempts to divide regulatory responsibilities for internet finance amongst relevant regulators. In doing so, it sets out a guiding principle of 'regulation according to law, moderate regulation, sectoral regulation, collaborative regulation, and innovative regulation'. Internet finance is divided into six sectors, namely online payment, online lending (which includes P2P and internet-based small-loan business, equity crowdfunding), online sale of investment funds, online insurance and online trust and consumer finance. As China's central bank, the PBOC has the responsibility for online payment;[14] the CBRC (now CBIRC) for online lending as well as online trust and consumer finance;[15] the CIRC (now CBIRC) for online insurance;[16] and the CSRC for equity crowdfunding and online sale of investment funds.[17]

The third part of the Guiding Opinions outlines eight regulatory propositions for the internet finance markets, serving as a basis for more detailed regulatory rules to be issued by relevant regulators in the future. This includes mandatory disclosures; disclaimers and warnings by internet finance firms about their models and the risks involved; compliance with anti–money laundering laws; online security and privacy; consumer protection rules; and the requirement that all internet finance platforms should entrust commercial banks with the management of their clients' capital.

1.3.2 Self-Regulatory Organization

Apart from governmental agencies, there exist a variety of self-regulatory organizations, which are subject to regulatory oversight by the relevant governmental regulatory agencies, and which have varying levels of responsibility for their respective markets and the conduct of their members. Each traditional industry in the financial market has its self-regulatory organization, such as the China Banking Association, the Insurance Association of China, and the Securities Association of China.

On 25 March 2016, the National Internet Finance Association of China (NIFAC) was established as a national self-regulatory organization in the field of internet finance in China.[18] The NIFAC has ten self-regulatory responsibilities, including[19]

---

[14] Ibid, art. 7.
[15] Ibid, art. 8, 12.
[16] Ibid, art. 11.
[17] Ibid, art. 9, 10.
[18] Official website of the National Internet Finance Association of China, www.nifa.org.cn /nifaen/2955866/2955892/index.html.
[19] Ibid.

1. To organize, guide and urge members to implement national policies and guiding principles concerning internet finance, follow relevant laws and regulations as well as regulatory and normative documents issued by regulatory bodies to ensure compliance in their business operations;
2. To formulate and organize members to sign and perform self-regulatory conventions, encourage fair competence and defend the interests of the industry; conduct research and provide solutions for existing problems in the internet finance service market through communication and consultation; establish dispute and complaint handling mechanism as well as penalty and feedback mechanism for violation of the charter and self-regulatory convention;
3. To coordinate relations between members and between NIFAC (and its members) and relevant authorities; assist the governing bodies in implementing related policies and measures; act as a link and a bridge;
4. To organize industry status surveys, formulate industrial standards and business codes and provide consulting and suggestions for mid- and long-term development plans; collect, gather, analyse and publish basic industry data on a regular basis; comprehensive statistical survey, monitoring and early warning in the field of internet finance while providing information sharing and consulting services; conduct research into innovative products and services in the field of internet finance;
5. To actively collect, sort out and study cases of risks in the field of internet financial services, inform NIFA members and the general public of relevant risks;
6. To formulate business and technical standards and codes, code for professional ethics and standard for consumer protection, and supervise their implementation; establish a consumer complaint handling mechanism for the industry;
7. To provide continuous education and on-job training for professionals as required by the development of the industry to enhance the competence of professionals in internet finance;
8. To enable the function of overall promotion and education of the industry; popularize the knowledge of internet finance; promote the concept of inclusiveness and innovation of internet finance;
9. To organize workshops on business operations among members, mediate disputes among members, and inspect behaviours of members;

10. To engage in interactions on the international level on behalf of internet finance service providers of China; strengthen international exchange and cooperation.

In practice, the aforementioned self-regulatory bodies have actively exercised their powers and played an important role in regulating the relevant markets. For instance, it was the Securities Association of China that issued an important consultation paper on equity crowding;[20] the NIFAC has issued implementing documents on information disclosure for P2P lending businesses,[21] and has also made great efforts to provide guidance on the issue of ICOs.[22]

1.3.3 Local Regulators

The local regulatory authority in charge of financial development and supervision generally refers to the financial work office or bureau established by the local government at the provincial or major-city level.

Taking Beijing's local regulatory authority as an example. It is called Beijing Local Financial Supervision and Administration (北京市地方金融监督管理局).[23] Established in March 2009, it is a municipal government agency responsible for promoting the city's financial development, financial services and financial market construction. Specifically, its main responsibilities include, but are not limited to the following:

1. To implement the national laws, regulations, rules and policies on finance; cooperate with the national financial management department in Beijing; formulate financial development plans and policies for Beijing, and take charge of their organization and implementation;
2. To guide and promote the development of the city's financial market;
3. To coordinate the promotion of corporate financing in the city; guide and promote regulatory development of venture capital funds, equity (industry) investment funds;
4. To coordinate and promote rural financial reforms and development; optimize the rural financial development environment;

[20] See Chapter 8.
[21] See Chapter 2.
[22] See Chapter 3.
[23] See the official website of the Beijing Local Financial Supervision and Administration, http://jrj.beijing.gov.cn/.

promote the construction of rural financial systems and product service innovation; guide the construction and development of rural financial comprehensive reform pilot zones; and coordinate and promote the enhancement of ability to support and benefit agriculture, rural areas and farmers of agricultural-related financial institutions and intermediary service agencies;

5. To coordinate and promote the development of the city's financial development environment, establish and improve a financial service system, and provide services for the state's financial management department and financial institutions in Beijing;

6. To coordinate financial institutions in Beijing to serve the economic development of the capital; provide financing support services for key projects, leading industries, important regional development, and development of SMEs;

7. To coordinate and guide financial services to the people's livelihood; guide and coordinate financial institutions to innovate service products, expand service scope, extend service areas, and improve service efficiency;

8. To promote the construction of the city's financial credit system; coordinate with related departments to promote the construction of corporate and personal credit information systems; participate in the establishment of credit information sharing exchange system and credit reward and punishment mechanism;

9. To study and formulate plans for the overall development of the financial industry in Beijing and promote the rational distribution of financial institutions;

10. To approve and supervise small-loan companies and other financing companies in Beijing;

11. To promote the reform and restructuring of municipal financial institutions; coordinate the campaigns of cracking down on illegal fundraising, illegal securities business activities, illegal futures businesses, illegal foreign exchange trading and anti–money laundering, and anti-counterfeit money work;

12. To guide and coordinate the development and management of financial talent resources and the construction of financial talent team in Beijing.

As shown above, the Beijing Local Financial Supervision and Administration has a wide range of responsibilities, which can be divided into three broad categories: providing regulatory assistance to the central-level regulators such as the CSRC and the CBIRC; exercising its own regulatory powers for certain issues such as the approval and supervision of small-loan companies; and formulate and implement policies for local financial developments. The local financial regulatory authority has played an increasingly important role in the development and regulation of the Fintech market in China.

2

Online P2P Lending

2.1 Introduction

By utilizing modern communication technologies, online peer-to-peer (P2P) lending may reduce certain transaction costs, rendering it economically viable to raise funds through small contributions from a large number of investors. As an attractive alternative to traditional bank financing, online lending has experienced exponential growth around the globe since Zopa.com, the world's first P2P platform, appeared in the United Kingdom in 2005. Within a short span of about ten years, the global online lending volume had reached more than USD 100 billion by the end of 2015 and has been projected to surpass USD 1 trillion by the end of 2025.[1]

The objective of this chapter is to contribute to the international discourse and debate on the aforementioned issue by examining the Chinese experience. On 17 August 2016, a host of Chinese financial regulators and government departments, led by the CBRC, jointly promulgated the Interim Measures for the Administration of the Business Activities of Online Lending Information Intermediary Institutions (2016 Interim Measures on Online Lending).[2] This is the very first time China has set up a relatively comprehensive and workable regulatory

---

[1] Charles Moldow, 'A Trillion Dollar Market by the People, for the People: How Marketplace Lending Will Remake Banking as We Know It', Foundation Capital submission to White House FinTech Summit, 2016, https://foundationcapital.com/wp-content/uploads/2016/07/TDMFinTech_whitepaper.pdf.

[2] Wangluo Jiedai Xinxi Zhongjie Jigou Yewu Huodong Guanli Zanxing Banfa (网络借贷信息中介机构业务活动管理暂行办法) [Interim Measures for the Administration of the Business Activities of Online Lending Information Intermediary Institutions], promulgated on 17 August 2016 by the CBRC and others. In April 2018, the CBRC and the China Insurance Regulatory Commission (CIRC) were merged to form the China Banking and Insurance Regulatory Commission (CBIRC), which oversees both the banking and the insurance markets. For convenience, however, this book still refers to the CBRC as the banking regulator, as it issued many relevant rules. For a discussion of the institutional structure of financial regulation in China, see Chapter 1.

framework specifically for the online lending industry. What mechanisms has this instrument put in place to balance financial innovation and consumer protection? Has the regulatory pendulum swung too far, or not far enough? How has the regime been enforced in practice to date? What factors may have contributed to the recent fall of the P2P lending industry? Are there any lessons to be learned from the Chinese experience? This chapter attempts to provide a contextual, comparative and critical examination of the Chinese experience and, based on such examination, draw implications for the development of China's online lending market and contribute to the international debate on the regulation of online lending.

2.2 The Rise of Online Lending in China: Key Drivers

China has seen a rapid development of online lending in the past decade. In 2005, Zopa.com, the world's first P2P lending platform, was set up in London, and China quickly followed suit with its first P2P lending platform, CreditEase.cn (Yi Xin), appearing in 2006. This good start ushered in a period of exponential growth for China's online lending industry, particularly after 2013, when the Chinese government explicitly resorted to internet finance as a general policy tool to stimulate China's slowing economy. As of January 2017, there were a total of 2,388 P2P platforms in China; the trading volume in 2015 reached USD 67 billion, which was about four times larger than that of the United States and ten times that of the United Kingdom.[3]

How should we account for the rise of online lending in China? In general, an online lending market requires three key factors to thrive: a large number of providers of funds seeking higher-return investments as compared to bank deposits, wide coverage of internet services, and a great demand for small-volume funds. Furthermore, it is important that these three elements emerge simultaneously.[4] It is submitted that China has had the simultaneous emergence of all three factors, thus providing fertile ground for the growth of its online lending market.

[3] Citi GPS, 'Digital Disruption: How FinTech Is Forcing Banking to a Tipping Point', 2016, p 54, https://ir.citi.com/SEBhgbdvxes95HWZMmFbjGiU%2FydQ9kbvEbHIruHR%2Fle%2F2Wza4cRvOQUNX8GBWVsV.

[4] This analytical framework is inspired by that Professor Gilson develops to explain the development of the venture capital market. Ronald J. Gilson, 'Engineering a Venture Capital Market: Lessons from the American' (2003) 55 *Stanford Law Review* 1067, 1076–1078.

2.2.1 High Online Penetration Rate

According to the official data released by the China Internet Network Information Centre, as of June 2019, China had a total of 854 million internet users. The online penetration rate in China reached 61.2 per cent.[5] Given China's large number of internet users, it is perhaps not surprising that China's internet economy has grown rapidly, becoming the world's largest retail e-commerce market. By 2013, China was already ranked as a global leader in terms of its contribution to the national gross domestic product (GDP).[6] In 2019, China accounted for 55.8 per cent of global retail e-commerce sales against a 15 per cent share occupied by the United States, and its share is projected to exceed 63 per cent by 2022.[7] The emergence of e-commerce giants, such as Alibaba and JingDong, provides a solid basis for the online lending platforms, many of which are their financial subsidiaries.

2.2.2 Large Supply of Funds

Furthermore, owing to strict control over the interest rate paid on deposits by traditional banks, Chinese investors are increasingly attracted to online lending, which can offer much higher rates of return. In 2004, China started to relax its interest rate control policy by allowing banks to set their loan rates at a discount of 10 per cent of the official base rate issued by the central bank, the PBOC. This reform process accelerated in the ensuing ten years. Government control over the loan rate was further relaxed to allow a discount of 20 per cent in June 2012 and a further 30 per cent in July 2012, culminating in a complete abolishment of the lower limit on the loan rate in July 2013. A similar reform pattern occurred regarding the deposit rate. In June 2012, the deposit rate given by commercial banks was allowed to be up to 10 per cent higher than the official base for the very first time. This floating-up range was widened successively to 20 per cent in November 2014, 30 per cent in

---

[5] China Internet Network Information Centre, 'Disishisici Zhongguo hulianwangluo fazhan zhuangkuang tongji baogao' (第44次中国互联网络发展状况统计报告) [The 44th Statistical Report on the Development of the Internet in China], 2019, www .cac.gov.cn/pdf/20190829/44.pdf.

[6] Jonathan Woetzel et al., 'China's Digital Transformation: The Internet's Impact on Productivity and Growth', McKinsey Global Institute, 2014, www.mckinsey.com/industries/technology-media-and-telecommunications/our-insights/chinas-digital-transformation.

[7] Emarketer, '2019: China to Surpass US in Total Retail Sales', 2019, www.emarketer.com /newsroom/index.php/2019-china-to-surpass-us-in-total-retail-sales/.

March 2015, and ultimately 50 per cent in May 2015. In August 2015, the cap was removed for the longer-than-one-year term deposit, and finally, in October 2015, the cap removal policy extended to all bank deposits.

It should be noted, however, that the formal removal of limits on the interest rate does not necessarily mean full liberalization or marketization. In practice, the PBOC continues to control or influence the lending businesses of commercial banks, including the setting of interest rates through informal or soft measures, such as the so-called window guidance (*chuangkou zhidao*). For instance, the PBOC may make a call to or organize a meeting with commercial banks to give them advice on the destination and structure of their loans.[8] Window guidance is an ad hoc mechanism usually employed in such special circumstances. One such example may arise when some commercial banks set grossly exorbitant interest rates with the possible or real effect of disrupting the order of the banking market or harming the interest of consumers. While window guidance is suasive and non-mandatory in nature, commercial banks will normally respect and follow the PBOC's advice, given the latter's regulatory role and power.

As such, although there are no formal restrictions on the interest rates commercial banks can set, they cannot deviate too far from the official base rate. In contrast, the interest rate offered by online lending is more marketized. For instance, statistics show that at the end of 2015, the general annualized interest rate of online lending was 12.45 per cent across China, and in some regions, such as the provinces of Shandong and Hubei, the rates were even higher than 16 per cent. This compares very favourably with the one-year term deposit base rate, which was only 1.5 per cent in 2015. The online lending rate dropped in 2016 but was still around 10 per cent. This has provided strong incentive for China's huge population of netizens to take part in the online lending market.

2.2.3   *Unmet Financial Demands*

Now let's turn to the last key element, namely the demand for a more inclusive financial system in China. After having galloped at an average of 9 per cent GDP growth rate over the past three decades, the Chinese economy is now at a crossroads. China's three decades of rapid growth were fuelled by capital investment, exports and consumption. With

---

[8] For certain industries, such as the housing market, the PBOC may still issue special rules on the lending activities of commercial banks.

growth now falling below 7 per cent, China's economy is in dire need of a makeover, and consequently, China has embarked on a national economic restructuring and upgrading strategy under the rubric of supply-side reform. A key element thereof is the national policy of encouraging entrepreneurship and innovation, which manifests itself largely in the growth of start-ups and SMEs. However, it has been notoriously difficult for start-ups and SMEs to obtain finance from China's traditional banking system. The inefficiency of the Chinese traditional banking system is mainly due to the long-standing problem of financial repression in China.

To start with, there has long been a general shortage of credit in the Chinese banking system. The Chinese financial system is over-dominated by the banking sector, which traditionally intermediates almost 75 per cent of the economy's capital, compared with a figure which is typically less than 20 per cent in developed countries.[9] This means that China depends too heavily on the banking system for capital allocation, resulting in an underdevelopment of other financing methods through the securities markets, such as bond and equity markets. Since the PBOC, as the central bank, controls the annual and quarterly quota of loans, commercial banks can, by reference to financial metrics such as the ratio of loan balance to deposit balance, extend the deposit reserve ratio and the total value of loans. In practice, the quota commercial banks receive is such that they can simply focus on higher-value and less-risky clients without the need to do business with others. The problem became more acute after the 2008 global financial crisis because the Chinese government tightened its monetary policy in the post-crisis era to control systemic risks and clamp down on a credit boom brought about by the government's controversial CNY 4 trillion economic revival measure.[10]

Second, when extending loans, the banks generally have a preference for state-owned enterprises (SOEs) or large firms. There are both political and economic reasons behind this. China's banking market has long been dominated by the banks, which are majority owned or otherwise controlled by the state. While government-brokered deals are not as common as in the past, it is still politically safer for those banks to lend to SOEs, even when repayment of the loan may be uncertain. Furthermore,

---

[9] Hui Huang, 'Institutional Structure of Financial Regulation in China: Lessons from the Global Financial Crisis' (2010) 10 (1) *Journal of Corporate Law Studies* 219.

[10] Hui Huang, 'China's Legal Responses to the Global Financial Crisis: From Domestic Reform to International Engagement' (2010) 12(2) *Australian Journal of Asian Law* 157.

2.3 FEATURES OF CHINA'S ONLINE LENDING MARKET 19

making a big loan to a large, more established firm also makes more business sense than lending to many new, small firms which lack qualified collateral and credit repayment records. Even if SMEs do secure loans from banks, whether state owned or not, the interest rates are significantly higher than those of large firms due to risk concerns.

As a result, SMEs, particularly start-ups, are left without easy access to finance from the traditional banking market. The World Bank estimated that only 25 per cent of China's SMEs received bank credit during the period 2011–2013;[11] a more recent report issued by the Development Bank of Singapore and Ernst and Young suggested that only 20–25 per cent of bank loans went to SMEs, even though they account for 60 per cent of GDP, 80 per cent of urban employment and 50 per cent of fiscal and tax revenues in China.[12] Many SMEs are forced to rely upon other sources of financing at exploitative rates. For instance, sometimes SMEs have to pay very high rates, ranging from 36 to 60 per cent, to borrow money from SOEs, which are able to obtain loans from the banking system.

In sum, there is a great need for a paradigm shift in entrepreneurial finance. This has prompted the Chinese government to resort to non-banking financing sources. For instance, in June 2016, China's securities market watchdog, the CSRC, set up a unit with the specific task of pushing forward a pilot programme to facilitate the issuance of corporate bonds to fund innovative and entrepreneurial activities. In October 2016, the first batch of two such bonds were issued to raise a total of RMB 55 million by two high-tech companies. Apart from the development of traditional financial tools, online lending as a key form of internet finance in China has also emerged to foster a more inclusive financial market in China.

2.3 Features of China's Online Lending Market

China has made great efforts to ride the international wave of internet finance to sustain its continued economic growth, seeing it as a significant resource for start-ups and middle- to lower-income citizens alike. Although online lending is a global phenomenon, the online lending market in China has exhibited distinctive features, which must be taken into account in designing and evaluating the regulatory regime in China.

---

[11] World Bank, 'Enterprise Surveys: China', 2013, https://microdata.worldbank.org/index.php/catalog/1559.

[12] Development Bank of Singapore and Ernst and Young, 'The Rise of Fintech in China: Redefining Financial Services', 2016, www.dbs.com/insights/uploads/20161202-03-Report-031-CHINA-FINTECH-LOWRES.pdf.

2.3.1 Highly Dispersed Market with Many Small Platforms

As discussed before, China's online lending market has undergone explosive growth in the past few years, producing a large number of online lending platforms. Most of the platforms, however, are operated by small and medium-sized firms. As of mid 2014, the average registered capital of the firms was about RMB 23.7 million, and the registered capital of most platforms was between RMB 5 million and 20 million.[13] As of mid 2015, only 29.7 per cent of platforms had more than RMB 50 million in registered capital. The market thus has become highly dispersed and competitive, with the largest 100 platforms as a group having only one-half to two-thirds market share. In contrast, the online lending markets in some overseas jurisdictions are far more concentrated. For instance, Lending Club and Prosper together have 98 per cent of the online lending market share in the United States;[14] similarly, up to 88.5 per cent of the British online lending market is in the hands of Zopa and Funding Circle.[15]

Furthermore, according to the identity of their largest shareholder or controller, the platforms could be classified into five groups, namely ordinary private investors, venture capital firms, banks, listed companies and SOEs. As of January 2017, a total of 2,007 platforms, or about 84 per cent of all platforms, were owned by ordinary private investors. They were relatively small platforms, and the aggregate of their trading volume accounted for only 20 per cent of the whole market. By contrast, although there were only fifteen bank-owned platforms, they were considerably bigger and together had about 18.9 per cent of the total trading volume in the online lending market.[16]

2.3.2 Concentrated in Economically More Developed Regions

Table 2.1 shows the geographical distribution of the platforms as of January 2017. The platforms were clearly concentrated in four economically more developed regions, namely Guangdong, Beijing, Shanghai and Zhejiang, which altogether had 1,505 platforms, or 63 per cent of all platforms in China. This is in line with the national policy that online

---

[13] Shen Wei, 'Internet Lending in China: Status Quo, Potential Risks and Regulatory Options' (2015) 31(6) *Computer Law & Security Review* 793, 800.

[14] 'P2P Lending: Banking without Banks', *The Economist*, 1 March 2014.

[15] CrowdfundingHub, 'Current State of Crowdfunding in Europe', 2016, p 63, www.crowdfundinghub.eu/the-current-state-of-crowdfunding-in-europe/.

[16] The figures were calculated using the data collected from Wang Dai Zhi Jia (网贷之家), www.wdzj.com/.

Table 2.1 *Geographical distribution of online P2P platforms*

Locality	Number	Percentage
Guangdong	461	19.3
Beijing	451	18.8
Shanghai	320	13.4
Zhejiang	273	11.4
Shandong	113	4.7
Jiangsu	96	4.0
Hubei	75	3.1
Sichuan	47	1.9
Others	552	23.1
Total	2,388	100

lending is to primarily provide an attractive alternative financing vehicle for entrepreneurial users, notably start-ups and SMEs, in China. In contrast, the online lending market in the United States mainly serves the needs of personal consumption, such as credit card and housing mortgage payments. In the United Kingdom, consumer lending also accounted for a greater proportion of the online lending market than business lending in 2012 and 2013.[17]

2.3.3 Transformation of Business Models

The International Organization of Securities Commissions (IOSCO) defines online lending as 'an online platform that matches lenders with borrowers to provide unsecured loans to individuals or projects'.[18] As it develops at an impressive rate, however, the online lending industry has generated a variety of business models, some of which deviate from the IOSCO's definition of online lending. Below is a survey of several popular business models of online lending.

[17] FCA, 'A Review of the Regulatory Regime for Crowdfunding and the Promotion of Non-readily Realisable Securities by Other Media', 2015, paras 17–18, www.fca.org.uk/publica tion/thematic-reviews/crowdfunding-review.pdf. In 2014, business loans surpassed personal loans in terms of value for the first time.

[18] Eleanor Kirby and Shane Worner, 'Crowd-funding: An Infant Industry Growing Fast', 2014, Staff Working Paper of the IOSCO Research Department, www.finextra.com/finex tra-downloads/newsdocs/crowd-funding-an-infant-industry-growing-fast.pdf.

22 ONLINE P2P LENDING

To begin with, the client segregated account model is a business model that adheres to the IOSCO definition of online lending. Under this model, the platform acts as an information intermediary by disseminating lending information and matching lenders and borrowers. To facilitate transactions, many platforms also provide other value-added services, such as conducting loan rating and borrowers' creditworthiness assessments, offering investment advice and managing repayment. The bottom line, however, is that lenders and borrowers stand in direct contractual relationships, while the platform itself is not a transacting party. On the platform, lenders can choose any businesses or projects according to the lenders' preferences and risk appetites. Once the transaction is consummated, the platform will collect a service fee from both parties. Importantly, all funds from lenders and borrowers are managed by a segregated account, which is separate from the platform's balance sheet. Hence, the funds of lenders and borrowers are not commingled with those of the platform and will not be affected even if the platform collapses. A good example of this model is Paipaidai (拍拍贷), which is one of the largest online lending companies in China. According to the platform's official website, the matching service provided by the platform does not guarantee the commercial merits of the lending transactions.[19]

Owing to information asymmetry, lenders and borrowers naturally lack trust in each other, and there is therefore a demand for the platform to provide more than just passive matching services. This has given rise to a number of business models which allow the platform to extend beyond being a purely informational intermediary. The first such transformation is the so-called guaranteed return model. Anxindai (安心贷) offers a useful example to illustrate how this model works. Guarantee companies owned by Anxindai provide guarantee services for online lending transactions made through the platform. Hence, in the event that borrowers default on loans, the guarantee company will be held jointly and severally liable. This effectively transfers the credit risk from lenders to the platform or its associated entities. The platform provides not only credit-related information but also the service of credit enhancement. As

---

[19] www.ppdai.com/. The so-called notary model is similar to the client segregated account model, in which the platform also acts as an intermediary between lenders and borrowers. The key difference is, however, that the work of originating loans will rest on a bank instead of the platform itself. After the required money proposed by the borrower is reached, the platform will then issue a note to the lender for his or her contribution to the loan, thus handing over proprietary interest. This note is, in general, a security and shifts the risk of non-payment of the loan from the bank to the lenders. The notary model is mainly adopted by online lending platforms in the United States, such as Prosper.

the platform plays a similar role to a traditional bank, this type of online lending is said to have 'bank-like functions'.[20]

The second and more widely practiced transformation is the 'platform lender model' or 'originate-to-distribute model', which clearly deviates from the IOSCO definition. Under this model, the platform is the one that originates loans to the borrowers. The credit funds of the platform are aggregated by managing a pool of assets on behalf of a group of investors through a collective investment scheme. The platforms commonly do so by repackaging borrowers' loans and selling them to investors. This arrangement enables the platform to originate loans to borrowers proactively without the need for the matches to actually occur. Thus lenders and borrowers do not have a direct contractual relationship but rather transact with the platform separately. The platforms profit from the spread between the loan's interest rate and the rate of return promised to the investors. This had been the most popular model in China before the 2006 Interim Measures on Online Lending. Since its nature is different from the traditional P2P definition, it is sometimes called 'marketplace lending'. Previously, CreditEase (宜信), one of the largest Chinese P2P lending platforms, adopted this model.

2.4 The 2016 Interim Measures on Online Lending: Main Elements

The 2016 Interim Measures on Online Lending is China's first instrument enacted specifically for the online lending market, setting up a regulatory regime in a comprehensive and systematic manner. It has a total of forty-seven articles which are divided into five parts, covering all important aspects of the online lending industry. Contravention of the 2016 Interim Measures on Online Lending may attract administrative penalties and even criminal liability.[21]

2.4.1 Business Scope of Online Lending Platform

According to Article 2 of 2016 Interim Measures on Online Lending, the term online lending is defined to mean direct lending made

---

[20] Tyler Aveni, 'New Insights into an Evolving P2P Lending Industry: How Shifts in Roles and Risk Are Shaping the Industry', 2015, p 19, www.findevgateway.org/sites/default/files/publications/files/new_insights_into_an_evolving_p2p_lending_industry_positive planet2015.pdf.

[21] 2016 Interim Measures on Online Lending, art. 40.

among individuals through the internet platform. Individuals include natural persons, legal persons and other organizations. Importantly, the role of the internet platform is restricted to just being an online lending information intermediary institution, whose function is to provide information-related services only, such as information search, information release, credit rating, information exchange and credit matching. In other words, the online lending platform cannot act as a financial intermediary.

The transaction between borrowers and lenders is direct lending in that the borrower pays the principal and interest directly to the lender. The online lending platform enters into agreements with the lender and the borrower in relation to the expense standards and payment modes for the information services it provides.[22] Lenders and borrowers that participate in online lending must be real-name registered users verified by the platform.[23] It is the lender who ultimately has the power to make the lending decision. Without the lender's authorization, the online lending platform cannot make decisions on behalf of the lender in any form.[24]

As a general principle, the platform cannot provide credit enhancement services, nor should it pool funds in a direct or indirect manner.[25] To assist with compliance, the 2016 Interim Measures on Online Lending enumerates a total of twelve specific activities that the online lending platform is not allowed to carry out, including but not limited to: directly or indirectly raise funds for the platform itself;[26] directly or indirectly accepting or pooling the lenders' funds;[27] providing credit enhancement services by directly or indirectly providing guarantee or promising guaranteed principal and interest to lenders;[28] conducting the asset securitization business or assigning claims in such forms as packaged assets, securitized assets, trust assets and fund shares.[29] Those prohibitions effectively outlaw other business models than the client segregated account model, such as the guaranteed return model and the platform lender model.

---

[22] Ibid, art. 20.
[23] Ibid, art. 11.
[24] Ibid, art. 25.
[25] Ibid, art. 3.
[26] Ibid, art. 10(1).
[27] Ibid, art. 10(2).
[28] Ibid, art. 10(3).
[29] Ibid, art. 10(8).

2.4.2 Registration Requirement of Online Lending Platforms

Under Article 5, setting up an online lending platform requires going through a three-step procedure: first, getting a usual business licence from the company registry which is the State Administration of Industry and Commerce and its local branches; second, conducting recordation and registration with the local financial regulatory authority at the place where it is based; third, applying for a relevant telecommunications business permit from the competent communications agency, which is the Ministry of Industry and Information Technology and its local branches. The business licence in the first step and the business permit in the third step are general in nature and thus are not very difficult to attain. The recordation and registration requirement in the second step is specific to the online lending business. However, it does not involve any substantive merit review, nor is there any special requirement in terms of minimum registered capital paid-up capital or capital reserve.

Hence, it represents a light-touch regulatory approach towards the establishment of online lending platforms. The purpose is to let market forces decide on the fate of online lending platforms. It is made clear that recordation and registration do not constitute the recognition and evaluation of the management capability, regulatory compliance degree and credit status of the online lending platform.[30]

On 28 November 2016, the CBRC, Ministry of Industry and Information Technology, and State Administration of Industry and Commerce, jointly issued the Guideline on the Administration of Recordation and Registration of Online Lending Information Intermediary Institutions (2016 Guideline on Online Lending Registration).[31] It provides detailed information on relevant issues in relation to registration, such as what the supporting documents are, how long the processing time is and how the materials should be processed. As the Chinese regime adopts a registration procedure rather than an approval process, the platform can get registered as long as they provide all relevant supporting materials. Local governments need to issue their own local rules to implement the national law, and local

---

[30] Ibid, art. 5(2).

[31] Wangluo Jiedai Xinxi Zhongjie BeiAn Dengji Guanli Zhiy in (网络借贷信息中介备案登记管理指引) [Guideline on the Administration of Recordation and Registration of Online Lending Information Intermediary Institutions] (issued by the CBRC, the Ministry of Industry and Information Technology, and the State Administration of Industry and Commerce on 28 November 2016).

26 ONLINE P2P LENDING

governments have raced to use this legislative power to make rules to promote the online lending industry in their regions.

On 14 February 2017, Guangdong Province firstly issued a consultation paper on the registration matter, providing further details on how the registration matter will be dealt with. Notably, it contains a provision under which the online lending platform is encouraged, albeit not required, to introduce strong legal person shareholders, increase their registered and paid-up capital to RMB 50 million and above, and hire persons with extensive work experience in financial institutions to be their senior managers.[32] Although this is an aspirational rather than mandatory provision, it clearly shows the intention of the Guandong government to make its online lending industry stronger and more professional.

2.4.3 *Lending Limits and Custodian Requirement*

As online lending is inherently risky, it is important that the lenders are suitable for the investment. In principle, the lender that participates in online lending should have investment risk awareness, risk identification capability and experience of investing in non-principal guaranteed financial products, and be familiar with the internet.[33] The online lending platform should remind lenders in a conspicuous manner of online lending risks and prohibited conduct for confirmation by lenders. And it is the duty of the platform to conduct due diligence assessment of the age, financial status, investment experience, risk appetite and risk tolerance, among others, of lenders. The online lending platform cannot provide trading services to any lender that has not been subject to risk assessment.[34]

To limit the exposure of investors to the risk of online lending, investment caps are imposed according to the types of investors. This is also consistent with the function of online lending which is to provide small funding to SMEs, start-ups and individual consumers. Specifically, the balance of loans of the same natural person on one online lending platform cannot be more than RMB 200,000 for a legal person or any other organization, the upper limit is set as RMB 1 million. Furthermore, there are caps on the total balance of loans obtained by the same person

---

[32] Guangdongsheng Wangluo Jiedai Xinxi Zhongjie Jigou BeiAn Dengji Guanli Shishi Xize (广东省网络借贷信息中介机构备案登记管理实施细则) [Guangdong Province Implementing Rules on the Administration of Recordation and Registration of Online Lending Information Intermediary Institutions] (issued on 14 February 2017).

[33] 2016 Interim Measures on Online Lending, art. 14.

[34] Ibid, art. 26.

from different online lending platforms: for natural persons, the cap is RMB 1 million, and for legal persons, it is capped at RMB 5 million.[35] It should be noted that the above limits for lenders are maximum, and the online lending platform can set stricter lending limits according to the risk assessment results of the specific lender.[36]

Furthermore, in response to the outbreak of scandals where platform owners absconded with funds in the past few years, it is required that the online lending platform separate its own funds and the funds of lenders and borrowers for management, and select a qualified banking financial institution as the custodian of the funds of lenders and borrowers.[37]

On 22 February 2017, the CBRC issued the Guideline on the Custodian Business for Online Lending Funds (2017 Guideline on Custodian Business), providing further details on how the custodian business can be carried out.[38] It clarifies that only commercial banks can provide fund custodian services for online lending businesses.[39] This precludes the possibility of having as custodians other types of banking institutions such as policy banks. The commercial bank should set up special custodian accounts and cannot outsource the relevant work such as account opening, trading information handling and trading password verification.[40] Furthermore, the online lending platform can hire only one custodian.[41] This effectively outlaws the so-called joint custodian model where banks and third-party payment institutions jointly act as custodians. As many banks are concerned about their potential liabilities arising from custodian businesses, it is made clear that as a general principle, custodians do not provide guarantees for online lending activities and will not be held liable for lending defaults.[42]

2.4.4 Information Disclosure

Information disclosure has long been the central plank of financial regulation with the important function of creating an efficient market and preventing fraud and other forms of market misconduct. The 2016

---

[35] Ibid, art. 17.

[36] Ibid, art. 26.

[37] Ibid, art. 28.

[38] Wangluo Jiedai Zijin Cunguan Yewu Zhiyin (网络借贷资金存管业务指引) [Guideline on the Custodian Business for Online Lending Funds] (issued by the CBRC on 22 February 2017).

[39] 2017 Guideline on Custodian Business, art. 5.

[40] Ibid, art. 12.

[41] Ibid, art. 14.

[42] Ibid, art. 2, 22.

Interim Measures on Online Lending devotes a whole chapter to the issue of information disclosure. The online lending platform should, on its official website, adequately disclose to lenders the borrowers' basic information, basic information on projects requiring funding, risk assessment and possible risks, utilization of funds in matched but unexpired projects, and other relevant information.[43] The platform is also required to publish its annual report in a designated section on its official website.[44]

Given the importance of information disclosure, there are three mechanisms to ensure the truthfulness, accuracy and completeness of the information disclosed. First, market intermediaries are introduced to act as gatekeepers. The information disclosure must be audited by an accounting firm on a periodic basis; the online lending platform should also introduce a law firm, an information system security assessment or any other third-party institution to assess the regulatory compliance and soundness of information systems of the institution.[45] Second, the online lending platform should submit information disclosure announcements and relevant documents for future inspection to the local financial regulatory authority at the place where it conducts industrial and commercial registration, and place them at the place of domicile of the institution for the public's reference.[46] Finally, the directors, supervisors and senior executives of the online lending platform should discharge their duties in a faithful and diligent manner, ensuring that the disclosed information is true, accurate, complete, timely and fair and contains no false records, misleading statements or material omissions.[47]

On 28 October 2016, the National Internet Finance Associate of China (NIFAC) issued two implementing rules on information disclosure, namely the Standard on Internet Finance Information Disclosure for Online Lending (2016 Standard on Information Disclosure)[48] and the NIFAC Rule on Self-regulation of Information Disclosure.[49] There are a total of ninety-six items for disclosure, of which sixty-five are mandatory and

---

[43] 2016 Interim Measures on Online Lending, art. 30.
[44] Ibid, art. 31.
[45] Ibid, art. 31.
[46] Ibid, art. 31.
[47] Ibid, art. 32.
[48] Hulianwang Jinrong Xinxi Pilu Geti Wangluo Jiedai (互联网金融信息披露个体网络借贷) [Standard on Internet Finance Information Disclosure for Online Lending] (issued by the National Internet Finance Associate of China on 28 October 2016).
[49] Zhongguo Hulianwang Jinrong Xiehui Xinxi Pilu Zilv Guanli Guifan (中国互联网金融协会信息披露自律管理办法) [NIFAC Rule on Self-regulation of Information Disclosure] (issued by the National Internet Finance Associate of China on 28 October 2016).

thirty-one are encouraged. They are divided into three categories. The first category is the institutional information about the online lending platform, including the basic information (e.g. the platform's name, registered and paid-up capital), governance information (e.g. directors, supervisors, senior management and actual controller), and accounting information and major events such as mergers, divisions and bankruptcy. The second category contains information related to the projects seeking funds, including the basic information of the borrower and the information about the project. The third category of information is statistics about the operation of the online lending platform, such as the total trading value, the total number of transactions, the total number of borrows, the total number of lenders and the total value of loans to be repaid.

About one year later, drawing upon the two implementing rules issued by the NIFAC, the CBRC promulgated the Guideline on Information Disclosure of the Business Activities of Online Lending Information Intermediary Institutions on 25 August 2017 (2017 Guideline on Information Disclosure).[50] Importantly, unlike the NIFAC which is a self-regulatory body, the CBRC has rule-making powers such that the 2017 Guideline on Information Disclosure carries the force of law. In terms of regulatory approach, the 2017 Guideline on Information Disclosure is broadly similar to the NIFAC rules, but with more detailed guidance and stricter rules on some matters. For instance, it further divides information disclosure requirements for the online lending platform into five categories, including registration information, organizational information, approval information, operational information and project information. Furthermore, it clarifies the definition of some important terms used in the information disclosure documents, such as defaulted loans, default volumes and default rates, in a bid to enhance the accuracy of information disclosure and facilitate comparability between different lending platforms.

2.5 Implications and Evaluations

2.5.1 The Online Lending Industry Facing A Big Reshuffle

As discussed earlier, China's online lending market has undergone a phase of explosive growth in the past few years, with online lending

---

[50] Wangluo Jiedai Xinxi Zhongjie Jigou Yewu Huodong Xinxi Pilu Zhiyin (网络借贷信息中介机构业务活动信息披露指引) [Guideline on Information Disclosure of the Business Activities of Online Lending Information Intermediary Institutions] (promulgated by the CBRC on 25 August 2017).

platforms having mushroomed across the country. In 2015, for example, the number of the platforms grew by almost 40 per cent, but the growth rate slowed down to about 10 per cent in 2016.[51] This is because the online lending market suffered from an outbreak of scandals in late 2015 and China started to tighten the regulation of the market from then on. For instance, in December 2015, it was exposed that an online lending platform called Fanya Metal Exchange had illegally raised more than RMB 40 billion; later in the same month, an even bigger scandal came to light involving a Shenzhen-based platform known as Ezu Bao which had reportedly bilked investors for more than RMB 50 billion in about one and a half year; and in April 2016, the Shanghai-based Zhongjin group was found to have illegally raised more than RMB 30 billion. As of June 2016, there were a total of 1,778 problematic platforms, representing 43.1 per cent of all platforms.[52]

It is against this background that the 2016 Interim Measures on Online Lending was promulgated as an effort to clean up the market. Further details are fleshed out by three important implementing rules, namely the 2016 Guideline on Online Lending Registration, the 2017 Guideline on Custodian Business and the 2017 Guideline on Information Disclosure. Together, within a short span of time, they have now set up a relatively complete regulatory regime for online lending in China, widely dubbed the 'one plus three' framework, putting an end to previous lawlessness which resulted in orderless growth of the underlying market. In general, this represents a positive development and has been welcomed by the market as evidenced by the rebound in trading volume in November 2016.

The newly established legal regime will undoubtedly have far-reaching implications for the online lending market in China. Although it is hard to predict with precision at this early stage, what is certain is that the online lending industry is going to face a storm of reshuffling. In fact, on 13 April 2016, four months before the promulgation of the 2016 Interim Measures on Online Lending, the CBRC had issued a notice to launch a campaign to manage the risks of online lending and crack down on fraudulent P2P lenders.[53] The valuable information and experience

---

[51] The figures were calculated using the data collected from Wang Dai Zhi Jia (网贷之家), www.wdzj.com/.

[52] See official website of the CBRC, www.cbrc.gov.cn/index.html.

[53] Guanyu Yinfa P2P Wangluo Jiedai Fengxian Zhuanxiang Zhengzhi Gongzuo Shishi Fangan de Tongzhi (关于印发P2P网络借贷风险专项整治工作实施方案的通知) [Notice on Issuing the Implementing Plan for the Work on Managing Risks of Online P2P Lending] (issued by the CBRC on 13 April 2016).

obtained from the campaign may have informed the drafting of the 2016 Interim Measures on Online Lending, and now the new regime provides a solid legal basis for continuing to carry out the campaign.

As discussed before, the role of the online lending platform is restricted to that of purely informational intermediaries and they therefore cannot function as financial intermediaries. It is not allowed to provide credit enhancement services, nor can it use securitization techniques. This effectively rules out the legality of other business models than the client segregated account model. It is estimated that more than half of China's online lending platforms will have to change their business models which can be a painful process for many. Coupled with the new requirements in relation to custodian, information disclosure and registration. it is likely that many small and weak platforms with poor internal control mechanisms may be driven out of the market. In principle, this is exactly what is needed, as those platforms are more likely to have problems in practice. From a comparative perspective, there are simply too many online lending platforms in China and the market needs to be more concentrated to allow the emergence of online lending giants which will become national champions and even compete on the international level.

2.5.2 More Collaboration between Online Lending Firms and Banks

Another important change brought about by the new regime might be that there will be more collaboration between online lending platforms and traditional banks. As discussed earlier, the online lending platform is required to appoint a custodian which will be commercial banks. In fact, due to the high incidence of problems and scandals, the online lending industry as a whole suffered significant reputational damage. Many platforms thus tried to have collaboration with banks, such as having banks act as custodians, in order to restore and improve their credibility. However, many banks were very reluctant to do so because they were concerned about the potential liability arising from the provision of custodian services. Before the promulgation of the 2017 Guideline on Custodian Business, only 4 per cent of online lending platforms succeeded in securing custodian services from banks.

Now, the 2017 Guideline on Custodian Business sets out detailed provisions on the role and responsibility of the custodian, thereby alleviating the liability concerns of the banks. It provides that fund custodians shall undertake the responsibilities for the formal examination of real-name account opening, performance of contractual agreements, and overall agreement of lending trade orders, and shall not undertake the substantive examination of the authenticity of information on projects needing funding and lending transactions.[54] Importantly, it is made clear that the custodian will not be held liable for lending defaults.

Hence, banks will be more willing to provide custodian services to online lending platforms. This actually presents a very attractive new business opportunity for banks whose traditional source of revenue, namely the spread between deposit rate and loan rate, has been narrowing significantly in recent years. To be sure, the custodian requirement introduces a new item of cost which will ultimately be transferred to the borrowers. This cost is, however, well justified as it can effectively prevent fraudulent activities, particularly the so-called runaway issue (*pao lu*, namely platform owners absconding with funds), which has occurred frequently in the past few years. For instance, in 2015 and 2016, there were a total of 3,056 cases of problematic platforms, and 32 per cent of them (982 platforms) were in the category of runaway issue.[55] The custodian fee that banks will charge is not regulated, but subject to the negotiation between the platform and its custodian bank. It is hoped that as many banks will likely enter into the custodian services market, competition amongst them will help drive down bank fees and keep them at a reasonable level.

2.5.3 The Central-Local Cooperative Regulatory Framework: Innovative but Uncertain

The 2016 Interim Measures on Online Lending sets up a multi-layered regulatory architecture which comprises multiple regulators at both the central and local level. Overall, the CBRC acts as the lead regulator for China's online lending market, empowered to develop rules for the supervision and administration of the business activities of online lending platforms as well as carry out conduct of business regulation.[56] The current financial regulatory framework in China has the defining feature of being sectors-based, with three sector-specific regulators responsible

---

[54] 2016 Interim Measures on Online Lending, art. 72(3).
[55] The figures were calculated using the data collected from Wang Dai Zhi Jia (网贷之家), www.wdzj.com/.
[56] The 2016 Interim Measures on Online Lending, art. 4.

2.5 IMPLICATIONS AND EVALUATIONS

for banking, securities and insurance, respectively, including the CBRC, the CSRC and the CIRC.[57] Online lending is considered something similar to banking businesses in China and hence falls within the jurisdiction of the CBRC.

In fact, the idea of assigning online lending to the jurisdiction of the CBRC is not initiated by the 2016 Interim Measures on Online Lending. As early as in 2011, the CBRC already claimed jurisdiction over online lending by issuing a notice on the potential risks of online lending.[58] As online lending operates outside of the traditional banking system, it is seen as part of the shadow banking system in China. In 2014, the Chinese central government, namely the State Council, promulgated an important document with respect to the regulation of shadow banking in China, known as Circular No. 107.[59] This instrument lays the groundwork for the allocation of regulatory responsibilities for shadow banking amongst different regulators, under the principle of 'separate operation, separate regulation'.[60] However, it does not specify who regulates internet finance businesses, largely because back then, the Chinese government was unsure of the proper way of regulating internet finance. Rather, it authorizes the central bank, namely the PBOC, to coordinate with other relevant regulators to work out how best to regulate internet finance businesses. One year later, in 2015, the PBOC led a group of ten government agencies, including, *inter alia*, the CBRC, CSRC and CIRC, which issued a rule to divide the regulatory responsibilities for various types of internet finance businesses.[61] For instance, the CSRC is tasked with regulating equity crowdfunding while online lending is assigned to the CBRC.

[57] Hui Huang, 'Institutional Structure of Financial Regulation in China: Lessons from the Global Financial Crisis' (2010) 10 (1) *Journal of Corporate Law Studies* 219.

[58] Zhongguo Yinjianhui Bangongting Guanyu Renrendai Youguan Fengxian Tishi de Tongzhi (中国银监会办公厅关于人人贷有关风险提示的通知) [Notice on Relevant Risks of Peer to Peer Lending by the General Office of China Banking Regulatory Commission] (issued by the CBRC on 23 August 2011).

[59] Guowuyuan Bangongting Guanyu Jiaqiang Yingzi Yinhang Jianguan Youguan Wenti de Tongzhi (国务院办公厅关于加强影子银行监管有关问题的通知) [Circular of the General Office of the State Council 2005 on Relevant Issues of Strengthening the Regulation of Shadow Banking] (State Council Circular No. 107, 2013) (hereinafter Circular No. 107).

[60] Hui Huang, 'The Regulation of Shadow Banking in China: International and Comparative Perspectives' (2015) 30 *Banking and Finance Law Review* 481.

[61] Guanyu Cujin Hulianwang Jinrong Jiankang Fazhan de Zhidao Yijian (关于促进互联网金融健康发展的指导意见) [Guiding Opinion on the Promotion of Healthy Development of Internet Finance Businesses] (issued by a group of ten government agencies led by the PBOC on 18 July 2015).

Hence, the 2016 Interim Measures on Online Lending just reaffirms the authority of the CBRC over the online lending market.

Furthermore, as online lending is a form of Fintech involving the application of technology, other governmental agencies also perform important regulatory functions. First, the Ministry of Industry and Information Technology has the responsibility of conducting supervision over the telecommunications business involved in the online lending business activities. Second, the Ministry of Public Security has power to conduct supervision over the security of internet services provided by online lending platforms, investigate and punish violations and crack down on financial crimes involved in online lending businesses. Third, the State Internet Information Office is responsible for conducting supervision over financial information services and internet information contents.

Importantly, the regulatory framework has a local dimension. Provincial governments are authorized to conduct recordation and registration of online lending platforms within their respective jurisdictions. In practice, this task will be performed by the agency called financial work office (*jinrong gongzuo bangongshi*) set up by the provincial people's governments. Apart from governmental agencies, self-regulatory bodies, notably the NIFAC, are involved in the supervision of the conduct of their members. It should be noted, however, that self-regulatory bodies in China are usually subject to the regulatory oversight of the relevant governmental regulatory agencies. For instance, the NIFAC is actually under the control of the PBOC.

This central-local cooperative supervisory arrangement is an innovative mechanism with a number of important advantages. The local authority is familiar with and proximate to the market within its jurisdiction. Compared to the central government, the local government should have a closer sense of the development and attendant risks in the market place. It may be privy to local information that the central government does not possess or pay adequate attention to. This is particularly important in a top-down society like China where the central government imposes tight control over the financial market on the basis of the limited information (sometimes false information) it obtains from local governments. For instance, the governor of LiaoNing Province has recently admitted that the province had faked its economic figures for years, dealing a massive blow to the national statistics' credibility.[62]

---

[62] Frank Tang, 'Chinese Province Admits to Cooking Its Books', *South China Morning Post*, 18 January 2017, www.scmp.com/news/china/economy/article/2063125/liaoning-governor-confirms-economic-data-faked-2011-2014.

Furthermore, the local government should be better equipped in adapting elements of its supervisory arrangements to meet the needs of the local market and its users through tailor-made rules. The local government has a natural intimacy with the local market and is likely to be more sensitive to the local conditions. They can respond to the local problems more quickly than the central government. On the legislative side, under China's lawmaking regime, it takes a considerably longer time to pass a national law than a local regulation. On the enforcement side, the proximity of the local authorities enables them to better monitor and supervise the market on a real-time basis.

The arrangement is, however, not without its challenges. Like the long-standing debate on the effect of the competition among American states for corporate charters, there are legitimate concerns over whether the local authorities will race to the top or the bottom in regulating its own online lending markets. The internet has no boundaries, which renders the place to set up the online lending platform unimportant. It is certainly possible that the local authority may try to attract more platforms to its region by setting more lax registration standards. Furthermore, under the arrangement, the local governments need to bear the cost of regulation.

Hence, the local government may pass the buck to the central government, particularly because the delineation of responsibility is not clear-cut. This may raise a raft of issues in practice. For instance, if an online lending platform commits misconduct, is it the responsibility of the local government or the central government? Who should come to handle the case, the local authority or the CBRC? The local authority is responsible for the registration process, but interestingly enough, it also has the power to impose penalties on misbehaving platforms.[63] In such case, how should the CBRC perform its regulatory role? Should the CBRC step in only when the local authority fails to regulate for various reasons, such as local protectionism? It will be a challenge to ensure that, sophisticated as it is, the central-local cooperation does not create regulatory conflicts, gaps and overlaps.

It is hoped that the above issues might be mitigated by the self-interest of the local government under the pressure of market competition. The law and finance literature has demonstrated strong correlation between efficient financial markets and economic growth. This is because, as a World Bank report shows, efficient financial markets can help overcome barriers to market entry, thereby facilitating economic growth and

---

[63] 2016 Interim Measures on Online Lending, art. 40.

reducing inequality.[64] Indeed, the local government is the beneficiary of the booming local market. The local regulatory arrangement may thus bestow a commercial incentive on the local government to ensure that it discharges supervisory responsibilities effectively through its vested interest in maintaining reputation and attracting investment.

2.5.4 Appropriateness of the Regulatory Approach: A Comparative Perspective

In essence, the significance of the 2016 Interim Measures on Online Lending lies in the legalization of online lending through a system of registration, disclosure, lending limit and obligation that is designed to achieve two main objectives, namely facilitating the growth of the online lending market and protecting financial consumers. The regulatory challenge, as always, is to prevent abuses without stifling market development and innovation. Fintech represents not only a shift in digital technology, but more importantly a paradigm change in finance and growth. Around the world, regulators are still getting to grips with the risks and realities of internet finance. This section will thus evaluate the appropriateness of China's regulatory approach from a comparative perspective.

2.5.4.1 Law and Development: Regulation or Prohibition?

At a fundamental level, China's regulatory approach towards online lending is consistent with its gradualist style of economic reform which is carried out on a trial-and-error basis. In the interest of providing ample room for the development of internet finance, China firstly adopted a *laissez faire* approach towards it. This may seem somewhat strange as China's financial regulation is traditionally characterized by conservatism and repression. To a large extent, before the promulgation of the 2016 Interim Measures on Online Lending, there was effectively a regulatory vacuum for online lending, leading to the 'wild west' quality of the existing online lending market. Nevertheless, it should be recognized that this loose regulatory environment had been conducive to the internet finance players thriving in areas such as online lending and online payments. A report issued by McKinsey Corporate Banking praised China's 'open, supportive regulatory environment' in making

---

[64] Stijin Claessens and Enrico Perotti, 'The Links between Finance and Inequality: Channels and Evidence' *Background Paper for World Development Report 2006*, 2005, www .rrojasdatabank.info/wir2006/claessens.pdf.

2.5 IMPLICATIONS AND EVALUATIONS 37

China the largest P2P lending marketplace in the world.[65] This 'development first and regulation later' approach has long been regarded as a successful experience of China's impressive economic development.

In Japan and Taiwan,[66] online lending is strictly prohibited to avoid its potential risks, but this approach is not an option for China. According to a report issued by Mr Liu Mingkang, the former chairman of the CBRC, despite the serious problems with online lending platforms, there is little need for a blanket prohibition on online lending, as the overall systemic risk currently posed by online lending in China is relatively small.[67] Indeed, regulation rather than prohibition should be a more appropriate approach. To be sure, a defect in the regulatory response to financial market scandals is that it is reactive rather than proactive. The law follows the impugned behaviour of the online lending platforms and changes to repair the things as done. This may come with significant costs, but the law does not seem to have the ability of foresight and cannot prevent the abuse before it occurs. The opportunity cost can be prohibitive if prophylactic rules were put in place to prevent rather than cure such abuses, particularly in an emerging area such as internet finance where innovation is highly valued. Internet finance such as online lending can be a very important tool to facilitate China's transition from financial repression to financial liberalization, and ultimately help realize its goal of 'Public entrepreneurship, innovation' (*dazhong chuangye, wanzhong chuangxin*).

2.5.4.2 United Kingdom: Special Licence and Minimum Capital Requirements

As noted before, the United Kingdom is the birthplace of online lending, with Zopa, the world's first P2P lending platform, being founded as early as 2004 (its first loan originated in 2005). Online lending platforms are required to be pure matchmakers, and client funds must be in the custody of a third party. Hence, online lending platforms in the United Kingdom

---

[65] Joseph Luc Ngai et al, 'Disruption and Connection: Cracking the Myths of China Internet Finance Innovation', McKinsey Greater China FIG Practice, 2016, www.mckinsey.com /~/media/mckinsey/industries/financial%20services/our%20insights/whats%20next% 20for%20chinas%20booming%20fintech%20sector/disruption-and-connection-cracking -the-myths-of-china-internet-finance-innovation.ashx.

[66] Eleanor Kirby and Shane Worner, 'Crowd-funding: An Infant Industry Growing Fast', *Staff Working Paper of the IOSCO Research Department*, 2014, p 32, www.finextra.com /finextra-downloads/newsdocs/crowd-funding-an-infant-industry-growing-fast.pdf.

[67] Liu Mingkang, 'Internet Finance and Regulation in China', Fung Global Institute Report, 2015, p 21, www.asiaglobalinstitute.hku.hk/storage/app/media/news%20and% 20insights/pdf/FGI-Report-Internet-Finance-part-I-Main-Report-2.pdf.

such as Zopa and Lending Circle adopt the client segregated account model for carrying on business.[68] The United Kingdom's current P2P regulatory framework came into existence in April 2014, when the Financial Conduct Authority (FCA) published the Policy Statement 14/4, entitled 'The FCA's Regulatory Approach to Crowdfunding over the internet, and the Promotion of Non-Readily Realisable Securities by Other Media: Feedback to CP13/13 and Final Rules'. This document sets out detailed rules specifically pertaining to loan-based (P2P) and investment-based crowdfunding (equity crowdfunding). It should be noted that separate rules apply to the two different types of crowdfunding platforms since the FCA considers online lending to be less risky than equity crowdfunding.

First, any firm wishing to enter the online lending market after 2014 'must first secure full authorization from the FCA'.[69] According to a later document the FCA issued, in deciding whether to grant authorization of crowdfunding businesses, the FCA will look at a range of factors, including planned activities and related risks, budget and resources (human, systems and capital), and a running website to demonstrate user interface.[70] Second, disclosure obligations are imposed on platforms, ensuring that 'customers interested in lending [...] had access to clear information, which would allow them to assess the risk and to understand who will ultimately borrow the money'.[71] Third and most notably, a minimum capital requirement has been introduced, under which online lending platforms are required to have at least 20,000 GBP in legal capital.[72]

There are some other regulatory requirements, including reporting requirements for firms to send information to the FCA, a plan to ensure that existing loans continue to be managed in case the platform crashes,

---

[68] Patrick Jenkins, 'US Peer-to-Peer Lending Model Has Parallels with Subprime Crisis: Credit Quality of Some Loans Is Triggering Concerns', *Financial Times*, 30 May 2016, www.ft.com/content/84f696ec-2436-11e6-9d4d-c11776a5124d.

[69] FCA, 'The FCA's Regulatory Approach to Crowdfunding over the Internet, and the Promotion of Non-Readily Realisable Securities by Other Media: Feedback to CP13/13 and Final Rules', 2014, p 6, www.fca.org.uk/publication/policy/ps14-04.pdf.

[70] FCA, 'A Review of the Regulatory Regime for Crowdfunding and the Promotion of Non-readily Realisable Securities by Other Media' (2015), para 44, www.fca.org.uk/publication/thematic-reviews/crowdfunding-review.pdf.

[71] Ibid, p 49.

[72] FCA, 'The FCA's Regulatory Approach to Crowdfunding over the Internet, and the Promotion of Non-Readily Realisable Securities by Other Media: Feedback to CP13/13 and Final Rules', 2014, para 12.3, www.fca.org.uk/publication/policy/ps14-04.pdf.

2.5 IMPLICATIONS AND EVALUATIONS

rules the firm must follow when holding clients' money and rules on dispute resolution. The FCA further supervises the platforms through engaging with senior management members, monitoring websites and reviewing monthly management information. If it notices irregularities, it has the power to step in and intervene to 'ensure proper protection of consumers'.[73] Apart from the regulation of the FCA, online lending platforms in the United Kingdom also establish a self-regulatory body called Peer-to-Peer Finance Association.

2.5.4.2 United States: Burdensome Securities Regulatory Process

In contrast with the United Kingdom, the United States does not restrict online lending to any particular business model. Prosper and Lending Club, the two main online lending platforms in the United States, both adopt the notary model where the work of originating loans rests on a partner bank instead of the platform itself and, based on the loan, the platform issues payment dependant notes to lenders.[74] Hence, unlike their counterparts in the United Kingdom, Prosper and Lending Club are not purely informational intermediaries.

Although the United States is one of the world's leading jurisdictions for development in the Fintech sector, its regulatory regime for P2P lending is overly complex, including both its federal and state requirements. At the state level, each individual state takes different approaches to regulation, ranging from a complete ban, to 'allowing platforms to elicit borrowers and sophisticated lenders only', to 'allowing activity in accordance to SEC regulatory criteria'.[75] The focus of discussion here is on the regulation at the federal level.

As early as in 2008, the US federal securities regulator, namely the Securities and Exchange Commission (SEC), exercised authority over online lending, by sending Prosper, one of the United States' largest P2P lending platforms, a cease and desist letter.[76] The SEC declared that P2P lending platforms such as Prosper must comply with the 1933 Securities Act, on the grounds that the loans/notes being offered by the platforms

---

[73] Ibid.

[74] US Government Accountability Office, 'Person-to-Person Lending: New Regulatory Challenges Could Emerge as the Industry Grows', 2011, p 13, www.gao.gov/new.items /d11613.pdf.

[75] Ibid, pp 26–30.

[76] Paul Slattery, 'Square Pegs in a Round Hole: SEC Regulation of Online Peer-to-Peer Lending and the CFPB Alternative' (2013) 30 *Yale Journal on Regulation* 233, 252.

constitute 'investment contracts' as defined in *SEC v. W.J. Howey Co.*,[77] and also 'notes' as found in *Reves v. Ernst & Young*.[78] Hence, it is necessary to register the loans/notes with the SEC, because it is 'unlawful to sell securities without an approved registration statement and prospectus'.[79] To become registered, 'more than 32 pieces of information' in addition to accounting records of the 'last 3 years of the company's business' are required. This is a very burdensome requirement which amounts to carrying out an initial public offer, thereby imposing significant compliance costs on online lending platforms. Most online lending platforms in the United States did not have the capital and resources to survive the securities regulatory process and eventually were pushed out of the market. Even the United Kingdom's Zopa chose to leave the United States altogether to avoid dealing with the stringent regulations.

The 2011 Dodd-Frank Wall Street Reform and Consumer Protection Act suggested an alternative approach in which P2P lending platforms would be regulated entirely through the Consumer Financial Protection Bureau (CFPB), a federal institution created as a result of the global financial crisis of 2008. The CFPB's 'broad discretion over financial entities' would allow it to adjust regulatory requirements where necessary, giving start-ups potential to enter into the market, and to effectively monitor these platforms more closely.[80] Unfortunately, a proposal to implement this idea did not pass in the US Congress. Now, with President Trump's desire to disempower the CFPB, it seems unlikely that P2P regulation in the United States will improve anytime soon.[81]

2.5.4.4 Hong Kong: Uncertain and Burdensome Rules under Existing Regulation

Hong Kong has not set up any specific regulations pertaining to online lending businesses, but rather relies on its existing law to regulate online lending. The actions and services online lending platforms provide could

---

[77] *Securities and Exchange Commission v. W. J. Howey Co.*, 328 US §§ 293, 301 (1946).

[78] *Reves v. Ernst & Young*, 494 US 56 (1990).

[79] Paul Slattery, 'Square Pegs in a Round Hole: SEC Regulation of Online Peer-to-Peer Lending and the CFPB Alternative' (2013) 30 *Yale Journal on Regulation* 233, 257.

[80] Ibid, p 261.

[81] Michelle Singletary, 'Trump's election does not bode well for the Consumer Financial Protection Bureau', *Washington Post*, 15 November 2016, www.washingtonpost.com/business/get-there/trumps-election-does-not-bode-well-for-the-consumer-financial-protection-bureau/2016/11/15/70618360-ab48-11e6-977a-1030f822fc35_story.html?utm_term=.4466d726a4bb.

2.5 IMPLICATIONS AND EVALUATIONS 41

potentially fall under some existing legislations depending on the model that the platform has chosen and how the loan was issued.

On 7 May 2014, the Hong Kong Securities and Futures Commission (SFC) issued Notice on Potential Regulations Applicable to, and Risks of, Crowd-funding Activities (2014 SFC Notice), warning that people who engage in crowdfunding activities may be subject to relevant securities laws and regulations.[82] In particular, financial return crowdfunding such as P2P lending and equity crowdfunding may be subject to the provisions of the Securities and Futures Ordinance (chapter 571) (SFO) and/or the Companies ('Winding Up and Miscellaneous Provisions) Ordinance (chapter 32) (C(WUMP)O).[83] It further suggested that other legislation such as the Money Lenders Ordinance (chapter 163) (MLO) and the Anti–Money Laundering and Counter Terrorist Financing (Financial Institutions) Ordinance (chapter 615) (AMLO), will apply when necessary.

Under section 103 of the Securities and Futures Ordinance (SFO), 'it is an offence under the SFO for a person to issue any advertisement, invitation or document which to his knowledge is or contains an invitation to the public to acquire securities or participate in a collective investment scheme, unless the issue has been authorized by the SFC or an exemption applies'. In the 2014 SFC Notice, the SFC specifically uses the term 'unsecured loan' to address P2P lending platforms, and it has stated in the past that any 'credit-linked note . . . where the return and redemption are linked to the credit risk of either a single reference entity or a basket of reference entities' would be considered a security.[84] Hence, online lending platforms following the notary model, such as Prosper and Lending Club in the United States which issue credit-linked notes, need to be licensed with the SFC.

Pursuant to section 7 of the MLO, 'no person shall carry on business as a money lender without a license' issued by the licensing court unless exemption apply. Under section 2 interpretation of the MLO, 'money

---

[82] SFC, 'Notice on Potential Regulations Applicable to, and Risks of, Crowd-funding Activities', 2014, www.sfc.hk/edistributionWeb/gateway/EN/news-and-announcements /news/doc?refNo=14PR53.

[83] The C(WUMP)O is less relevant to debt crowdfunding (online lending) than equity crowdfunding in that online lending platforms do not usually issue debentures within the meaning of securities. The prospectus requirement for securities offerings is mainly based on relevant disclosure sections in the C(WUMP)O, including s. 38, s. 38B, and s. 38D for companies incorporated in Hong Kong, and s. 342 and s. 342C for companies incorporated outside of Hong Kong.

[84] Adrian Fong, 'Regulation of Peer-to-Peer Lending in Hong Kong: State of Play' (2015) 9 (4) *Law and Financial Market Review* 251, 254.

lender means every person whose business (whether or not he carries on any other business) is that of making loans or who advertises or announces himself or holds himself out in any way as carrying on that business'. Thus, lenders who engage in traditional P2P lending platforms will highly likely fall afoul of the MLO since it is impossible for individual investors to obtain a money lenders licence. However, Schedule 1 Part 2 of the MLO provides certain loan exemptions which the lenders may rely on. Under Schedule 1 Part 2, the fifth exemption states that 'A loan made by a company or a firm or individual whose ordinary business does not primarily or mainly involve the lending of money, in the ordinary course of that business' will be excluded from the application of section 7 of the MLO.[85] Nevertheless, the applicability of this exemption to P2P lenders remains unclear and probably requires interpretation by the Hong Kong courts. As a result, it is highly risky to operate traditional P2P lending platforms in Hong Kong due to the uncertain legality of investors engaging in such activities as an unlicensed lender.

Given the uncertainties and burdensome applications under the existing regulatory regime, the operation of P2P lending business in Hong Kong is highly restricted and has to be carefully devised to work around the regulation. In 2016, a newly established firm called MoneySQ.com found an innovative way to carry out its online lending business, claiming itself as the first legitimate P2P lending platform in Hong Kong. It essentially adopts the platform lender model: MoneySQ.com has a money lenders license under the MLO, and then partners up with Bridgeway, an assets management company properly licensed by the SFC, to manage assets.[86] Through Bridgeway, MoneySQ issues its investment invitations to 'professional investors' to raise funds, which is exempted from the authorization and prospectus requirement. MoneySQ.com then uses the funds to originate microloans to borrowers with interest rates ranging from 6 per cent to 15 per cent, and the professional investors participating in the collective investment scheme expect to receive a fixed rate of return of about 5 per cent or 5.5 per cent.

Sophisticated as it is, the MoneySQ arrangement does not come without problems. As only professional investors are allowed to participate in the lending business, MoneySQ is not a typical form of debt crowdfunding. More importantly, the arrangement is not entirely free of legality concerns, particularly in relation to the promising of 'a fixed rate

---

[85] Sch. 1, pt. 2, (v) of MLO.
[86] Official website of MoneySQ, www.moneysq.com/.

2.5 IMPLICATIONS AND EVALUATIONS 43

of return' by the platform.[87] Since the platform was established in March 2016, the SFC has not expressed any objection to the MoneySQ arrangement. This however does not mean categorical consent from the SFC. The legal uncertainty issue, like the Sword of Damocles, may descend at any moment, thus impeding the development of the online lending market in Hong Kong.[88]

2.5.4.5   A Matter of Balance: The Case of China

As noted earlier, China's new regulatory regime is intended to encourage the healthy development of the online lending industry to provide an alternative source of finance for entrepreneurship and innovation, while at the same time protect investors from predatory and fraudulent activities. This is a matter of balance which needs to be handled with care according to the local conditions in China.

To start with, the Chinese law requires that online lending platforms perform the role of purely informational intermediaries and appoint third-party custodians to keep client funds. This means that China's online lending platforms can only adopt the client segregated account model. From a comparative perspective, it follows the UK approach, and differs from the US practice. Is this a right choice? The answer is in the positive. While the restriction on the business model may impede the development of the market, it is necessary to achieve the goal of protecting investors and controlling systemic financial risks. In the United States, where the notary model is used, several recent high-profile scandals in the online lending market have attracted widespread attention. For instance, Renaud Laplanche, the former CEO of Lending Club, was forced to resign due to his mismanagement of investors' assets.[89] Patrick Jenkins, a financial journalist of Financial Times, further describes the

---

[87] The promise may be misleading to the extent that investment made to a collective investment scheme is never risk-free. It thus may constitute an offense of fraudulently or recklessly inducing people to invest money pursuant to s. 107 of the SFO which may attract criminal or civil liabilities.

[88] The lukewarm reception online lending has got in Hong Kong is partly because online lending is seen by many as playing a less important role in Hong Kong's highly developed financial system.

[89] Michael Erman and Joy Wiltermuth, 'Lending Club CEO Resigns after Internal Probe, Shares Plummet', Reuters, 9 May 2016, www.reuters.com/article/us-lendingclub-results/lending-club-ceo-resigns-after-internal-probe-shares-plummet-idUSKCN0Y01BK; also see US Department of the Treasury, 'Opportunities and Challenges in Online Marketplace Lending', 2016, www.treasury.gov/connect/blog/Documents/Opportunities_and_Challenge s_in_Online_Marketplace_Lending_white_paper.pdf.

current P2P lending bubble in the United States as parallel with the subprime mortgage crisis in 2008.[90] This has prompted the US Treasury to recommend tighter regulations for P2P lending business in their recent report.[91]

If the United States has difficulty handling the above problem, it can only be worse in China where regulatory capacity is more limited. In fact, the high proportion of problematic platforms in China shows that the risks of online lending have already manifested under the transformation of business model. At the very least, it is sensible for China to impose the restriction at this stage of market development. It should be noted that in recognition of the acute problem of lack of trust between borrowers and lenders, online lending platforms are still allowed to invite third parties such as guarantee companies and insurance companies to provide guarantee for lending transactions. This is a pragmatic compromise which facilitates the growth of the market while controlling the risk exposure of platforms.

The lending limit is the key regulatory tool introduced under the 2016 Interim Measures on Online Lending, which gives technical effect to the regulatory objectives. Conceptually, imposing lending limits is not surprising given that online lending is seen as a form of inclusive financial innovation which is meant to provide small-value finance to start-ups, SMEs and individual consumers. Nevertheless, it has generated a heated debate over its appropriateness, with many complaints from the industry that it may unduly restrict the amount of credit to be provided and ultimately stifle the contribution of the online lending market to economic growth.

The author recognizes the difficulty in achieving a workable balance between market growth and investor protection, but believes that the lending limit is well justified under China's local conditions. First, the lending limit clearly helps control the risks of online lending, particularly default risk and systemic risk. This is important in China where there is generally a lack of big data of credit history. Even worse, due to its relatively brief track record of operation, China's online lending market has yet to accumulate the depth of data and experience on which

---

[90] Patrick Jenkins, 'US Peer-to-Peer Lending Model Has Parallels with Subprime Crisis: Credit Quality of Some Loans Is Triggering Concerns', *Financial Times*, 30 May 2016, www.ft.com/content/84f696ec-2436-11e6-9d4d-c11776a5124d.

[91] US Department of the Treasury, 'Opportunities and Challenges in Online Marketplace Lending', 2016, www.treasury.gov/connect/blog/Documents/Opportunities_and_Challeng es_in_Online_Marketplace_Lending_white_paper.pdf.

traditional lenders rely. China's central bank, namely the PBOC, has established a national credit reference centre since March 2006, but online lending platforms are not yet covered in the system at the time of writing.[92] It is important for China to move without delay to build a credit reference system for internet finance, or include internet finance within the PBOC's existing system.

Second, the lending limit is closely related to the existing law on illegal fundraising, namely Interpretation of the Supreme People's Court of Several Issues on the Specific Application of Law in the Handling of Criminal Cases about Illegal Fund-raising (SPC Interpretation on Illegal Fundraising).[93] Under section 3(1) of this instrument, criminal liability may arise if an individual absorbs public savings of not less than CNY 200,000 illegally or in disguised form, or an entity absorbs public savings of not less than CNY 1 million illegally or in disguised form. The lending limits mesh well with the criteria for criminal sanctions against illegal fundraising. This can prevent traditional offline illegal fundraising activities from migrating online under the cloak of online lending and financial innovation. Indeed, many online lending platforms previously adopted the so-called offline plus online model to consummate transactions: the transactions were marketed offline and then executed online. For instance, CreditEase reportedly employed more than 30,000 salespersons to advertise its services and find suitable borrowers.[94] This strategy is useful because face-to-face marketing is more acceptable for Chinese people, particularly those living in economically less developed regions. But this may allow illegal private lending in the disguise of online lending, and thus is now prohibited.[95]

Third, although there is no such rule in the United Kingdom and the United States, the Chinese online lending regulation does not have

---

[92] See official website of the Credit Reference Centre of the PBOC, www.PBOCcrc.org.cn/zxzx/index.shtml.

[93] Zuigao Renmin Fayuan Guanyu Shenli Feifa Jizi Xingshi Anjian Juti Yingyong Falv Ruogan Wenti de Jieshi (最高人民法院关于审理非法集资刑事案件具体运用法律若干问题的解释) [Interpretation of the Supreme People's Court of Several Issues on the Specific Application of Law in the Handling of Criminal Cases about Illegal Fundraising] (issued by the Supreme People's Court of the PRC on 13 December 2010, effective 4 January 2011).

[94] Tyler Aveni, 'New Insights into an Evolving P2P Lending Industry: How Shifts in Roles and Risk Are Shaping the Industry', 2015, p 23, www.findevgateway.org/sites/default/files/publications/files/new_insights_into_an_evolving_p2p_lending_industry_positive planet2015.pdf.

[95] The 2016 Interim Measures on Online Lending, art. 10(4).

relevant requirements adopted in those jurisdictions. As discussed before, the Chinese online lending platforms only need to register themselves with the local authorities, and there are no substantive requirements such as minimum capital requirements. Online lending platforms are not required to have special financial services licences, apart from a general telecommunication licence which can be easily obtained. In contrast, the UK regime contains licence and minimum capital requirements. The lending limit may perform similar functions as those requirements in protecting investors and controlling financial systemic risks.

Finally, as a matter of commercial reality, the loans made through online lending platforms are generally small in value even in jurisdictions that do not impose lending limits. For instance, in the United Kingdom, the average loan amount borrowed by personal consumers via online lending platforms in 2014 was GBP 5,471; the average loan amount borrowed for business purposes in 2014 was GBP 73,222.[96]

Hence, the lending limit is theoretically sound and fits well into the exiting legal regime in China. Its practical effect may not be unduly restrictive to the point of stifling the development of the market at present. It is also flexible in the sense that the numerical limits can be adjusted to stay aligned with market developments in the future. Based on the above analysis, it is suggested that in addition to the lending limits, there should also be limits on investments in online lending so as to better protect investors by limiting their risk exposure.

2.6 Recent Developments: What Went Wrong?

2.6.1 Special Rectification Campaign

In response to the worsening situation of P2P lending irregularities, in December 2017, the CBRC and other fourteen ministries and commissions jointly set up a task force to carry out the so-called Special Rectification Campaign to clean up the market and facilitate the implementation of the '1+3' regulatory regime for P2P lending.[97] It was hoped

---

[96] FCA, 'A Review of the Regulatory Regime for Crowdfunding and the Promotion of Non-readily Realisable Securities by Other Media', 2015, paras. 20 and 26, www.fca.org.uk /publication/thematic-reviews/crowdfunding-review.pdf.

[97] Guanyu Zuohao P2P Wangluo Jiedai Fengxian Zhuanxiang Zhengzhi Zhenggai Yanshou Gongzuo De Tongzhi (关于做好P2P网络借贷风险专项整治整验收工作的通知) [Notice on Carrying Out Work on Special Rectification and Acceptance of P2P Online Lending Risks] (issued by the leading group for the special rectification campaign against P2P online lending risks on 8 December 2017).

that upon completion of the campaign, the P2P lending platforms would be able to get through the recordation and registration process. The Special Rectification Campaign was initially scheduled to be completed by the end of June 2018, but the deadline has been postponed again and again. Even today, the campaign is still ongoing, and the objective has changed from rectification to termination, resulting in the fall of the P2P lending market. As at the end of March 2020, there were only 139 P2P platforms nationwide in operation.[98]

There are many reasons behind the failure of the Special Rectification Campaign. To start with, some of the substantive requirements do not properly reflect the commercial reality of the P2P lending market, and thus have a stifling effect on the market. For instance, the Special Rectification Campaign stresses that the platforms as an information intermediary can only introduce third-party guarantees and are not allowed to set up their own risk guarantee funds to cover the default risks for investors. However, as I argued elsewhere, China should consider allowing the P2P lending platforms to introduce different models of the so-called risk guarantee fund scheme (RGFS).[99] The RGFS in online P2P lending refers to the arrangement under which the lending platform will pay the lender in the event of loan default by the borrower. It aims to protect the principal and interest of the lender cum investor, thereby controlling their risk exposure and facilitating the consummation of online P2P lending business. The Special Rectification Campaign puts a blanket ban on RGFS, confining lending platforms strictly to the role of informational intermediaries. While this prohibition helps control the financial risks posed by the RGFS, it represents the traditional philosophy of command and control, with inadequate attention paid to the important economic function of the RGFS in facilitating capital formation as well as the practical need for the RGFS in China's online P2P lending industry. In practice, lending platforms have to adopt various types of RGFS in disguise, with differences in capital composition, custodial modes, coverage degrees and transfer rules. Hence, China should not ban RGFS completely, but should rather adopt a dual-track regulatory regime so that lending platforms can choose whether to adopt RGFS according to their own particular circumstances. If they choose to adopt, there will be additional regulatory requirements such as minimum capital requirements. The dual-track regime can help

---

[98] www.wdzj.com/news/hangye/6119604.html.

[99] Robin Hui Huang, Wangluo Jiedai Pingtai de Fengxian Baozhangjin Jizhi Yanjiu (网络借贷平台的风险保障金机制研究) ['A Study of Risk Guaranty Fund Scheme in Online P2P Lending'] (2018) 12(6) *Qinghua Faxue* (清华法学)*[Tsinghua University Law Journal]* 43–58.

achieve multiple objectives of financial regulation, including financial security, financial development and investor protection.

2.6.2 Rethinking the Central-Local Cooperative Regulation

On the other hand, the central-local cooperative regulatory regime has not operated to achieve the purpose for which it was established. As discussed earlier, the CBRC and its local offices are responsible for the overall regulation of P2P lending platforms, and specifically the business-conduct regulation; the local governments oversee these institutions within their territories, particularly the recordation and registration of P2P platforms. Under the Special Rectification Campaign, the online lending platforms are required to pass a compliance review before recordation and registration with the local financial regulatory authority. This review is a three-step process.[100] First, the platform and the industry association are responsible for institutional self-assessment and self-discipline inspection respectively, according to the '1+3' regulatory regime. Second, the self-assessment reports should be submitted to the provincial office of the leading group for the Special Rectification Campaign where the P2P platform is located. Third, the local leading group will verify the authenticity of the reports and relevant data, and then issue a final report that needs to be signed by the financial regulatory authority of the local government and the local branch of the CBRC.

In October 2019, the financial work bureau of Hunan Province made a shocking announcement that all online lending businesses within the province would be terminated.[101] According to the announcement, all twenty-four P2P platforms in the province were found to be not fully compliant with relevant laws and regulations, and thus cannot be approved by or registered with the local financial regulatory authority. Consequently, all the platforms would be required to cancel their industrial and commercial registrations or change their names and business scope to retreat from the P2P lending business. Hunan was the first province in China to announce the termination of all P2P platforms in its jurisdiction. Nine

---

[100] Guanyu Kaizhan P2P Wangluo Jiedai Jigou Hegui Jiancha Gongzuo de Tongzhi (关于开展 P2P网络借贷机构合规检查工作的通知) [Notice on Commencing the Work of Compliance Review for P2P Online Lending Institutions] (issued by the leading group for the special rectification campaign against P2P online lending risks on 13 August 2018), pts 3–4.

[101] http://dfjrjgj.hunan.gov.cn/dfjrjgj/xxgk_71626/tzgg/gggs/201910/t20191016_10485618 .html.

other provinces and cities soon followed suit in the same year, announcing that all the P2P platforms in their jurisdictions failed to satisfy regulatory requirements and thus would be required to close down. As of the end of August 2020, up to nineteen provinces, representing more than half of China, had made similar announcements.[102]

Furthermore, some P2P lending platforms in other regions declared that they would voluntarily withdraw from the online lending business. For example, Shenzhen and Xinjiang announced their lists of online lending platforms that would exit the market on a voluntary basis.

Finally, the P2P lending platforms are encouraged to transform into small-loan companies, according to a document issued in November 2019 under the Special Rectification Campaign.[103] If a P2P lending platform meets certain requirements in relation to its operation, shareholders and management team and advanced financial technology, it can submit relevant materials to the local financial regulatory authority to apply for business transformation and get a temporary licence for doing the small-loan business. After the platform obtains the approval document, it should clean up the existing online lending business in accordance with the transformation plan, report the implementation progress to local regulators weekly, and eliminate risks in an appropriate manner.[104] The local authority is empowered to formulate specific rules regarding the business transformation, set stricter standards in light of local conditions, and take responsibility for supervision over small-loan companies. On 13 May 2020, the local financial regulatory bureau of Xiamen City approved the transformation of two online lending institutions into small-loan companies.[105]

As noted earlier, the Special Rectification Campaign has not yet completed and it remains to be seen how China's P2P market will eventually look like after it. One thing is certain, however, that is, the number of P2P

---

[102] They are Hunan, Shandong, Chongqing, Henan, Sichuan, Yunnan, Hebei, Gansu, Shanxi, Inner Mongolia, Shanxi, Jilin, Heilongjiang, Jiangxi, Anhui, Hubei, Jiangsu, Ningxia and Fujian.

[103] Guanyu Wangluo Jiedai Xinxi Zhongjie Jigou Zhuanxingwei Xiaoe Daikuan Gongsi Shidian De Zhidiao Yijian (关于网络借贷信息中介机构转型为小额贷款公司试点的指导意见) [Guiding Opinions on the Pilot Project of Transforming Online Lending Information Intermediaries into Micro-credit Companies] (issued by the leading group for the special rectification campaign against Internet finance risks and the leading group for the special rectification campaign against P2P online lending risks on 15 November 2019).

[104] Ibid, pts 2–3.

[105] See the official website of Xiamen municipal financial regulatory bureau, http://jr .xm.gov.cn/zfxxgk/zfxxgkml/tzgg/bmtz/202005/t20200515_2447130.htm; http://jr .xm.gov.cn/zfxxgk/zfxxgkml/tzgg/bmtz/202005/t20200515_2447179.htm.

lending platforms will be drastically reduced and the role of P2P lending as a financing tool will never be the same as before. More research is needed to examine the reasons behind the fall of the Chinese P2P market, in particular the pros and cons of the central-local cooperative regulatory regime. Indeed, in the early stage, the cooperative regulation seemed to work well, with the local regulatory authorities showing great interest and enthusiasm in the development and regulation of their local P2P markets. Later, however, they completely reversed their attitudes, gradually shunning the P2P market and finally choosing to close it down altogether. When the dust settles and more information becomes available, it would be interesting to look back and draw lessons from it.

2.7 Conclusion

Internet Finance such as online lending has been promoted as an important vehicle to foster a more inclusive financial system in China under its national strategy of supply-side reform (*gongjice gaige*). The arguably overzealous encouragement of the Chinese government, coupled with the fact that there was effectively a regulatory vacuum before 2016, helped China's online lending market grow rapidly over the past few years, but also gave rise to many gaping problems therein.

The promulgation of the 2016 Interim Measures on Online Lending marks a watershed in the history of China's online lending regulation. This has been followed by three implementation rules which were issued in quick succession to flesh out more details. Together, they have now made up a relatively complete regulatory regime for online lending, widely dubbed the 'one plus three' framework, consisting of the 2016 Interim Measures and three guidance documents on registration, custodian and information disclosure. It has far-reaching implications and ushers in a new era for the development of China's online lending market, with platforms facing a period of reshuffling. It also provides opportunities for more collaboration between online platforms and traditional banks.

In essence, the significance of the new regulatory regime lies in the legalization of online lending through a system of registration, disclosure, lending limit and obligation that is designed to achieve two main objectives, namely facilitating the growth of the online lending market, and protecting financial consumers. These two objectives may be consistent in some instances, while in other situations they may be diametrically opposed. Hence, the challenge of finding the best possible way to regulate online lending consists of nothing more than trying to strike a balance between the two regulatory objectives. Importantly, the balance is a delicate one and needs to be adjusted according to local conditions.

The Chinese experience contributes to the international debate on the way in which online lending should be regulated to maintain the right balance. While the *laissez faire* policy taken by the Chinese government before 2016 generated significant costs as evidenced by the high proportion of problematic platforms, it provided ample room for the online lending market to grow. A total prohibition on online lending is simply not a viable option for China. Furthermore, the objectives are illustrated in some significant regulatory elements, particularly the lending limit. Based on a comparative analysis of the Chinese experience with those in other jurisdictions such as the United States, the United Kingdom and Hong Kong, it is submitted that the Chinese regime is generally sound and less onerous. The central-local cooperative supervisory arrangement is innovative, but not without concerns. The recent developments of the regulation and the market have cast doubt on the efficacy of the central-local cooperative supervision, which is an area for future research.

3

Initial Coin Offerings

3.1 Introduction

'Initial coin offering' (ICO), or 'token sales', refers to a new fundraising tool which allows organizations, mainly entrepreneurs or start-ups, to launch a business based on distributed ledgers or blockchain technologies to raise operating funds. The ICO funding model is generally believed to have been first introduced by J. R. Willett, who launched the first ICO called Mastercoin (now called Omni) in 2013 and raised USD 500,000 worth of Bitcoins.[1] Since then, there has been a flood of new ICOs being launched every other day. In 2018, more than USD 14 billion have been raised from ICOs.[2] The tremendous amount of capital raised by ICOs have called into question the adequacy of financial regulations at a national and international level. To date, few jurisdictions have established comprehensive regulations on ICOs and the relevant transactions. Nevertheless, great efforts are being made by many jurisdictions in defining the nature of ICOs and developing relevant regulations and guidelines.

Since many jurisdictions have been slowly seeking to test the waters in this regulatory whirlpool, the legal status of ICOs and applicable laws has been discussed and announced by some regulators. Except for the United Kingdom and the European Union (EU), both of which are highly friendly to new and innovative technology, jurisdictions such as those in China, the United States, Canada, Australia, Singapore and Hong Kong are progressively tightening regulation around ICOs. Among these jurisdictions, China is the only one imposing an outright ban on ICOs while the financial regulators in the United States, Canada,

---

[1] Laura Shin, 'Here's The Man Who Created ICOs and This Is the New Token He's Backing', *Forbes*, 21 September 2017, www.forbes.com/sites/laurashin/2017/09/21/heres-the-man-who-created-icos-and-this-is-the-new-token-hes-backing/#294a92171183.

[2] Mathias Fromberger and Lars Haffke, 'ICO Market Report 2018/2019 – Performance Analysis of 2018's Initial Coin Offerings', p 3, https://papers.ssrn.com/sol3/papers.cfm?abstract_id=3512125.

Australia, Singapore and Hong Kong are adopting a similar approach and are looking at the possibility of applying securities laws to ICOs.

China's ICO ban caused chaos to the cryptocurrencies market and has been criticized for disrupting financial innovation even though it is an efficient movement towards protecting investors from fraudulent projects. However, this may only be a temporary ban given the facts that economic development is a major strategy of the Chinese government and nations are competing to be the next big hub of financial technology (Fintech). Therefore, the objective of this chapter is to contribute to the proposal for regulating and governing ICOs rather than banning them outright.

The chapter is structured as follows. Section 3.2 will provide a general overview of the workings of ICOs with their two key technical elements. The evolution of ICO regulations in China, especially the ICO ban and its effects, and the current situation of ICOs in China will also be discussed in this section in light of recent notifications issued by Chinese authorities. This is followed in Section 3.3 by an economic analysis of ICO's benefits and risks to explain why some jurisdictions are open to it while others are not. This section will also look at risks and benefits which may be specific to China. The chapter then turns to the more important question of how China may proceed with the reform of a regulatory framework for ICOs. Section 3.4 looks at some relevant experiences in and lessons learned from overseas jurisdictions which have advanced economies, including those of the United States, Canada, Australia, Singapore and Hong Kong in terms of the legal status of ICOs and possible laws applicable to ICOs. The current position in the United Kingdom and the EU will also be discussed even though the regulators in the United Kingdom and the EU have been regarded as more 'ICO-friendly' than other jurisdictions and thus no instructive guidelines have been issued yet. This section conducts a comparative analysis of these jurisdictions with a view to furthering an appropriate reform of China's financial regulations on ICOs as discussed in Section 3.5. Section 3.6 gives concluding remarks.

3.2 Background to ICO Regulation in China

3.2.1 Overview of the Workings of ICOs

It is beyond the scope of this chapter to provide a comprehensive explanation of the inner workings of the cryptocurrency system.[3] The aim of

---

[3] For a fuller discussion of the nature and utility of crypto-currency, see Chapter 6.

this sub-section is to give a generalized overview of the normal process of ICO, the goal of ICO and the two key technical ICO attributes that allow for ICOs to better understand and regulate them.

Put simply, ICOs could be regarded as a means of crypto-crowdfunding via the use of cryptocurrency, also called digital currency, coin or token, or 'virtual currencies',[4] which is launched on decentralized platforms based on blockchain technology to raise funds.[5] It is a type of fundraising activity whereby new cryptocurrencies are issued, usually in exchange for payment in other widely accepted cryptocurrencies or for real money. Normally, start-ups need to publish an ICO white paper, a document which may appear to be similar to a prospectus, detailing their planned project and the parameters of the ICO as required by ICO platforms. The funds raised through the ICO would be used to develop the project as explained in their white paper. The reasons that investors participate in ICOs may vary, for instance they may be speculative, helping start-ups develop their projects or expecting to obtain some related rights. After an ICO has been completed, a newly issued cryptocurrency will usually start trading on cryptocurrency exchanges, after which investors can choose to hold their coins on the start-up's platform or transfer them onto a cryptocurrency exchange for trading.

To date, the most popular and well-respected cryptocurrency as well as the first decentralized cryptocurrency is Bitcoin, which was invented by Satoshi Nakamoto in 2009 and can only be generated through mining, a process done by the use of computer processing power and through which transactions are verified and new Bitcoins are released.[6] In 2017, the Luxembourg House of Financial Technology and the Stellar Development Foundation provided a good review of the ICO life cycle process in their research paper, which can be represented as that in Figure 3.1.[7]

The two key technical attributes of ICOs are cryptocurrency and blockchain. First, cryptocurrency is akin to fiat currency in the sense that cryptocurrency has value and it can be exchanged or traded on the

---

[4] For the purposes of this chapter, 'cryptocurrency', 'digital currency', 'digital coin', 'digital token', 'virtual currency; etc. have the same meaning and are used interchangeably. The term 'virtual currency' is commonly used in courts.

[5] Nirupama Devi Bhaskar et al, 'Bitcoin IPO, ETF, and Crowdfunding', in David Lee Luo Chuen (ed), *Handbook of Digital Currency: Bitcoin, Innovation, Financial Instruments, and Big Data* (Elsevier Academic Press, 2015), p 529.

[6] Satoshi Nakamoto, 'Bitcoin: A Peer-to-Peer Electronic Cash System', 2008, https://bitcoin.org/bitcoin.pdf.

[7] Luxembourg House of Financial Technology (LHoFT) and Stellar Development Foundation (SDF), 'Understanding Initial Coin Offerings: Technology, Benefits, Risks, and Regulations', 2017, www.lhoft.com/uploads/editor/files/news/WhitePaper.pdf.

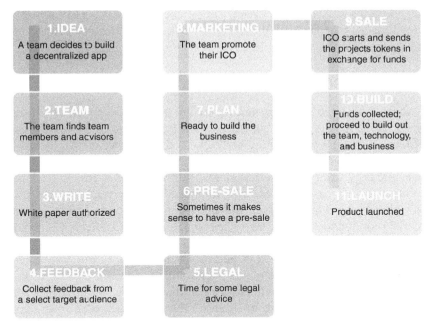

Figure 3.1 ICO life cycle process.

market and can be used as a medium of exchange. The two main distinguishing factors compared with traditional currencies are that cryptocurrency is entirely non-tangible as it only exists in a digital space, and there is no administrative influence from a regulatory authority as is the case with traditional currencies.[8] Investors can keep their cryptocurrencies in their wallet, a software program where cryptocurrencies are stored.

In order for cryptocurrencies to run, there must be a blockchain, which can be regarded as a kind of public ledger recording all the transactions executed and verified during a given period of time. A block in the blockchain is like a page from a ledger and once a block is 'completed', it is added to the chain at each node and gives way to a new block in the blockchain.[9] Therefore, the blockchain is in essence a decentralized and distributed

---

[8] Mitsuru Iwamura et al, 'Is Bitcoin the Only Cryptocurrency in the Town? Economics of Cryptocurrency and Friedrich A. Hayek', 2014, Discussion Paper Series from Institute of Economic Research, Hitotsubashi University no 602, http://hermes-ir.lib.hit-u.ac.jp/rs/bitstream/10036/26493/1/DP602.pdf.

[9] Don Tapscott and Alex Tapscott, *Blockchain Revolution: How the Technology Behind Bitcoin Is Changing Money, Business and the World* (Portfolio Penguin 2016).

database, or so-called shared ledger, without the need for a central authority, recording a secure list of all the transactions that have been stored at nodes on the peer-to-peer network since the very beginning.[10]

3.2.2 The Evolution of ICO Regulation in China

ICOs have emerged in China since the second half of 2016. As the size of the financial market in China is quite huge, there have been increasing numbers of Chinese people participating in ICOs. In the first half of 2017, China-based ICOs raised around RMB 2.6 billion (USD 400 million) through sixty-five offerings from Chinese investors, with a secondary market whose transaction volumes exceeded RMB 100 billion.[11] However, although ICO is a global phenomenon, given the fact that China is one of the biggest markets for cryptocurrencies and 90 per cent of ICOs operated in China are highly suspected of being associated with illegal fundraising or fraud while only 1 per cent of funds raised through ICOs are used for the development of blockchain projects,[12] this makes it substantially different from its counterparts overseas. It may be due to the fact that the opening up of China's capital market is quite late compared to other developed economies, and therefore China's financial regulation and the development of a supportive legal framework has been lagging behind in terms of applying international standards. The consequence is that there is no sound law to regulate the mobilization of capital via ICO and license the cryptocurrency exchanges in China. Accordingly, ICOs have resulted in increasing fraud, Ponzi schemes and other scams which will be discussed in more detail in the risk section.

Faced with the surge in ICOs in China, Chinese regulators have been trying to closely monitor the movements of cryptocurrencies, especially Bitcoin, and have gradually developed a regulatory approach since then, before the central bank issued a sharp ban on ICOs in China. This section will outline the development of regulations on cryptocurrencies and their

---

[10] Pedro Franco, *Understanding Bitcoin: Cryptography, Engineering and Economics* (John Wiley, 2015).

[11] Guojia hulianwang jinrong anquan jishu zhuanjia weiyuanhui (国家互联网金融安全技术专家委员会) [National Committee of Experts on Internet Financial Security Technology]: '2017 shangbannian guonei ICO fazhan qingkuang baogao' (2017 上半年国内 ICO 发展情况报告) [2017 First Half Domestic ICO Development Situation Report], 2017, www.ifcert.org.cn/res/web_file/1501062824386085029.pdf.

[12] 'ICO was characterized as illegal fundraising, crush of overnight dreams', 2 September 2017, www.finet.hk/Newscenter/news_content/59aa5805e4b0d1966a2a57e1 (resources from the study of most ICO White Books conducted by the PBOC).

3.2 BACKGROUND TO ICO REGULATION IN CHINA

related transactions and financing activities, and examine the current regulatory environment for ICOs in China.

3.2.2.1 Before the 2017 Ban

In December 2013, the PBOC and four associated ministries jointly issued the Circular on Prevention of Risks Associated with Bitcoin[13] (2013 Bitcoin Circular). The circular clearly defined Bitcoin as 'a specially designated virtual commodity or good' and made it clear that Bitcoin did not have the same legal status as fiat currency.[14] The 2013 Bitcoin Circular also prohibited financial and payment institutions from engaging in any Bitcoin-related activities or services and specified detailed requirements on Bitcoin-related anti–money laundering obligations.[15] As domestic Bitcoin transactions warmed up in 2015 and ushered in a bull market in 2016, the PBOC promulgated the *Yinfa* [2016] No. 201,[16] requiring financial institutions to strengthen their monitoring and give early warning of suspicious and illegal fundraising, and especially prompting financial institutions to monitor the sale of virtual currency by way of pyramid schemes.[17] In response to the emergence of five ICO platforms in China at the end of 2016 and the price volatility of Bitcoin, the PBOC took the lead with various regulatory authorities in meeting with the three leading platforms – OKCoin, Huobi and BTCChina, to ensure that they would operate in accordance with the laws and regulations of China.[18]

The surge in ICOs in the first half of 2017 increased concerns with the regulatory authorities about fraud and illegal activities. In order to curb ICO-related risks and strengthen supervision of the financial sector, the Legislative Affairs Office of the State Council released the Exposure Draft of the Regulations on the Handling of Illegal Fundraising ('the

---

[13] Guanyu Fangfan Bitebi Fengxian de Tongzhi (关于防范比特币风险的通知) [Circular on Prevention of Risks Associated with Bitcoin] (promulgated on 5 December 2013 by the People's Bank of China and others).

[14] Ibid.

[15] Ibid.

[16] Guanyu Jinyibu Jiaqiang Dui Shexian Feifa Jizi Zijin Jiaoyi Jiance Yujing Gongzuo de Zhidao Yijian (关于进一步加强对涉嫌非法集资资金交易监测预警工作的指导意见 (银发【2016】201号)) [Directive Opinion on Further Strengthening the Monitoring and Early Warning of Financial Transactions Involving Possible Illegal Fundraising] (promulgated in September 2016 by the People's Bank of China).

[17] Ibid.

[18] John Riggins, 'PBOC Meets with Leading Chinese Bitcoin Exchanges amid Price Volatility', *Bitcoin Magazine*, 2017, https://bitcoinmagazine.com/articles/pboc-meets-with-leading-chinese-bitcoin-exchanges-amid-price-volatility-1483717475/.

Draft')[19] drafted by the CBRC on 24 August 2017 for public comment. The Draft provides for an administrative investigation into illegal fundraising in the name of 'issuing virtual currency' in Article 15(2) and the 'sale of goods, provision of services [...] project investment, sale-and-rent' in Article 15(3),[20] which clearly indicates the legislative intent to regulate ICOs in China. However, in Article 2, fundraising refers to an activity which promises to pay off a principal sum plus interest or promises a reward.[21] Accordingly, it is possible to conclude that an ICO does not qualify as illegal fundraising, provided no promises of future value or price appreciation are or will be made with respect to the cryptocurrency issued. This relates to the legal status of an ICO which will be discussed in detail in Section 3.5.

3.2.2.2 The 2017 Ban and Its Problems

In September 2017, China issued an outright 'ICO ban', causing turbulence in the virtual currencies market, as China is one of the biggest markets. On 2 September 2017, the Internet Financial Risk Special Rectification Work Leading Group Office issued the Notification Concerning the Undertaking of Clean-up and Rectification Work for ICO (2017 ICO Work).[22] It clearly defined ICO as 'a form of unapproved illegal public financing' highly suspected of facilitating 'illegal fundraising, illegal securities offerings, illegal sale of virtual currencies [...] as well as other illegal criminal activities such as financial fraud and pyramid selling that severely disrupt the economic and financial order'.[23] This can be literally interpreted to mean that the ICOs themselves are illegal no matter what their nature or legal status.

Almost immediately after the issuance of the 2017 ICO Work, the PBOC along with six associated ministries collectively issued the Notice

---

[19] Chuzhi Feifa Jizi Tiaoli (Zhengqiu Yijiangao) (处置非法集资条例（征求意见稿）) [Exposure Draft of the Regulations on the Handling of Illegal Fundraising] (promulgated on 24 August 2017 by the Legislative Affairs Office of the State Council of the PRC, effected from 24 August 2017 to 24 September 2017).

[20] Ibid.

[21] Ibid.

[22] Guanyu Dui Daibi Faxing Rongzi Kaizhan Qingli Zhengdun Gongzuo de Tongzhi (关于对代币发行融资开展清理整顿工作的通知) [Notification Concerning the Undertaking of Clean-up and Rectification Work for ICO] (promulgated on 2 September 2017 by the *Hulianwang Jinrong Fengxian Zhuanxiang Zhengzhi Gongzuo Lingdao Xiaozu Bangongshi* (互联网金融风险专项整治工作领导小组办公室) [Internet Financial Risk Special Rectification Work Leading Group Office].

[23] Ibid. See also China Banking News, 'China Declares Initial Coin Offerings Illegal', 2017, www.chinabankingnews.com/2017/09/04/china-declares-initial-coin-offerings-illegal/.

3.2 BACKGROUND TO ICO REGULATION IN CHINA 59

on Preventing Risks Associated with ICOs[24] (2017 ICO Notice) on 4 September 2017. In consistency with the 2017 ICO Work, Article 1 of the 2017 ICO Notice states that[25]

> financing through coin offerings refer to financing bodies raising virtual currencies such as Bitcoin or Ethereum from investors through illegal sales and circulation of crypto currency or tokens. Such offerings, in essence, are unauthorized and illegal public fundraising and are suspected of involving in criminal activities such as illegal selling of tokens, illegal issuance of securities, illegal fundraising, financial fraud and pyramid schemes.

Hence, the 2017 ICO Notice explicitly mentions the raising of Bitcoins, Ethers and other virtual currencies through illegal sales and circulation of cryptocurrencies, and ICOs are essentially an unauthorized fundraising tool or unauthorized illegal fundraising activity. The 2017 ICO Notice also emphasized that no cryptocurrencies have any legal status equivalent to money.[26] Furthermore, Article 2 of the 2017 ICO Notice clearly prohibits organizations or individuals from illegally conducting ICO financing activities.[27]

The 2017 ICO Notice, based on the 2013 Bitcoin Circular, gives a number of instructions as summarized in the following four points: (1) all ICOs being conducted in Mainland China are to stop their financing activities with immediate effect; (2) organizations and individuals that have completed fundraising through ICOs in Mainland China must make relevant arrangement to return funds; (3) all ICO platforms and cryptocurrency exchange platforms (including websites and apps) based in Mainland China are to halt the provision of services, including trading cryptocurrencies for fiat currencies and providing related information; (4) financial institutions and non-bank payment agencies are not allowed to carry out any ICO-related businesses (such as opening accounts, registration, settlement, clearing and trading).[28]

However, the 2017 ICO Notice is still not fully clear on a number of important matters. First and foremost, although the 2017 ICO Notice bans ICOs in China, there are some ambiguities over what amounts to an

---

[24] Guanyu Fangfan Daibi Faxing Rongzi Fengxian de Gonggao (关于防范代币发行融资风险的公告) [Notice on Preventing Risks Associated with ICOs] (promulgated on 4 September 2017 by the People's Bank of China and others).

[25] Ibid, para 1.

[26] Ibid, para 1.

[27] Ibid, para 2.

[28] Ibid.

ICO. It mentions 'illegal sale of virtual currencies', suggesting that the sale of virtual currencies can be either legal or illegal, depending on the particular circumstances of each case. However, it does not provide further guidance on what constitutes a 'legal' or 'illegal' sale of virtual currencies. There seems to be a possibility that as long as the sale of virtual currencies is legal, it may not be classified as an ICO. Probably for this reason, the 2017 ICO Work states that the rectification work and assessment will be carried out with respect to ICOs on a case-by-case basis while all new ICOs must be called off. In practice, as a self-regulatory industry body in the field of internet finance, the NIFAC has issued its opinions on specific cases from time to time.

Second, the 2017 ICO Notice does not give a clear view on regulations over cross-border ICO activities and does not mention issues regarding the location of where investors are based. Accordingly, it seems practically impossible to regulate cross-border ICO activities if both the platform and the financing entity are outside of Mainland China and to ban domestic investors from investing in overseas ICOs or trading cryptocurrencies for either fiat currencies or other cryptocurrencies through overseas platforms or institutions. Besides, it is ambiguous in terms of how to determine whether an issuer has a basis in Mainland China and what elements, such as marketing place, website location or location of sale agency, should be taken into account.

3.2.3   Effects of the 2017 ICO Ban

As ICOs have been treated as a form of illegal public fundraising in China, any ICO launched after the ICO ban may constitute a breach of the relevant laws, such as securities laws and, consumer protection laws, and may even constitute criminal offences under the Criminal Law of the People's Republic of China (PRC) if such an activity qualifies as an 'illegal taking savings from public or such an equivalent activity'.[29]

---

[29] Art. 176, Zhonghua Renmin Gongheguo Xingfa (中华人民共和国刑法) [Criminal Law of the PRC] (adopted on 1 July 1979 at the Fifth National People's Congress; revised on 14 March 1997 at the Eighth National People's Congress; promulgated on 14 March 1997 by Order No. 83 of the President of the PRC and effected from 1 October 1997). See also the four requirements in art. 1, Gaunyu Feifa Jizi Xingshi Anjian Juti Yingyong Falv Ruogan Wenti de Jieshi (Fa Shi [2010] No. 18) (关于非法集资刑事案件具体应用法律若干问题的解释 (法释【2010】18号)) [Judicial Interpretations on Several Issues Concerning Implementation of Laws in Trial of Criminal Cases Relating Illegal Fundraising] (promulgated on 13 December 2010 by the Supreme People's Court of China and effected from 4 January 2011).

3.2 BACKGROUND TO ICO REGULATION IN CHINA 61

Even though the 2017 ICO Notice is not clear enough, the ICO ban did achieve a remarkable effect, not only in the domestic market, but also with two non-Chinese ICO platforms – TokenCapital, on which Chinese domestic ICO projects are launched, had to close down its website;[30] and Allcoin, a Canadian-based platform, was made to deal with Chinese domestic ICO project refunds.[31] Despite the 2017 ICO Notice requiring all ICO exchange platforms to cease all services from its release date, it seems that the regulators did imply a buffer term after the release date for the platforms to finish the clearance and settlement of funds and assets. This extra time can be seen as a protective measure for domestic investors, allowing them to deal with Bitcoins in their accounts since the Bitcoin price had dropped by 20 per cent after the announcement of the ICO ban.[32]

In reality, even though the 2017 ICO Notice stated that all requirements would take effect on its release date (4 September 2017), all clearances and transactions of cryptocurrencies were actually finished off by October and most platforms had shut down.[33] In order to tighten control over cryptocurrency transactions and payments, on 17 January 2018, the Payment and Settlement Office within the Business Administration Department of the PBOC issued a notice requiring each unit to carry out a thorough self-examination and rectification work so as to make sure that no services for cryptocurrency transactions were provided.[34] All units and branches of the PBOC shall close down payment channels for cryptocurrencies once discovered and report to the Business Management Department on 20 January 2018.[35] In practice, some platforms were found to continue to

[30] See the main page of TokenCapital, https://tokencapital.io/, which has been closed down.

[31] Michael House et al, 'China Halts ICOs and Token Sales and China-Based Trading Platforms Suspend Trading Amid Reports of Additional Government Restrictions'. 2017, www.virtualcurrencyreport.com/2017/09/china-halts-icos-and-token-sales-and-china-based-trading-platforms-suspend-trading-amid-reports-of-additional-government-restrictions/.

[32] Chao Deng and Paul Vigna, 'China to Shut Bitcoin Exchanges', *Wall Street Journal*, 11 September 2017, www.wsj.com/articles/china-to-shut-bitcoin-exchanges-sources-1505100862.

[33] Lou Yun, 'Bitcoin Exchanges Follow Up: Clearance and Settlement', *Asia Finance*, 2017, www.asiafinance.cn/jmnc/110064.jhtml.

[34] Guanyu Kaizhan Wei Feifa Xuni Huobi Jiaoyi Tigong Zhifu Fuwu Zicha Zhenggai Gongzuo de Tongzhi (关于开展为非法虚拟货币交易提供支付服务自查整改工作的通知) [Notification on Carrying Out Self-examination and Rectification Reform Work on Providing Payment Services for Illegal Virtual Currency Transactions] (promulgated on 17 January 2018 by the Payment and Settlement Office of the PBOC's Business Administration Department).

[35] Ibid.

provide a gateway for mining cryptocurrencies and opening wallets for clients to store their cryptocurrencies.[36] However, to play safe, a vast majority of platforms have chosen to migrate elsewhere, notably Singapore and Hong Kong. In short, it is not fully clear whether the mining and storage of cryptocurrencies are completely banned as a result of the 2017 ICO ban, but as a matter of fact, the Chinese market for cryptocurrencies has virtually gone with the wind.

3.3 Economic Analysis of ICO: Benefits and Risks

3.3.1 Benefits of ICO

This section examines what benefits can be brought by ICOs. The benefits are not restricted to start-ups or companies and investors who participate in them, but instead apply to society as a whole, in the sense that the projects can help develop Fintech and create beneficial and innovative projects. Those benefits can be seen as one of the reasons why the United Kingdom and the EU still remain reluctant to regulate ICOs.

3.3.1.1 Low Cost and Low Requirement

ICOs are especially attractive to start-ups and small businesses.[37] They can be regarded as a combination of traditional initial public offerings (IPOs) and online crowdfunding, which provides blockchain start-ups with low-cost, fast and unregulated early-stage financing.[38] While ICOs work similar to IPOs in a sense that investors in return receive rewards, ICOs avoid the high cost, long waiting period and strict regulations imposed on IPOs. Traditional IPOs and transactions are based on a trust model that has the inherent weakness of the inability to make non-reversible payments for non-reversible transactions, as financial institutions are always trying to mediate disputes.[39] The consequence is that

---

[36] Lou Yun, 'Bitcoin Exchanges Follow Up: Clearance and Settlement', *Asia Finance*, 2017, www.asiafinance.cn/jmnc/110064.jhtml.

[37] Aleksei Churilov, 'The Nature of Bitcoin and Some Practical Aspects of Its Use by Business', *Proceedings of International Academic Conferences no 3605453*, 2016, International Institute of Social and Economic Sciences, Prague, www.iises.net/proceed ings/23rd-international-academic-conference-venice/table-of-content/detail?article=bit coins-and-business-the-best-friends-or-the-worst-enemies.

[38] Octavian Nica et al, 'Cryptocurrencies: Economic Benefits and Risks', *FinTech Working Paper no 2*, 2017, University of Manchester, https://papers.ssrn.com/sol3/papers.cfm? abstract_id=3059856.

[39] Satoshi Nakamoto, 'Bitcoin: A Peer-to-Peer Electronic Cash System', 2008, https://bitcoin .org/bitcoin.pdf.

transaction costs will get higher, the minimum practical transaction size gets limited, and the possibility for small casual transactions gets cut off.[40] However, the decentralized nature of blockchain makes it possible for purely peer-to-peer cryptocurrency transactions to be conducted and accordingly allows for those cryptocurrencies to not be tied to any particular nation, government or financial institution.[41] Therefore, ICOs based on the blockchain technology enjoy the benefits of much lower costs and fewer regulatory requirements compared to traditional ways. Due to this, entrepreneurs may feel freer to invent or produce more innovative projects as financing is not a big problem at all.

3.3.1.2   Efficiency, Reliability and Anonymity

In addition, as the decentralization of blockchain frees the ties with authorities or intermediaries, ICOs save a lot of time that would be requested in traditional transactions, and accordingly foster efficiency for transactions across borders and between institutions to take place. Time can also be saved through quicker verification because network nodes can verify transactions for themselves.[42] Besides, benefits of the trust-based model remain despite the detachment from the central authority. Firstly, the credibility and proper controls of the circulation process can be realized by a system of digital signatures and a complex validation process set up on the blockchain.[43] Secondly, similar to the level of information released by stock exchanges, privacy can be better protected by keeping public keys anonymous, without information linking transactions to any individual parties.[44]

3.3.1.3   Profit and Liquidity

Aside from start-ups, investors are also interested in ICOs because they can see potential gains more quickly and pull profits more easily[45]

---

[40] Ibid.

[41] Don Tapscott and Alex Tapscott, *Blockchain Revolution: How the Technology Behind Bitcoin Is Changing Money, Business and the world* (Portfolio Penguin, 2016).

[42] Satoshi Nakamoto, 'Bitcoin: A Peer-to-Peer Electronic Cash System', 2008, https://bitcoin .org/bitcoin.pdf.

[43] Gianni Bonaiuti, 'Economic Issues on M-Payments and Bitcoin', in Gabriella Gimigliano (ed), *Bitcoin and Mobile Payments: Constructing a European Union Framework* (Palgrave Macmillan, 2016).

[44] Satoshi Nakamoto, 'Bitcoin: A Peer-to-Peer Electronic Cash System', 2008, https://bitcoin .org/bitcoin.pdf.

[45] Richard Kastelein, 'What Initial Coin Offerings Are, and Why VC Firms Care', *Harvard Business Review*, 24 March 2017, https://hbr.org/2017/03/what-initial-coin-offerings-are-and-why-vc-firms-care.

although it is hard to prove that an ICO project will definitely succeed and therefore will increase the value of the cryptocurrency issued by the ICO project. In addition to profit, the liquidity of cryptocurrency is another benefit that is attractive to investors.[46] After all, once an ICO has finished, the cryptocurrencies can be freely traded on the exchanges as well as converted to other accepted cryptocurrencies, such as Bitcoins and Ethers, or even fiat currencies, rather than being locked in the account of the ICO equity.

3.3.2 Risks of ICO

Despite these benefits, due to the different sound levels of regulatory systems in different jurisdictions, risks rooted in ICOs may cause varying degrees of problems. These may be the reasons why China has banned ICOs and why the United States, Canada, Australia, Singapore and Hong Kong have started to look into ICOs' regulations.

3.3.2.1 Risks of Inadequate Regulatory Compliance

While the decentralized, open and cryptographic nature of blockchain allows for anonymity and privacy of customers when making transactions online, the feature could at the same time be used for fraudulent purposes if users can avoid linking their identities to their online 'wallets' such that they can trade illegal products online without being traced. One typical example is *United States v. Ross William Ulbricht*,[47] also referred to as the *Silk Road* case. Ulbricht was convicted of drug trafficking and other crimes related to the use of the Silk Road, an online marketplace for users to trade illegal goods and services while using Bitcoins.[48] Even though every transaction was recorded on the blockchain, Bitcoin anonymity techniques make it impossible for the Federal Bureau of Investigation to trace the identities of the sellers and the buyers. As a consequence, there is a high risk of ICOs getting involved in illegal activities such as the trading of illegal products, and even capital flight, money laundering, tax evasion and so on.

3.3.2.2 Risks of Inadequate Investor Protection

The anonymity and irreversible nature of cryptocurrency transactions can also be used for phishing purposes by fraudulently impersonating an entity

---

[46] Ibid.
[47] Docket No. 15-1815 CA (2nd Cir. 31 May 2017).
[48] Ibid.

conducting an ICO and subsequently transferring received funds to a non-traceable account. In addition to potential risks caused by anonymity, the exclusion of a supervisory authority also makes investors vulnerable to risks. Given that no trustful authority or third party has been there to apply the rules and penalties for auditing ICOs as yet, the lack of proper due diligence under the terms of an ICO's white book and the uncertain status of the legality of the white book can cause considerable risks. Besides, as the cryptocurrency value can fluctuate drastically and it is possible for hackers to steal[49] or use ransomware to attack investors' computers,[50] the risk of losing on investment is very high. In summary, the lack of regulations on ICOs and the unclear nature of ICOs have left many areas uncertain, including what legal rights investors have and what remedies they may seek. Risks like these consequently put investors in a vulnerable position.

3.3.2.3   Risks of Market

Since no adequate regulations or policies have been imposed to protect investors, market risks further aggravate the vulnerable position of investors when they invest in ICOs. The three main market risks are related to the stability of cryptocurrencies, manipulation of price and the supply of cryptocurrencies. Firstly, the governance structure of ICOs without a central authority to stabilize the 'currency' again brings about a risk of price volatility of cryptocurrency.[51] As the basis for cryptocurrency valuation is uncertain and algorithms cannot take into account all the factors that affect the supply and demand of cryptocurrencies,[52] the price of a cryptocurrency is volatile and may be easily manipulated. This relates to the second point, that is, that the market for ICOs is very opaque and susceptible to price manipulation.[53] This is also why investors

---

[49] See e.g. the DAO Attack – a hacker stole USD 55 million of Ether. The full story is at Matthew Leising, 'The Ether Thief', *Bloomberg*, 13 June 2017, www.bloomberg.com /features/2017-the-ether-thief/.

[50] The Ransomware attack in 2017, which encrypts victims' files and demands a ransom payment through Bitcoins to decrypt them.

[51] Joseph Bonneau et al, 'Research Perspectives and Challenges for Bitcoin and Cryptocurrencies', MIT Computer Science and Artificial Intelligence Laboratory, 2015, https://courses.csail.mit.edu/6.857/2015/files/BMCNKF15-IEEESP-bitcoin.pdf.

[52] David S. Evans, 'Economic Aspects of Bitcoin and Other Decentralized Public-Ledger Currency Platforms', *Coase-Sandor Institute for Law & Economics Working Paper no. 685*, 2014, https://chicagounbound.uchicago.edu/cgi/viewcontent.cgi?article=2349&context= law_and_economics.

[53] Jay Clayton, 'Governance and Transparency at the Commission and in Our Markets', 2017, US Securities and Exchange Commission, www.sec.gov/news/speech/speech-clayton-2017-11-08.

may be tricked by Ponzi schemes. Thirdly, as ICOs are based on the technology which is designed in such a way as to create a free market, it accordingly prevents any government or central authority from intervening in the supply of cryptocurrency.[54] The various programming and algorithms of different cryptocurrencies allows the total amount of supply to be capped differently or without limit. For example, the supply of Bitcoin is capped at 21 million and people can get Bitcoins by receiving them from others, or by earning them by way of awards from investments or through running a node and generating blocks, that is, mining.[55] While Bitcoin set a limit for the total Bitcoin volume at the time it was launched, Ethereum has set its limit for a total supply of 230 million Ethers until 2017[56] in response to the monetary policy announced by the Ether network.[57] However, the trustworthiness of the authority releasing the 'monetary policy' is dubious. Therefore, it is unclear as to how much cryptocurrency can be produced if there is no authoritative party to regulate it.

3.3.3 Benefits and Risks of ICOs in a Chinese Context

In addition to the general risks as mentioned above, some risks may be more serious in China. The value basis of cryptocurrencies is known to be not clearly defined, prices of cryptocurrencies are volatile and the ICO market is quite speculative. Given the specific circumstances of the Chinese ICO market, 90 per cent of China-based ICOs are said to be scams[58] taking advantage of investors' lack of knowledge about how ICO works. It is because of the unique character of China's national situation, including the short growth period of the financial regulatory regime and the high population density which makes it much harder to educate investors, that Chinese investors are more vulnerable to losses and the government

---

[54] David Yermack, 'Is Bitcoin a Real Currency? An Economic Appraisal', in David Lee Luo Chuen (ed), *Handbook of Digital Currency: Bitcoin, Innovation, Financial Instruments, and Big Data* (Elsevier Academic Press, 2015).

[55] Satoshi Nakamoto, 'Bitcoin: A Peer-to-Peer Electronic Cash System', 2008, https://bitcoin.org/bitcoin.pdf.

[56] ETCDEV TEAM, 'A Joint Statement on Ethereum Classic's Monetary Policy', 2017, https://medium.com/@ETCChina/monetarypolicy-1b9c73568081.

[57] ECIP, 'Monetary Policy and Final Modification to the Ethereum Classic Emmission Schedule', 2016, https://github.com/ethereumproject/ECIPs/blob/master/ECIPs/ECIP-1017.md.

[58] 'ICO Was Characterized as Illegal Fundraising, Crush of Overnight Dreams', 2 September 2017, www.finet.hk/Newscenter/news_content/59aa5805e4b0d1966a2a57e1 (resources from the study of most ICO White Books conducted by the PBOC).

3.3 ECONOMIC ANALYSIS OF ICO

is more sensitive regarding the ICO market. Even though it is said that all ICOs have to post a white paper stating detailed information about their project, as there is no existing legal framework to regulate what information is necessary, project assets and information disclosure may be ambiguous. The consequence is that the ICOs are of dubious quality and could potentially be fraudulent scams. Besides, as the Chinese government prioritizes economic stability and sustainable development, the increasing prices of cryptocurrencies has alerted the government to the risk of a cryptocurrency bubble.

However, even though these risks put China in a particularly precarious position, we believe that it may not be the best option for the Chinese government to regain overall control of the ICO craze and reduce the risks by prohibiting ICOs. The most significant concern for the Chinese government in its decision to halt ICOs in September 2017 may have been political. Since President Xi Jinping had been emphasizing the significance of the development of a financial system and financial security, and the nineteenth National Congress of the Communist Party of China was going to be held in October 2017, the ICO ban issued in September 2017 was consistent with the central government's stated policy of maintaining financial order.[59] However, an ICO prohibition is not the only way to address the problem that ICOs operated in China are mostly unregulated and potentially fraudulent and to protect poorly educated investors from being taken advantage of and maintain political stability. From the perspective of this chapter, these risks can be reduced or controlled by regulations. Besides, there are many benefits which are contributable to China's overall development.

In addition to the general benefits which have been discussed above, there are a few benefits of ICOs that may be more specific to China. During recent years, China has almost accomplished digital transformation and is already a global leader in the digital economy.[60] At the nineteenth National Congress of the Communist Party of China, President Xi Jinping emphasized the significance of digital economy,

---

[59] Michael House et al, 'China Halts ICOs and Token Sales and China-Based Trading Platforms Suspend Trading amid Reports of Additional Government Restrictions', 2017, www.virtual currencyreport.com/2017/09/china-halts-icos-and-token-sales-and-china-based-trading-platforms-suspend-trading-amid-reports-of-additional-government-restrictions/.

[60] Mckinsey Global Institute, 'Digital China: Powering the Economy to Global Competitiveness', 2017, www.mckinsey.com/featured-insights/china/digital-china-powering-the-economy-to-global-competitiveness.

internet, informatization and intellectualization for China's development in the future and he also mentioned that Cyber Superpower, Digital China and Smart Society were important directions for China's overall development.[61] As ICOs operate on blockchain technology and some of them aim at innovating the current societal system or Fintech, a prohibition of ICO would definitely impair their contribution to China's digital development.

For example, before the ICO ban, the most successful ICO in China was possibly the NEO, also called Antshares, a company raising funds to develop a decentralized protocol designed to realize a 'smart economy' by digitizing real-world assets into digital assets and allow users to register, trade and circulate via a peer-to-peer network.[62] In addition to its project objective of providing a platform for people to digitize their assets, NEO also aimed to become the platform for decentralized applications, smart contracts, as well as ICOs. Because of the anonymity of blockchain, serious concerns were raised in government about the potential risks, whereupon NEO also solved this problem by utilizing a digital identity – a verifiable identity in digital form.[63] From the example of NEO, it can be seen that ICOs can indeed bring about benefits which are consistent with China's future strategy and can contribute much to a Digital China. However, due to the ICO ban, NEO has had to return all the funds collected from Chinese investors as well as other ICO projects. Therefore, a ban does not only impair the development of those individual ICO projects, but also prohibits the contributions of ICOs to the development of a Digital China.

3.4 International Experiences

In 2017, regulators in the United States, Canada, Australia, Singapore and Hong Kong paved the way towards exercising jurisdiction over ICOs, progressively tightening regulation around ICOs. Compared to

---

[61] Xi Jinping, 'Secure a Decisive Victory in Building a Moderately Prosperous Society in All Respects and Strive for the Great Success of Socialism with Chinese Characteristics for a New Era', 2017, www.xinhuanet.com/english/download/Xi_Jinping's_report_at_19th_CPC_National_Congress.pdf.

[62] NEO, 'NEO White Paper: A Distributed Network for the Smart Economy', 2017, https://bravenewcoin.com/insights/neo-white-paper-a-distributed-network-for-the-smart-economy.

[63] Noam Levenson, 'NEO versus Ethereum: Why NEO might be 2018's strongest cryptocurrency', 2017, https://hackernoon.com/neo-versus-ethereum-why-neo-might-be-2018s-strongest-cryptocurrency-79956138bea3.

3.4 INTERNATIONAL EXPERIENCES 69

China's outright ban, the financial regulators in those jurisdictions issued statements on the legal status of ICOs as well as possible laws and regulations that could apply to this sector. Unlike these five jurisdictions, the United Kingdom and the EU, which have been known to be FinTech-friendly, have not shown any indication of their intention to regulate this sector at this time even though they have published a warning about ICO-related risks. In this section, the current state of ICO regulations in all the jurisdictions mentioned above will be explored.

3.4.1 United States

Perhaps the United States is the first country to look into potential regulatory oversight in this booming area and take steps towards legitimizing cryptocurrency. Various US government agencies and several court rulings in different states have classified cryptocurrency as a medium of exchange that functions as a currency, a security, a commodity or a property. This sub-section looks at the steps taken by the US state courts as well as the US financial regulator, the SEC, to regulate ICO-related activities.

3.4.1.1 Cryptocurrency Is Not the Equivalent of Money

The legal status of cryptocurrency has been murky since the United States first classified cryptocurrency in 2013 as a 'virtual currency' and the term was reaffirmed in *The State of Florida v. Michell A. Espinoza (Espinoza)*,[64] which concerned a seller of Bitcoin accused of money laundering and operating an unlicensed money services business. Judge Pooler ruled that Bitcoin was not money even though it may 'have some attributes in common with what we commonly refer to as money' and dismissed the two charges.[65] As per Pooler J's comments, 'Bitcoin has a long way to go before it is the equivalent of money' due to its decentralized system and high volatility and 'with such volatility they have a limited ability to act as a store of value'.[66] This has set a benchmark in the judicial branch but it is unclear how long the ruling in *Espinoza* will stand. The ruling is in line with the position which is taken by the Internal Revenue Services (IRS). The IRS treats virtual currency as property for federal tax purposes and defines virtual currency as 'a digital representation of value that functions

---

[64] No. F14-2923 (11th Cir. 2016).
[65] Ibid.
[66] Ibid.

as a medium of exchange, a unit of account, and/or a store of value' and lacks the 'legal tender status'.[67] In its guidance, the IRS also refers to the 2013 Financial Crimes Enforcement Network (FinCEN) Guidance emphasizing that virtual currency, which functions similar to and can be exchanged for real currencies as 'convertible virtual currency', is not money in itself.[68]

3.4.1.2 The Howey Test

The US SEC, on 25 July 2017, for the first time issued pronouncements that federal securities laws may apply to ICOs although they had argued for this position in the courts several times. The SEC issued a Report of Investigation Pursuant to section 21(a) of the Securities Exchange Act of 1934: The DAO (the DAO Report). They concluded that DAO tokens, offered and sold in the ICO by the DAO and executed on Ethereum as a means for raising capital, were securities.[69] The DAO, also called the Decentralized Autonomous Organization, was based on the concept of a smart contract system. It was designed to function as a community-managed venture fund, without having any owner, manager or analyst, and generated approximately 12 million Ethers, which was valued at approximately USD 150 million at the time the offering closed.[70] Investors paid Ethers to the DAO and received the right to vote on and become investors in venture projects proposed by start-ups, based on Ethereum.[71] A security, which is defined in the 1933 Securities Act and the 1934 Securities Exchange Act, means 'any note, stock, treasury stock, security future, security-based swap, bond [...] or investment contract [...]'.[72]

The US SEC based their findings that DAO tokens were to be regarded as securities under an 'investment contract' (be it a contract, transaction or scheme) on the *Howey* test, which was articulated in the Supreme

---

[67] Internal Revenue Service, Notice 2014–21, 2014.

[68] Ibid. For a more comprehensive description of convertible virtual currencies, see Financial Crimes Enforcement Network (FinCEN), *Guidance on the Application of Fin CEN's Regulations to Persons Administering, Exchanging, or Using Virtual Currencies,* FIN-2013-G001, 18 March 2013.

[69] US SEC, *Report of Investigation Pursuant to Section 21(a) of the Securities Exchange Act of 1934: The Dao,* Release No. 81207, 2017.

[70] Ibid.

[71] Ibid.

[72] Section 2(a)(1), Securities Act of 1933 (enacted on 27 March 1933 by the US Congress); the Securities Exchange Act of 1934 contains a definition of security virtually identical to that contained in the Securities Act of 1933.

Court case – *SEC v. W.J. Howey*.[73] The test establishes 'whether it is an investment of money in a common enterprise with a reasonable expectation of profits to be derived from the entrepreneurial or managerial efforts of others'.[74]

Indicators as to whether an arrangement is an investment contract comprise four prongs, according to the *Howey* test. First, there should be an investment of money. The meaning of 'money' for the purposes of ICOs is a question of fact, not of law. In *SEC v. Shavers*,[75] concerning the use of Bitcoins raised through an ICO and the misuse and misappropriation of investors' Bitcoins, the investment of Bitcoins was held to meet the *Howey* test.[76] It can be inferred that Bitcoin is regarded as 'money' for the purposes of ICOs even though it does not have the equivalent status of money. Therefore, it is reasonable to conclude that Ethers paid by investors into the DAO should also be regarded as 'money' for the purposes of ICOs and thus the first prong is satisfied.

Second, there should be a common enterprise. Even though there is no consensus among the circuit courts in the United States and the US Supreme Court has not reached a clear definition of 'common enterprise', this term has been interpreted broadly.[77] Case law strongly points to the multiple investors' test for common enterprises, that is, a common enterprise is an enterprise shared among a promoter and multiple investors.[78] In *Reves v. Ernst & Young*,[79] an offering to a broad segment of the public, involving multiple investors, is held to represent a common enterprise.[80] The DAO must therefore clearly qualify as a common enterprise.

A third requirement is that an investor expects profits from his investment, whereby 'profits' do not need to be the sole reason for investing and any increase in value, dividends, and other periodic payments can amount to 'profits'.[81] In the DAO, since the objective of pooling Ethers was to fund projects in exchange for a return, the third prong can be

---

[73] 328 US 293, 301 (1946).
[74] Ibid; *SEC v. Edwards*, 540 US 389, 393 (2004).
[75] No. 4: 13-CV-416, 2014 WL.
[76] Ibid.
[77] Stephen M. Maloney, 'What Is a Common Enterprise – A Question of Legislative Intent' (1990) 11 *Mississippi College Law Review* 125.
[78] *SEC v. Howey*, 328 US 293, 301 (1946); *Marine Bank v. Weaver*, 455 US 551 (1982); *Reves v. Ernst & Young*, 494 US 56, 68 (1990); *SEC v. Edwards*, 540 US 389, 393 (2004).
[79] 494 US 56, 68 (1990).
[80] Ibid.
[81] See *SEC v. Edwards*, 540 US 389, 393 (2004); US SEC, *Report of Investigation Pursuant to Section 21(a) of the Securities Exchange Act of 1934: The Dao*, Release No. 81207, 2017.

easily met as well. The last prong is that profits come from the entrepreneurial or managerial efforts of others. Under this prong, the issue is 'whether those efforts made by those other than the investors are the undeniably significant ones which can affect the success or failure of the enterprise'.[82]

The US SEC first looked at the role of the DAO creators who had been responsible for promoting the ICO, for providing information about the DAO, for closely monitoring the forum discussing the DAO, and for selecting persons to serve as Curators, and for vetting projects based on their expertise for the first round. The SEC concluded that these activities had substantially contributed to the success of the DAO.[83] In addition, the SEC analysed the contributions made by investors and concluded that the mere exercise of their voting rights to decide whether or not to fund a project did not constitute a significant managerial effort.[84] Another reason was that the quasi-anonymous nature of the investors' identities prohibited them from contacting each other or forming alliances so as to exert managerial control. In addition, with Curators vetting projects before they could be voted on by investors, this substantially reduced the investors' contribution. Therefore, by meeting the *Howey* test, the investment in the DAO creates an investment contract which qualifies as a security and is thus subject to securities law and regulations.

3.4.1.3 Implications of the DAO Report

The announcement made by the US SEC that ICOs may be governed by securities laws means that any ICO may have to either demonstrate, by providing evidence, that its digital coins are not *de facto* securities or that they fall under the US SEC's regulatory scrutiny. In the DAO Report, the US SEC clarified what type of ICO would be regarded as an offering of securities, and therefore would be subject to securities laws. However, two issues have to be addressed here. First, for a newly issued digital coin to fall within the regulatory scope of securities laws, the cryptocurrency paid in exchange for the newly issued one has to be classified as 'money' in the first place for the purposes of ICOs. As ICOs are operated on blockchain technology, a newly issued digital coin and the one paid in exchange, most of the time as either Bitcoin or Ether, inevitably share the same features. It is therefore dubious to impose two legal natures

---

[82] See *SEC v. Glenn W. Turner Enterprises*, 474 F.2d 476 (1973).

[83] US SEC, *Report of Investigation Pursuant to Section 21(a) of the Securities Exchange Act of 1934: The Dao*, Release No. 81207, 2017.

[84] Ibid.

simultaneously upon cryptocurrency – that is, being both 'money' and security. However, under this reasoning, a cryptocurrency could be regarded as 'money' only when it is used as a medium of exchange for the purposes of ICOs.

The second issue is that an ICO could fall outside the scope of securities law if the issuer has declared that the ICO is not to make a profit but only serves a specific purpose and utility. In other words, an ICO might escape the US SEC's regulatory scrutiny by declaring it not being for profit so as to quash investors' expectation of profits and fail the *Howey* test, and therefore may not be classified as an issue of securities. However, the second issue might be clear when seen in light of the most recent press release issued by the US SEC. On 2 April 2018, the US SEC halted an ICO called 'Centra' and charged the two co-founders with fraud and violation of the federal securities laws because they had used false or misleading marketing materials to promote their ICO.[85] Even though the issued 'Centra Token' had the utility component that, as they alleged, allows holders to use the Centra product line and ecosystem, including the option of instant conversion of cryptocurrencies into legal tender,[86] this ICO allegedly violated securities laws. It appears that as long as the issued cryptocurrency has an investment component, which is similar to traditional shareholders' interests or rights, a financial authority is likely to assume that the issued cryptocurrency is an unregistered security.

3.4.1.4 Possibility of Being Regulated as Commodity?

Despite the DAO Report reaching a conclusion that an ICO may be regarded as an offering of securities under federal law, this does not end the possibility of it being subjected to regulatory inquiry because cryptocurrency could also be regulated as other items. In 2015, the US Commodity Futures Trading Commission (CFTC) took the position in the Coinflip case, which involved a platform marketing Bitcoin derivatives, that Bitcoin and other virtual currencies were properly defined as commodities and should be subject to the Commodity Exchange Act.[87]

---

[85] Centra, 'White Paper – Version 3.0 Centra Wallet System', 2017, https://cryptorating.eu/whitepapers/Centra/CentraWhitepaper.pdf.

[86] SEC, 'SEC Halts Fraudulent Scheme Involving Unregistered ICO', 2018, www.sec.gov/news/press-release/2018-53.

[87] CFTC, 'CFTC Orders Bitcoin Options Trading Platform Operator and Its CEO to Cease Illegally Offering Bitcoin Options and to Cease Operating a Facility for Trading or Processing of Swaps without Registering', 2015, www.cftc.gov/PressRoom/PressReleases/7231-15.

This position is consistent with China's current classification of crypto-currency as a 'virtual commodity'.

However, the reasoning behind classifying cryptocurrency as a commodity in the Coinflip case is different from that used by the Chinese authorities. In this case, Bitcoin was regarded as a commodity because derivative contracts or options had been offered based on the value of Bitcoin. Since then, the CFTC has had the authority to oversee cryptocurrency futures and options and platforms for cryptocurrency derivatives and futures must be registered as a Swap Execution Facility or a Designated Contract Market.[88] In July 2017, the US CFTC for the first time granted LedgerX, a trading platform providing trading services for crypto-currency derivatives and clearing services for fully collateralized cryptocur-rency swaps, to be registered as both a Swap Execution Facility and a derivatives clearing organization in accordance with the Commodity Exchange Act.[89] Based on the facts and circumstances of the two examples, it can be argued that the US CFTC may only treat cryptocurrencies as a commodity for the purposes of cryptocurrency derivatives.

Even though it is understandable that some cryptocurrencies can be (exclusively) generated through online mining which is somewhat simi-lar to mining gold and other metals, it is still dubious why the underlying cryptocurrencies cannot be treated as a type of security for the purposes of cryptocurrency derivatives. In order to address this problem, a distinction must be made between cryptocurrencies generated through mining and cryptocurrencies issued through ICOs. It is worth noting that the platforms that the US CFTC have held to be governed by the Commodity Exchange Act to date only provide trading and clearing services for swaps and options on Bitcoins, a cryptocurrency that can only be generated through mining.[90] Given that cryptocurrencies which are issued by ICOs are not generated through mining alone, it is reason-able to conclude that cryptocurrencies for the purposes of ICOs will not be regarded as a commodity. In other words, the possibility of regarding

---

[88] Ibid.

[89] CFTC, 'CFTC Grants SEF Registration to LedgerX LLC', 2017, https://mondovisione.com /media-and-resources/news/cftc-grants-sef-registration-to-ledgerx-llc/; CFTC, 'CFTC Grants DCO Registration to LedgerX LLC', 2017, www.cftc.gov/PressRoom/ PressReleases/7592-17.

[90] Ibid. See also CFTC, 'CFTC Orders Bitcoin Options Trading Platform Operator and its CEO to Cease Illegally Offering Bitcoin Options and to Cease Operating a Facility for Trading or Processing of Swaps without Registering', 2015, www.cftc.gov/PressRoom/ PressReleases/7231-15; Satoshi Nakamoto, 'Bitcoin: A Peer-to-Peer Electronic Cash System', 2008, https://bitcoin.org/bitcoin.pdf.

cryptocurrencies that can only be generated through mining, such as Bitcoin, as a commodity for the purposes of Bitcoin-based derivatives may not affect the ICO regime.

However, things became murky again on 19 January 2018 when the US CFTC filed three civil enforcement actions in the US District Court against three cryptocurrency operators.[91] They were charged with engaging in fraudulent schemes to solicit Bitcoin and money from members of the public, misrepresenting information and misappropriating those members' funds in violation of federal commodities laws. Five days after the three charges, the US CFTC filed another similar action in the federal court charging My Big Coin Pay Inc. with misappropriating over USD 6 million from customers and using this for personal purchases.[92] The fact that fraudulent cryptocurrency schemes are charged by the US CFTC rather than by the US SEC indicates that the US regulators are attempting to classify cryptocurrency under such schemes as a commodity. Despite the fact that cryptocurrency is to potentially be classified as a commodity, for the purposes of ICO, it is more likely to be categorized as a security instead. This is because on 30 January 2018, the US SEC alleged that the ICO launched by AriseBank, an algorithmic trading application, was based on fraud, and had obtained a court order to halt and freeze funds raised by the ICO.[93] Therefore, despite the murky categorization of cryptocurrency, for the purposes of ICO, cryptocurrency is more likely to be regulated as a security rather than a commodity if an ICO raises the US regulators' concerns.

3.4.2 Canada

Canada followed in the footsteps of the United States, and Canada's financial regulator, the Canadian Securities Administrators (CSA), released an

---

[91] See CFTC, CFT Charges Patrick K. McDonnell and His Company Cabbage Tech, Corp. d/b/a Coin Drop Markets with Engaging in Fraudulent Virtual Currency Scheme', 2018, www.cftc.gov/PressRoom/PressReleases/pr7675-18; CFTC, 'CFTC Charges Colorado Resident Dillon Michael Dean and His Company, the Entrepreneurs Headquarters Limited, with Engaging in a Bitcoin and Binary Options Fraud Scheme', 2018, www .cftc.gov/PressRoom/PressReleases/pr7674-18; Reuters, 'US CFTC Sues Three Virtual Currency Operators for Fraud', 19 January 2018, www.reuters.com/article/us-usa-cftc-bitcoin/u-s-cftc-sues-three-virtual-currency-operators-for-fraud-idUSKBN1F81K9.

[92] CFTC, 'CFTC Charges Randall Crater, Mark Gillespie, and My Big Coin Pay, Inc. with Fraud and Misappropriation in Ongoing Virtual Currency Scam', 2018, www.cftc.gov /PressRoom/PressReleases/pr7678-18.

[93] SEC, 'Press Release – SEC Halts Alleged Initial Coin Offering Scam', 2018, www.sec.gov /news/press-release/2018-8.

76 INITIAL COIN OFFERINGS

announcement on 24 August 2017 stating that securities law may apply to ICOs.[94] The announcement referred to the CSA Staff Notice 46-307 on Cryptocurrency Offerings (CSA Notice), in which items such as how securities law requirements may apply to ICOs and what obligations may apply under securities laws are addressed.

3.4.2.1 The Four-Prong Test

The CSA Notice clarifies that a facts-and-circumstances-type inquiry will apply to all ICOs since 'every ICO is unique and must be assessed on its own characteristics'.[95] Similar to the United States, a lengthy but non-exhaustive definition of 'security' is provided in the Canadian securities laws – Securities Act (Ontario), which states that an 'investment contract' is a type of 'security'. This definition captures a purchase of digital coins where the value of such digital coins is tied to the future profits or success of a business regardless of whether they represent the shares in a company or similar ownership interests. To determine whether an ICO would be viewed as an investment contract, the well-established four-prong test originating in the US case *SEC v. W.J. Howey*[96] was adopted in Canada as stated in *Pacific Coast Coin Exchange v. Ontario Securities Commission ('Pacific Coast')*.[97] It requires a purposive interpretation while bearing in mind the objective of investor protection.[98] In this case, Pacific Coast sold silver coins on TV and traded in 'commodity account agreements' for the purchase of silver coins on margin.[99] Investors entered into 'commodity account agreements' with Pacific Coast but most investors never paid the purchase price in full so they never took possession of any silver coins.[100] Investors' return depended fully on fluctuations in the market price for silver and they would either realize a profit or suffer a loss when they closed their accounts.[101]

---

[94] CSA, 'Canadian Securities Regulators Outline Securities Law Requirements That May Apply to Cryptocurrency Offerings', 2017, www.osc.gov.on.ca/en/NewsEvents_nr_20170824_cryptocurrency-offerings.htm.

[95] Ibid.

[96] 328 US 293, 301 (1946).

[97] [1978] 2 SCR 112.

[98] CSA, 'Canadian Securities Regulators Outline Securities Law Requirements That May Apply to Cryptocurrency Offerings', 2017, www.osc.gov.on.ca/en/NewsEvents_nr_20170824_cryptocurrency-offerings.htm.

[99] *Pacific Coast*, [1978] 2 SCR 112.

[100] Ibid.

[101] Ibid.

3.4 INTERNATIONAL EXPERIENCES

The Supreme Court of Canada held that 'commodity account agreements' were 'investment contracts', a term included in the statutory definition of securities for the purposes of the Securities Act (Ontario).[102] The court looked at *Howey* and endorsed the four-prong test in determining whether or not an investment contract exists. In other words, they look at whether an arrangement involves the following: (1) an investment of money (2) in a common enterprise (3) with the expectation of profit (4) to come significantly from the efforts of others.[103] Since Pacific Coast was clearly a common enterprise which was responsible for management and operation and investors deposited money into their accounts with the expectation of an increase in the market price for silver, the four-prong test was satisfied and therefore the 'commodity account agreements' were held to be securities.[104]

It can be argued that the Canadian approach is almost the same as the US approach over ICO regulation. Therefore, it can be concluded that once an ICO is regarded as involving investors investing their money in a common enterprise with the expectation of profit to come significantly from others' efforts, the ICO will be subject to securities laws.

3.4.2.2   Other Possibilities

The CSA Notice also states the possibility of treating an ICO as a derivative under applicable securities laws and for it to be subject to derivatives laws if the ICO meets the criteria of issuing derivatives adopted by the Canadian authorities.

3.4.3   Australia

Among jurisdictions that are relatively friendly to innovative and new Fintech, Australia takes a fast step in looking into the ICO regime and has proposed relatively clear guidelines aimed at both individuals and businesses. The Australian Securities & Investment Commission (ASIC) proposed guidelines (INFO 225) on ICOs in September 2017 and clarified that an ICO could be an offer of a managed investment scheme, a share in a company, a derivative or a non-cash payment facility and

---

[102] Ibid.

[103] CSA, 'Canadian Securities Regulators Outline Securities Law Requirements That May Apply to Cryptocurrency Offerings', 2017, www.osc.gov.on.ca/en/NewsEvents_nr_2017 0824_cryptocurrency-offerings.htm.

[104] *Pacific Coast*, [1978] 2 SCR 112.

could be subject to the relevant law.[105] Therefore, it is worth having a closer look at the ICO regime in Australia.

3.4.3.1 Managed Investment Schemes

According to ASIC, most ICOs are likely to constitute a managed investment scheme, or can be referred to as a managed fund or a collective investment fund, and are therefore subject to the Corporations Act.[106] A managed investment scheme is defined in the Corporations Act and INFO 225 provides the basic indicators in accordance with the Corporations Act to be as follows:

> (1) people contribute assets (such as digital currency) to obtain an interest in the scheme; (2) the assets are pooled together with one or more other contributors or used in a common enterprise to produce financial benefits or interests in property; and (3) the contributors do not have day-to-day control over the operation of the scheme but, at times, may have voting rights or similar rights.[107]

As the law looks at substance rather than form, even though some ICOs have labelled the funds raised by them as a receipt for services purchased, as long as the value of the cryptocurrency is affected by 'the pooling of funds from contributors or use of those funds under the arrangement', then the ICO is likely to be regarded as a managed investment scheme.[108]

However, what does 'interest' mean under the criteria for a managed investment scheme? According to section 9 of the Corporations Act, "interest' in a managed investment scheme means a right to benefits produced by the scheme (whether the right is actual, prospective or contingent and whether it is enforceable or not)'.[109] It is a very broad definition and a cryptocurrency issued by an ICO is highly likely to fall within the definition of 'interest' as long as it can bring benefits to the cryptocurrency holder.

Compared to the *Howey* test for investment contracts, the INFO 225 test for managed investment schemes is much broader. Firstly, it does not mention 'money' but uses 'investment of assets' instead. Given that the term 'asset' has a very broad meaning which includes many different things, it is unclear how the ASIC will clarify the nature of cryptocurrency

---

[105] ASIC Information Sheet 225.
[106] Corporations Act 2001 (amended and in force on 1 January 2018).
[107] ASIC Information Sheet 225.
[108] Ibid.
[109] Corporations Act 2001, section 9.

even though it must be an asset. Secondly, INFO 225 does not require 'the expectation of profits' as an element but uses 'obtain an interest' instead, in which 'interest' is deemed to include 'profits'. Additionally, even though 'common enterprise' has been interpreted broadly in the *Howey* test, the Corporations Act makes it clear that no matter which form an 'entity' takes, as long as there is a pool of assets contributed by one or more contributors (in the *Howey* test, there should be more than one contributor), the arrangement can amount to a managed investment scheme. Accordingly, since the test for managed investment schemes is broader than the *Howey* test, if the DAO had operated in Australia, it is likely that it would have definitely been regarded as a managed investment scheme.

Besides, according to the definition of an investment contract adopted in *Howey*, it covers any contract, transaction or scheme. That is to say, investment contracts also include managed investment schemes. In this sense, an ICO that qualifies as a managed scheme will also be regarded as a security and therefore be subject to securities laws. Since the Corporations Act in Australia combines many laws, including securities law and company law, it does not mean that managed investment schemes, if they are governed by the Corporation Act, should be governed by company law in other jurisdictions.

3.4.3.2 Issue of Shares

According to ASIC, the objective of ICOs and the rights attached to the digital coins are the two aspects that ASIC focuses on. An ICO is highly likely to fall within the definition of a share if, first of all, the objective of the ICO is to fund a company (or to fund an undertaking that looks like a company), and secondly, if the rights attached to the digital coins issued by the ICO are similar to the rights commonly attached to a share, such as ownership of the body, voting rights in decisions of the body, some rights to receive dividends, or promises to share in future profits.[110] As long as the two prongs are satisfied, an ICO is likely to be a *de facto* IPO and therefore will be held to the requirements of conducting an IPO and will be governed by securities laws as well.

3.4.3.3 Derivatives or Non-Cash Payment Facilities

Similar to the CSA Notice, INFO 225 also states the possibility of treating a digital coin issued by an ICO as a derivative if the digital coin is 'priced based on factors such as a financial product or underlying market or asset

---

[110] ASIC Information Sheet 225.

price moving in a certain direction before a time or event which resulted in a payment being required as part of the rights or obligations attached to the coin [...]'.[111] Even though unlikely, the ASIC also discusses the possibility of an ICO being a non-cash payment facility. However, for the purposes of this chapter, digital coins offered under an ICO are highly unlikely to involve a non-cash payment facility unless they are structured under a specific condition, which is outside the scope of this chapter. Therefore, as it is not structured as the normal ICOs discussed in this chapter, it is out of the scope of this book.

3.4.3.4 ICOs to Be Distinguished from Crowd-Sourced Funding

According to the Corporations Amendment (Crowd-Sourced Funding) Act 2017 that took effect on 29 September 2017, crowd-sourced funding is now regulated by the Corporations Act in Australia. However, crowd-sourced funding only applies to small unlisted companies, enabling them to raise up to AUD 5 million through issuing ordinary shares to retail clients without going through the burdensome IPO procedures.[112] Based on the requirements, it is clear that an ICO is not a type of crowd-sourced funding because the objects are registered companies and the financing method is arranged by issuing ordinary shares. These two factors definitely distinguish ICOs from crowd-sourced funding in Australia because ICOs are usually launched by start-ups and they issue digital coins, the definition of which is based on facts and circumstances, to the public. Additionally, ASIC has made it clear that ICO is not a type of crowd-sourced funding[113] and thus the Corporations Amendment (Crowd-Sourced Funding) Act 2017 does not apply to ICOs.

Even though ICOs have been launched in Australia since the release of the guidelines on ICO, for example Power Ledge, the first ICO to be launched since the release of the guidelines raising AUD 17 million half in cash and another half in cryptocurrencies, which was designed to create a renewable energy trading marketplace for households to trade surplus solar power, the ASIC remains silent as to how to regulate such an ICO. Therefore, it is still unclear how the Australian authorities will regulate ICOs in practice.

---

[111] Ibid.
[112] Corporations Amendment (Crowd-Sourced Funding) Act 2017.
[113] ASIC Information Sheet 225.

3.4 INTERNATIONAL EXPERIENCES

3.4.4 *Singapore*

3.4.4.1 Applicability of Securities Laws

Similar to the United States, Australia and Canada, Singapore's financial regulator, the Monetary Authority of Singapore (MAS), issued A Guide to Digital Token Offerings (ICO Guide) on 14 November 2017 and last revised it on 26 May 2020, declaring that ICOs may be subject to Singapore's Securities and Futures Act (SFA). According to the ICO Guide, an ICO may be regulated by MAS if it constitutes a type of capital markets product, which includes 'any securities, units in a collective investment scheme, derivatives contracts and spot foreign exchange contracts for purposes of leveraged foreign exchange trading'.[114] Under the Prospectus Requirements of the ICO Guide, once an ICO constitutes a capital markets product, it 'must be made in or accompanied by a prospectus that is prepared in accordance with the SFA and is registered with MAS'.[115]

In deciding what constitutes an ICO, some other laws are also relevant. Under section 2(1) of the SFA, the term 'capital markets products' includes any securities (which includes shares, debentures and units in a business trust), units in a collective investment scheme, derivatives contracts (which includes derivatives of shares, debentures and units in a business trust), spot foreign exchange contracts for the purposes of leveraged foreign exchange trading, and such other products as MAS may prescribe as capital markets products.[116] Furthermore, the Payment Services Act came into effect on 28 January 2020, providing a framework for the regulation of payment systems and payment service providers in Singapore. This act defines a 'digital payment token' as any digital representation of value (other than an excluded digital representation of value) that[117]

1. is expressed as a unit;
2. is not denominated in any currency, and is not pegged by its issuer to any currency;
3. is, or is intended to be, a medium of exchange accepted by the public, or a section of the public, as payment for goods or services or for the discharge of a debt;

---

[114] Monetary Authority of Singapore, 'A Guide to Digital Token Offerings', 26 May 2020, www.mas.gov.sg/regulation/explainers/a-guide-to-digital-token-offerings.

[115] Ibid.

[116] SFA, s2(1).

[117] Payment Services Act 2019 (No. 2 of 2019), s2.

82 INITIAL COIN OFFERINGS

4. can be transferred, stored or traded electronically;
5. satisfies such other characteristics as the Authority may prescribe.

The act gives 'digital payment tokens' an expansive definition which encompasses the different forms of cryptocurrencies.[118] However, there is no clear-cut definition of 'cryptocurrency' or 'ICO' in the act.[119]

3.4.4.2 Exemptions

Even though an ICO may constitute a security or a unit in a collective investment scheme, the ICO Guide provides four conditions for an ICO to be exempted from the Prospectus Requirements.[120] The four conditions are as follows:

> (1) the Offer is a small offer (must be a personal offer) of securities of an entity, or units in a collective investment scheme, that does not exceed SGD 5 million within any 12-month period; (2) the Offer is a private placement offer made to no more than 50 persons within any 12-month period; (3) the Offer is made to institutional investors only; or (4) the Offer is made to accredited investors.[121]

Since most ICOs are offered to the public neither in person nor in private, it is unlikely for an ICO in the current form to obtain the exemption benefits. However, as exemption from the registration requirements can save substantial time and cost, maybe future ICOs will be structured in a form to meet the four criteria in Singapore.

3.4.4.3 Application of Regulatory Sandbox to ICOs

However, in order not to stifle the development of Fintech, the Singapore authorities seem to be reluctant to impose strict regulations upon those technological start-ups, in spite of the announcement of the ICO Guide. The managing director of the MAS, Ravi Menon, said that ICOs which had the potential to be held as securities may well be the first to be tested in the regulatory sandbox, implying that those types of ICOs would not be banned or held to the IPO regulatory requirements in the first place.[122] This shows an ICO- or FinTech-friendly position in Singapore and it

---

[118] Lin Lin, 'Regulating FinTech: The Case of Singapore' (2019) 35 *Banking and Finance Law Review* 94–119, at 110.
[119] Ibid.
[120] ICO Guide.
[121] Ibid.
[122] Laura Noonan, 'Singapore Keen on Initial Coin Offering', *Financial Times*, 15 November 2017, www.ft.com/content/17173c92-c9e6-11e7-ab18-7a9fb7d6163e.

3.4 INTERNATIONAL EXPERIENCES

seems unlikely for securities laws to be applied to ICOs in Singapore in the near future. Since the regulatory sandbox was first introduced by the United Kingdom's regulator in May 2016, an explanation of what is meant by a regulatory sandbox will be briefly discussed under the UK part.

3.4.4.4 Situation of ICOs in Singapore

Due to its FinTech-friendly position, Singapore has emerged as the leading hub for ICOs in Asia and the third-largest ICO hub in the world.[123] Several ICOs have been launched successfully in Singapore, such as Digix and TenX. The ICO of Digix, issuing DGX as its own cryptocurrency, raised 465,134 Ethers, which was worth around USD 5.5 million at that time.[124] It tokenizes gold on the Ethereum blockchain and provides a platform for people to own, save and trade gold in tokenized form.[125] Every DGC represents one gram of gold.[126] The other successful ICO of TenX raised 245,832 Ethers which was worth close to USD 80 million in June 2017.[127] It is a blockchain start-up aiming at developing a cryptocurrency payment system which can convert different cryptocurrencies into fiat currencies so that people can use cryptocurrencies for their daily payment.[128] There are many other ICOs that have been launched successfully in Singapore and a few are going to be launched in the near future.[129]

This could result in a positive cycle for Singapore's Fintech development: as more good ICOs are launched successfully in Singapore, Singapore is likely to become a more favoured destination for blockchain start-ups, and the MAS regulatory sandbox will develop a more advanced and mature regulation for ICOs, and finally the overall development of

---

[123] Fintechnews Singapore, 'Singapore: Asia's Leading ICO Hub?', 2017, http://fintechnews .sg/14927/blockchain/singapore-ico-asia-hub/.

[124] Jack Ellis, 'Digix Gets $1.3m Seed Funding to Turn Gold into Cryptocurrency', 2017, www.techinasia.com/digix-seed-funding.

[125] See Digital Global's main website at https://digix.global/.

[126] Ibid.

[127] CryptoNinjas, 'TenX Raises Roughly $80 million for Cryptocurrency Payment System for Everyday Life', 2017, www.cryptoninjas.net/2017/06/28/tenx-raises-roughly-80- million-cryptocurrency-payment-system-everyday-life/.

[128] Julian Hosp et al, 'COMIT – Cryptographically-secure Off-chain Multi-asset Instant Transaction Network', 2017, https://arxiv.org/abs/1810.02174.

[129] Lin Lin, 'The Law and Practice of Fintech in Singapore', in JD Finance Research Centre (ed), *2018 Jinrong keji baogao: hangye fazhan yu falv qianyan* (2018金融科技报告：行业发展与法律前沿) [Global Fintech Report 2018: Industry Development and Legal Frontier] (Law Press China, 2018).

84 INITIAL COIN OFFERINGS

Fintech and the regulatory environment will contribute to Singapore's economy.

3.4.5 Hong Kong

As a financial centre, unlike Mainland China where the authority has just issued an overall ban on ICOs, the Hong Kong regulatory authority, the SFC, made an announcement in September 2017 in their statement on initial coin offerings (HK Statement) which claims that ICOs will fall under the HK SFC's regulatory scope if the digital coins issued under an ICO are *de facto* securities of the issuer.[130]

Very similar to the ICO Guide issued by the Singapore MAS, the HK Statement provides three typical examples – shares, debentures and interests in a collective investment scheme where a cryptocurrency issued under an ICO constitutes an ICO and will be subject to the securities laws of Hong Kong. Therefore, if the digital coins offered in an ICO represent any equity or ownership interests, they would be categorized as shares; if they represent any debt or liability owed by the issuer, they would be categorized as debentures and then both would be regulated by securities laws.[131] As for a 'collective investment scheme', as defined in Schedule 1 of the SFO, the requirements are similar to those set by the Australian authority ASIC and the Singapore authority MAS, although there are slight differences.[132] In summary, the guidelines on ICOs in Hong Kong are almost the same as Singapore's in the sense that they are subject to Hong Kong's securities laws.

In addition, in order to find a balance between avoiding the setting of strict regulations regarding Fintech development and introducing the necessary rules to protect investors and govern illegal activities, the Hong Kong regulatory authorities have launched several regulatory

---

[130] SFC, 'Statement on Initial Coin Offerings', 2017, www.sfc.hk/web/EN/news-and-announce ments/policy-statements-and-announcements/statement-on-initial-coin-offerings.html.

[131] Ibid.

[132] Generally a collective investment scheme has four elements: '(1) it must involve an arrange- ment in respect of property; (2) participants do not have day-to-day control over the management of the property; (3) the property is managed as a whole by or on behalf of the person operating the arrangements, and/or the contributions of the participants and the profits or income from which payments are made them are pooled; and (4) the purpose of effect of the arrangement is for participants to participate in or receive profits, income or other returns from the acquisition or management of the property'; see also SFC, 'Statement on Initial Coin Offerings', 2017, www.sfc.hk/web/EN/news-and-announcements/policy- statements-and-announcements/statement-on-initial-coin-offerings.html.

sandboxes. The Hong Kong Monetary Authority (HKMA) launched the Fintech Supervisory Sandbox in September 2016,[133] while the SFC launched the SFC Regulatory Sandbox in September 2017.[134] These Sandboxes may allow ICOs to operate within a relatively relaxed regulatory environment during their development stage and help Hong Kong become one of the hubs for Fintech and innovative products.

Although Hong Kong has not had any grand campaigns like the United States or Singapore, it has witnessed several ICOs conducted by local start-ups. Simple Token, a start-up aimed at providing services of cryptocurrency creation, sale, distribution and maintenance to companies, raised 46,828 Ethers which was worth approximately USD 21 million in 2017.[135] On 10 October 2017, AirSwap launched its ICO and raised 119,511 Ethers, valued at around USD 36 million.[136] This organization is going to build a cryptocurrency exchange providing better privacy and security and making it easier for investors to find, price and trade cryptocurrencies.[137]

3.4.6   United Kingdom and European Union

3.4.6.1   FinTech-Friendly Stance in the United Kingdom and the EU

The UK FCA and the European Securities and Markets Authority (ESMA) have been known to be very Fintech-friendly. Unlike the jurisdictions mentioned above which issued substantive guidelines on how to regulate ICOs, there is no clear guideline on how an ICO will be regulated according to either the financial authority in the United Kingdom or the EU. Even though no announcement about how to regulate ICOs has been issued, the innovation-friendly stances of the UK FCA and ESMA have been demonstrated by their statements warning against ICO-related risks and highlighting the risks of investing in ICOs that investors should be aware of. However, there is no indication that this sector is going to be regulated at this stage.

---

[133] Hong Kong Monetary Authority, 'Fintech Supervisory Sandbox (FSS)', 2018, www .hkma.gov.hk/eng/key-functions/international-financial-centre/fintech-supervisory-sandbox.shtml.

[134] SFC, 'Circular to Announce the SFC Regulatory Sandbox', 2017, www.sfc.hk /edistributionWeb/gateway/EN/circular/doc?refNo=17EC63.

[135] See Simple Token's website at https://sale.simpletoken.org/.

[136] See AirSwap's website at www.airswap.io/.

[137] Ibid.

The UK FCA released a statement entitled 'Consumer Warning about the Risks of Initial Coin Offerings ("ICOs")' on 12 September 2017, which showed that the UK regulator was taking a 'wait-and-see' approach. The statement consists of only one page and contains a brief explanation of ICOs and the risks that investors may run. In addition to this, it just simply states that 'many ICOs will fall outside the regulated space' and some ICOs may involve regulated investments if their proposed structure 'has parallels with IPOs, private placement of securities, crowdfunding or even collective investment scheme'.[138]

Compared to the UK FCA, the EU ESMA seems to be even more generous to ICOs. In addition to giving some warnings about the risks of investing in ICOs,[139] ESMA merely provides four possibly related directives for issuers of ICOs, which are the Prospectus Directive, the Markets in Financial Instruments Directive, the Alternative Investment Fund Managers Directive and the Fourth Anti–Money Laundering Directive (AMLD).[140] Then, the EU ESMA asks companies or issuers to look at the directives for themselves and see whether they are involved in any regulated investment activities.[141] However, even though it may seem vague to just position the four directives, this might implicitly suggest the possibility for the EU regulator to regulate ICOs in accordance with the laws governing IPOs, investment funds, other financial instruments and money laundering in the future.

3.4.6.2   The United Kingdom's Regulatory Sandbox Program

In May 2016, the United Kingdom took the initiative to put into practice the regulatory sandbox which allowed not only financial institutions but also start-ups to test their innovative financial products in a regulatory sandbox with real consumers and under a relaxed degree of regulatory

---

[138] Financial Conduct Authority, 'Consumer Warning about the Risks of Initial Coin Offerings ("ICOs")', 2017, www.fca.org.uk/news/statements/initial-coin-offerings.

[139] European Securities and Markets Authority, 'ESMA Alerts Investors to the High Risks of Initial Coin Offerings (ICOs)', 2017, www.esma.europa.eu/sites/default/files/library/esma50-157-829_ico_statement_investors.pdf. It lists five risks of investing in ICOs: (1) unregulated space, vulnerable to fraud or illicit activities; (2) high risk of losing all of the invested capital; (3) lack of exit options and extreme price volatility; (4) inadequate information; and (5) flaws in the technology.

[140] European Securities and Markets Authority, 'ESMA Alerts Firms Involved in Initial Coin Offerings (ICOs) to the Need to Meet Relevant Regulatory Requirements', 2017, www.esma.europa.eu/document/esma-alerts-firms-involved-in-initial-coin-offerings-icos-need-meet-relevant-regulatory.

[141] Ibid.

oversight and support.[142] In order to not add too much burden on the regulators, only those companies or firms that could meet the criteria set by the authority could apply for entry into the sandbox. The establishment of the regulatory sandbox may be a reason why the United Kingdom's financial regulator has not yet considered setting up rules for ICOs. When it is a test phase for the early development of new financial innovations, it is also a test phase for the financial authority to strike a balance between early intervention so as to promote public security and the liberty for innovative ideas to promote Fintech development.

3.4.7 Summary

After a thorough look at regulatory measures and experiences in the above jurisdictions, one common feature is that they all have a relatively friendly environment for ICOs. Even though some jurisdictions such as the United States, Canada, Australia, Singapore and Hong Kong have announced the possibility of regulating ICOs as a type of issuance of securities,[143] only one case – the DAO in the United States, has been classified as issuing securities. Except for the US regulators' position in the DAO and AriseBank, jurisdictions are willing to provide a friendly environment for genuine ICOs, or at least they seem willing to take a very liberal view and supervise such a new type of fundraising means within a regulatory sandbox. None of the jurisdictions mentioned show any indication of prohibiting ICOs as they know how much benefit they would gain and how crucial it would be for them to become a Fintech hub in the world today. These may be the reasons why the United Kingdom and the EU still remain silent on whether ICOs should be regulated as the means of offering securities.

3.5 Going Forward: Reform Suggestions for China

3.5.1 Regulation Rather than Prohibition

Since the announcement of the ICO ban in China, it has been heavily criticized. For the most part, the criticism points to its adverse impact on

---

[142] UK Financial Conduct Authority, 'Regulatory Sandbox', 2015, www.fca.org.uk/firms/innovation/regulatory-sandbox.

[143] Aurelio Gurrea-Martínez and Nydia Remolina, 'The Law and Finance of Initial Coin Offerings', *Ibero-American Institute for Law and Finance, Working Paper Series 4/2018*, 2018, https://papers.ssrn.com/sol3/papers.cfm?abstract_id=3182261 (calling this regulatory model as 'selective control *ex ante*').

the development of new blockchain applications, which can bring many benefits to a currency financial system, such as improving security, data storage, financial transactions and documentation and legal transactions. In addition to these general benefits, some are more specific to China at this stage as becoming a digital superpower, which is one of the national strategies for the near future.

With the considerable benefits brought in by ICOs, even if they pose certain risks to the market, regulations to reduce and prevent these risks are needed, rather than an outright ban. Indeed, risks of ICOs can be reduced or controlled by proper regulations. As discussed earlier, not one of the advanced economies mentioned in this chapter has prohibited ICOs. Instead, they have been trying to establish a sound regulatory framework to regulate ICOs, protect investors and maintain stability in the financial markets. Therefore, it would be advisable for the Chinese government to regulate ICOs rather than prohibit them. The present section is going to set out suggestions for the way in which China might craft its regulatory regime for ICOs.

3.5.2   Typology of ICOs and Regulatory Responses

The legal status of an ICO should be dependent on the facts and circumstances of an ICO, such as how the ICO is structured and what rights are attached to the cryptocurrency issued under the ICO. In line with the regulatory suggestions and experiences provided in the jurisdictions above, this section is going to see how ICOs may be regulated in China and what laws and regulations may apply to ICOs based on different facts and circumstances. Six non-exhaustive possible classifications of ICOs are discussed below and a modified five-prong *Howey* test will be provided.

3.5.2.1   Pre-Sale of Goods or Services

The first category of ICOs based on their legal status may be classified as the pre-sale of goods or services, and the digital coins issued under such ICOs should be regarded as 'virtual commodities'. In order to be classified under this category, the issuer has to make sure there is only a right to access and use of the goods or services provided by the project attached to the newly issued digital coin but no other rights or interests similar to those attached to any type of security.

Perhaps the most famous ICO of this type to date is that of Ethereum in 2014, which issued Ethers in exchange for Bitcoins. Ether is intended for 'paying transaction fees or building or purchasing decentralized application services on the Ethereum platforms'.[144] There is no voting right over anything attached to Ether and there is no guarantee of Ether's future value as this is totally decided by the market itself.[145] By looking at Ethereum, the typical features of this type of ICO can be concluded as consisting of four parts. Firstly, the digital coin issued under the ICO only grants its holders the right to access and use the platform or the right to use the digital coin to pay for services or products provided by other users on the platform. Secondly, there is no guarantee of the digital coin's future value and it will be purely decided by the market once the ICO ends. Thirdly, holders can spend or transfer the digital coin but once it has been used or transferred, the process is non-reversible. Lastly, the platform is based on blockchain technology.

By analogy, if an ICO meets the four criteria listed above, it is unlikely for it to be regarded as an offering of securities. The *Howey* test could be applied to confirm its legal status. There seems to be no doubt that such an ICO can satisfy the second prong of the 'common enterprise'. However, in terms of 'an investment of money' and 'investors expect profits from the investment', as the digital coin is only used for buying products or using services provided on the platform and there is no guarantee of the digital coin's future value, it is not appropriate to call such an activity an investment. Even if it could be proved that investors indeed expect an increase in the digital coin's value, it is still unlikely for it to pass the fourth prong, which requires such an increase in value as is the result of others' entrepreneurial or managerial efforts, whereas the price is actually decided by its supply and demand on the market. Therefore, in respect of its legal status, it may be more appropriate to define an ICO of this type as the pre-sale of goods or services, whereby there is a contract between the issuer and holders of the newly issued digital coins for the future provision of services or products.

As the legal status has been defined, what must then be considered is which law is applicable to govern such ICOs. The crowdfunding example of a Kickstarter campaign for Asylum Bicycle Playing Card may provide some hints. This campaign was launched by Altius Management in 2012 and raised USD 25,146 from 810 backers.[146] Kickstarter is a crowdfunding platform for gathering money from the public. In this case, the court held

---

[144] Vitalik Buterin, 'Launching the Ether Sale', 2014, https://blog.ethereum org/2014/07/22/launching-the-ether-sale/.
[145] Ibid.
[146] *State of Washington v. Altius Management, LLC*, No. 14-2-12425-2 SEA 2015.

that Altius Management was liable for violating the state Consumer Protection Act by failing to deliver the promised playing cards to the backers.[147] Even though a campaign was launched on a crowdfunding platform for gathering money, which is different from ICOs in the sense that these are built on blockchain technology and sell the newly issued digital coins to investors in exchange for widely accepted cryptocurrencies like Bitcoin or Ether instead of real money, the cryptocurrencies paid in this case can be regarded as 'money' for the purposes of ICOs according to both the judicial authority and the government in the United States and Canada. In addition, in both cases, there is a similar kind of agreement, that is, money is prepaid for services or goods provided in the future.

Therefore, in China, the Law of the PRC on the Protection of Consumer Rights and Interests[148] could be used to govern such ICOs. Alternatively, the Contract Law of the PRC[149] may be applicable if an ICO project fails to deliver on the terms provided in its white paper in terms of the provision of services or goods.

3.5.2.2 Offering of Shares

When a newly issued cryptocurrency is structured to represent a share in the issuing company and is a digital representation of a cryptocurrency holder's ownership in the company, such a cryptocurrency will constitute a share as governed by the securities laws.

A typical example in China might be NEO, also called Antshares, a company raising funds to develop a decentralized protocol designed to digitalize real-world assets into digital assets and allow users to register, trade and circulate via a peer-to-peer network.[150] It issues two cryptocurrencies, NEO (or 'Antshares') and NeoGas (or 'Antcoins'). Antshares, which is indivisble and transferable and the smallest unit of

---

[147] Ibid.

[148] Zhonghua Renmin Gongheguo Xiaofeizhe Quanyi Baohufa (中华人民共和国消费者权益保护法) [Law of the PRC on the Protection of Consumer Rights and Interests] (adopted on 31 October 1993 at the Eighth National People's Congress; promulgated on 31 October 1993 by Order No. 11 of the President of the PRC and effected from 1 January 1994).

[149] Zhonghua Renmin Gongheguo Hetongfa (中华人民共和国合同法) [Contract Law of the PRC] (adopted on 15 March 1999 at the Eighth National People's Congress; promulgated on 15 March 1999 by Order No. 15 of the President of the PRC and effected from 1 October 1999).

[150] NEO, 'NEO White Paper: A Distributed Network for the Smart Economy', 2017, https://bravenewcoin.com/insights/neo-white-paper-a-distributed-network-for-the-smart-economy.

which is one, represents ownership of the blockchain protocol, the right to manage the network, and the right to receive Antcoins. Antcoins, by contrast, is divisible and only represents the right to use the blockchain protocol.[151] Since Antcoins functions similar to Ethers, which has a similar usage and could be regarded as 'money' for the purposes of ICOs, it is possible to regard the distribution of Antcoins to Antshares holders as the distribution of dividends, i.e., a form of award. In accordance with Article 4 of the Company Law of the PRC,[152] 'the shareholders of a company shall enjoy such rights as return on assets, participation in major decision-making and selection of managers according to the law'. By taking into account that the offering is open to public investors, Antshares holders can receive Antcoins by way of profits, Antshares represents ownership of the platform and the right to manage the network, the smallest unit of Antshares is one and Antshares are transferable, the ICO of Antshares could be considered as an issue of shares.

Therefore, the offering of Antshares may need to comply with the relevant registration requirements that apply to IPOs and in accordance with the Securities Law, the company may also very likely be required to hold a financial licence for carrying on business in the regulated activity of dealing in securities. However, since there are still some differences in the ownership rights between holding Antshares and holding shares issued by registered companies, it is not certain how broad the judicial and statutory authorities are going to interpret the item of ownership rights.

3.5.2.3   Issue of Debentures

If a newly issued cryptocurrency represents the right of an investor, being the creditor of a loan which has been extended to the issuer, such an ICO may be treated as an offering of debentures, and the cryptocurrency may therefore constitute a security governed under the securities law. According to Article 15 of the Company Law of PRC, when a 'company agrees to repay, together with interest, within a definite time limit', such 'securities' will be classified as 'corporate bonds'. Therefore, it is necessary to see how the company structures its terms regarding the rights attached to the cryptocurrency that they put in their white paper of the ICO. If it

---

[151]   Ibid.

[152]   Zhonghua Renmin Gongheguo Gongsifa (中华人民共和国公司法) [Company Law of the PRC] (adopted on 29 December 1993 at the Eighth National People's Congress; amended on 28 December 2013 at the Twelfth National People's Congress and effected from 1 March 2014).

promises to repay the principal together with interest within a specified time, an obligation arises and thus the cryptocurrency may constitute a debenture and is subject to the securities laws.

3.5.2.4 Issue of Derivatives

A newly issued cryptocurrency could be regarded as a derivative if its future value were dependent on fluctuations in the underlying assets, all of which have certain elements in common, including stocks, currencies, commodities and indexes or other cryptocurrency market prices. It may be called by other names such as financial derivatives product, financial derivative instrument or derivative security. Whatever name it goes by, it is a type of investment contract and shall be subject to securities laws.

3.5.2.5 Collective Investment Schemes

The DAO seems to be the first ICO that could be regarded as a collective investment scheme. Both the *Howey* test and the Australian test for the managed investment schemes could be applied to see whether or not an ICO should be classified as a collective investment scheme.

However, there is no clear definition of what constitutes a collective investment scheme in the PRC law but since there is no general definition of 'security' in the Securities Law of the PRC[153] either, a collective investment scheme is highly likely to be treated as a security and therefore should be subject to securities laws in China. There are several factors that may trigger the regulator's concern about whether an ICO should be regarded as a collective investment scheme. Firstly, there is the element of common enterprises pooling funds raised from the offering of cryptocurrency and using these funds to invest in portfolios of investment in various projects or companies. Secondly, holders of the cryptocurrency will not have the right to manage the day-to-day operation the platform even though they may have voting rights to select portfolio managers or select projects to be added to the portfolio. Thirdly, profits generated from the investment of a portfolio will be pooled and distributed as awards to cryptocurrency holders. On this basis, the cryptocurrency issued under the ICO is likely to represent a unit in a collective management scheme and therefore should be subject to securities laws.

---

[153] Zhonghua Renmin Gongheguo Zhengquanfa (中华人民共和国证券法) [Securities Law of the PRC] (adopted on 29 December 1998 at the Ninth National People's Congress, last amended in 2019).

3.5.2.6 Crowdfunding

Crowdfunding, which is normally based on the internet, by its very nature, should be a regulated financial activity and subject to securities laws, but there is no relevant law in China to govern such an activity yet. In jurisdictions such as the United States, Canada, Australia, the EU and the United Kingdom, regulations on crowdfunding have been established but none of them have applied any relevant regulations to ICOs. While there is a very broad academic definition of crowdfunding,[154] the Legislative Council of Hong Kong has issued an Information Note on the regulation of crowdfunding, in which four types of crowdfunding are given:

> donation-based [. . .] for charitable causes; reward-based or presales-based where goods or services are delivered in return for fund contribution; equity crowdfunding where investors acquire shares of a business investment for financial return; and peer-to-peer ('P2P') lending where debts are issued to borrowers for interest in return.[155]

By looking at this classification, it is unlikely that ICOs will fall within the first criteria for charitable usage, nor is it likely for them to fall in the last category of P2P lending (which has special regulatory treatment in China), given the features of current ICOs. In terms of the second and the third types of crowdfunding, each can be said to correspond with the classification of ICOs as stated above. The reward-based or pre-sales-based crowdfunding is analogical to the pre-sale of goods or services in Section 3.5.2.1 and equity crowdfunding has a number of features in common with the offering of shares in Section 3.5.2.2. In terms of the reward-based or pre-sales-based crowdfunding, it may be appropriate for them to be treated together with the first type of ICO, such as the one in the Kickstarter campaign for playing cards as discussed in Section 3.5.2.1, and therefore they may be subject to consumer protection laws as well as contract laws.

In respect of equity crowdfunding, according to the provisions of the Implementation Plan for Special Rectification on Risks in Equity

---

[154] Armin Schwienbacher and Benjamin Larralde, 'Crowfunding of Entrepreneurial Ventures', in Douglas Cumming (ed), *The Oxford Handbook of Entrepreneurial Finance* (Oxford University Press, 2012); Ethan Mollick, 'The Dynamics of Crowdfunding: An Exploratory Study' (2014) 29(1) *Journal of Business Venturing* 1.

[155] Research Office of the Legislative Council of HKSA, 'Regulation of Crowdfunding in Selected Place', Information Notice IN17/16–17, 2017, www.legco.gov.hk/research-publications/english/1617in17-regulation-of-crowdfunding-in-selected-places-20170721-e.pdf.

94 INITIAL COIN OFFERINGS

Crowdfunding,[156] any public offering of shares to the public or to a total of more than 200 investors should be reported to the relevant authority to obtain approval, or would otherwise be classified as an illegal issue of shares.[157] Therefore, ICOs qualifying as equity crowdfunding shall also be subject to the relevant securities laws.

3.5.2.7 A Modified Howey Test

The classification of the six types of ICO above is not exhaustive but only provides the most likely forms of ICOs. Since technology is developing very fast and companies may design their offerings of cryptocurrencies in different ways, the *Howey* test will be helpful when an ICO does not fall under any form of ICO discussed above. However, since the *Howey* test is not clear enough and needs to defer to a courts' interpretation and judgement where applicable, a modified *Howey* test may be provided by taking into account several features of ICOs and regulatory experiences in other jurisdictions, in addition to those of the United States.

The modified test consists of five prongs, namely does the arrangement involve any of the following: (1) an investment of money or cryptocurrencies (2) to obtain a right to benefits in a common enterprise, (3) in which the right can be actual, prospective or contingent regardless of whether it is enforceable or not, (4) with the expectation of financial benefits or interest in property by investors (5) to come significantly from the efforts of others. Even though this chapter agrees with the rationale of treating cryptocurrency as money when it is used as a medium of exchange or payment for a newly issued cryptocurrency, it may cause confusion if the authority has already announced that cryptocurrency is not the equivalent of money.

Therefore, this modified test adds cryptocurrencies as a payment for investment in addition to real money. The test also adds one more element as shown in the third prong to better protect investors as issuers of ICOs may avoid liability by asserting that the right is not enforceable or is only prospective or contingent as stated in the white paper. If an ICO satisfies all five prongs of this modified *Howey* test, it should be treated as a regulated financial activity and therefore should be governed by securities laws.

---

[156] Guquan Zhongchou Fengxian Zhuanxiang Zhengzhi Gongzuo Shishi Fangan (股权众筹风险专项整治工作实施方案) [Implementation Plan for Special Rectification on Risks in Equity Crowdfunding] (promulgated on 14 October 2016 by the China Securities Regulatory Commission and others).
[157] Ibid.

3.6 Conclusion

It is without a doubt that ICOs must be regulated, but an outright ICO ban in China may stifle innovation and is not conducive to the development of Fintech and blockchain technology. It is clear that the Chinese government has been trying to develop China's economy to become a hub for Fintech. However, it is unclear how the Chinese government hopes to regulate ICOs rather than ban it. This presents the challenge of drawing up a relatively complete regulatory regime for ICOs that can achieve both objectives, namely to facilitate the development of Fintech and the ICO market, as well as protect investors against fraudulent projects.

In order to strike a balance between these two objectives, thorough research has been done on relevant experiences in and lessons from overseas jurisdictions that have advanced economies. A common trait of regulatory authorities in the United States, Canada, Australia, Singapore and Hong Kong is their effort to control certain ICOs and regulate them under securities laws. What we have learned from them is that, based on the facts and circumstances, there are six types of ICOs, namely the pre-sale of products or services, offering of shares, issue of debentures, issue of derivatives, collective investment schemes and crowdfunding. If an ICO cannot be classified as any one type out of the six, a modified five-prong *Howey* test shall apply to see whether the cryptocurrency issued under an ICO constitutes securities. If an ICO is regarded as a pre-sale of products or services according to the relevant features and requirements, such an ICO should be subject to the laws on the protection of consumer rights and interests or, alternatively, contract law. If an ICO could be classified as any other of the five types of financial activities, or it could pass the five-prong test, that ICO should be governed by securities laws.

In addition to finding relevant laws to regulate the different types of ICO, this chapter also suggests the relevance of setting up a modest regulatory scheme so as to allow for a healthy growth of ICOs and related activities. Establishing a regulatory sandbox for innovative financial products and services may be a preferable method to encourage incentives for developments in the Fintech area. Exactly how this can be done and what criteria such a project project will have to meet in order to enter the sandbox is a different and new research area. However, as the jurisdictions that have been discussed in this chapter have already established their own regulatory sandbox, China may seek to collaborate with those regulatory authorities. As a first step, due to the historical and intense relationship between the regulatory and financial activities in China and Hong Kong, the preferred option may be to seek collaboration with Hong Kong's regulatory sandbox.

4

Cryptoassets

4.1 Introduction

Although generalized under one wide umbrella categorization, cryptoassets, or known as virtual assets, comprise a myriad of different products, each with different features. Indeed, since Bitcoin was first created in 2008,[1] cryptoassets have been widely used in raising capital through ICOs and in peer-to-peer electronic cash systems, which allow online payments to be made between parties without the need for a financial intermediary.[2] This polymorphic nature rationalizes the particular difficulty faced by regulators in devising a framework which comprehensively captures all cryptoassets and applies the appropriate regulations according to their features.[3] At the international level, different jurisdictions have adopted different regulatory approaches[4] in an attempt to achieve the right balance between ensuring effective investor protection and supporting cryptoasset market development. As of 30 June 2020, there were 2,718 types of cryptoassets available in the global market and the total market capital amounted to over USD 261 billion.[5]

In Hong Kong, cryptoassets have traditionally been regulated by the SFC under the existing securities law framework. Over the years, the SFC has displayed a rather cautious stance towards cryptoassets, and has adopted a piecemeal approach to dealing with the regulatory issue. As the cryptoasset market grows, this piecemeal approach has become increasingly inadequate as evidenced in the issues of regulatory gaps and regulatory arbitrage. Owing

---

[1] Satoshi Nakamoto, 'Bitcoin: A Peer-to-Peer Electronic Cash System', 2018, https://bitcoin.org/bitcoin.pdf.

[2] For a more detailed discussion of the concept of cryptoassets, see Section 4.2.

[3] Laurin Arnold et al, 'Blockchain and Initial Coin Offerings: Blockchain's Implications for Crowdfunding', *Research Center Finance & Information Management*, 2018, p 22, www.fim-rc.de/Paperbibliothek/Veroeffentlicht/843/wi-843.pdf.

[4] Sarah Jane Hughes and Stephen T. Middlebrook, 'Advancing a Framework for Regulating Cryptocurrency Payments Intermediaries' (2015) 32 *Yale Journal on Regulation* 495, 512.

[5] CoinMarketCap website, https://coinmarketcap.com/all/views/all/.

98   CRYPTOASSETS

to the growing concerns of investor protection, the SFC issued the Statement
on Regulatory Framework for Virtual Asset Portfolios Managers, Fund
Distributors and Trading Platform Operators (2018 Statement on
Regulatory Framework) on 1 November 2018.[6] This is the first time that
the SFC has issued a special rule on cryptoassets, representing a significant
development in the regulatory approach towards cryptoassets in
Hong Kong. Under this rule, the SFC uses interchangeably the terms
cryptoasset, virtual asset, cryptocurrency, digital token and so on, as does
the present chapter.

The objective of this chapter is to critically evaluate the new regulatory
regime for cryptoassets in Hong Kong as established by the 2018 Statement
on Regulatory Framework. Given that cryptoasset regulation presents itself
as a challenge to worldwide regulators, the implication of this evaluation
extends beyond Hong Kong, providing important lessons for overseas
jurisdictions to draw on. As a global financial centre, Hong Kong should
not only embrace the future of cryptoassets, but also shape it.

4.2   Background: Concept, Nature, Risks and Benefits

In order to appraise the appropriateness of different regulatory approaches,
it is necessary to first understand the workings of cryptoassets and their
inherent characteristics, which give rise to relevant risks and benefits.

4.2.1   Basic Concepts and Typology of Cryptoassets

In general, a cryptoasset is a cryptographically secured digital representation of value which employs some form of DLT, and can be transferred,
stored or traded electronically. DLT is a technology which enables the
sharing and updating of information in a distributed and decentralized
way. The term 'blockchain' is often used interchangeably with DLT and
refers to a specific way of structuring data on a DLT platform. In the
context of cryptoassets, a blockchain serves as a public ledger which
includes a full record of transactions on the network. Each user of the

---

[6] SFC, 'Statement on Regulatory Framework for Virtual Asset Portfolio Managers, Fund
Distributors and Trading Platform Operators', 2018, www.sfc.hk/web/EN/news-and-
announcements/policy-statements-and-announcements/reg-framework-virtual-asset-port
folios-managers-fund-distributors-trading-platform-operators.html. To provide more guidance, this new regulation contains Appendix 1 (Regulatory Standards for Licensed
Corporations Managing Virtual Asset Portfolios) and Appendix 2 (Conceptual Framework
for the Potential Regulation of Virtual Asset Trading Platform Operators).

blockchain keeps a copy of the entire ledger, which is updated and synchronized with a new block added every time a new transaction occurs.[7] This feature removes the need for a third-party intermediary as in conventional transactions, as transactions are verified by users and permanently recorded on an immutable ledger accessible by all network participants.[8] It should be noted that cryptoassets are just one application of DLT, with other common examples including smart contracts, asset storage and transaction validation.[9]

Depending on the design of the underlying blockchain, the purposes for which the cryptoasset is created, and the rights it grants its owners, can vary greatly in terms of their features. While the UK Cryptoassets Taskforce has observed that there 'is not a single widely agreed definition of a cryptoasset',[10] the UK FCA has defined cryptoassets as 'any publicly available electronic medium of exchange that features a "permissionless" distributed ledger and a decentralised system for exchanging value'.[11]

Existing cryptoassets can be broadly categorized into three types, namely exchange tokens, security tokens and utility tokens. Exchange tokens are used as a means of exchange or for investment, and are not backed by a central body. Security tokens usually provide rights such as ownership, the repayment of a specific sum, or an entitlement to a share in future profits. Utility tokens can be redeemed for access to a specific product or service that is typically provided when using a DLT platform.

---

[7] Hossein Kakavand, Nicolette Kost De Sevres and Bart Chilton, 'The Blockchain Revolution: An Analysis of Regulation and Technology Related to Distributed Ledger Technologies' 2017, p 7, https://papers.ssrn.com/sol3/papers.cfm?abstract_id=2849251. In the process of synchronization, new transactions between users are broadcast across the network, verified by cryptographic algorithms, and grouped into blocks. The blocks are then added to the blockchain and can no longer be altered.

[8] Randolph A. Robinson, 'The New Digital Wild West: Regulating the Explosion of Initial Coin Offerings' (2018) 85(4) *Tennessee Law Review* 897, 908.

[9] European Securities and Markets Authority, 'Discussion Paper: the Distributed Ledger Technology Applied to Securities Markets', ESMA/2016/773, 2016, p 8, www.esma.europa .eu/sites/default/files/library/2016-773_dp_dlt.pdf.

[10] HM Treasury, 'Cryptoassets Taskforce: Final Report', 2018, p 11, https://assets .publishing.service.gov.uk/government/uploads/system/uploads/attachment_data/file/ 752070/cryptoassets_taskforce_final_report_final_web.pdf.

[11] Financial Conduct Authority, 'Discussion Paper on Distributed Ledger Technology', DP17/ 3, 2017, p 11, www.fca.org.uk/publication/discussion/dp17-03.pdf. A 'permissionless' network is one which anyone is allowed to validate and add new records to the existing set of records. This is in contrast to 'permissioned' networks, where only users with specific rights can perform the same actions.

Cryptoassets are commonly used as a means of exchange, for investment and to support the raising of capital through ICOs.[12]

4.2.2   The Nature of Cryptoassets: Currency or Property?

As will be discussed later, the cryptoasset is officially considered as commodity or asset rather than currency or money in Hong Kong. This position is however not without challenges. Indeed, there has been a heated debate on the nature of the cryptoasset, and indeed cryptoassets are also termed by some as cryptocurrency, or virtual currency. Several recent cases in the United States have well demonstrated the divergence of views on this issue and its important implications in practice.

In the course of deciding whether the operation of Bitcoin forms a money transmission business, *US v. Faiella*[13] decided that 'Bitcoin can be easily purchased in exchange for ordinary currency, act as a denominator of value, and be used to conduct financial transactions' and as such Bitcoin is "money"'.[14] This was followed in *US v. Murgio*[15] by stating that Bitcoin fits the definition of 'funds' and 'money'. The SEC in the United States also came to the same conclusion through *SEC v. Shavers* that Bitcoin is a currency meeting the definition of an investment contract.[16] However, in the case of *Hastfast v. Lowe*, the Bankruptcy Court of the Northern District of California 'declared that Bitcoins are not U.S. dollars and should be considered as intangible property or commodity for bankruptcy procedures'.[17]

From a technological point of view, a cryptocurrency is 'a decentralized system for interacting with virtual money in a shared global ledger'.[18] Again, taking Bitcoin as an example, the blockchain serves as 'the public registry of all Bitcoin transactions being maintained as

---

[12] Ibid.

[13] *United States v. Faiella*, 39 F.Supp.3d 544 (SDNY 2014) 2 [2].

[14] Ibid.

[15] *United States v. Murgio*, No. 15-CR-769 (AJN) (SDNY 2016).

[16] Seth Litwack, 'Bitcoin: Currency or Fool's Gold: A Comparative Analysis of the Legal Classification of Bitcoin' (2015) 29 *Temple International & Comparative Law Journal*, 309, 333–334.

[17] Olena Demchenko, 'Bitcoin: Legal Definition and Its Place in Legal Framework' (2017) 3 (1) *Journal of International Trade, Logistics and Law* 23, 32.

[18] Kevin Delmolino, Mitchell Arnett, Abmed Kosba, Andrew Miller and Elaine Shi, 'Step by Step towards Creating a Safe Smart Contract: Lessons and Insights from a Cryptocurrency Lab', University of Maryland, 2015, p 2, https://eprint.iacr.org/2015/460.pdf.

a distributed peer-to-peer network'.[19] Tracking of Bitcoin transactions is viable as each Bitcoin owns a unique serial number.[20] In general terms, 'Bitcoin is created through mining activities that use the power of computers to solve mathematical problems, which in turn, releases blocks of bitcoin'.[21] Some academics have categorized Bitcoin as a 'decentralized peer-to-peer virtual currency' and other well-known virtual currencies include 'Litecoin, Namecoin, Auroracoin, Peercoin and Dogecoin'.[22] According to them, the main characteristic of the cryptoasset is that it is not 'denominated by any national currency' and 'does not require third party to validate its transactions'.[23] In this respect, some say that 'Bitcoin seeks to separate money from the state's regulatory power'.[24]

However, the key question here is what the central feature of money is and whether cryptoasset possesses it. It is widely known that since the start of human history, there have been different forms of 'currencies' to facilitate transactions. The early money was usually a commodity or commodity money that has intrinsic value such as food, livestock and precious metal in the historic barter economy.[25] Money in the form of papers did not have any intrinsic value, but it represented underlying assets such as gold and could be exchanged for a fixed quantity of these underlying assets.[26] Nowadays in modern economies, similar forms of currencies called 'fiat' money are used but they are completely different from commodity-backed money as they can no longer be exchanged for commodity.

According to the European Central Bank (2012), 'fiat money is any legal tender designated and issued by a central authority'.[27] In the United States, the Financial Crimes Enforcement Network (FinCEN) has usefully defined

---

[19] The Clearing House and Independent Community Bankers of America, 'Virtual Currency: Risks and Regulation', 2014, p 9, https://buckleyfirm.com/wp-content/uploads/2014/06/ICBA-TCH-VirtualCurrencyWhitePaperJune2014.pdf.

[20] Ibid.

[21] Tracey A. Anderson, 'Cryptocurrency: The Wild, Wild Web: Analogies to the American and Canadian Wild, Wild West – Will History Repeat?' (2018) 33(4) *Journal of International Banking Law and Regulation* 113.

[22] Matthew P. Ponsford, 'A Comparative Analysis of Bitcoin and other Decentralised Virtual Currencies: Legal Regulation in China, Canada and the United States' (2015) 9 *Hong Kong Journal of Legal Studies* 29, 30.

[23] Ibid.

[24] Daniela Sonderegger, 'A Regulatory and Economic Perplexity: Bitcoin Needs Just a Bit of Regulation' (2015) 47 *Washington University Journal of Law & Policy* 175, 177.

[25] Glyn Davies, *A History of Money from Ancient times to the Present Day* (University of Wales Press, 2002), p 10.

[26] European Central Bank, 'Virtual Currency Schemes', 2012, p 9, www.ecb.europa.eu/pub/pdf/other/virtualcurrencyschemes201210en.pdf.

[27] Ibid.

currency as 'the coin and paper money of the United States or of any other country that is designated as legal tender and that circulated and is customarily used and accepted as a medium of exchange in the country of issuance'.[28]

It is believed that state credit is a defining feature of currency or money. Because of trust in the central authority, people are willing to accept it in exchange for goods and services. Considering fiat money, it is issued by the government but not commodity backed and has no intrinsic value, yet it has in general a stable value because of the credibility of government. The term 'credibility' is referred to the belief individuals have that 'the government will not attempt to exploit this source of seigniorage to the point where money becomes worthless'.[29] There are many economics or political theories for the arguments on credibility, which will not be discussed in detail in this paper. If, just for a brief moment, a government prints too much of its money, it will generate serious inflation such that the price of goods in terms of that particular currency will be very high and will keep increasing consistently over time. The public will stop using the currency as money for transactions. In contrast, there is no central issuer or authority to control the supply of cryptocurrency.[30] Taking Bitcoin as an example, the total supply of Bitcoin is limited to 21 million.[31] Even if the credibility of Bitcoin is developed such that most people are willing to accept it for transactions, regardless of its unstable value, it would attract investment and other speculative activities and people would tend to retain them for an investment return after the increase in value with its finite supply rather than use it the same way as the legal currency. In this case, Bitcoin could be viewed as a new type of 'gold' or 'diamond' that is valuable, but one that does not facilitate the operations of economic activities like fiat money does.

Furthermore, currency or money serves three basic functions, including as a medium of exchange, a store of value and a unit of account.[32]

---

[28] Department of the Treasury Financial Crimes Enforcement Network, 'Application of FinCEN's Regulations to Persons Administering, Exchanging, or Using Virtual Currencies', 2013, p 1, www.fincen.gov/sites/default/files/shared/FIN-2013-G001.pdf.

[29] Joseph A Ritter, 'The Transition from Barter to Fiat Money' (1995) 85 *American Economic Review* 134, 135.

[30] Financial Action Task Force, 'FATF Report Virtual Currencies Key Definitions and Potential AML/CFT Risks', 2014, p 5, www.fatf-gafi.org/media/fatf/documents/reports/Virtual-currency-key-definitions-and-potential-aml-cft-risks.pdf.

[31] William J. Luther and Lawrence H. White, 'Can Bitcoin Become a Major Currency?', *George Mason University Working Paper in Economics No. 14–17*, 2014, p 4.

[32] European Central Bank, 'Virtual Currency Schemes', October 2012, p 10, www.ecb.europa.eu/pub/pdf/other/virtualcurrencyschemes201210en.pdf.

Cryptocurrency can serve as a medium of exchange as it is commonly known that there are many things in the world that have gone digital such as music and books, hence let alone money with computer technology nowadays. Legal currency has its digital form and is becoming more popular in daily transactions because of its benefits over its physical form, examples of which are portability and convenience. PayMe[33] is a mobile application launched by HSBC that facilitates peer-to-peer money transactions where one can send money to another through a mobile device after registering for a bank account or a credit card. It is not hard to imagine a world without physical fiat money in the near future. Cryptocurrency can also serve as a unit of account, which is a common measure of the value of goods and services in the economy. Cryptocurrency, with its digital nature, serves as a store of value well as it won't 'deteriorate' compared to any forms of physical money, but its value fluctuation could be an issue. There are many forms of money including metals, stones and so forth; while they all, to a certain extent, also serve the three basic functions of money, they fall short in other areas, such as portability, compared to paper money. Considering only the digital nature of cryptocurrency, it has many advantages over physical fiat money; however, digital form of fiat money share the same benefits. One of the key features of money material is the stability of its value that highlights the core difference between the fiat money and cryptocurrency.

When the value of a currency is not stable like most of the cryptocurrencies nowadays, it will not be an ideal option to be used as money. Firstly, the public will not use it as a medium of exchange if they know that the value of the currency fluctuates vigorously: Consumers will keep the cryptocurrency as an asset and sell it for a profit if the value rises; it is also a poor option as a store of value because of the instability of its value. On the other hand, price in terms of it being a unit of account does not give useful signals for market activities as it will change frequently.

Hence, although no consensus has been reached so far regarding the nature of cryptocurrency, namely whether it is a form of currency or property, we are inclined to agree with the FinCEN that the cryptoasset 'operates like a currency in some environments but does not have ... legal tender status in any jurisdiction'.[34] The next issue is regarding the

---

[33] The Hongkong and Shanghai Banking Corporation Limited, 'How It Works', 2018, https://payme.hsbc.com.hk/how-it-works.

[34] Department of the Treasury Financial Crimes Enforcement Network, 'Application of FinCEN's Regulations to Persons Administering, Exchanging, or Using Virtual Currencies', 2013, p 1, www.fincen.gov/sites/default/files/shared/FIN-2013-G001.pdf.

risks and benefits of the cryptoasset, whether or not it is regarded as a legal tender.

4.2.3 Risks Associated with Cryptoassets

Cryptoassets carry a number of inherent risks due to their characteristics and the operations of cryptoasset funds and trading platforms.[35] The IOSCO has in fact recognized the potential conduct and market integrity risks of cryptoassets as one of its top priorities.[36] In addition, while some risks are not at present significant, they can proliferate through time and pose a threat to financial stability, and are therefore worth addressing at an early stage.[37]

4.2.3.1 Market Immaturity Risks

The market for cryptoassets is far from mature, usually with high levels of price volatility, which poses significant risks for their use or investment therein. For instance, the price of Bitcoin since its launch in 2009 had been relatively stable before 2013, with a steady appreciation in value until 2017, upon when there has been a drastic increase in value from USD 1,000 to approximately USD 19,000, followed by a dramatic drop to USD 8,000.[38] This price volatility poses a difficulty to pricing goods and services based on cryptoassets and hence limits their potential widespread application.[39] Indeed, cryptoassets have a highly speculative nature, due to the lack of backing by any physical items.

Furthermore, as a relatively new market, immature market infrastructures give rise to concerns with liquidity and a difficulty in price valuation. This is particularly the case for less widely traded cryptoassets where there is no guarantee of liquidity in the secondary market. It has also been observed in the United Kingdom that cryptoasset exchanges, trading platforms and wallet providers can charge high and variable fees,

---

[35] UK Parliament, 'The Treasury Committee, Digital Currencies Inquiry on 22 February 2018', 2018, para 10, https://publications.parliament.uk/pa/cm201719/cmselect/cmtreasy/910/91002.htm.

[36] The IOSCO is an association of securities regulators, which acts as the global standard-setter for worldwide securities regulation.

[37] Schlomit Azgad-Tromer, 'Crypto Securities: On the Risks of Investments in Blockchain-Based Assets and the Dilemmas of Securities Regulation' (2018) 68 *American University Law Review* 69, 104.

[38] Bitcoin.com, 'Bitcoin Price', 2018, https://charts.bitcoin.com/chart/price.

[39] Daniela Sonderegger, 'A Regulatory and Economic Perplexity: Bitcoin Needs Just a Bit of Regulation' (2015) 47 *Washington University Journal of Law & Policy* 175, 186.

4.2 BACKGROUND

of which consumers may not be made aware.[40] There is no agreed standard on the assessment of the value of cryptoassets under current accounting frameworks, in relation to obtaining audit evidence for cryptoassets and judging the reasonableness of valuations.[41]

Finally, the market immaturity risks may be intensified by vicious market competition. As Fintech companies often race to launch products ahead of their peers, their trial-and-error mode of innovation may result in the release of immature products to the market. It has been suggested that network effects tend to amplify risks, which cause substantial financial losses and result in operational risks and compliance issues.[42]

4.2.3.2   Market Abuse Risks

The novel nature of the cryptoasset market means that market abuses may arise easily, such as the dissemination of misleading information and price manipulation.[43] Indeed, compared to traditional financial markets, there is a heightened risk of market abuse in relation to cryptoassets.

Disclosure problems have already been well documented in traditional financial markets. For instance, the 2008 Lehman Minibond Saga in Hong Kong made it clear that where the disclosure of product information is ineffective, investors are likely to be exposed to little or no protection and the available remedies may be limited.[44] For cryptoassets,

---

[40] HM Treasury, 'National Risk Assessment of Money Laundering and Terrorist Financing', 2018, p 37, https://assets.publishing.service.gov.uk/government/uploads/system/uploads/attachment_data/file/655198/National_risk_assessment_of_money_laundering_and_terrorist_financing_2017_pdf_web.pdf.

[41] SFC, 'Statement on Regulatory Framework for Virtual Asset Portfolio Managers, Fund Distributors and Trading Platform Operators', 2018, www.sfc.hk/web/EN/news-and-announcements/policy-statements-and-announcements/reg-framework-virtual-asset-portfolios-managers-fund-distributors-trading-platform-operators.html.

[42] HKEX, 'Research Report: Financial Technology Applications and Related Regulatory Framework', 2018, p 19, www.hkex.com.hk/-/media/HKEX-Market/News/Research-Reports/HKEx-Research-Papers/2018/CCEO_Fintech_201810_e.pdf.

[43] HM Treasury, 'Cryptoassets Taskforce: Final Report', 2018, p 37, https://assets.publishing.service.gov.uk/government/uploads/system/uploads/attachment_data/file/752070/cryptoassets_taskforce_final_report_final_web.pdf.

[44] SFC, 'Issues Raised by the Lehmans Minibonds Crisis: Report to the Financial Secretary', 2008, pp 2, 16, 35, 37, www.sfc.hk/web/doc/EN/general/general/lehman/Review%20Report/Review%20Report.pdf. The Lehman Minibonds were an unlisted investment product which led to significant investor losses in 2008. Investigations by the SFC showed that although disclosure on the marketing leaflet complied with the law, the intermediaries adopted improper selling practices and were given inadequate financial advice, which resulted in investors purchasing unsuitable products that were overly complex and risky.

disclosure issues can be aggravated by their novelty and complexity. In the context of ICOs, for instance, due to the lack of standardization of 'white paper' documents which accompany ICOs, there are numerous cases of inadequate disclosure and even false or misleading disclosure.[45] Even if there are warnings regarding the risks of cryptoassets, it can be very difficult for investors to truly understand them, let alone to accurately factor them into the pricing process. A 2018 research has found that almost 25 per cent of ICOs are fraudulent, and 46 per cent of ICOs issued in 2017 had failed by end of 2018.[46]

Furthermore, without having access to adequate information about the products and their risk profiles, investors are prone to purchasing unsuitable products which do not match their risk profile and needs or those which may be of poor value, due to unclear price formation and pricing practices, high fees and the difficulty in assessing their fundamental value.[47] For secondary trading of cryptoassets on exchanges, there are also potential conflicts of interest, as cryptoasset exchanges may act both as agents for their customers and as principal dealers trading with their own book.

4.2.3.3 Security Risks

Security risks refer to the risks of loss or theft during a security breach or technological failure, fraud or unauthorized use.[48] Losses suffered by cryptoasset holders may result from disruptions to cryptoasset systems.[49] Investors may also suffer from errors caused by cryptoasset intermediaries,[50] as transactions involving cryptoassets are often

---

This catastrophe exposed the weaknesses of the disclosure-based regulatory model, particularly for more complex and opaque financial products.

[45] Schlomit Azgad-Tromer, 'Crypto Securities: On the Risks of Investments in Blockchain Based Assets and the Dilemmas of Securities Regulation' (2018) 68 *American University Law Review* 69, 109; Dirk A. Zetzsche et al, 'The ICO Gold Rush: It's a Scam, It's a Bubble, It's a Super Challenge for Regulators', *University of Luxembourg Law Working Paper No 11/2017*; *UNSW Law Research Paper No 17-83*, *University of Hong Kong Faculty of Law Research Paper No 2017/035*, 2017, p 15, https://papers.ssrn.com/sol3/papers.cfm?abstract_id=3072298.

[46] Bank for International Settlements, 'BIS Annual Economic Report', 2018, p 107, www.bis.org/publ/arpdf/ar2018e.pdf.

[47] Ronald J. Gilson and Reinier H. Kraakman, 'The Mechanisms of Market Efficiency' (1984) 70 *Virginia Law Review* 549, 552.

[48] The Clearing House and Independent Community Bankers of America, 'Virtual Currency: Risks and Regulation', 2014, pp 4–5, www.theclearinghouse.org/~/media/Files/Research/20140623%20Virtual%20Currency%20White%20Paper.pdf.

[49] International Monetary Fund, 'Virtual Currencies and Beyond: Initial Considerations', 2016, p 28, www.imf.org/external/pubs/ft/sdn/2016/sdn1603.pdf.

[50] Ibid.

irreversible, and there is no third party to absorb risks due to the decentralized nature of cryptoassets.[51] A new form of cybercrime known as 'cryptojacking' has also emerged, which involves the hijacking of customers' computer processing power to mine cryptoassets without their explicit knowledge and permission.[52]

Not surprisingly, security risks are not limited to retail investors. Owing to the ineffective security measures adopted by exchanges and wallet providers in safeguarding consumer assets, cryptoasset intermediaries are common targets for cybercrimes such as hacking and theft.[53] A further concern of regulators relates to the safe custody of cryptoassets by exchanges, particularly in light of cybersecurity breaches and hacks.[54] A number of major platform hacks have occurred in Japan, with 850,000 Bitcoins stolen from Mt Gox in 2014,[55] USD 540 million from Coincheck in January 2018, and USD 60 million from Zaif in September 2018.[56] Similar incidents have been reported in Canada, with USD 654,000 worth of cryptoassets stolen from Flexcoin in 2014.[57] Due to the international nature and the variable traceability of cryptoassets, it is often difficult for law enforcement agencies to track stolen assets and take action against perpetrators, which render resultant consumer losses irrecoverable. The need for an effective regulation of intermediaries is evident.

4.2.3.4 Financial Crime Risks

Cryptoassets have a high level of anonymity as owners are 'not identified by name on the ledger, but [only] letters and numbers representing their

---

[51] Ibid, p 29.

[52] National Cyber Security Centre, 'The Cyber Threat to UK Business', 2018, p 25, www.sbrcentre.co.uk/media/3055/cyber-threat-to-uk-business-2018.pdf.

[53] Averie Brookes, 'US Regulation of Blockchain Currencies: A Policy Overview' (2018) 9 *American University Intellectual Property Brief* 75, 84.

[54] SFC, 'Statement on Regulatory Framework for Virtual Asset Portfolio Managers, Fund Distributors and Trading Platform Operators', 2018, www.sfc.hk/web/EN/news-and-announcements/policy-statements-and-announcements/reg-framework-virtual-asset-portfolios-managers-fund-distributors-trading-platform-operators.html.

[55] Jen Wieczner, 'The Surprising Redemption of Bitcoin's Biggest Villain' (2018) 177(5) *Fortune* 68, 70.

[56] Samburaj Das, 'Licensed Crypto Exchange Zaif Plans Compensation after 6,000 Bitcoins, $60 Million Crypto Theft', CNN, 20 September 2018, www.ccn.com/licensed-crypto-exchange-zaif-plans-compensation-after-6000-bitcoins-60-million-crypto-theft.

[57] Matthew P. Ponsford, 'A Comparative Analysis of Bitcoin and Other Decentralised Virtual Currencies: Legal Regulation in the People's Republic of China, Canada, and the United States' (2015) 9 *Hong Kong Journal of Lega Studies* 29, 30.

108   CRYPTOASSETS

public [cryptoasset] address'.[58] Anonymity-based abuse risks then arise as cryptoassets may be used in facilitating unlawful activities, which are very difficult to detect and trace. In 2017, the UK National Risk Assessment reported on the role which cryptoassets can play in laundering proceeds of crimes conducted through computer technology, as a method of payment between criminals and the purchase of illicit goods or services. Increasing signs of cryptoassets being used as a means to handle illicit proceeds from offline crime have also been observed since 2017.[59] This rise of illicit use in money laundering is not only linked to the inherent anonymity of users and the privacy features of some cryptoassets, but also to their growing accessibility.[60] A lack of effective regulation can only exacerbate these anti–money laundering (AML) concerns. Infamous examples include the 'Silk Road' digital black market which made use of the anonymity and high-tech feature of Bitcoin to trade illegal drugs on its website, and the online criminal marketplace AlphaBay which traded illegal drugs, hacking tools and firearms.

Furthermore, at the international level, cryptoassets have raised terrorist financing concerns due to their accessibility, global reach and anonymous nature.[61] There have been cases in which terrorist groups have used social media to solicit donations and post Bitcoin addresses for payment, such as a group that claimed to be supporting Syrian fighters.[62] These raise concerns over combating the financing of terrorism (CFT) and call for effective regulation.

4.2.3.5   Financial Stability Risks

The Financial Stability Board (FSB) has assessed the financial stability implications of the use of cryptoassets, adopting the view that cryptoassets

---

[58] Omri Marian, 'A Conceptual Framework for the Regulation of Cryptocurrencies' (2015) 82 *University of Chicago Law Review Dialogue* 53, 56.

[59] HM Treasury, 'National Risk Assessment of Money Laundering and Terrorist Financing', 2017, p 40, https://assets.publishing.service.gov.uk/government/uploads/system/uploads/attachment_data/file/655198/National_risk_assessment_of_money_laundering_and_terroris t_financing_2017_pdf_web.pdf.

[60] Averie Brookes, 'US Regulation of Blockchain Currencies: A Policy Overview' (2018) 9 *American University Intellectual Property Brief* 75, 82; Shaen Corbet et al, 'Cryptocurrencies as a Financial Asset: A Systematic Analysis' (2019) 62 *International Review of Financial Analysis* 182, 193.

[61] Peter Twomey, 'Halting a Shift in the Paradigm: The Need for Bitcoin Regulation' (2013) 16 *Trinity College Law Review* 67, 72.

[62] Travis J. Tritten, 'The Dark Side of Bitcoin: Terror Financing and Sanctions Evasion', *Washington Examiner*, 16 January 2018, www.washingtonexaminer.com/the-dark-side-of-bitcoin-terror-financing-and-sanctions-evasion.

did not pose a material risk to global financial stability in October 2018.[63] However, owing to rapid market evolution, risks to financial stability may emerge in the future and regulators must remain vigilant to potential 'transmission channels', through which risks from the cryptoasset market may leak into the formal financial system.[64] These include the use of cryptoassets in payment and settlement, the exposure of systemically important financial institutions to cryptoassets, and links between cryptoasset markets and systemically important markets.[65] Fintech companies which have achieved a 'critical mass' will become systemically important institutions, and may threaten financial stability if their inherent business model is not sufficiently robust. It would therefore be sensible for regulators to plan ahead and design their regulatory approaches in such a way which allows for effective oversight of the transmission channels and the mitigation of any potential risks to financial stability as the market grows.[66]

4.2.4 Benefits of Cryptoassets

While there are various risks associated with cryptoassets, they have important benefits. The UK Cryptoassets Taskforce is of the view that although there is so far limited evidence of the current generation of cryptoassets delivering benefits, the potential for benefits to materialize in the future has been recognized.[67] The International Monetary Fund (IMF), while acknowledging the risks, has expressed a similarly favourable stance towards cryptoassets regarding their potential.[68] A closer look

---

[63] Financial Stability Board, 'Crypto-Asset Markets: Potential Channels for Future Financial Stability Implications', 2018, p 14, www.fsb.org/wp-content/uploads/P101018.pdf. The FSB is an international body which monitors and makes recommendations for the global financial system. It should be noted that this view may change in light of the rapid developments of technology in this field.

[64] Ibid, p 8.

[65] HM Treasury, 'Cryptoassets Taskforce: Final Report', 2018, p 38, https://assets .publishing.service.gov.uk/government/uploads/system/uploads/attachment_data/file/ 752070/cryptoassets_taskforce_final_report_final_web.pdf.

[66] Dirk A. Zetzsche et al, 'The ICO Gold Rush: It's a Scam, It's a Bubble, It's a Super Challenge for Regulators', *University of Luxembourg Law Working Paper No 11/2017, UNSW Law Research Paper No 17-83, University of Hong Kong Faculty of Law Research Paper No 2017/ 035*, 2017, p 17, https://papers.ssrn.com/sol3/papers.cfm?abstract_id=3072298.

[67] HM Treasury, 'Cryptoassets Taskforce: Final Report', 2018, p 31, https://assets .publishing.service.gov.uk/government/uploads/system/uploads/attachment_data/file/ 752070/cryptoassets_taskforce_final_report_final_web.pdf.

[68] International Monetary Fund, 'What Are Cryptocurrencies, Finance & Development', 2018, p 26, www.imf.org/external/pubs/ft/fandd/2018/06/pdf/fd0618.pdf.

110   CRYPTOASSETS

at these potential benefits sheds light on the embracive, albeit cautious stance adopted by regulators.

4.2.4.1   Efficient Financial Transactions

Cryptoassets enable efficient and inexpensive financial transactions through the reduction of a third party such as a trusted 'bank, credit card company, escrow agent, or recording agency' which is required in validating traditional transactions, and transaction costs are substantially reduced.[69] This reduction of 'costs or charges in connection with the currency exchange rates and other governmental barriers'[70] is particularly advantageous to smaller businesses and 'nations without developed financial sectors'.[71] The peer-to-peer exchange platform offered by cryptoassets also fosters greater speed and efficiency in making payments, in particular for cross-border transactions.[72] It is commonplace for retail cross-border payments to be completed 'instantly and securely' and not requiring 'third party approval or support',[73] whereas the same transaction would require one to two days under a traditional payment system.

In addition, cryptoasset transactions are securely and permanently recorded on a ledger which improves the transparency and traceability of transactions, thanks to the underlying DLT.[74] These features have far-reaching implications for the financial sector and beyond, with potential applications capable of benefiting record-intensive industries such as the health care and property sectors. A noteworthy idea is the process of 'tokenization', which means the representing of existing assets as tokens on DLT platforms to improve processes around trading in and the transfer of the assets.[75] In this way, cryptoassets can be used as a means to boost efficiency in traditional transactions.

[69] Omri Marian, 'A Conceptual Framework for the Regulation of Cryptocurrencies' (2015) 82 *University of Chicago Law Review Dialogue* 53, 55.
[70] Daniela Sonderegger, 'A Regulatory and Economic Perplexity: Bitcoin Needs Just a Bit of Regulation' (2015) 47 *Washington University Journal of Law & Policy* 175, 183.
[71] Ibid, p 177.
[72] International Monetary Fund, 'Virtual Currencies and Beyond: Initial Considerations', 2016, p 5, www.imf.org/external/pubs/ft/sdn/2016/sdn1603.pdf.
[73] Ferdinando M. Ametrano, 'Hayek Money: The Cryptocurrency Price Stability Solution', 2016, p 10, https://papers.ssrn.com/sol3/papers.cfm?abstract_id=2425270.
[74] di Anderson K. Braeden, 'Regulating the Future of Finance and Money: A Rational US Regulatory Approach to Maximizing the Value of Crypto-Assets and Blackchain Systems' (2018) 11 *Bocconi Legal Papers* 1, 9.
[75] HM Treasury, 'Cryptoassets Taskforce: Final Report', 2018, p 13, https://assets .publishing.service.gov.uk/government/uploads/system/uploads/attachment_data/file/ 752070/cryptoassets_taskforce_final_report_final_web.pdf.

4.2.4.2 Diversification of Financial Landscapes

As a form of Fintech innovation, cryptoassets have the potential to widen access to new and different types of financial products and services, thereby creating new fundraising and investment opportunities. In particular, cryptoasset benefits are most likely to materialize through their use as a capital raising tool in ICOs.[76] Not only does this facilitate a more streamlined and cost-efficient capital raising process, ICOs also support innovation and incentivize improvements in traditional capital raising processes by introducing more competition, which ultimately results in improvements to the market as a whole.[77] The global accessibility of ICOs may also unlock new sources of capital, particularly for high-risk, early-stage projects which would likely struggle to raise funds under the traditional fundraising model.

Moreover, cryptoassets will not completely eliminate the need for trusted intermediaries such as brokers and bankers, but their use will lead to a diversification of the financial landscape with a better balance between centralized and decentralized service providers. With more diversification, this would create a financial ecosystem that is more efficient and resistant to threats. Importantly, this supports the idea of incorporating cryptoassets into existing financial systems, which has emerged as a common theme in cryptoasset regulation.[78]

4.3 The Regulatory Regime in Hong Kong

As shown above, cryptoassets have both risks and benefits, and the goal of the regulation is to maximize the benefits while controlling the risks. The challenges in designing a suitable regulatory framework are closely linked to the risk-benefit profile of cryptoassets. It is important to note that while most potential benefits are to be harvested by the market and its users, it is the investors who bear the most imminent risks. Indeed, concerns about market integrity arise due to a combination of factors such as market immaturity, market

---

[76] Ibid, p 32.

[77] European Securities and Markets Authority, 'Advice to ESMA: Own Initiative Report on Initial Coin Offerings and Crypto-Assets', ESMA22-106-1338, 2018, p 9, www.esma.europa.eu/sites/default/files/library/esma22-106-1338_smsg_advice_-_report_on_icos_and_crypto-assets.pdf.

[78] Maria Demertzis and Guntram B. Wolff, 'The Economic Potential and Risks of Crypto Assets: Is a Regulatory Framework Needed', 2018, p 2, http://bruegel.org/wp-content/uploads/2018/09/PC-14_2018.pdf.

112   CRYPTOASSETS

abuse and security risks, which may affect the effective operation of the market and damage user confidence.[79]

Hence, investor protection should be given sufficient attention in the regulation. Yet, the novelty and complexity of cryptoassets have posed difficulties for their regulation under traditional frameworks, and there is a great need for finding a new way to effectively regulate cryptoassets.

4.3.1 Overview

In Hong Kong, cryptoassets do not qualify as money and are not regulated as legal tender. On 11 February 2015, the HKMA, which is the central bank and banking regulator in Hong Kong, stated in a press release that 'Bitcoin is not a legal tender but a virtual "commodity"', and its spokesperson confirmed again that 'bitcoin and other similar virtual commodities are not regulated by the HKMA' and the public should be 'aware of the risks associated with Bitcoin'.[80] Similarly, Customs and Excise Department confirmed that Bitcoin and other virtual currencies are not 'money' and thus they are not under the supervision of the department.[81]

The SFC has been the primary authority that ventures to regulate cryptoassets in Hong Kong. Prior to the introduction of the 2018 Statement on Regulatory Framework, cryptoassets had generally been regulated by the SFC under pre-existing securities laws. On 5 September 2017, the SFC issued a statement to the effect that under the Securities and Futures Ordinance (Cap 571) (SFO) cryptoassets may constitute a 'security' based on their terms and features, and parties engaging in a 'regulated activity' associated with securities must be licensed or registered with the SFC, so long as such activities target the Hong Kong public.[82] ICOs and the secondary trading of cryptoassets on

---

[79] European Banking Authority, 'Report with Advice for the European Commission on Crypto-Assets', 2019, p 17, https://eba.europa.eu/documents/10180/2545547/EBA +Report+on+crypto+assets.pdf.

[80] Hong Kong Monetary Authority, 'The HKMA Reminds the Public to Be Aware of the Risks Associated with Bitcoin', 11 February 2015, www.hkma.gov.hk/eng/news-and-media/press-releases/2015/02/20150211-3/.

[81] Customs and Excise Department Money Service Supervision Bureau, 'Statement in Relation to Bitcoin and Money Service Operator License', April 2014, https://eservices .customs.gov.hk/MSOS/downloadFile?id=41214.

[82] SFC, 'Statement on Initial Coin Offerings', 2017, www.sfc.hk/web/EN/news-and-announcements/policy-statements-and-announcements/statement-on-initial-coin-offer ings.html.

4.3 REGULATORY REGIME IN HONG KONG

exchanges must similarly comply with registration or authorization requirements.[83]

On 11 December 2017, the regulation was extended to cover derivatives of cryptoassets falling under the definition of 'securities' and 'futures contracts' (SF cryptoassets).[84] It was made clear that while Bitcoin itself is not considered a 'security', Bitcoin futures contracts are regulated under the SFO as 'futures contracts', and intermediaries must possess a Type 2 (dealing in futures contracts) licence and observe the relevant 'suitability' and 'conduct' requirements. Importantly, the licensing requirements also apply to funds investing in Bitcoin futures contracts and other forms of cryptoasset-related investment products which are regarded as 'securities', and cover marketing, managing and advising activities.

Furthermore, the extension of notification requirements to all cryptoassets on 1 June 2018,[85] which required intermediaries to notify the SFC of any changes in their cryptoasset-related trading and asset management activities, highlighted the SFC's growing concern with regard to the effectiveness of intermediaries in discharging their gatekeeping function, and the lack of regulation over cryptoassets which are not regarded as 'securities' or 'futures contracts' (non-SF cryptoassets).

In summary, cryptoassets are broadly divided into SF cryptoassets and non-SF cryptoassets in Hong Kong, and it is hard to regulate both of them via a piecemeal approach under the traditional framework. Hence, as noted earlier, the SFC issued the 2018 Statement on Regulatory Framework (with two appendices), reflecting a more holistic approach to the regulation of cryptoassets. Two points are worth noting here. First, the new regime is still based largely on the existing securities regulation, and not on a stand-alone, specific regime for cryptoassets. Mr Ashley

---

[83] Registration requirements refer to the prospectus regime for securities such as shares under Parts II and XII of the Companies (Winding Up and Miscellaneous Provisions) Ordinance (Cap 32) (CWUMPO), while the authorization requirement under Part IV of the SFO means SFC authorization for collective investment scheme products such as funds.

[84] SFC, 'Circular to Licensed Corporations and Registered Institutions on Bitcoin Futures Contracts and Cryptocurrency-Related Investment Products', 2017, www.sfc.hk /edistributionWeb/gateway/EN/circular/doc?refNo=17EC79.

[85] SFC, 'Circular to Intermediaries on Compliance with Notification Requirement', 2018, www.sfc.hk/edistributionWeb/gateway/EN/circular/doc?refNo=18EC67. Under section 4 and Schedule 3 to the Securities and Futures (Licensing and Registration) (Information) Rules (Cap 571S), intermediaries are required to notify the SFC of any 'significant changes' in the nature of their business and the types of service they provide. Importantly, the notification requirements cover all cryptoassets, regardless of whether they qualify as securities or not.

114   CRYPTOASSETS

Alder, the CEO of the SFC, has stated that it is too early at this point to introduce legislation that is specific to cryptoassets, with international consensus on regulatory standards yet to crystallize.[86] Second, under the new regime, investments in cryptoasset funds are largely restricted to professional investors only, who are traditionally better positioned to assess and bear risks from investment in sophisticated and risky financial products.

This reflects the cautious and gradualist approach that the SFC takes towards cryptoassets, with an emphasis on risk control and investor protection. More specifically, to give technical effect to this regulatory principle, the new regime provides an elevated regulatory standard for managers and distributors of funds investing in cryptoassets, and opens up the SFC Regulatory Sandbox to operators of cryptoasset trading platforms. These key elements will be discussed below in turn.

4.3.2   Managed Funds with Cryptoassets Portfolio

4.3.2.1   Portfolio Managers

The new regime imposes new standards on managers of funds investing in non-SF cryptoassets. First, a Type 1 licence (dealing in securities) is required for firms *managing* and *distributing* funds solely investing in non-SF cryptoassets. Second, firms already licensed for Type 9 regulated activity (asset management) may manage portfolios investing solely or partially (subject to the *de minimis* requirement)[87] in non-SF cryptoassets. It should be noted that while the portfolio managers of funds solely investing in non-SF cryptoassets (where the managers do not also distribute the funds) and those of portfolios with less than 10 per cent GAV investment in non-SF cryptoassets are not subject to the requirements in this section, such funds are regulated through their distribution under the requirements to be discussed in the next section, which apply to all cryptoasset funds.

---

[86] Ashley Alder, 'Fintech: Meeting the Regulatory Challenges: Keynote Speech at Hong Kong FinTech Week 2018', 2018, p 7, www.sfc.hk/web/EN/files/ER/PDF/Speeches/Ashley%20HK%20FinTech%20Week.pdf.

[87] SFC, 'Statement on Regulatory Framework for Virtual Asset Portfolio Managers, Fund Distributors and Trading Platform Operators', 2018, www.sfc.hk/web/EN/news-and-announcements/policy-statements-and-announcements/reg-framework-virtual-asset-portfolios-managers-fund-distributors-trading-platform-operators.html. The *de minimis* requirement provides that only portfolio managers who intend to invest 10 per cent or more of the gross asset value (GAV) of their portfolios in cryptoassets will be subject to the SFC's oversight in this way.

The management activities of the two types of funds above investing in non-SF cryptoassets will be overseen by the SFC through the imposition of licensing conditions, subject to the same standard as that currently applied to portfolio managers investing in traditional SF products (Existing Requirements).[88] This is regardless of whether the portfolios invest solely or partially in cryptoassets, and whether the cryptoassets concerned are SF or non-SF.[89]

To provide additional clarity, the SFC has provided a set of standard terms and conditions (Terms and Conditions), which outlines the essential terms of the existing requirements.[90] The Terms and Conditions will be applied in a principles-based manner, with the possibility of minor variations and elaborations being made, so as to adapt to the business model of the particular cryptoasset portfolio manager.[91]

---

[88] Ibid. The Existing Requirements refer to existing requirements under the SFO, the Code of Conduct for Persons Licensed by or Registered with the Securities and Futures Commission (Code of Conduct), the Fund Manager Code of Conduct, and guidelines, circulars and frequently asked questions issued by the SFC.

[89] Ibid.

[90] In essence, the Terms and Conditions cover the following:

1. *The type of investors and disclosure to investors*: portfolio managers should ensure that only 'professional investors' are permitted to invest into cryptoasset portfolios (subject to the *de minimis* requirement), and ensure risk disclosure to investors and distributors.
2. *Safeguarding of assets*: portfolio managers should select appropriate custodial arrangements by assessing the accessibility and security of stored assets. A duty of care, skill and diligence is imposed. Additional requirements covering insurance and disclosure apply to cases of self-custody.
3. *Portfolio valuation*: with no generally accepted valuation principles for cryptoassets, managers should select reasonably appropriate valuation methodologies in the best interests of investors.
4. *Risk management*: managers should set appropriate limits for each product, market and counterparty, conduct periodic stress testing, and assess the reliability and integrity of cryptoasset exchanges.
5. *Auditors*: managers should appoint an independent auditor with capability in cryptoassets to audit the financial statements of funds.
6. *Liquid capital*: different levels of liquid capital requirement are imposed on managers depending on whether they hold client assets.

SFC, Appendix 1 (Regulatory Standards for Licensed Corporations Managing Virtual Asset Portfolios) of 'Statement on Regulatory Framework for Virtual Asset Portfolios Managers, Fund Distributors and Trading Platform Operators', 2018, pp 3–6, www .sfc.hk/web/EN/files/ER/PDF/App%201%20-%20Reg%20standards%20for%20VA% 20portfolio%20mgrs_eng.pdf.

[91] Ibid, p 5.

116 CRYPTOASSETS

Third, licence applicants and licensed firms are required to inform the SFC if they are presently managing or planning to manage portfolios investing in cryptoassets. This is not subject to the *de minimis* requirement and covers all firms with cryptoasset portfolios. The SFC will consider the firm's business activities, and provide the firm with a set of proposed terms and conditions which will be imposed as part of the licensing conditions. Non-compliance with licensing conditions will likely be considered as misconduct under the SFO, which may affect the intermediary's fitness and properness, or even attract regulatory action. Licence applicants that do not agree to the terms and conditions will have their application rejected, and licensed firms will be required to unwind their relevant cryptoasset portfolios within a reasonable period of time.[92]

4.3.2.2 Fund Distributors

The new regime also imposes new standards on the distribution of cryptoasset funds. Firms which distribute funds investing solely or partially in cryptoassets in Hong Kong will require a licence or registration for Type 1 regulated activity (dealing in securities). This is regardless of whether the underlying cryptoassets are SF or non-SF. The distribution of these funds will be overseen by the SFC and the standard is that of the existing requirements.[93] Hence, the distribution requirements serve as a catch-all measure to ensure protection for funds which are not regulated through their portfolio management as noted earlier.

In addition, on 1 November 2018 the SFC issued, together with the 2018 Statement on Regulatory Framework, the Circular to Intermediaries: Distribution of Virtual Asset Funds (2018 Circular on Fund Distribution).[94] Under this circular, intermediaries which distribute cryptoasset funds are required to ensure compliance with paragraph 5.2 of the Code of Conduct as supplemented by the suitability obligations.[95] In effect, intermediaries must ensure that the suitability of the recommendation or solicitation for clients is reasonable in all the circumstances, having regard to information about the client through due diligence.[96]

---

[92] Ibid.

[93] Ibid.

[94] SFC, 'Circular to Intermediaries: Distribution of Virtual Asset Funds', 2018, www.sfc.hk /edistributionWeb/gateway/EN/circular/doc?refNo=18EC77. The statement contains further regulations that cryptoasset fund distributors are subject to.

[95] Ibid. The suitability obligations for fund distribution refer to the Frequently Asked Questions on Compliance with Suitability Obligations by Licensed or Registered Persons, and the Frequently Asked Questions on Triggering of Suitability Obligations.

[96] Ibid, p 1.

Furthermore, intermediaries are required to follow a set of additional requirements if they distribute cryptoasset funds that are not authorized by the SFC (subject to the *de minimis* requirement, except where the intermediary has been advised that the fund manager intends to shortly reduce the fund's investment in cryptoassets to below 10 per cent of the fund's GAV). These additional requirements encompass the following:[97]

1. *Selling restrictions and concentration assessments*: distribution is limited to professional investors. Except for institutional professional investors, distributors should assess client knowledge in cryptoassets, act in their best interests, and ensure that their aggregate investment in cryptoassets is reasonable.
2. *Due diligence on cryptoasset funds that are not authorized*: distributors should conduct due diligence on cryptoasset funds, their fund managers and counterparties such as custodians.
3. *Information for clients*: information disclosure and warning statements regarding the risks of cryptoassets.

4.3.3 Platform Operators

4.3.3.1 The Situation before 2019

Compared to distributors and managers of cryptoasset funds, platform operators present far greater difficulties for the SFC, due to their various business models and the inherent characteristics of the underlying technology of cryptoassets. The SFC has shown determination and a willingness to explore ways of regulating platform operators.

To begin with, the SFC looks at licensing as a possible regulatory approach. The 2018 Statement on Regulatory Framework states that '[i] f the SFC is minded to license any virtual asset trading platforms, it is proposed that the standards of conduct regulation for virtual asset trading platform operators should be comparable to those applicable to existing licensed providers of automated trading services'.[98] To facilitate the licensing idea, the new regime opens up the SFC Regulatory Sandbox mechanism previously set up on 29 September 2017 to cryptoasset

---

[97] Ibid, p 2.

[98] SFC, 'Statement on Regulatory Framework for Virtual Asset Portfolio Managers, Fund Distributors and Trading Platform Operators', 2018, p 6, www.sfc.hk/web/EN/news-and-announcements/policy-statements-and-announcements/reg-framework-virtual-asset-port folios-managers-fund-distributors-trading-platform-operators.html. Automated trading services are Type 7 regulated activities under the SFO.

trading platform operators.[99] The sandbox adopts an opt-in approach, in the sense that platform operators have the freedom to choose to participate in the sandbox. Through joining the sandbox, platform operators may 'set themselves apart from other platforms' by taking a head start in obtaining a licence.[100]

The sandbox regulatory experimentation is split into two stages. First, in the initial exploratory stage, the SFC does not grant participating platforms a licence, but instead observes their live operations under the SFC's expected regulatory standards, and considers the effectiveness of the proposed regulatory requirements in addressing risks and providing investor protection. The main purpose at this stage is for the SFC to consider whether cryptoasset trading platforms are appropriate to be regulated by the SFC. Importantly, participation in the sandbox in the initial stage is to be kept confidential. In the case that the SFC positively determines that cryptoasset platforms are suitable for regulation, it would consider granting a licence to qualified operators, which imposes licensing conditions and moves the operator to the second stage of the sandbox.[101] In the second stage, the operator will be subject to more frequent reporting, monitoring and reviews by the SFC, with the aim of enhancing internal controls and addressing the SFC's concerns associated with the conduct of its business. After a minimum 12-month period, the operator may apply to the SFC for removal or variation of some licensing conditions and exit the sandbox. The licensing status of the operator will be made public at this point. The standards of conduct regulation to be applied to platform operators will likely be comparable to the existing standards for automated trading services.[102]

It should be noted that there are entry requirements for platform operators intending to participate in the sandbox.[103] First, at this stage, the sandbox will only be open to those platforms that provide trading,

---

[99] Securities and Futures Commission, 'Circular to Announce the SFC Regulatory Sandbox', 2017, www.sfc.hk/edistributionWeb/gateway/EN/circular/doc?refNo=17EC63.

[100] Ibid, p 6.

[101] Ibid, p 7. The licensing conditions include five mandatory 'core principles', and a list of 'proposed terms and conditions' which may be modified based on discussions between the SFC and the platform operator. SFC, 'Conceptual Framework for the Potential Regulation of Virtual Asset Trading Platform Operators', 2018, pp 3–5, www.sfc.hk/web/EN/files/ER/PDF/App%202_%20Conceptual%20framework%20for%20VA%20trading%20platform_eng.pdf.

[102] Ibid, p 6.

[103] Ibid, p 2.

4.3 REGULATORY REGIME IN HONG KONG

clearing and settlement services for cryptoassets and have control over investors' assets. Other platforms which only provide a direct peer-to-peer marketplace for transactions by investors who retain control over their own assets, or trade cryptoassets for clients but do not provide automated trading services themselves, are not invited to participate in the sandbox. Second, they must operate an online trading platform in Hong Kong, and offer trading of at least one cryptoasset categorized as 'securities' on its platform.

4.3.3.2 The 2019 Position Paper

After the completion of the first stage of 'exploratory analysis', the SFC announced its determination to regulate platform operators on 6 November 2019, when it published the 2019 Position Paper on Regulation of Virtual Asset Trading Platforms (2019 Position Paper).[104] The SFC concluded that the same regulatory standards for licensed automated trading service providers and securities brokers can be applied to regulate cryptoasset trading platforms, and it now accepts licensing applications from qualified platform operators.[105]

The 2019 Position Paper broadly defines virtual asset as '*digital representations of value which may be in the form of digital tokens (such as digital currencies, utility tokens or security or asset-backed tokens), any other virtual commodities, cryptoassets or other assets of essentially the same nature, irrespective of whether they amount to "securities" or "futures contracts" as defined under the SFO'.*[106] As for the virtual asset that falls under the 'securities' or 'futures contracts' as defined under the SFO, they are referred to as 'security tokens'.

A firm operating a centralized virtual asset trading platform (VATP) by offering trading of at least one securities may apply for a license from the SFC for Types 1 (regulating activities of dealing with securities) and 7 (regulating activities of providing automated trading services).[107] Upon becoming licensed, a platform operator will be moved to the second stage

---

[104] SFC, 'Position Paper: Regulation of Virtual Asset Trading Platforms', 2019, www.sfc.hk/web/EN/files/ER/PDF/20191106%20Position%20Paper%20and%20Appendix%201%20to%20Position%20Paper%20(Eng).pdf.

[105] Ibid, pp 6–7. Cryptoasset platform operators which operate a centralized online trading platform and offer trading of at least one security token on its platform are regulated by the SFC, and require a licence for Type 1 (dealing in securities) and Type 7 (providing ATS) regulated activities.

[106] Ibid, note 2.

[107] Ibid, para 82.

of the SFC Regulatory Sandbox, where its internal controls and risk management are further improved under the SFC's close supervision.[108]

Applicants are expected to comply with all relevant regulatory requirements. On the one hand, the general requirements for other types of licensed firms apply, including but not limited to, the Code of Conduct for Persons Licensed by or Registered with the Securities and Futures Commission (Code of Conduct),[109] relevant circulars and regulatory statements set out by the SFC. On the other hand, the SFC imposes several licensing conditions specific to the regulation of VATP. One condition is to only provide services to professional investors who are more experienced and own a certain amount of capital. Another condition is to comply with the terms and conditions set out under the licensing conditions and terms and conditions for virtual asset trading platform operators (terms and conditions for VATP). In essence, the terms and conditions cover the following:[110]

1. *Safe custody of assets*: platform operators should hold client assets on trust, predominantly in cold wallets, have in place procedures for handling cryptoasset transfers, procure insurance and safely manage private keys for digitally signing transactions.
2. *Know-your-customer (KYC)*: platform operators should comply with KYC requirements, ensure clients have sufficient knowledge of cryptoassets and associated risks before providing trading services or otherwise provide training, and assess concentration risks by setting trading or position limits.
3. *AML and CFT*: platform operators should implement adequate AML/CFT systems, regularly review and enhance them based on SFC guidance and Financial Action Task Force (FATF) recommendations, for example by deploying cryptoasset tracking tools.
4. *Prevention of market manipulative and abusive activities*: platform operators should implement written policies and controls for the

---

[108] Ibid, p 15.

[109] SFC, 'Code of Conduct for Persons Licensed by or Registered with the Securities and Futures Commission', www.sfc.hk/web/EN/assets/components/codes/files-current/web/codes/code-of-conduct-for-persons-licensed-by-or-registered-with-the-securities-and-futures-commission/code-of-conduct-for-persons-licensed-by-or-registered-with-the-securities-and-futures-commission.pdf.

[110] SFC, Appendix 1 (Licensing Conditions and Terms and Conditions for Virtual Asset Trading Platform Operators) of 'Position Paper: Regulation of Virtual Asset Trading Platforms', 2019, www.sfc.hk/web/EN/files/ER/PDF/20191106%20Position%20Paper%20and%20Appendix%201%20to%20Position%20Paper%20(Eng).pdf.

proper surveillance of activities, take immediate steps to restrict or suspend trading upon discovery of manipulative or abusive activities.

5. *Accounting and auditing*: platform operators should select and appoint auditors with experience and track record in virtual asset related businesses.

6. *Risk-management*: platform operators should have a risk-management framework to identify, measure, monitor and manage risks and require customers to pre-fund their accounts.

7. *Conflicts of interest*: platform operators should not engage in proprietary trading or market-making activities except at arm's length via an independent external party, and regulate employees' dealings.

8. *Virtual assets for trading*: platform operators should set up a function to establish, implement and enforce the rules on cryptoasset issuers, the criteria for cryptoasset inclusion, and the criteria for halting, suspending and withdrawing cryptoassets from trading, and perform due diligence.

The licensed VATP must obtain prior written approval from the SFC for any plan to introduce new service or to make any material change to an existing service or to add any product to its trading platform. The licensed VATP is also required to report monthly to the SFC and engage an independent professional firm to conduct annual review and report the same to the SFC as regards to the compliance with the licensing conditions. Any breach or non-compliance of the above licensing requirements and conditions will affect the fitness and properness of the licensed VATP and potentially lead to revocation of license or even disciplinary action.

It should be noted that there are two limitations on the application of the licensing regime. First, it only applies to the exchanges where at least one type of cryptoassets traded falls within the definition of 'securities' or 'futures contracts' under the SFO. This is because, as a securities regulator, the SFC only has jurisdiction over what may constitute securities, and non-securities tokens cannot be directly regulated by the SFC. However, once a platform is licensed, the SFC has a remit over all of its trading activities, including both security and non-security tokens, even if only a small part of its business involves the activities in security tokens. Second, it only applies to the centralized exchanges where the investors' funds are not controlled by investors themselves but rather by virtual assets trading platforms, and does not apply to decentralized exchanges on which the investors trade on a direct peer-to-peer basis.

4.4 Evaluating the Hong Kong Experience: Strengths and Merits

As discussed above, the new regime in Hong Kong represents great efforts made to regulate cryptoassets, addressing the lacunas that existed in the preceding framework. Through a comparison with four major Fintech jurisdictions, including Mainland China, the United States, the United Kingdom and Singapore, this section will conduct a multi-faceted examination of the new Hong Kong regime. The inclusion of Mainland China is for the apparent reason that there is an increasingly strong economic integration between it and Hong Kong; the United States and the United Kingdom are included owing to their leading roles in the regulation of cryptoassets, and Singapore is Hong Kong's long-time arch-rival in becoming the top financial centre in Asia and beyond.

4.4.1 Is Ban a Solution? Lessons from Mainland China

To start with, the choice of regulation over prohibition is a sensible one, and the new SFC regime should be a welcoming move for the Hong Kong cryptoasset market. While the majority of overseas jurisdictions have embraced cryptoasset business activities and put forth regulatory responses, jurisdictions such as Mainland China have gone the opposite way by banning cryptoassets altogether.[111]

Having defined cryptoassets to be without legal status as fiat currency, Mainland China has all along adopted a considerably cautious and sceptical approach.[112] The curb on cryptoassets was intensified when requirements for the monitoring of suspicious and illegal fundraising activities were heightened in September 2016,[113] and investigative powers were

---

[111] South Korea also imposes an outright ban. Jennifer Carlson and Anne Selin, 'Initial Coin Offerings: Recent Regulatory and Litigation Developments' (2018) 25(3) *Invest Lawyer* 18, 23.

[112] Guanyu Fangfan Bitebi Fengxian de Tongzhi (关于防范比特币风险的通知) [Notice or Precautions against the Risks of Bitcoins] (promulgated on 5 December 2013 by the People's Bank of China and others). In December 2013, the PBOC issued the Notice or Precautions Against the Risks of Bitcoins, which defines Bitcoin as a 'specialized virtua commodity' without legal status as fiat currency. Financial institutions are prohibitec from engaging in Bitcoin-related business activities and must observe Bitcoin-relatec AML obligations.

[113] Guanyu Jinyibu Jiaqiang Dui Shexian Feifa Jizi Zijin Jiaoyi Jiance Yujing Gongzuo de Zhidao Yijian (Yinfa 2016 No. 201) (关于进一步加强对涉嫌非法集资资金交易监测 预警工作的指导意见 (银发 2016 201号)) [Further Strengthening the Monitoring and Early Warning of Suspected Illegal Raising Fund Transactions] (promulgated on 9 September 2016 by the People's Bank of China).

4.4 EVALUATING THE HONG KONG EXPERIENCE   123

enhanced in August 2017.[114] On 2 September 2017, ICOs were declared to be a form of 'unapproved illegal public financing', with rectification work and assessments to be conducted on ICOs on a case-by-case basis, and all new ICOs must be called off.[115] This quickly escalated two days later on 4 September 2017, when the Announcement on Preventing the Financing Risks of ICOs was made by the PBOC, effectively amounting to an absolute ban which outlawed all fundraising activities through ICOs.[116] On 17 January 2018, the PBOC followed up by requiring each of its units to conduct self-examination to ensure that no payment services were being provided for cryptoasset transactions.[117]

Compared to the outright ban approach as adopted in Mainland China, the choice of regulation is more suitable for Hong Kong. First and foremost, as discussed before, cryptoassets have important benefits to offer and may be one of the most important financial innovations for the future. Indeed, it has been suggested that even China's ban is likely to be only temporary, owing to the fact that economic development is a major strategy of the Mainland Chinese government.[118]

Second, China's particular concern with cryptoassets inevitably relates to its less well-developed market regulations and infrastructure as compared to other more economically advanced jurisdictions. This is partly attributable to the late opening up of its capital market and its generally less sophisticated investors. The situation is quite different in Hong Kong, with its markets having been developed on par with

---

[114] Chuzhi Feifa Jizi Tiaoli (Zhengqiu Yijiangao) (处置非法集资条例(征求意见稿)) [Exposure Draft of a Regulation to Handle Illegal Fundraising Released] (promulgated on 24 August 2017 by the China Banking Regulatory Commission).

[115] Guanyu Dui Daibi Faxing Rongzi Kaizhan Qingli Zhengdun Gongzuo de Tongzhi (关于对代币发行融资开展清理整顿工作的通知) [Notification Concerning the Undertaking of Cleaning-up and Rectification Work on ICOs (Notification No. 99)] (promulgated on 2 September 2017 by the Office of the Leading Group for the Special Campaign against Internet Financial Risks).

[116] Guanyu Fangfan Daibi Faxing Rongzi Fengxian de Gonggao (关于防范代币发行融资风险的公告) [Announcement on Preventing the Financing Risks of Initial Coin Offerings] (promulgated on 4 September 2017 by the People's Bank of China and other departments).

[117] Guanyu Kaizhan Wei Feifa Xuni Huobi Jiaoyi Tigong Zhifu Fuwu Zicha Zhenggai Gongzuo de Tongzhi (Yinguan Zhifu 2018 No. 11) (关于开展为非法虚拟货币交易提供支付服务自查整改工作的通知 (银管支付 (2018) 11号) [Notification on Self-inspection and Rectification Work on the Provision of Payment Services for Illegal Virtual Currency Transactions] (promulgated on 17 January 2018 by the People's Bank of China).

[118] Hui Deng et al, 'The Regulation of Initial Coin Offerings in China: Problems, Prognoses and Prospects' (2018) 19 *European Business Organization Law Review* 465, 466, 493.

124 CRYPTOASSETS

international standards. Regulation is therefore a sufficient and more appropriate means of addressing cryptoasset-related concerns.

Finally, if Hong Kong were to maintain and consolidate its status as a global financial centre, cryptoassets are certainly something that it cannot afford to miss. In fact, the ban in Mainland China has led to substantial business opportunities being diverted to the Hong Kong cryptoasset market. Following the ban, many Mainland Chinese issuers have flocked to Hong Kong and Singapore to seek ICO opportunities.[119] Singapore, the arch-rival of Hong Kong in the area of financial services, already ranks as the top ICO hub in Asia.[120] The key for Hong Kong to win this race is to face up to the risks of cryptoassets and explore ways to establish a robust regulatory regime.[121]

4.4.2 Enhanced Investor Protection

4.4.2.1 Lacunas in the Previous Regulatory Regime

Prior to 1 November 2018, it was evident that significant regulatory gaps existed in the preceding framework. While the 5 September 2017 statement and the 11 December 2017 circular set out the regulatory standard for SF cryptoassets and their derivative products, non-SF cryptoassets remained largely unregulated and were only subject to the notification requirements under the 1 June 2018 circular. Despite active enforcement against non-compliant intermediaries,[122] the SFC has acknowledged its potential lack of jurisdiction over cryptoasset exchanges and ICO issuers that have no nexus with Hong Kong, or provided trading services for non-SF cryptoassets. Investors have also been warned not to invest, unless they are 'prepared for a significant loss'.[123]

---

[119] Coco Liu, 'Forget China: Hong Kong, Singapore are New Kids on the Blockchain', *South China Morning Post*, 23 April 2018, www.scmp.com/week-asia/business/article/2142682/forget-china-hong-kong-singapore-are-new-kids-blockchain.

[120] 'Why Singapore Ranks as the Third Most Favourable Country in the World of ICOs', *Singapore Business Review*, 2018, p 1, https://sbr.com.sg/sites/default/files/singaporebusinessreview/print/SBR_2018_AugSept-26-28.pdf.

[121] Enoch Yiu and Georgina Lee, 'Cryptocurrency Rules Unveiled by SFC as Hong Kong Aims to Become Major Trading Hub', *South China Morning Post*, 1 November 2018, www.scmp.com/business/banking-finance/article/2171157/cryptocurrency-rules-be-unveiled-sfc-hong-kong-aims-become.

[122] SFC, 'SFC's Regulatory Action Halts ICO to Hong Kong Public', 2018, www.sfc.hk/edistributionWeb/gateway/EN/news-and-announcements/news/doc?refNo=18PR29.

[123] SFC, 'SFC Warns of Cryptocurrency Risks', 2018, www.sfc.hk/edistributionWeb/gateway/EN/news-and-announcements/news/doc?refNo=18PR13.

In addition, investors have been exposed to cryptoassets through their investment in funds.[124] Without protection by the SFO, non-SF cryptoassets are traded on unregulated exchanges and funds investing in non-SF cryptoassets are managed by unregulated portfolio managers. In addition to the lack of scrutiny over their fitness, properness, financial soundness and competence, there is no regulation to ensure the safe custody of assets and market fairness, both of which are items of particular concern in the context of cryptoassets.[125] This weakness is evinced by the numerous investor complaints received by the SFC regarding significant losses arising from the misappropriation of assets, market manipulations and technical breakdowns of cryptoasset exchanges.[126] Upon suffering a loss, investors are also likely to have little or no recourse due to the limited regulatory scope and extraterritorial nature of exchanges.

4.4.2.2 Improved Investor Protection

The new regime provides comprehensive regulatory coverage for all types of cryptoassets, addressing the issue of regulatory gaps and regulatory arbitrage which existed in the previous framework. To start with, investor protection has been significantly enhanced through the imposition of regulations on non-SF cryptoassets, effectively closing much of the regulatory gaps under the previous framework, particularly in relation to funds. Under the new regime, regulation is extended to cover the management and distribution activities of non-SF cryptoasset funds, applying standards equal to those applied to traditional funds. Not only does the new regime result in enhanced protection for investors, it furthermore provides a pathway through which cryptoasset funds can be effectively incorporated into the existing financial regulatory framework.

As all types of cryptoassets are subject to the same regulatory standard, the new regime gets around the previous difficulty of categorizing cryptoassets under the SF-based taxonomy, and the associated problem of regulatory arbitrage where certain SF cryptoassets may opportunistically

---

[124] Ashley Alder, 'Fintech: Meeting the Regulatory Challenges: Keynote Speech at Hong Kong FinTech Week 2018', 2018, p 5, www.sfc.hk/web/EN/files/ER/PDF/Speeches/Ashley%20HK%20FinTech%20Week.pdf.

[125] SFC, 'Statement on Regulatory Framework for Virtual Asset Portfolio Managers, Fund Distributors and Trading Platform Operators', 2018, p 1, www.sfc.hk/web/EN/news-and-announcements/policy-statements-and-announcements/reg-framework-virtual-asset-portfolios-managers-fund-distributors-trading-platform-operators.html.

[126] Rosario Girasa, *Regulation of Cryptocurrencies and Blockchain Technologies: National and International Perspectives* (Palgrave Macmillan, 2018), p 217.

morph into non-SF ones to avoid regulation. In particular, a major challenge faced by global regulators has been the characterization of cryptoassets under their applicable laws and regulations.[127] As the FSB critically points out, whether a cryptoasset is a security, commodity or some other financial product is a threshold question in financial regulation.[128]

As a starting point, 'security' is defined in the SFO to include, *inter alia*, shares, debentures and interests in a collective investment scheme.[129] The test for determining whether a particular cryptoasset or derivative product fits within the definition of a 'security' has also been set out in the landmark US Supreme Court case of *SEC v. W. J. Howey Co.*[130] to be 'an investment of money in a common enterprise with an expectation of profits solely from the efforts of others'. This is however not a straightforward question at all, particularly when cryptoassets are designed to be used in multiple economic activities. A representative illustration is that cryptoassets are regulated in the United States both as securities and as commodities, with much murkiness still remaining in this distinction. The same issue exists in the United Kingdom where it is difficult to determine whether a cryptoasset falls under a 'regulated activity' and is consequently subject to regulation.[131]

This provides room for regulatory arbitrage where the issuers deliberately design cryptoassets to avoid relevant regulation. Furthermore, regulatory confusion may arise in cases where the nature of cryptoassets may morph over time. Under the *Howey* test, a cryptoasset can be considered to have transformed from a security to a commodity when its value is no longer based primarily on the efforts of others, but on its own intrinsic value. For instance, the US SEC stated in June 2018 that Ethereum is not a security, as it started as a security offering upon its ICO, but subsequently morphed into a non-security due to its decentralized nature and establishment of clear utility.[132] In summary, such a cryptoasset will be regulated as

[127] Iris M. Barsan, 'Legal Challenges of Initial Coin Offerings' (2017) 3 *Revue Trimestrielle de Droit Financier* 54, 54.

[128] Financial Stability Board, 'Crypto-Assets: Report to the G20 on Work by the FSB and Standard-Setting Bodies', 2018, p 5, www.fsb.org/wp-content/uploads/P160718-1.pdf.

[129] Securities and Futures Ordinance (Cap. 571), sch. 1, pt. 1, section 1.

[130] *SEC v. W. J. Howey Co.*, 328 US 293 (1946), p 293.

[131] In the United Kingdom, cryptoasset-related activities are only subject to regulation if they are considered to be 'regulated activities' under the Financial Services and Markets Act 2000 (Regulated Activities) Order (RAO) and the Payment Services Regulation 2017. Andrew Bailey, 'Letter on the FCA Powers and Perimeter', 2018, p 1, www.parliament.uk/documents/commons-committees/treasury/Correspondence/2017-19/FCA-powers-perimeter-300118.pdf.

[132] Securities and Exchange Commission, 'Digital Asset Transactions: When Howey Met Gary (Plastic)', 2018, www.sec.gov/news/speech/speech-hinman-061418.

a security by the SEC in its earlier stages, but as a commodity by the CFTC thereafter.

In contrast, through imposing the same standard on both SF and non-SF cryptoassets, the new regime in Hong Kong ensures that all cryptoassets are regulated, regardless of whether they qualify as securities or not. This helps to avoid the difficult, and somehow artificial, task of categorizing a cryptoasset, and to eliminate the problems of regulatory gaps and regulatory arbitrage. Investor protection is thus improved as a result of the comprehensiveness of the new regime in Hong Kong.

4.4.3 Innovative Regulatory Sandbox

Although the concept of a regulatory sandbox is nothing new, the two-staged sandbox for cryptoasset platform operators in Hong Kong is the first of its kind as an attempt to develop a robust regulatory framework for cryptoasset exchanges. The SFC's concept is rather innovative, in the sense that instead of testing novel financial products, the sandbox is deployed to explore and fine-tune the regulatory approach for cryptoasset exchanges itself. Indeed, among the jurisdictions examined in this chapter, while the United Kingdom and Singapore have applied regulatory sandboxes in cryptoasset regulation, their objectives are to test innovative financial products. Furthermore, the SFC sandbox is exclusively applied to cryptoasset exchanges, while the United Kingdom and Singapore ones are broadly applied to Fintech innovations.

A direct comparison reveals a number of differences in features between the United Kingdom, Singapore and Hong Kong sandboxes. First, the SFC sandbox resembles more closely the Singaporean counterpart in adopting a more ad hoc approach and accepting applications on a rolling basis; while the United Kingdom conducts testing in prescribed cohorts with predefined milestones. Second, the UK sandbox has a broader range of supportive mechanisms available, such as the possibility to waive certain FCA rules and even issue no enforcement action letters; in contrast the SFC and Singaporean sandboxes provide support mainly by relaxing certain regulatory requirements. Third, while both the UK and Singapore sandboxes have set out similar methods in determining the eligibility of applicants, this has not been done in the SFC sandbox. Fourth, while both the Singaporean and SFC sandboxes categorize regulatory requirements to be imposed on participants into core and non-core requirements, the SFC core requirements are notably more

128 CRYPTOASSETS

restrictive, such as limiting trading to professional investors and established ICOs, and requiring investments to be pre-funded.

Overall, the SFC sandbox possesses features that are comparable to its counterparts in the United Kingdom and Singapore, in imposing requirements to ensure financial soundness, proper custody of customer assets, and AML and CFT compliance. In line with its customer protection mandate, the SFC sandbox places more emphasis on maintaining a fair market and proper customer treatment.

4.4.4 Enhanced AML and CFT Standards

Another achievement of the new Hong Kong regime lies in the enhanced protections through elevated AML and CFT standards, which are key regulatory challenges in cryptoasset regulation. Often offering features such as user anonymity and transactions without a third-party intermediary, cryptoassets are often prone to AML and CFT concerns. For example, the strong market reaction of Bitcoin following the shutdown of Silk Road, a major marketplace for illegal drugs in October 2013, points towards the existence of large-scale illicit activities based on cryptoassets.[133] Despite having emerged only a decade ago, the cryptoasset industry has experienced rapid growth, in terms of both market size and product sophistication. It is clear that regulatory standards must catch up at a similar pace in order to remain effective.

In view of this, international standard-setting bodies have led regulatory developments on a global level. Other than the aforementioned IMF and FSB, which have monitored cryptoasset-related risks and called for heightened AML and CFT standards, the FATF has similarly revised its recommendations in October 2018 to call for the regulation of cryptoasset service providers such as trading platforms, with a particular emphasis on imposing AML and CFT obligations.[134] As a member state of the FATF, it is only a matter of time before Hong Kong updates its cryptoasset regulations to reflect these enhanced standards. A similar response is seen worldwide, with Singapore enacting a new Payment

---

[133] Bank for International Settlements, 'BIS Annual Economic Report', 2018, p 107, www .bis.org/publ/arpdf/ar2018e.pdf.

[134] Financial Action Task Force, 'International Standards on Combating Money Laundering and the Financing of Terrorism & Proliferation: The FATF Recommendations', 2018, p 15, www.fatf-gafi.org/media/fatf/documents/recommendations/pdfs/FATF% 20Recommendations%202012.pdf. The FATF is an intergovernmental organization and the global standard setter for AML and CFT regulations.

4.5 REMAINING CONCERNS AND THE WAY FORWARD

Services Bill in 2019 that imposes licensing requirements and AML and CFT obligations on cryptoasset exchanges.[135]

The new Hong Kong regime answers the FATF's call for elevated AML/CFT standards, as is evident from the AML/CFT obligations imposed on platform operators in the sandbox, which cover areas such as KYC obligations, customer due diligence and transaction monitoring.[136] Interestingly, the model terms and conditions proposed by the SFC apply in a principles-based manner, which is generally seen as an effective way to deal with complex problems. Principles-based regulation sets general objectives that are linked to risks, and devolves responsibility for achieving the objectives to the industry, allowing each intermediary to respond to the regulator's principles in its own internal policies.[137] This allows for less prescriptive regulation and enables the regulator to engage in risk-based regulation more freely.

4.5 Remaining Concerns and the Way Forward

4.5.1 Problems with Regulatory Scope

While the new regime represents an overall improvement in investor protection, a number of lacunas remain unaddressed. First, as noted before, the distribution of cryptoasset funds and the trading of cryptoassets on regulated exchanges are restricted to only professional investors. The combined implication of these two factors is that retail investors who are eager to access cryptoassets may end up trading directly on unregulated exchanges, which exposes them to further risk. This may be a lacuna under the new regime, which needs to be mitigated in the next stage of regulatory reform, potentially by broadening the regulatory scope on exchanges. The SFC has already hinted

---

[135] Ong Ye Kung, 'Payment Services Bill Second Reading Speech', 2019, Monetary Authority of Singapore, www.mas.gov.sg/news/speeches/2019/payment-services-bill.

[136] SFC, Appendix 2 (Conceptual Framework for the Potential Regulation of Virtual Asset Trading Platform Operators) of 'Statement on Regulatory Framework for Virtual Asset Portfolios Managers, Fund Distributors and Trading Platform Operators', 2018, p 6, www.sfc.hk/web/EN/files/ER/PDF/App%202_%20Conceptual%20framework%20for%20VA%20trading%20platform_eng.pdf.

[137] Bryane Michael, 'Does Objectives-Based Financial Regulation Imply a Rethink of Legislatively Mandated Economic Regulation? The Case of Hong Kong and Twin Peaks Financial Sector Regulation', 2015, p 21, www.econstor.eu/bitstream/10419/107579/1/Rethinking%20Economic%20and%20Financial%20Regulation%20-%20Hong%20Kong%20and%20Twin%20Peaks.pdf.

that the restriction on professional investors may be relaxed in the next stage of regulation.[138]

Second, certain cryptoasset exchanges remain unregulated under the new regime. If a cryptoasset exchange offers the trading of non-SF cryptoassets as opposed to SF cryptoassets, it will not be subject to the regulation of the SFC.[139] The reason is that, as a securities and futures regulator, the SFC only has power to regulate what falls within the definition of securities or futures. Hence, as the SFC acknowledged, '[s]ome of the world's largest virtual asset trading platforms have been seen operating in Hong Kong, but they fall outside the regulatory remit of the SFC'.[140] In contrast, as noted earlier, the 2018 Statement on Regulatory Framework enables the SFC to regulate all distributors and managers of funds investing in cryptoassets, irrespective of whether the cryptoassets are classified as SF cryptoassets or not. This is on the premise that cryptoassets, as an asset class, have similar features and risk characteristics, whether or not they amount to 'securities' or 'futures contracts'. As the SFC has general jurisdiction over funds, it has the power to regulate all types of cryptoasset funds.

At a fundamental level, the above problem stems from the sectoral financial regulatory structure in Hong Kong. The sectoral regulatory model demarcates regulatory responsibilities based on financial sectors, with the securities, banking and insurance sectors being regulated by different regulators separately.[141] In the case of Hong Kong, the SFC is responsible for regulating securities and futures, while other financial products fall under the purview of other regulators, including the HKMA as the banking regulator and the Insurance Authority as the insurance regulator.[142] For the time being, a practical solution would be to strengthen the regulatory cooperation between the SFC and other relevant regulators. Indeed, there have been numerous occasions on which the SFC and other regulators,

---

[138] Ashley Alder, 'Fintech: Meeting the Regulatory Challenges: Keynote Speech at Hong Kong FinTech Week 2018', 2018, pp 5–6, www.sfc.hk/web/EN/files/ER/PDF/Speeches/Ashley%20HK%20FinTech%20Week.pdf.

[139] SFC, 'Statement on Regulatory Framework for Virtual Asset Portfolios Managers, Fund Distributors and Trading Platform Operators', 2018, p 6, www.sfc.hk/web/EN/news-and-announcements/policy-statements-and-announcements/reg-framework-virtual-asset-portfolios-managers-fund-distributors-trading-platform-operators.html.

[140] Ibid.

[141] Robin Hui Huang and Dirk Schoenmaker Schoenmaker (eds), *Institutional Structure of Financial Regulation: Fundamental Theories and International Experiences* (Routledge, 2015), p 251.

[142] Ibid, p 225.

4.5 REMAINING CONCERNS AND THE WAY FORWARD   131

notably the HKMA, have collaborated in cross-sectoral regulation, and a similar approach can be adopted for cryptoasset regulation. In the long run, Hong Kong may consider a structural reform of financial regulation, changing from the sectoral model to the twin-peaks model under which the SFC will become a business-conduct regulator, with powers and regulatory scope to be expanded to cover all financial products, including all types of cryptoassets.

4.5.2 Applicability of Traditional Regulatory Standards to Non-SF Cryptoassets

A common challenge for cryptoasset regulators has been the operational difficulty in policing cryptoasset-related activities. As the Bank for International Settlements has pointed out, cryptoassets can largely function in isolation from existing institutions and infrastructure, and consequently lack a legal entity or person that can be brought into the regulatory perimeter, with a legal domicile that may be offshore or impossible to be established clearly.[143] A solution is to regulate cryptoassets indirectly by targeting infrastructure providers which offer services specific to cryptoassets, for instance crypto wallets and institutions exchanging cryptoassets into sovereign currencies.[144] In resonance with this theory, the new Hong Kong regime has effectively targeted infrastructural service providers as a means of indirect regulation. A considerable regulatory burden has been shifted from the SFC to intermediaries by applying standards of traditional securities regulation on cryptoasset service providers. An example is that portfolio managers are now vested with the responsibility to select appropriate custodians and auditors.[145]

While it is a rational and convenient approach to apply the same regulatory standards over traditional financial products and their cryptoasset counterparts, there can be both philosophical and practical problems. On the one hand, the appropriateness of applying traditional regulatory standards to non-SF cryptoassets depends on the validity of

---

[143] Bank for International Settlements, 'BIS Annual Economic Report', 2018, p 107, www.bis.org/publ/arpdf/ar2018e.pdf.

[144] Ibid.

[145] SFC, Appendix 1 (Regulatory Standards for Licensed Corporations Managing Virtual Asset Portfolios) of 'Statement on Regulatory Framework for Virtual Asset Portfolios Managers, Fund Distributors and Trading Platform Operators', 2018, pp 3–5, www.sfc.hk/web/EN/files/ER/PDF/App%201%20-%20Reg%20standards%20for%20VA%20portfolio%20mgrs_eng.pdf.

the view that Fintech only upgrades the delivery channels of traditional financial products but does not alter their nature and content.[146] On the other hand, the current lack of industry standards and inadequate infrastructure in the cryptoasset industry mean that it may be significantly more difficult for intermediaries to ensure compliance. Indeed, the SFC has acknowledged that cryptoasset funds face a unique challenge due to the limited availability of qualified custodian solutions.[147] A further illustration is the obligation placed on fund distributors in conducting due diligence on funds, their managers and counterparties.[148] In view of the lack of developed standards in the cryptoasset industry, the rather onerous obligations to examine the fund's constitutive documents, procure due diligence questionnaires, make enquiries concerning fund managers, and examine counterparties may pose significant difficulties and costs on distributors with less resources.

These scenarios seem to cast doubt on the applicability of the regulatory standards of traditional securities products to their cryptoasset equivalents. Consider the case of portfolio managers holding non-SF cryptoassets for clients, who must now maintain a minimum liquid capital of HKD 3 million pursuant to the liquid capital requirements under the new regime.[149] This will most likely dissuade portfolio managers who were previously relying on the lowest liquid capital requirement of HKD 100,000 without holding client assets.[150] In summary, the likely result of this regulatory move is that less well-resourced intermediaries may be forced out of the cryptoasset fund market, eventually leading to an overall concentration of the market.

4.5.3 Issues with the SFC Sandbox

While the SFC Regulatory Sandbox represents a bold move by the SFC to develop a sustainable regulatory model for cryptoasset trading platforms

---

[146] HKEX, 'Research Report: Financial Technology Applications and Related Regulatory Framework', 2018, p 21, www.hkex.com.hk/-/media/HKEX-Market/News/Research-Reports/HKEx-Research-Papers/2018/CCEO_Fintech_201810_e.pdf.

[147] SFC, 'Statement on Regulatory Framework for Virtual Asset Portfolio Managers, Fund Distributors and Trading Platform Operators', 2018, p 2, www.sfc.hk/web/EN/news-and-announcements/policy-statements-and-announcements/reg-framework-virtual-asset-portfolios-managers-fund-distributors-trading-platform-operators.html.

[148] Ibid, Appendix 1, pp 3–4.

[149] Ibid, p 6.

[150] Ibid. Portfolio managers are generally required to maintain increased liquid capital where they hold 'client assets'. Under the new regime, the holding of non-SF cryptoassets will also trigger this requirement.

it is not without concerns. Several features critical to the successful operation of a sandbox can be distilled from the UK's experience, and are worth considering by the SFC.

First, an effective two-way communication and close liaison are the key to a smooth sandbox process. It is highly desirable for the SFC to assign case officers to participating platform operators, particularly in the initial authorization stage where many participants have experienced difficulties with navigating the regulatory framework.[151] Second, the difficulty with pre-assessing the ability of sandbox applicants in meeting authorization conditions may be particularly relevant to the SFC sandbox. This difficulty is associated with the differently structured operations of Fintech innovations, as compared to traditional business models. Indeed, cryptoasset exchanges operate substantially differently from traditional stock exchanges, with which the SFC possesses ample experience. Third, the UK experience has revealed the usefulness of the sharing of lessons learned in the sandbox journey with the wider industry, as a means of providing general guidance and levelling the playing field for non-participants.[152]

Having said that, participating platform operators are able to enjoy the usual benefits felt by sandbox participants, such as a better understanding of the regulatory environment, enhanced client confidence and a quicker, smoother licensing process. As the next step, the SFC should consider introducing more favourable features to its sandbox exercise, such as to enhance support for participants and facilitate better experience sharing.

4.5.4 Balancing Investor Protection and Market Development

A common challenge in financial regulation lies in determining the appropriate regulatory strength, and this is no different in the context of cryptoassets. An effective regulatory framework is one which can protect consumers, maintain financial stability and combat illicit usage, while being able to preserve long-term incentives for innovation.

---

[151] In the UK sandbox, multiple participants have emphasized the importance of having dedicated case officers to maintain a close dialogue, facilitate engagement with FCA subject-matter experts, and obtain feedback. This is particularly the case for less regulatory savvy start-ups. Deloitte, 'A Journey through the FCA Regulatory Sandbox: The Benefits, Challenges, and Next Steps', 2018, p 4, www2.deloitte.com/content/dam/Deloitte/uk/Documents/financial-services/deloitte-uk-fca-regulatory-sandbox-project-innovate-finance-journey.pdf.

[152] Ibid, p 9.

134

CRYPTOASSETS

Although the new SFC regime undoubtedly represents a positive step from the previous framework, a better balance between investor protection and the promotion of innovation could be achieved.

While the new regime provides for enhanced investor protection, it lacks attractive features that stand out from regional rivals such as Singapore, which is highly supportive of innovation. For instance, Singapore provides for carve-outs under its securities laws which furnish reduced regulatory scrutiny for ICOs so long as investor protection is not jeopardized, and takes significant steps to incorporate cryptoassets into day-to-day financial services.[153] The Hong Kong regime, on the other hand, remains confined to safeguarding investor protection and is rather weak in attracting business opportunities. To fulfil its ambition in becoming a leading cryptoasset hub, Hong Kong must learn from its rivals and strengthen its support for market development.

This fundamentally different regulatory philosophy is evident upon a comparison of the diverging regulatory development between Hong Kong and Singapore. The new Hong Kong regime extends existing regulation to non-SF cryptoassets with the primary aims being investor protection and risk containment. The Singaporean framework, on the other hand, attempts to universalize the use of cryptoassets through incorporation into everyday financial activities, such as the application of cryptoassets to payment services under the new Singaporean Payment Services Act (S-PSA) which upgrades the financial system as a whole.[154] According to the MAS, '[t]hrough the introduction of the S-PSA, [it] aims to consolidate payment services regulations under one piece of legislation, elevate the standards of AML and CFT requirements, and improve the application of cryptoassets beyond a store of value, through extension to cross-border payment and remittance applications'.[155] Thus, the MAS seems to represent a more forward-looking and embracive stance towards cryptoassets.

This divergence is also apparent from a comparison of the sandbox objectives. Rather than to shield investors from risks, the MAS introduced

---

[153] Monetary Authority of Singapore, 'Fintech Regulatory Sandbox Guidelines', 2016, p 3, www.mas.gov.sg/-/media/MAS/Smart-Financial-Centre/Sandbox/FinTech-Regulatory-Sandbox-Guidelines-19Feb2018.pdf?la=en&hash=1F4AA49087F9689249FB8816A11AEA A6CB3DE833.

[154] Payment Services Act 2019 (No. 2 of 2019). It was passed by the Singaporean Parliament on 14 January 2019 and came into effect on 28 January 2020.

[155] Monetary Authority of Singapore, 'Consultation Paper on Proposed Payment Services Bill, 2017, P021-2017, p 3, www.mas.gov.sg/-/media/MAS/resource/publications/consult_pa pers/2017/Consultation-on-Proposed-Payment-Services-Bill-MAS-P0212017.pdf.

the sandbox with the primary motivation to prevent the potential stifling of innovation, in situations where financial institutions are uncertain if new Fintech will comply with regulatory requirements, and tend to 'err on the side of caution and choose not to implement' innovations.[156] This is rather different to the Hong Kong regime which has been introduced primarily to guarantee investor protection. While Hong Kong has always been ahead of Singapore in the regulatory development of traditional securities, this does not seem to be the case for cryptoassets.

4.6 Conclusion

Owing to their unique characteristics, cryptoassets are often widely accessible worldwide and pose significant challenges to regulators in adopting a comprehensive strategy to ensure both existing and emerging species of cryptoassets are captured within their regulatory net. In particular, it is crucial to apply an appropriate regulatory strength which achieves the optimal balance between investor protection, on the one hand, and allowing for innovation and development on the other. Cryptoasset regulation is effectively a global exercise which requires international jurisdictions to develop compatible regulatory regimes, and overseas experiences are consequently of great value in the assessment of regulatory effectiveness.

In Hong Kong, cryptoassets have been regulated by the SFC under existing securities laws, effectively leaving behind a large lacuna with non-SF cryptoassets being largely unregulated. The SFC effectively responded to this issue through the introduction of a new regime on 1 November 2018, which extended its regulatory net to cover non-SF cryptoasset funds and enhanced the regulation of platform operators. To assess the new regime, four major overseas jurisdictions with cryptoasset experience have been selected for comparison, including Mainland China, the United States, the United Kingdom and Singapore.

As a starting point, it is not in Hong Kong's interest to follow Mainland China's footsteps in imposing an outright ban on cryptoassets. Through extending regulation to non-SF cryptoassets, the new regime has generated a significant enhancement in investor protection, and placed Hong Kong ahead of the United States and the United Kingdom. Furthermore, AML and CFT obligations have also been elevated in line

---

[156] Official website of the Money Authority of Singapore for the sandbox, www.mas.gov.sg /Singapore-Financial-Centre/Smart-Financial-Centre/FinTech-Regulatory-Sandbox.aspx.

with heightened international standards. On the other hand, a number of potential limitations of the new regime were revealed. The restriction on the type of investors in cryptoassets will need to be reconsidered as the market grows. The capability of the SFC, in regulating all aspects of cryptoassets outside its areas of expertise, is called to question. While the features of the sandbox are largely appropriate in achieving its aim of exploring cryptoasset platform regulation, reference can be made to international experiences to maximize its benefits and function.

Overall, the new regime is a positive development for Hong Kong, addressing the issues of regulatory gaps and regulatory arbitrage that existed under the previous framework as well as introducing enhanced regulatory standards. This has the effect of improving investor protection, but as a matter of regulatory philosophy there is a need for striking a delicate balance between investor protection and market development.

5

Mobile Payment

5.1 Introduction

The last decade witnessed a profound change in the payment landscape, with the widespread use of mobile payment having significantly transformed our lives and habits. Although mobile payment did not originate in China, China has successfully placed itself at the forefront of the global market in terms of the scale and market volume. According to PricewaterhouseCoopers's Global Consumer Insight Survey 2019,[1] the penetration rate of mobile payment in China is 86 per cent, whereas the global penetration rate stands at 34 per cent. Mobile payments can be seen in use in almost every corner of China, accepted by both humble street vendors and luxury brand stores. Even beggars accept mobile payment by displaying a quick-response (QR) code printed on cardboard to pedestrians.[2]

Probably due to the rapidly evolving nature of the mobile payment industry, however, there is today no universal definition of what exactly constitutes a mobile payment. The European Commission offers one useful definition, under which mobile payments refer to 'payments for which the payment data and the payment instruction are initiated, transmitted or confirmed via a mobile phone or device. This can apply to online or offline purchases of services, digital or physical goods'.[3] Despite the large variety of forms a mobile payment may take, its essential function is to resolve the lack of trust between payors (such as consumers) and payees (such as merchants) by having the payment platform

---

[1] PricewaterhouseCoopers, 'Global Consumer Insights Survey 2019 – It's Time for a Consumer-Centred Metric: Introducing "Return on Experience"', www.pwc.com/gx/en/consumer-markets/consumer-insights-survey/2019/report.pdf.

[2] Prachi Gupta, 'Beggars with QR Code: Chinese Poor Collect Alms in Mobile Wallets, Ditch Tin Bowls', www.financialexpress.com/industry/beggars-with-qr-code-chinese-poor-collect-alms-in-mobile-wallets-ditch-tin-bowls/1641567/.

[3] 'Green Paper: Towards an Integrated European Market for Card, Internet and Mobile Payments', European Commission, 22 June 2015, https://eur-lex.europa.eu/legal-content/en/TXT/?uri=CELEX:52011DC0941.

serve as an intermediary between them. The sum given by the consumer payor for the goods would be first forwarded to the payment platform and would only be transferred to the merchant payee when the transaction has been completed and confirmed by the payors.[4]

From the perspective of financial innovation and regulatory challenge, mobile payment is very different from online banking and thus both forms should be distinguished. Online banking is essentially 'old wine in a new bottle', insofar as it provides traditional banking services through internet-based channels. Third-party mobile payments, on the other hand, represent an innovative and potentially disruptive financial service. Moreover, while banks have long been subject to the conventionally well-established supervisory system,[5] the emerging third-party mobile payment service providers, mainly tech firms, present new regulatory challenges. Hence, this chapter will be focused on the issue of third-party (non-bank) mobile payment.

The rapid development of mobile payment can be largely attributed to the significant advantages it possesses vis-à-vis the traditional payment.[6] Consumers can enjoy the convenience and speed of a cashless society, no longer restricted by geographical factors when transferring money or paying for goods. Merchants, on the other hand, can reduce their transaction costs and attract more consumers via a mobile payment platform. Meanwhile, the development of mobile payment has brought a range of legal, regulatory and risk-management challenges, such as fund security, cybersecurity and privacy issue.[7] Regulators are facing unprecedented difficulties; products and services related to mobile payments are increasingly complex and interdependent. It is not an easy task for regulators to balance multiple competing interests, such as financial stability, technological innovations and consumer rights. Onerous regulations may stifle innovation and impede the growth of the industry, while loose regulations may leave consumers unprotected.

---

[4] Goldman Sachs, 'The Rise of China Fintech-Payment: The Ecosystem Gateway' 7 August 2017, p 30, https://hybg.cebnet.com.cn/upload/gaoshengfintech.pdf.

[5] In general, there are three-tiered regulations over banking in China, including the legislation on the banking enacted by the National People's Congress, the administrative rules and regulations enacted by the State Council, and the PBOC'S and the China Banking Insurance Regulatory Commission (the merged regulatory of China's banking and insurance sector)'s guidelines, notices and rules. For further details, see Dongyue Chen and Yixin Huang, 'Banking Regulation in China', Global Legal Insights, www.globallegalinsights.com /practice-areas/banking-and-finance-laws-and-regulations/china#chaptercontent3.

[6] For a more detailed discussion, see Section 5.2.2.

[7] For a more detailed discussion, see Section 5.2.3.

Following this introduction, Section 5.2 will first briefly introduce the current mobile payment market, and then explore the key enablers that contribute to the success of mobile payment in China. It will also discuss the various risks inherent in mobile payment, risks that call for regulatory attention. Section 5.3 will give an overview of the current regulatory regime in China, focusing on four aspects: the entry threshold and exit mechanism, restrictions on the management of consumer fund, crackdown measures on financial crimes (primarily for anti–money laundering), and consumer protection (data security and the liability distribution upon the unauthorized payment). Although China has in many ways led the world in the development of its mobile payment infrastructure, it is of crucial importance to look to the experiences of other jurisdictions to gain some insights, given that speed and scale do not necessarily entail quality and sustainability in the payment system. Section 5.4 will thus examine regulations affecting mobile payment in four other jurisdictions: the United States, the United Kingdom, Singapore and Hong Kong. This is followed by Section 5.5, which evaluates the Chinese law from a comparative perspective, pointing out its strengths and weaknesses, as well as making suggestions for improvement. Section 5.6 provides a unifying conclusion.

5.2 Background: The Market, Enablers and Risks

5.2.1 The Market and Typology of Mobile Payment

In recent years, markets around the world have embraced the unstoppable global trend toward mobile payment. The global mobile payment market was worth USD 368 billion in 2017. Over the next two years, it surpassed USD 745.7 billion.[8] As a global frontrunner in this area, China has the biggest mobile payment market, accounting for almost half of the world.[9] In 2017, approximately 65 per cent of all mobile users in China used their mobile phones as their wallets. Around RMB 38 trillion was spent through mobile payment in 2016.[10] According to the data of the PBOC, the Chinese central bank, China saw 101.43 billion mobile

---

[8] Alex Rolfe, 'Global Mobile Wallet Market Value Set to Reach $1 Trillion in 2020' 26 February 2020, www.paymentscardsandmobile.com/global-mobile-wallet-market-value-set-to-reach-1-trillion-in2020/#:~:text=According%20to%20new%20data%2C%20the,market%20reaching%20%242.1%20trillion%20value.

[9] 'The Age of the Appacus; Fintech in China', Economist, 25 February 2017, www.economist.com/finance-and-economics/2017/02/25/in-fintech-china-shows-the-way.

[10] Ibid.

payment transactions in 2019, with a total value of CNY 347.11 trillion.[11] The US mobile payment market, although showing an incremental year-on-year growth, is six times smaller than that of China.[12] Alipay, a Chinese mobile payment platform associated with the e-commerce giant of Alibaba group, is the world's biggest mobile payment platform now with over 1.2 billion active users.[13]

In general, mobile payments can be classified into two broad categories, namely: (1) remote mobile payments and (2) proximity payments. Each category can be further divided into several subgroups based on the technologies involved.

Remote mobile payments can be made through premium short message services (SMS) or the internet. SMS payment is the simplest method of mobile payment. Consumers are required to create an account with a mobile network operator to link their accounts to their bank accounts.[14] To make a mobile payment, SMSs are sent between users and the mobile network operator to provide transaction details; once the user verifies the payment by entering his password, the mobile network operator will transfer the funds from payor to payee.[15] Although this method is somewhat simpler than the other payment methods discussed below, SMS can suffer from transmission delays between users and mobile network operators and even potential SMS transmission failures,[16] which hampers the use of SMS mobile payments in the global markets.

Remote mobile payments can also be made through the internet, namely the Wireless Application Protocol (WAP).[17] The WAP is a technical standard used in wireless devices for accessing and transmitting information over a mobile wireless network. In WAP mobile payments, mobile applications are created by financial institutions; the various players in mobile payment, such as merchants, third-party mobile payment service providers, and consumers, are all linked to

---

[11] 'Online Payments Transactions Processed by Chinese Banks Rise 37.14% YoY in 2019, Mobile Payments up 67.57%', *China Banking News*, March 2020.

[12] 'Amazing Stats Demonstrating the Unstoppable Rise of Mobile Payments Globally', Merchant Savvy, www.merchantsavvy.co.uk/mobile-payment-stats-trends/.

[13] Ibid.

[14] Meena Aharam Rajan, 'The Future of Wallets: A Look at the Privacy Implications of Mobile Payments' (2012) 20 (2) *CommLaw Conspectus* 445, at 448–449.

[15] Ibid.

[16] Ibid, pp 450–451.

[17] Tanai Khiaonarong, 'Oversight Issues in Mobile Payments', *International Monetary Fund Working Paper*, 2014, p 7, www.imf.org/external/pubs/ft/wp/2014/wp14123.pdf.

5.2 BACKGROUND

these mobile applications.[18] In China, the most-used WAP mobile payment applications include Alipay and Tenpay.[19]

Proximity payment, also called mobile at the point of sale payment, involves the use of mobile phones to pay for goods in shops: the retailer uses a piece of hardware that can interact with the hardware in consumers' mobile phones.[20] Currently, near-field communications (NFC) and QR codes are the most common technologies used in proximity payments.

The NFC is a 'wireless protocol which allows for an encrypted exchange of payment and other data at a close range'.[21] NFC hardware, embedded in the customer's mobile phone by its manufacturer, is scanned by the retailer's NFC reader, installed at the point of sale. The NFC reader scans the consumer's payment account credentials when he taps or swipes his mobile phone on the reader.[22] Typically, NFC technology is used alongside some form of mobile wallet, either prepaid cards or accounts that are saved in a mobile application. The NFC uses a 'secure element' to record consumers' payment credentials on their mobile phones for access to retail shops.[23]

---

[18] Timothy R. McTaggart and David W. Freese, 'Regulation of Mobile Payments' (2010) 127 (6) *Banking Law Journal* 485, at 488.

[19] Alipay was launched in 2004 by Alibaba Group to support online payment. It is run by Ant Financial Services Group, an affiliate company of the Chinese Alibaba Group. Alipay took off mainly due to its tight linking to the online shopping platform of Taobao. However, Alipay did not stand still as a mere payment method, the core value of which is being part of the Alibaba ecosystem. It introduced a wide range of services to its platform, including financial, leisure, and transportation services, in order to meet the users' daily life needs. Data from IResearch Consulting Group shows that it retains its leadership position with a market share of over 50 per cent. Tenpay, owned by Tencent, includes WeChat Pay and Mobile QQ Wallet, both of which are incorporated into one of the most common social media platforms in China. It launched a new product named 'Red Envelope', allowing the user to give lucky money or red packets to close friends, has successfully wrapped up the popularity. Leveraging its large user network, it is a formidable competitor of Alipay in China, with a market share of around 38.9 per cent. [The data of Tenpay and Alipay aforementioned is from IResearch, 2020Q1&Q2中国第三方支付市场数据发布报告(China's Third-Party Payment Industry Report for the First Two Quarters), www.iresearch.com.cn/Detail/report?id=3601&isfree=0

[20] Chris Hill, 'Mobile Payments: Technological, Contractual and Regulatory Convergence', *Kemp Little Annual Update*, 26 January 2017, www.kemplittle.com/wp-content/uploads/2018/12/Mobile-payments-January-2017.pdf.

[21] Robert C. Drozdowski, Matthew W. Homer, Elizabeth A. Khalil, and Jeffrey M. Kopchik, 'Mobile Payments: An Evolving Landscape', Federal Deposit Insurance Corporation, Winter 2012, p 5, www.fdic.gov/regulations/examinations/supervisory/insights/siwin12/mobile.html.

[22] Erin Fonte, '2017 US Regulatory Overview of Mobile Wallets and Mobile Payments' (2017) 17 (4) *Wake Forest Journal of Business and Intellectual Property Law* 549, at 559.

[23] Ibid.

NFC technology is considered the predominant mobile payment method adopted in the global market; it is used as a primary technology in Apple Pay, Samsung Pay, Google Pay etc.

The QR code was originally developed as a 'mobile advertising tool' but has now extended to the use of mobile payments.[24] The QR code is a two-dimensional barcode where information or credential may be encrypted; the QR code can be read by barcode or QR code readers. The use of QR codes may sometimes require the use of another type of mobile payment technology, cloud-based technology. Credentials are stored in the cloud and controlled by a third party rather than on the mobile phone itself. Using cloud-based technologies, static QR codes may be used and stored in the user's mobile device. 'Dynamic QR codes' are unique codes to each transaction but are linked to the user's same payment account and can be used through cloud-based technology.[25] Since QR codes can be printed and be read by mobile phones instead of special devices installed at the point of sale, QR code technology is sometimes classified as a remote mobile payment.[26]

Although mobile payments can be classified into different categories and different technologies can be used, these categories are not mutually exclusive and can be used by the same user or in one mobile application. For example, Apple Pay includes both remote and proximity mobile payment options, and an NFC mobile payment option is available for Apple mobile phones with NFC chips installed.[27] In short, all mobile payments discussed above contain four basic elements, namely (1) a handset, which can be a mobile phone or a device to read codes; (2) an account having the user's funds; (3) a means to communicate the user's request to transfer funds; and (4) a channel which connects the user's (payor's) account to the payee's account.[28]

---

[24] PricewaterhouseCoopers, 'Mobile Proximity Payment: 5 Things Retailers Should Know', PricewaterhouseCoopers Italy, 2016, p 3, www.pwc.com/it/it/publications/assets/docs/mobile-proximity.pdf.

[25] Erin Fonte, '2017 US Regulatory Overview of Mobile Wallets and Mobile Payments' (2017)17 (4) *Wake Forest Journal of Business and Intellectual Property Law* 549, at 560–561.

[26] PricewaterhouseCoopers, 'Mobile Proximity Payment: 5 Things Retailers Should Know', PricewaterhouseCoopers Italy, 2016, p 3, www.pwc.com/it/it/publications/assets/docs/mobile-proximity.pdf.

[27] Ibid, p 9.

[28] Chris Hill, 'Mobile payments: technological, contractual and regulatory convergence', *Kemp Little Annual Update*, 26 January 2017, p 3, www.kemplittle.com/wp-content/uploads/2018/12/Mobile-payments-January-2017.pdf.

5.2 BACKGROUND 143

5.2.2 The Key Enablers

Mobile payment did not originate in China, but it did take off in China's market. There are several drivers behind its rapid development, including technological advancement leading to the wide availability of accessible internet and affordable smartphones; the wide acceptance of mobile payment by Chinese consumers; and competitive advantages of mobile payment vis-à-vis the traditional payment.

5.2.2.1 Technological Advancement

With wide coverage of the internet (around 54.6 per cent) and high smartphone penetration (up to 56 per cent),[29] Chinese payment service providers tried all means to render the mobile payment as the first option for consumers in transferring money or paying for goods. For example, Tenpay introduced "red packet", a money transfer function that immediately went viral among Chinese users, including the elderly. Giving physical red envelopes to the younger generation during holidays or special occasions is a traditional Chinese custom. According to Tenpay's official report, around 823 million people during the 2019 Chinese Lunar New Year sent or received digital red envelopes via the WeChat platform.[30]

The use of QR codes in China has also drastically enhanced user experiences. No special equipment is needed, only software. Merchants, particularly small stores, are more willing to support QR code in lieu of the credit card payment, given that installing the POS machines to support credit card payment is a high cost. It is much easier for merchants to keep payment records, which serve as reliable supporting documents when it comes to applying for bank loans and even IPOs on the securities market. Consumers also gain in convenience as payment is completed with a few taps on a mobile device. This is particularly true in the supermarket, where self-checkout has become more popular.[31]

Additionally, compared to US mobile platforms that are more focused on their payment business, the majority of the Chinese mobile payment platforms offer full-service lifestyle functions. Alipay, for example, apart

---

[29] '2019 J. P. Morgan Global Payment Trends – E-Commerce Payments Trends: China', www.jpmorgan.com/merchant-services/insights/reports/china.

[30] 'Wechat published data report on 2019 Chinese Lunar New Year' CNR News, 11 February 2019, http://tech.cnr.cn/techgd/20190211/t20190211_524506987.shtml.

[31] Fumiko Hayashi and Terri Bradford, 'Mobile Payments: Merchants' Perspectives' (2014) 99 *Economic Review* 5–30, at 44.

from being a payment channel for shopping in-store and online, is integrated with a wide spectrum of financial services, e-commerce, leisure and travel services. The users can make financial investments, buy insurance, order food, book tickets, hail taxis, and so on.

5.2.2.2 The Wide Acceptance by the Local Consumer

While other countries have switched from cash to credit cards and are now switching to mobile payments, China's ability to skip the second step namely the absence of a habit of using credit cards in daily consumption has allowed China to go straight from cash to mobile payment.[32]

In addition, the Chinese people are arguably less concerned with or sensitive about privacy issues than Westerners for various reasons, such as a Confucian cultural tradition and the prevalent pragmaticism adopted in the recent economic reform era.[33] Given that data privacy is one of the most serious risks of mobile payment, it is much easier for mobile payment to gain popularity in China than in Western jurisdictions.[34]

Also, one striking feature of mobile payment in China is that payment institutions can leverage their sizeable customer bases in e-commerce or social media networks. This is well illustrated by some major players in the mobile payment industry, including Alipay (supported by its sister platforms Taobao), Tenpay (it relies on its popular social platform-WeChat), JD Lingqianbao (linked with JD E-Commence platform), and Ping An's Yiqian Bao (backed up by its insurance business). This is a critical point, as one of the major difficulties in developing mobile payment is that not many people are willing to take a remote transaction without a face-to-face verification, nor do they often wish to transfer money to a virtual account.[35] The third-party platforms have successfully

---

[32] 'The Mobile Payment Revolution in China', Asia Pacific Foundation of Canada, p 14 www.asiapacific.ca/sites/default/files/publication-pdf/mobile_payment_report.pdf.

[33] 'In China, Consumers Are Becoming More Anxious about Data Privacy', *Economist* 25 January 2018. Based on our own experiences and interviews with others, there may be another reason behind the phenomenon: many Chinese people believe that the data privacy issue in China is so serious that their personal data might have already been, or would inevitably be leaked out, and thus it is not really meaningful to care about data privacy only in the context of mobile payment. Online interviews with two mobile payment users in each of the three cities of Beijing, Shanghai and Shenzhen, on 18 September 2020.

[34] For a more detailed discussion of the data privacy issue of mobile payment, see Robin Hui Huang et al, 'Protecting Data Privacy for Mobile Payment under the Chinese Law: Comparative Perspectives and Reform Suggestions', working paper. available at https://papers.ssrn.com/sol3/papers.cfm?abstract_id=3767317

[35] Torben Hansen, 'Understanding Trust in Financial Services: The Influence of Financial Healthiness, Knowledge, and Satisfaction' (2012) 15(3) *Journal of Service Research* 280–295.

5.2.2.3 Competitive Advantages over Traditional Payment Services

There has long been a serious mismatch between consumers' high demands for payment services and banks' short supplies of such services in China. Mobile payment does not require the expensive infrastructure and buildings that traditional banks entail, and can help resolve the long-term shortage of financial services in rural areas. More generally, it offers a good alternative to unsatisfactory banking services, particularly for small consumers, as they may not be as valued by the bank as big clients are.[36] Hence, mobile payment operators have seized such an opportunity to provide convenient payment services under the rubric of an 'inclusive financial system'.

As noted earlier, China's mobile payment platforms are usually associated with existing business giants, which affords them the leverage required to gain the trust of consumers. Through sharing consumer data, such as consumer patterns of behavior and preference, with their associated business, payment service platforms can provide more targeted services to suit the needs of individual consumers.[37] In turn, this can generate more nuanced data on the consumers' creditworthiness than can traditional banking.[38] It shall be noted that in the eyes of the platform operators, mobile payment is the means and not the end, given that the profit made directly from the payment service is thin in China due to the low fees charged under fierce competition.[39] Hence, what providers are actually trying to do is build a financial ecosystem via the gateway of payment service.[40] Take Alipay as an example. A wealth management product called 'Yu'e Bao' was introduced with Alipay acting as a conduit for consumers to invest the money left in their Alipay accounts; because it offers much better returns than the bank's savings account while having the same flexibility of withdrawals as the latter, it quickly gained huge popularity and became the largest money market fund in the world just four years after its

---

[36] Dirk A. Zetsche, Ross P. Buckley, Douglas W. Arner and Janos N. Barberis, 'From FinTech to TechFin: The Regulatory Challenges of Data-Driven Finance' (2017) 14 *New York University Journal of Law & Business* 393.

[37] Ibid.

[38] Mikella Hurley and Julius Adebayo, 'Credit Scoring in the Era of Big Data' (2016) 18 *Yale Journal of Law & Technology* 148.

[39] Goldman Sachs, 'The Rise of China Fintech-Payment: The Ecosystem Gateway', 7 August 2017, p 30, https://hybg.cebnet.com.cn/upload/gaoshengfintech.pdf.

[40] Ibid.

introduction, surpassing JP Morgan's US government money market fund with USD 150 billion under management.[41]

It is also important to note that the rapid development of mobile payment in China can be partly attributed to the issue of regulatory arbitrage. Mobile payment platforms are treated as non-financial institutions and thus are not subject to costly banking regulation, despite the fact that they compete with banks in offering financial services. Indeed, at the initial stage of development of mobile payment in China, the third-party platforms were effectively operating in a legal vacuum, gaining competitive advantages over the traditional payment institutions in terms of regulatory burden. As the mobile payment industry grew and many problems emerged, China has since 2010 started to tighten its regulation of mobile payment by gradually introducing an array of relevant regulations and rules, as well as strengthening law enforcement. In short, the initial light-touch regulatory approach was important for the take-off of the mobile payment industry in China, reflecting the policy support of the Chinese authorities for the concept of financial inclusion.[42]

5.2.3 Risks of Mobile Payments

While mobile payment brings many important benefits to our society, there are serious risks associated with it, risks that call for regulatory attention. Indeed, the goal of our regulatory regime is to encourage the development of mobile payment in a beneficial way while controlling the attendant risks. It is thus necessary to examine the risks of mobile payment.

5.2.3.1 Unauthorized Transactions and Fraud

'Unauthorized electronic fund transfer' is defined as 'electronic fund transfer from a consumer's account initiated by a person other than the consumer without actual authority to initiate such transfer and from which the consumer receives no benefit'.[43] The degree of data security provided by a mobile payment app is closely related to the issue of unauthorized transactions and fraud. If a weak authentication system is

---

[41] Louise Lucas, 'Chinese Money Market Fund Becomes World's Biggest', *Financial Times*, 26 April 2017, www.ft.com/content/28d4e100-2a6d-11e7-bc4b-5528796fe35c.

[42] Peter Sparreboom and Eric Duflos, 'Financial Inclusion in the People's Republic of China: An Analysis of Existing Research and Public Data', CGAP and Working Group on Inclusive Finance in China, *China Papers on Inclusiveness No. 7*, August 2012, pp 1–45.

[43] Electronic Fund Transfer Act s.903(12).

adopted by a mobile payment app, fraudsters may easily enter into the user's account by hacking and conduct unauthorized transactions resulting in financial loss.

Unauthorized transactions have been one of the major concerns regarding mobile payment, with cases of unauthorized transactions reported in different regions in recent years. In 2017, it was reported in Guangdong province in China that around RMB 90 million was stolen through QR code scams; also, a man was arrested for stealing RMB 900,000 in the city of Foshan by replacing merchants' QR codes with fake ones which contained a malware to steal consumers' personal information.[44]

Compared to traditional payment, the risk of unauthorized transactions is more serious and harder-to-address in the context of mobile payment. When unauthorized transactions occur, it is necessary to determine which party should be responsible for the fault and whether the user will bear the whole financial loss.[45] Since mobile payment involves multiple players including banks, mobile network operators, and third-party agents, and transactions are conducted quickly with information stored in digital form in different players' systems,[46] it is difficult to trace where the problem occurred, and it can be only more difficult to determine which player is liable for the loss. Moreover, when a consumer complains that an unauthorized payment is made from his account, he may have difficulty in providing any proof because most of the data are held by mobile network operators and third-party mobile payment service providers, but not the user.[47]

Also, when an unauthorized transaction is detected, coordination among the parties in the mobile payment system plays an important role in stopping further unauthorized transactions. However, since multiple parties are involved and each of them may have different communication mechanisms and agreements with other parties, the party who detects the problem may not simultaneously notify other parties about

---

[44] Li Tao, 'QR code scams rise in China, putting e-payment security in spotlight', *South China Morning Post* [Hong Kong], 21 March 2017, www.scmp.com/business/china-business/article/2080841/rise-qr-code-scams-china-puts-online-payment-security.

[45] Rhys A. Bollen, 'Recent Developments in Mobile Banking and Payments' (2009) 24 (9) *Journal of International Banking Law and Regulation* 454, at 466–467.

[46] Tanai Khiaonarong, 'Oversight Issues in Mobile Payments', *International Monetary Fund Working Paper*, 2014, p 6, www.imf.org/external/pubs/ft/wp/2014/wp14123.pdf.

[47] Yongqing Yang, Yong Liu, Hongxiu Li, and Benhai Yu, 'Understanding Perceived Risks in Mobile Payment Acceptance' (2015) 115 (2) *Industrial Management Data Systems* 253, at 258.

148   MOBILE PAYMENT

the problem and the informed party may not take any precautionary measures to minimize the loss suffered by the users. For example, if a user lost his phone, he may try to report the loss to his mobile network operator but the mobile network operator may not relay the message to third-party mobile payment service providers.[48]

5.2.3.2   Money Laundering and Terrorist Financing

From the perspectives of anti–money laundering (AML) and CFT, mobile payment may be useful in reducing the use of cash from unknown sources, because mobile payment transactions are more traceable than traditional cash-based transactions.[49] Also, restrictions and monitoring policies can be imposed on mobile payments to make it more difficult to conduct money laundering or other illicit activities than with traditional payment methods.[50] Yet, the complexity of mobile payment and the involvement of more parties in the system provide opportunities for fraudsters or terrorists to conduct money laundering activities and terrorist financing.[51]

Similar to unauthorized transactions, money launderers and terrorism financiers can gain access to users' accounts by stealing mobile phones with inadequate security setting, or by phishing to obtain mobile payment users' financial account information or by hacking the mobile payment application.[52] Money launderers and terrorism financiers may then create fake transactions to transfer dirty money to a mobile payment platform and subsequently transform the dirty money into funds with an apparently legal origin. For example, they may use dirty money to purchase weapons in online games and then sell those online items to earn a profit.[53]

Again, compared to traditional payment, a mobile payment could be more vulnerable to money laundering and terrorism financing than a traditional payment because of an absence of face-to-face meetings and insufficient consumer identity verification during mobile payment service

---

[48] Ibid.
[49] Tanai Khiaonarong, 'Oversight Issues in Mobile Payments', *International Monetary Fund Working Paper*, 2014, p 17, www.imf.org/external/pubs/ft/wp/2014/wp14123.pdf.
[50] Ibid.
[51] Ibid.
[52] Erin F. Fonte, 'Mobile Payments in the United States: How Disintermediation May Affect Delivery of Payment Functions, Financial Inclusion and Anti-Money Laundering Issues' (2013) 8 (3) *Washington Journal of Law, Technology & Arts* 419, at 437–438.
[53] James Whisker and Mark Eshwar Lokanan, 'Anti-Money Laundering and Counter-terrorist Financing Threats Posed by Mobile Money' (2019) 22 (1) *Journal of Money Laundering Control* 158, at 160–161.

registrations.[54] Also, mobile payment usually involves non-bank institutions and other players that the traditional payment system lacks. These new parties may not be regulated at all or maybe regulated at a lower level than banking institutions; this may lead to insufficient 'recordkeeping, screening and reporting' mechanisms to monitor money laundering, terrorism financing and other illicit activities.[55]

5.2.3.3 Data Security and Privacy Issues

Since mobile payment involves many players and each player may require different information, a large number of data are collected and held by different parties.[56] In a mobile payment transaction, some or even all of the players may have access to user information such as name, age, gender, identification number or bank account passwords, and so on. Notably, mobile payment also allows different players, especially mobile application providers, to collect information about users' purchasing habits which could not be easily obtained in traditional payment.

As mobile payment usually involves large amounts of data collection, it attracts fraudsters hoping to hack into the system to get data. For example, in the WAP form of mobile payment, the wireless network may be insecure, allowing malware to be secretly downloaded to a mobile phone without the owners' knowledge; as for NFC mobile payments, hackers may be able to steal users' information using an NFC reader when the mobile phone and the reader are in close distance.[57] Interestingly, according to the European Parliament, about 15 per cent of cyberattacks that gain access to corporate networks are done by damaging physical equipment such as storage devices, routers and servers.[58] In 2015, it was estimated that consumers' information was stolen from around 200 online stores and payment platforms in China.[59] According to a study conducted

---

[54] Tanai Khiaonarong, 'Oversight Issues in Mobile Payments', *International Monetary Fund Working Paper*, 2014, p 17, www.imf.org/external/pubs/ft/wp/2014/wp1423.pdf.

[55] Ibid.

[56] Robin Hui Huang et al, 'Protecting Data Privacy for Mobile Payment under the Chinese Law: Comparative Perspectives and Reform Suggestions', working paper.

[57] Meena Aharam Rajan, 'The Future of Wallets: A Look at the Privacy Implications of Mobile Payments' (2012) 20(2) *CommLaw Conspectus* 445, at 452–453.

[58] Valant Jana, 'Consumer Protection Aspects of Mobile Payments', European Parliament, 22 June 2015, pp 4–5, www.europarl.europa.eu/RegData/etudes/BRIE/2015/564354/EPRS_BRI(2015)564354_EN.pdf.

[59] Mo Wanyou (莫万友), Yi Dong Zhi Fu De Fa Lu Wen Ti Ji Qi Jie Jue Ban Fa (移动支付的法律问题及其解决办法) [Legal Problems of Mobile Payment and Their Solutions] (2017) 10 *Lanzhou xuekan* (兰州学刊) [*Lanzhou Academic Journal*] 142, at 145.

by the US Federal Reserve, 42 per cent of consumers were concerned about data protection and data security was the main reason why consumers did not prefer to use mobile payment.[60]

5.2.3.4 Operational Mistakes and Misconduct

In the ordinary course of their business, mobile payment platforms may make operational mistakes and even commit misconduct, including payment errors and misappropriation of client funds.

Payment errors, such as payment delay, overpayment and transfer of funds to a wrong payee, may occur. These errors can be caused by user error such as entry of incorrect payee details, an incorrect payment amount or pressing the wrong button resulting in incomplete transactions and the like. Payment errors may also result from system errors computer viruses or other factors under the mobile payment operator's control. Wrong payment and delay in payment may cause a breach of the contracts entered between mobile payment users and their payees, and thus mobile payment users may be liable for damages or overdue payment fees.

Another issue lies in the management of client funds, namely the fund that is pre-received from clients to the mobile payment platform and then paid to the merchants according to the transaction order. Payment institutions can generate profitable interest rewards from the fund. Some entities seized such a lucrative opportunity to gain illicit profits by misappropriating consumer funds, which became the focus of regulators. For instance, Kayou Payment Services Co. Ltd was found to have mismanaged customer deposits and was punished by the PBOC with a fine of over CNY 25.8 million.[61]

The problem of misappropriating client funds can be more acute in relation to so-called dormant funds. User funds or assets are usually stored in the mobile payment platform until that user makes a transaction. There are various reasons why funds in mobile payment platforms can become dormant. For example, the access code or password to the mobile payment account are only known to the user, so the

---

[60] Federal Trade Commission Staff, *Paper, Plastic ... or Mobile? An FTC Workshop on Mobile Payments*, March 2013, p 11, www.ftc.gov/sites/default/files/documents/reports/paper-plastic-or-mobile-ftc-workshop-mobile-payments/p0124908_mobile_payments_workshop_report_02-28-13.pdf.

[61] Quan Yue and Fran Wang, 'Central Bank Fines Payment Providers for Flouting Rules', *Caixin*, 31 July 2018, www.caixinglobal.com/2018-07-31/central-bank-fines-payment-providers-for-flouting-rules-101310293.html.

death of the user can lead to the loss of access to mobile payment accounts, and as a result, the funds stored in the account would remain in the mobile payment platform without notice to others.

Although the amount of funds which can be stored by each individual in their mobile wallets is relatively small, the aggregate amount of funds stored in a mobile payment platform can be enormous, especially for mobile payment platforms which have high market shares. If there is ineffective governance or regulation of dormant funds in the mobile payment platforms, the dormant funds could be vulnerable to misappropriation by the mobile payment platforms, which can harm the interests of users and reduce the credibility of the mobile payment industry.[62]

5.3 The Regulatory Regime in China

5.3.1 Overview

There is no uniform or specific law for regulating the mobile payment industry in China. Instead, relevant rules are scattered around a wide array of laws and regulations with supervisory powers shared by multiple regulators. The overall regulatory aim is to establish a safe, robust and sustainable mobile payment system, striking a proper balance between the efficiency of the system and consumer protection.[63]

The explosive growth of mobile payment is largely due to a supportive regulatory environment at the initial developing stage. It was not until 2010 that the Chinese government became aware of the risks associated with mobile payment and as a result established a systematic regulatory framework. Chief among the first set of regulations on non-bank payment services is *Administrative Measures for the Payment Services of Non-financial Institutions* (2010 Measures on Third-Party Payment Service)[64]

---

[62] Valant Jana, 'Consumer Protection Aspects of Mobile Payments', European Parliament, 22 June 2015, p 7, www.europarl.europa.eu/RegData/etudes/BRIE/2015/564354/EPRS_BRI(2015)564354_EN.pdf.

[63] ShuSong Ba(巴曙松), Yang Biao(杨彪), 'Di San Fang Zhi Fu Guo Ji Jian Guan Yan Jiu Ji Jie Jian (第三方支付国际监管研究及借鉴) [The International Comparison over Third-Party Payment]', (2012) 4 *Cai Zheng Yan Jiu*(财政研究) [*Financial Research*] 72–75, at 72.

[64] Fei Jin Rong Ji Gou Zhi Fu Fu Wu Guan Li Ban Fa (非金融机构支付服务管理办法) [Administrative Measures for the Payment Services of Non-financial Institutions] (issued by the People's Bank of China on 14 June 2010). Several months later, an implementing rule was issued to provide more guidance. Fei Jin Rong Ji Gou Zhi Fu Guan Li Ban Fa Shi Shi Xi Ze (非金融机构支付服务管理办法实施细则) [Implementing Rules for the Administrative Measures for Payment Services of Non-Financial Institutions] (promulgated by the People's Bank of China on 1 December 2010).

and its implementing rules which were both issued by the PBOC in 2010. It was also confirmed that the PBOC would play a leading regulatory role, responsible for the overall regulation and supervision on the payment services of non-financial institutions (i.e. the third-party mobile payment platforms), as well as facilitating coordination and cooperation of multiple regulatory bodies in this area. Then, due to the increased misappropriation of clients' reserve by the mobile payment platforms, the PBOC introduced a specific regulation regarding the protection of clients' reserve in 2013. To combat the problem of money laundering, the PBOC introduced a real-name system[65] and specified the daily operation requirements in terms of the large-sum transactions and suspicious transactions from 2015 to 2016.[66] Since 2017, the PBOC has made greater efforts to tighten its regulation of mobile payment, particularly in relation to the management of clients' reserve and the customer reserve requirements.[67]

5.3.2 Entry Threshold and Exit Mechanism

The primary tool to control market access is via a licensing scheme. To provide payment services, payment institutions must obtain a licence pursuant to the 2010 Measures on Third-Party Payment Service.[68] They must satisfy a list of criteria, some of which are noted here. First, the payment institution shall be a limited liability company or stock limited company established in China with a status of the non-financial legal person and with adequate registered capital.[69] The payment institutions providing national payment service shall provide minimum RMB 100 million registered capital, while those providing province-wide service shall offer RMB 30 million.[70] Second, the major investors, those holding not less than 10 per cent interest in the company or actually controlling the company, must have provided the

---

[65] Article 6, Fei Yin Hang Zhi Fu Ji Gou Wang Luo Zhi Fu Ye Wu Guan Li Ban Fa (非银行支付机构网络支付业务管理办法) [Administrative Measures for Online Payment Business Operated by Non-Banking Payment Institutions] (issued by the People's Bank of China on 28 December 2015).

[66] Jin Rong Ji Gou Da E Jiao Yi He Ke Yi Jiao Bao Gao Guan Li Ban Fa (金融机构大额交易和可疑交易报告管理办法) [Administrative Measures on Reporting of Large-Sum Transactions and Suspicious Transactions by Financial Institutions] (first issued by the People's Bank of China on 14 November 2006 and having undergone two revisions, on 28 December 2016 and 26 July 2018, separately).

[67] For further details, see Section 5.3.

[68] 2010 Measures on Third-Party Payment Service, art. 3.

[69] Ibid, art. 8.

[70] Ibid, art. 9.

relevant services and made profits for more than two years.[71] Third, the applicants shall have a robust organizational structure and internal risk control system.[72] Procedurally, the applicant shall first be examined by the local branch of the PBOC in the location where the applicant is domiciled, and then be referred to the PBOC for approval. Although the PBOC confirmed that there would be no other quantitative requirements than those specified requirements,[73]the PBOC did not approve any licensing applications over a long period of time, on the grounds that the suspension of the licensing approval was intended to restore and maintain the market order.[74] The term of the licence is five years and the subsequent renewal is allowed upon the PBOC's approval.[75]

5.3.3 Management of Clients' Reserves

The PBOC has endeavoured to mitigate the risk of mobile payment platforms misappropriating clients' reserves. In recent years, numerous scandals of platform collapse have harmed client funds and overall financial stability. The relevant measures taken by the PBOC in this regard are discussed below.

First, the 2010 Measures on Third-Party Payment Service confirms that customers retain the legal title of the fund and payment institutions are mere custodians.[76] The payment institutions shall open a deposit account exclusively for clients' reserves only at one branch of a commercial bank.[77] The custodian service agreement shall specify the rights, obligations, and responsibilities and the related document shall be filed with the PBOC.[78] The proportion of the paid-up capital shall at least maintain 10 per cent against its daily average balance of clients' deposits.[79] The payment institutions are

---

[71] Ibid, art. 10.

[72] Ibid, art. 18.

[73] Zhong Guo Ren Min Yin Hang You Guan Bu Men Fu Ze Ren Jiu Fei Jin Rong Ji Gou Zhi Fu Fu Wu Guan Li Ban Fa You Guan Wen Ti Da Ji Zhe Wen (中国人民银行有关部门负责人就《非金融机构支付服务管理办法》有关问题答记者问) [The PBOC Answers Questions of Reporters on Rules on the Administration of Payment Services Provided by Non-Financial Institutions] (issued on 24 June 2010), www.gov.cn/zwhd/2010-06/24/content_1635734.htm.

[74] Wan Jun, 'Internet Finance In China', Han Kun Law Office, 2017, www.hankunlaw.com /downloadfile/newsAndInsights/770b77b61e634d1384389f3f5d1b2af8.pdf.

[75] 2010 Measures on Third-Party Payment Service, art. 13.

[76] Ibid, art. 24.

[77] Ibid, art. 26.

[78] Ibid.

[79] Ibid, art. 30.

154   MOBILE PAYMENT

not allowed to appropriate the fund in any form without approval.[80] The collaborative commercial banks also have a duty to supervise the usage of the fund and report to the PBOC when there is any suspicion.[81]

In 2013, the PBOC issued a further rule specifically governing clients' reserves.[82] The rule imposes more restrictions on payment platforms in terms of gathering, using and transferring the clients' funds. For example, payment institutions are required to account and draw a certain percentage of risk reserves to secure the clients' reserves, the amount of which depends on the number of partner banks.[83] And the risk reserves shall likewise be preserved in the special purpose account at a reserve bank.[84] Under this rule, payment platforms are still allowed to deposit the funds in the form of time deposits, entity notice deposits or other forms approved by the PBOC.[85] However, this method has changed dramatically since the 2017 Notice discussed below was issued.

In 2017, the PBOC issued a notice requiring all online payment transactions to settle via a centralized network platform called *NetsUnion (WangLian)*. This platform operates in the form of a company (2017 Notice).[86] The biggest shareholder of NetsUnion is the PBOC, while the remaining shares are held by private institutions.[87] This was a watershed event in the development of the mobile payment market in China, marking the end of the period when third-party payment platforms could negotiate with different banks and bargain for the best offer. After the 2017 reform, there are only two clearing options for payment institutions: UnionPay (a traditional state-backed clearance system) and NetsUnion.

The 2017 Notice was intended to address the concern that some big payment platforms were able to form closed financial ecosystems with

---

[80] Ibid, art. 24.

[81] Ibid, art. 29.

[82] Zhi Fu Ji Go Uke Hu Bei Fu Jin Cun Guan Ban Fa (支付机构客户备付金存管办法) [Measures for Deposit of Reserves of Payment Institutions' Clients] (issued by the People's Bank of China on 6 July 2013).

[83] Ibid, art. 29.

[84] Ibid.

[85] Ibid, art. 16.

[86] Zhong Guo Ren Min Yin Hang Zhi Fu Jie Suan Si Guan Yu Jiang Fei Yin Hang Zhi Fu Ji Gou Wang Luo Zhi Fu Ye Wu You Zhi Lian Mo Shi Qian Yi Zhi Wang Lian Ping Tai Chu Li De Tong Zhi (中国人民银行支付结算司关于将非银行支付机构网络支付业务由直连模式迁移至网联平台处理的通知) [Notice on Migrating the Online Payment Business of Non-bank Payment Institutions from Direct Connection Mode to Network Platform Processing] (issued by the People's Bank of China on 4 August 2017).

[87] Ibid.

5.3 REGULATORY REGIME IN CHINA 155

absolute control of consumer data and thus bypassed the supervision of the PBOC. The centralization of transaction settlements enables the PBOC to access relevant data, keep track of capital flows, and increase its ability to supervise the industry. More importantly, the establishment of a centralized clearinghouse symbolized the effort of the Chinese authority to take more direct control of the mobile payment industry, which had been until then dominated by private firms. Furthermore, by engaging with private firms, the government managed to find a new way to build the mobile payment infrastructure with mixed public and private ownership.

The payment institutions were initially required to put at least 20 per cent of clients' reserves under central management.[88] The required amount has been increased to 50 per cent by April 2018,[89] but then to 100 per cent since 14 January 2019.[90] It indicated that all third-party payment institutions should cancel the specified account for the customer and shift the sum to the designated central bank account.[91] The PBOC initially decided that no interest would be offered for the central custody of funds, leading to a great loss for payment institutions and invoking much controversy. But then in January 2020, the PBOC announced that it would pay an annual interest rate of 0.35 per cent to the payment institutions.[92]

The PBOC also issued a notice that payment institutions should suspend service when the user account is not used for twelve months.[93]

[88] Zhong Guo Ren Min Yin Hang Ban Gong Ting Guan Yu Diao Zheng Zhi Fu Ji Gou Ke Hu Bei Fu Jin Ji Zhong Jiao Cun Bi Li De Tong Zhi (中国人民银行办公厅关于调整支付机构客户备付金集中交存比例的通知) [The Circular on Adjusting the Proportion of the Collective Deposit of Clients' Reserve Funds by Payment Institutions] (promulgated by the People's Bank of China on 13 January 2017).

[89] Zhong Guo Ren Min Yin Hang Ban Gong Ting Guan Yu Diao Zheng Zhi Fu Ji Gou Ke Hu Bei Fu Jin Ji Zhong Jiao Cun Bi Li De Tong Zhi (中国人民银行办公厅关于调整支付机构客户备付金集中交存比例的通知) [The Circular on Adjusting the Centralized Deposit Percentage of Clients' Reserves of Payment Institutions], promulgated by the People's Bank of China on 29 December 2017.

[90] Zhong Guo Ren Min Yin Hang Ban Gong Ting Guan Yu Zhi Fu Ji Gou Ke Hu Bei Fu Jin Quan Bu Ji Zhong Jiao Cun You Guan Shi Yi De Tong Zhi (中国人民银行办公厅关于支付机构客户备付金全部集中交存有关事宜的通知) [Notice of the General Office of the People's Bank of China on Matters concerning Complete Centralized Deposit of the Funds of Pending Payments of Clients of Payment Institutions] (promulgated by the People's Bank of China on 29 June 2018).

[91] Ibid, section 2(4).

[92] 'Chinese Central Bank to Pay Interest on Centralised Customer Deposits of Payments Companies', *China Banking News*, January 2020, www.chinabankingnews.com/2020/01/08/chinese-central-bank-to-pay-interest-on-centralised-customer-deposits-of-payments-companies/.

[93] Zhong Guo Ren Min Yin Hang Guan Yu Jin Yi Bu Jia Qiang Zhi Fu Jie Suan Guan Li Fang Fan Dian Xin Wang Luo Xin Xing Wei Fa Fan Zui You Guan Xiang De Tong Zhi (中国人民银行

But there is no further detail as to the ownership of the asset in the deactivated account after its closure.

5.3.4 AML Measures

The Chinese AML regime is based on three overarching principles the protection of financial integrity, anti-corruption and harmonization with international standards. Considering the substantial incidence of money laundering via mobile payment account, PBOC introduced the Measures on Anti–Money Laundering and Anti-Terrorist Financing through Payment Institutions in 2012[94] in accordance with the general AML law. Simply put, the payment institutions are required to establish an effective internal risk control system, encompassing adequately conducting customer due diligence making suspicious transaction reports and setting up an AML specialized agency.[95]

Another prominent rule regulating mobile payment also touches on the AML aspect – the Administrative Measures for Online Payment Business Operated by Non-Banking Payment Institutions (2015 Measures),[96] which lays out specific guidance on how mobile payment business should be conducted. Particularly, payment institutions are required to follow the 'know-your-customer' requirement, under which a real-name system should be implemented for account management.[97] Payment institutions are banned from opening payment accounts for financial institutions or other related businesses.[98] Additionally, the PBOC would evaluate AML measures via a scoring system, under which lower scorers might be subject to a higher level of scrutiny.[99]

关于进一步加强支付结算管理防范电信网络新型违法犯罪有关项的通知) [Notice by the People's Bank of China of Matters concerning Further Strengthening Administration of Payment and Settlement to Prevent New Types of Telecommunications and Online Illegal and Criminal Activities] (issued by the People's Bank of China on 22 March 2019).

[94] Zhong Guo Ren Min Yin Hang Guan Yu Yin Fa Zhi Fu Ji Gou Fan Xi Qian He Fan Kong Bu Rong Zi Guan Li Ban Fa De Tong Zhi (中国人民银行关于印发《支付机构反洗钱和反恐怖融资管理办法》的通知) [Notice of the People's Bank of China on Issuing the Measures for Administration of Anti-Money-Laundry and Anti-terrorism by Payment Institutions] (issued by the People's Bank of China on 5 March 2012).

[95] Ibid, art. 5–6.

[96] See note 64.

[97] Ibid, art. 6.

[98] Ibid, art. 8.

[99] Ibid, art. 32.

5.3 REGULATORY REGIME IN CHINA

It was not until 2016 that the PBOC extended the reporting requirement of large-sum and suspicious transactions to the non-financial institutions.[100] Payment institutions are obliged to report cash transactions exceeding RMB 50,000 or equivalent value of USD 10.000.[101] The reporting threshold set for non-natural-person clients or cross-border transfer is much higher.[102]

5.3.5 Consumer Protection

After the reinforcement of the consumer identity authentication requirement, there has been an increasing demand for data protection, including the collection, processing and transfer of the consumer's personal information as well as the data generated from the payment record.

The PBOC enacted relevant rules to safeguard the consumer's data security and privacy.[103] For instance, the 2015 Measures require payment institutions to establish effective internal data management and a risk control system and to strictly comply with the 'minimal collection' principle when collecting data.[104] Also, centralized management by NetsUnion can prevent the misuse of clients' data, because the data accompanying the transaction would be transferred to NetsUnion as well.[105]

In order to strengthen the protection of personal financial information, the PBOC has recently issued the *Technical Specification for Protection of Personal Financial Information*,[106] categorizing personal information into three types: C1, C2 and C3, with an increasing level of

---

[100] See note 65.

[101] Ibid, art. 5.

[102] Ibid.

[103] The issue of protecting data privacy will be examined in more detail in Chapter 6.

[104] Zhong Guo Ren Min Yin Hang Ban Gong Ting Guan Yu Diao Zheng Zhi Fu Ji Gou Ke Hu Bei Fu Jin Ji Zhong Jiao Cun Bi Li De Tong Zhi (中国人民银行办公厅关于调整支付机构客户备付金集中交存比例的通知) [The Circular on Adjusting the Proportion of the Collective Deposit of Clients' Reserve Funds by Payment Institutions] (promulgated by the People's Bank of China on 13 January 2017).

[105] Zhong Guo Ren Min Yin Hang Zhi Fu Jie Suan Si Guan Yu Jiang Fei Yin Hang Zhi Fu Ji Gou Wang Luo Zhi Fu Ye Wu You Zhi Lian Mo Shi Qian Yi Zhi Wang Lian Ping Tai Chu Li De Tong Zhi (中国人民银行支付结算司关于将非银行支付机构网络支付业务由直连模式迁移至网联平台处理的通知) [Notice on Migrating the Online Payment Business of Non-bank Payment Institutions from Direct Connection Mode to Network Platform Processing] (issued by the People's Bank of China on 4 August 2017).

[106] Ge Ren Jin Rong Xin Xi Bao Hu Ji Shu Gui Fan (个人金融信息保护技术规范) [Technical Specification for Protection of Personal Financial Information] (issued by the People's Bank of China on 13 February 2020).

sensitivity.[107] Detailed requirements are laid out regarding the entire cycle of information handling, including collection, storage, use, sharing and deletion of personal information.[108] No entities without relevant qualifications or licences would be allowed to collect C2 and C3 information, despite being on behalf of the payment institutions.[109] Furthermore, the transfer, saving, use, or deletion of C2 or C3 information are subject to the more stringent requirement as the leak of that information would cause more harm to the individuals due to increased sensitivity, particularly when there is mounting concern regarding the increasing use of facial or fingerprint recognition. Such biometric information is subject to the highest level of protection as C3 information.[110]

Some general laws also govern this aspect of mobile payment, including the PRC Criminal Law which imposes the highest penalties for infringement of personal information.[111] The 2016 Cybersecurity Law,[112] as the first national-level law on data protection, is focused on information that can be used to identify individual citizens as well as information concerning the personal privacy of citizens. The legislation mainly targets the network operators and operators of 'critical information infrastructure' (CII), and mobile payment institutions are very likely to fall within the scope of the CII.

Mobile payment also increases security risks such as fraud and hacking. The rule dealing with unauthorized payment is also of primary concern to consumers. The 2015 Measures require the payment institutions to advance full compensation for consumers' capital losses before the investigation is completed.[113] However, there is no other specific rule on this issue. In practice, the related disputes are normally addressed by

---

[107] Ibid, section 4.2.

[108] Ibid, section 6.

[109] Ibid, section 6.1.

[110] Ibid, section 4.2.

[111] Xing Fa Xiu Zheng An Jiu (刑法修正案(九)) [Amendments to the Criminal Law of the People's Republic of China (9) (Ninth Amendment)] (issued by the Standing Committee of the National People's Congress on 29 August 2015), art. 253-1, 286-1. Also see Guan Yu Ban Li Qin Fan Gong Min Ge Ren Xin Xi Xings Hi An Jian Shi Yong Fa LÜ Ruo Gan Wen Ti De Jie Shi (关于办理侵犯公民个人信息刑事案件适用法律若干问题的解释) [SPC and SPP Judicial Interpretation on Several Issues Concerning the Application of Law in the Handling of Criminal Cases Involving Infringement of Citizens' Personal Information] (8 May 2017, effective 1 June 2017).

[112] Zhong Hua Ren Min Gong He Guo Wang Luo An Quan Fa (中华人民共和国网络安全法) [Cyber Security Law of the People's Republic of China] (issued by Standing Committee of the National People's Congress on 7 November 2016).

[113] 2015 Measures, art. 19.

the PRC Contract Law[114] or the PRC Tort law,[115] under which the burden of proof is on the plaintiff, namely the consumer side.

5.4 International Experiences

5.4.1 The United States

Mobile payment is classified as a Money Service Business in the United States according to the *Bank Secrecy Act*,[116] which is administered by the Financial Crimes Enforcement Network (FinCEN). Unlike similar entities in China, Money Service Business providers in the United States are treated as financial institutions and are thus subject to the regulatory regime for financial institutions.

The regulatory regime for financial institutions in the United States has two levels, federal and state. In respect to the entry threshold, federal and state licences are both required for participants. The applicants shall register with the FinCEN on the online e-filing system, which are mainly used to collect initial information rather than to impose any onerous requirement in terms of bonding or net worth.[117] In contrast, states may impose substantive requirements, which is often pointed to as an obstacle for payment institutions to enter the national market.[118] For example, under the Uniform Money Service Act (UMSA),[119] a model law adopted by twelve states,[120] applicants are required to provide security of USD 50,000, plus USD 10,000 for each location (up to an additional USD 250,000).[121] The security can take the form of bonds, cash or letter

---

[114] Zhong Hua Ren Min Gong He Guo He Tong Fa (中华人民共和国合同法) [Contract Law of the People's Republic of China] (issued by the National People's Congress on 15 March 1999).

[115] Zhong Hua Ren Min Gong He Guo Qin Quan Ze Ren Fa (中华人民共和国侵权责任法) [Tort Law of the People's Republic of China] (issued by the Standing Committee of the National People's Congress on 26 December 2009).

[116] Public Law 91-508, effective on 26 October 1970.

[117] 'Registration of Money Services Business (RMSB) Electronic Filing Instructions' (Version 1.0). Financial Crimes Enforcement Network, July 2014, pp 1–6.

[118] Kathryn L. Ryan and Christopher Robins, 'Navigating State Money-Transmission Laws', *C-Suite Financial Services Review*, Fall 2018.

[119] Uniform Money Service Act (UMSA), amended in 2004.

[120] Uniform Law Commission, '2019–2022 Guide to Uniform and Model Act', www.uniform laws.org/HigherLogic/System/DownloadDocumentFile.ashx?DocumentFileKey=01c556bd-ec9b-0fab-3805-7715f0eb9344&forceDialog=0.

[121] UMSA, section 204.

of credit.[122] A minimum net worth of at least USD 25,000 is required as well.[123] The licence granted is effective for one year and annual renewal is expected.[124]

As for the exit mechanism, Article 8 of the UMSA specifies the circumstances under which the superintendent may take disciplinary actions against the licensee, such as suspending or revoking its license. Importantly, the action shall be taken only after a hearing procedure.[125] However, if regulators reasonably hold that the business of the licensee is likely to cause irreparable and immediate harm, they can take immediate action without prior notice or a hearing procedure.[126]

Regarding the customer deposit, the 'pass-through insurance' of the Federal Deposit Insurance Corporation's (FDIC) can cover the fund deposited in banks, share accounts and share draft accounts at credit unions, provided that the relevant requirements are met.[127] The amount of insurance is up to USD 250,000 per depositor, per institution and per ownership category.[128] However, it does not guarantee consumer protection in the event of bankruptcy or insolvency of the payment institutions.[129] The payment institutions are also allowed to invest the fund in permissible projects that are highly liquid and safe.[130] Different states implemented different unclaimed property laws concerning a dormant asset. In general, holders of tangible or intangible property which is owned by others are required to 'escheate' the property to the 'state comptroller, treasurer, or other designated agency' if the legal owner cannot be found within the statutory abandonment period.[131]

Furthermore, the United States has tried very hard to combat money laundering and terrorism financing. The current AML regime for

---

[122] 'Uniform Money Services Act with Predatory Note and Comments', National Conference of Commissioners on Uniform State Law, 25 February 2005, p 34.

[123] UMSA, section 207.

[124] Ibid, section 206.

[125] Ibid, section 801.

[126] Ibid.

[127] The Federal Deposit Insurance Act (12 USC 1811 et seq.); also see C. D. Robert, W. H. Matthew and A. K. Elizabeth, 'Mobile Payments: An Evolving Landscape' (2012) 9(2) *Supervisory Insights* 3–11.

[128] For a more detailed discussion, see the guidance provided by FDIC, www.fdic.gov /deposit/diguidebankers/documents/single-accounts.pdf.

[129] C. D. Robert, W. H. Matthew and A. K. Elizabeth, 'Mobile Payments: An Evolving Landscape' (2012) 9(2) *Supervisory Insights* 3–11, at 9.

[130] UMSA, section 701.

[131] Erin Fonte, 'US Regulatory Overview of Mobile Wallets and Mobile Payments' (2017) 17 (4) *Wake Forest Journal of Business and Intellectual Property Law* 549, at 586.

payment institutions is mainly comprising three legal instruments: the Bank Secrecy Act,[132] the Money Laundering Suppression Act[133] and the USA PATRIOT Act.[134] Given the complexity and intricacy of the AML process, all investigatory agencies, including federal, state, local and even foreign law agencies, can request that the FinCEN share certain information obtained from financial institutions.[135]

Finally, consumer protection in the United States is secured by the existing legal regime, under which the level of protection largely depends on the method of payment.[136] For instance, if a mobile payment is linked to a credit card account, the transaction would be governed by the Federal Truth in Lending Act[137] and Regulation Z.[138] If the payment is made through a debit card or bank account, then it is protected under the federal *Electronic Funds Transaction Act* (EFTA),[139] which is further implemented by *Regulation E*.[140]

In terms of an unauthorized payment, if a phone is lost or stolen, the consumer might be liable for USD 50 if reporting to the institution within two business days, while the maximum amount would extend to USD 500 if there is any undue delay.[141] If the unauthorized payment occurs on the bank statement and no phone is missing, then the consumer would take no liability provided notification is given within sixty days.[142] To address the uncertainty and ambiguity of the statute, the CFPB, which is responsible for US consumer protection in the financial sector, has the authority to interpret the relevant rules and determine relevant issues on a case-by-case basis.[143]

The issues of data privacy and security are dealt with under the Gramm–Leach–Bliley Act.[144] Notably, clients are entitled to reject the

---

[132] Public Law 91-508, effective 26 October 1970.
[133] Public Law 103-325, issued in 1994.
[134] Public Law 107-56, issued in 2001.
[135] Section 314(a) of the USA PATRIOT Act. For more details, see FECEN official website, www.fincen.gov/resources/law-enforcement-overview.
[136] Suzanne Martindale and Gail Hillebrand, 'Pay at Your Own Risk? How to Make Every Way to Pay Safe for Mobile Payments' (forthcoming) *Banking & Finance Law Review*.
[137] 15 USC §§ 1601–1666(j) (2012).
[138] 12 CFR §§ 226.1, 226.59 (2012).
[139] 15 USC §§ 1693a–1693p (2012).
[140] Electronic Fund Transfers (Regulation E), 12 CFR pt. 1005 (2017).
[141] The Regulation E, section 6(b).
[142] Ibid.
[143] Erin F. Fonté, 'Mobile Payments in the United States: How Disintermediation May Affect Delivery of Payment Functions, Financial Inclusion and Anti-Money Laundering Issues' (2012) 8 *Washington Journal of Law, Technology & Arts* 419, at 426.
[144] 15 USC §§ 6801–6809 (2012).

request of their payment institutions to share their personal information with third parties. Such an option must not be excluded in the consumer service agreement.[145]

5.4.2 The United Kingdom

Mobile payment in the United Kingdom is mainly governed by the Payment Services Regulations 2017 (PSR 2017)[146] and the Electronic Money Regulations 2011 (EMR).[147] The Payment Systems Regulator (PSR), established in 2013 as a subsidiary of the FCA, is an independent regulator that oversees the payment systems industry in the United Kingdom. Notably, the PSR is the world's first dedicated regulator for the payment sector, and is charged with both competition and regulatory powers, aiming to 'ensure that payment systems are operated and developed in a way that considers and promotes the interests of all the businesses and consumers that use them', 'promote effective competition in the markets for payment systems and services', and 'promote the development of and innovation in payment systems'.[148]

To provide payment services, institutions shall first comply with the registration or authorization requirement under the PSR 2017 and EMR unless they fall within an exemption.[149] The registration category and the specific application requirement depend on the type and scale of the business involved.[150] For instance, a mobile payment services provider with a considerable scale of business needs to apply for the status of the Electronic Money Institution (EMI), as the electronic storage of funds would fall under its definition. Apart from assessing the relevant information listed in the statutory form, the regulatory authority can request additional information if necessary.[151] An intentional or reckless material fault or misleading information disclosure may expose the applicants to the criminal offence.[152] In addition, payment service providers are

---

[145] Ibid. § 6802(b).

[146] Payment Services Regulations 2017 (SI 2017/752), www.legislation.gov.uk/uksi/2017/752/contents/made.

[147] The Electronic Money Regulations 2011 (SI 2011/99), www.legislation.gov.uk/uksi/2011/99/made.

[148] See the official website of the PSR, www.psr.org.uk/.

[149] The PSR 2017, art. 6 and sch. 2; the EMR, art. 6.

[150] Ibid.

[151] 'Payment Services and Electronic Money – Our Approach' (version 4), *Financial Conduct Authority*, June 2019, chapter 3, pp 3.10–3.20.

[152] The PSR 2017, art. 142; the EMR, art. 66.

5.4 INTERNATIONAL EXPERIENCES

required to meet the initial capital requirement.[153] A normal-sized EMI is required to hold at least EUR 350,000.[154] It must also satisfy the minimum required capital requirement at all times.[155] The additional amount of capital would be required if the EMI increases the provision of an unrelated payment service.[156]

To safeguard customer funds, the payment institutions shall fulfil the safeguarding obligations in two ways: segregating the fund or offering insurance or comparable guarantee.[157] Any segregated funds shall be kept in a separate account with an authorized credit institution or shall be invested in secure liquid assets.[158] In exceptional circumstances, other investment forms may be approved with sufficient justification.[159] Unlike in China, there is no requirement of one specific account for storing the clients' funds. One payment institution may have several accounts, but its associated companies cannot share the accounts.[160]

Regarding the AML approach, in addition to the PSR 2017 and the EMR, there are some other legislations that the payment institutions shall comply with.[161] The most typical one is *the Money Laundering, Terrorist Financing, and Transfer of Funds (Information on the Payer) Regulations 2017*.[162] The novelty of the system is that it does not merely rely on the public effort, but also the participation of private sectors. The Joint Money Laundering Steering Group (JMLSG) is a private association that consists of all leading UK trade associations in the financial industry.[163] The JMLSG publishes guidance to the firms regarding how to fulfil their AML obligations. The guidance is not mandatory but still

---

[153] The PSR 2017, art. 6(3) and para. 3, sch. 2; the EMR, art. 6(3) and para. 3, sch. 1.

[154] 'Payment Services and Electronic Money – Our Approach', *Financial Conduct Authority* (version 4), June 2019, chapter 3, p 3.46.

[155] Ibid, chapter 3, pp 3.46–3.48.

[156] Ibid.

[157] Ibid, chapter 10, p 10.29.

[158] Ibid, chapter 10, p 10.35.

[159] Ibid, chapter 10, pp 10.46–10.48.

[160] Ibid, chapter 10, pp 10.41–10.44.

[161] Money Laundering, Terrorist Financing and Transfer of Funds (Information on the Payer) Regulations 2017 (MLRs); EU Regulation 2015/847; etc.

[162] The Money Laundering, Terrorist Financing, and Transfer of Funds (Information on the Payer) Regulations 2017, 2017 No. 692, passed by parliament on 22 June 2017. For more details, see Financial Conduct Authority (FCA), 'Payment Services and Electronic Money – Our Approach', June 2019, p 8.57, www.fca.org.uk/publication/finalised-guidance/fca-approach-payment-services-electronic-money-2017.pdf.

[163] See the official website of the Joint Money Laundering Steering Group (JMLSG), https://jmlsg.org.uk/joint-money-laundering-steering-group-jmlsg/about-us/who-we-are/.

164 MOBILE PAYMENT

important as a benchmark of industry practice for the court and the regulatory authorities to refer to.

The protection of consumers is of great priority for the UK regulators. Except for the security of consumer funds and the minimum capital required in the licence as mentioned above, the law also provides a detailed list of business-conduct requirements that the institutions shall comply with.[164] They can be broadly summarized into two categories: (1) information disclosure before and after the transaction; and (2) the right and obligation of respective parties. Besides, consumer rights are protected for unauthorized payment. As in the United States, the maximum consumer liability would be capped at £35 in the case of the mobile device being stolen or lost.[165] Consumers are also given the right to rectify unauthorized transactions and defective transactions if they notify the relevant service provider within a certain period.[166] In principle, consumers would not be liable for any loss unless otherwise proved by the payment institutions.[167] Furthermore, if there is any complaint or dispute, the consumer can address their problems through various channels. They can complain to the payment institution, which must respond within a specified time limit.[168] Other options include the financial ombudsman service, a statutory or informal dispute-resolution forum.[169]

Consumer data are protected by the PSR 2017, the Data Protection Act 2018,[170] and the General Data Protection Regulation (GDPR).[171] The GDPR is claimed to be the world's most far-reaching data privacy regulation, setting out considerable provisions to safeguard data protection and provide individuals with stronger rights. In general, it introduced six vital data processing principles. For example, personal data must be processed lawfully, fairly, and transparently; and must be collected for a legitimate and necessary purpose; Compared to other jurisdictions, the GDPR is

---

[164] 'Payment Services and Electronic Money – Our Approach', *Financial Conduct Authority* (version 4), June 2019, chapter 8.

[165] Ibid, chapter 8, p 8.218.

[166] The PSR 2017, art. 74.

[167] Ibid, art. 77.

[168] 'Payment Services and Electronic Money – Our Approach', *Financial Conduct Authority* (version 4), June 2019, chapter 11, pp 11.16–11.21.

[169] Ibid, chapter 11.

[170] The Data Protection Act 2018 (c 12), www.legislation.gov.uk/ukpga/2018/12/contents.

[171] Regulation (EU) 2016/679 of the European Parliament and of the Council of 27 April 2016 on the protection of natural persons with regard to the processing of personal data and on the free movement of such data, and repealing Directive 95/46/EC [2016] OJ L119/1, art. 20.

claimed to impose much more onerous obligations on the payments service providers. For instance, prior consent is needed before collecting any personal data, and the users' right to withdraw their consent at any time is also highlighted.[172] Any breach of the GDPR may incur significantly high administrative fines. For breach of certain important provisions, the fines can amount up to EUR 20 million or 4 per cent of global annual turnover.[173]

5.4.3 Singapore

Singapore, striving to become a Fintech hub, was one of the earliest countries to respond to the development of Fintech with regulation.[174] The primary relevant legal instrument is the *Payment Services Act 2019* (PSA), which came into effect on 28 January 2020. The PSA and its implementing rules together lay out a comprehensive regulatory regime for mobile payment in Singapore. The MAS, which is the central bank and integrated financial regulator in Singapore, is the main regulator regarding mobile payment.[175]

The PSA introduces two parallel regulatory frameworks: a licensing regime and a designation regime. Under the licensing regime, there are three kinds of licences, namely money-changing licences, standard payment institution licences, major payment institution licences, according to the types and numbers of the services provided, and the business volume of the firms. Besides, the MAS is empowered to designate a payment system for four statutory reasons: financial stability, public confidence, public interest and the efficiency and competition of the payment service. Hence, the MAS adopts a risk-based approach under which only those posing significant risks would be required for licensing, while the low-risk firms are exempted, to build a more accessible payment ecosystem.[176] The MAS can designate a payment institution to meet the licensing requirement in the interest of the public if it is satisfied that they may pose risks to the system even though they may otherwise not subject to the licensing requirement.[177]

---

[172] GDPR, art. 7.

[173] Ibid, art. 83.

[174] Pei Sai Fan, 'Singapore Approach to Develop and Regulate FinTech', in *Handbook of Blockchain, Digital Finance, and Inclusion*, vol. 1 (Academic Press, 2013), pp 347–357.

[175] The MAS official website, www.mas.gov.sg/who-we-are/What-We-Do.

[176] The MAS, 'FAQs – Payment Services Act 2019', p 8, www.mas.gov.sg/regulation/faqs/faqs-on-payment-services-act-2019.

[177] Ibid, p 6.

MOBILE PAYMENT

To safeguard consumer interest from flight risk, the MAS requires the payment institutions to submit a certain amount of security for the due performance of their obligations.[178] The MAS has clarified that the security was not intended to cover all losses of the customers, which otherwise, might impose too high of a burden on the businesses.[179] Regarding the clients' reserve, the major payment institutions are required to adopt safeguard measures: a deposit in a trust account, an undertaking or guarantee by a safeguarding institution or any other prescribed manner by the MAS.[180] Furthermore, the MAS imposes a cap on the amount of fund that the consumers can store in their e-wallet accounts to maintain the crucial economic function that the banks perform in the financial system.[181]

In relation to the settlement of unauthorized transactions, the *E-payments User Protection Guidelines*[182] identify the situations where users and payment institutions should take liability arising from unauthorized transactions, respectively. For example, the user will bear the actual loss if the loss is mainly caused by the user's recklessness;[183] while mobile payment platforms will be liable for loss caused by fraud, negligence or non-compliance of regulations imposed by the MAS.[184] Besides, if the user's account has a balance of more than USD 500 at any time and is used for electronic payments, the user will not be liable for any loss in an unauthorized transaction which does not exceed USD 1,000.[185]

To address the cybersecurity concern, the MAS issued several guidelines, including the *Notice PSN05 Technology Risk Management*[186] and the *Notice PSN06 Cyber Hygiene*.[187] PSN05 sets out that payment

---

[178] The PSA, section 22. 'Flight risk' refers to the risk that someone accused of a crime will try to escape out of the country or area before their trial begins.

[179] The MAS, 'FAQs – Payment Services Act 2019', p 17, www.mas.gov.sg/regulation/faqs/faqs-on-payment-services-act-2019.

[180] The PSA, section 23.

[181] The MAS, 'FAQs – Payment Services Act 2019', p 23, www.mas.gov.sg/regulation/faqs/faqs-on-payment-services-act-2019.

[182] The MAS, E-payments User Protection Guidelines, 28 January 2020, www.mas.gov.sg/-/media/MAS/Regulations-and-Financial-Stability/Regulations-Guidance-and-Licensing/Payment-and-Settlement-Systems/PSOA-Guidelines/E_payments-User-Protection-Guidelines-WEF-28-January-2020.pdf.

[183] Ibid, sections 5.2–5.4.

[184] Ibid, sections 5.5–5.6.

[185] Ibid.

[186] Published on 5 December 2019, www.mas.gov.sg/regulation/notices/psn05.

[187] Ibid.

institutions should maintain a sufficiently high degree of availability and recoverability in the critical systems (the failure of which may cause significant disruption to the operation of payment service).[188] The specific measures the payment institutions shall take include restricting the maximum unscheduled downtime for each critical system for not more than four hours, reporting the relevant incidents in time, and implementing IT controls to protect customer information. PSN06 aims to protect users from cyber threats. The payment institutions are required to implement and maintain robust security for IT systems via timely updates to address the security flaws, and strengthen user authentication.

The last highlight is the MAS's solution to reduce the fragmentation of the payment industry.[189] The MAS launched the Singapore Quick Response Code (SGQR), the world's first unified payment code that combined multiple payment codes into a single one. Merchants can use a single QR code to link with different payment service apps. The customers can check the merchant name and choose one of the payment platforms such as Alipay, Remo, EZ-Link, that the merchant has contracted with. Under the PSA, the MAS has further power to impose interoperability measures, including requiring the large institutions to allow the third parties to access their system; mandating any major payment institutions to participate in a common platform or adopt common standards such as the SGQR.[190]

In short, the MAS attempts to build a simple, secure and accessible payment regulatory regime, streamlining the regulation under one single legislation with other accompanying instruments. The MAS adopts a risk-based approach to regulationand, maintains the flexibility to deal with the particular circumstances of individual cases.

5.4.4 Hong Kong

Hong Kong, one of the world's top financial hubs, has been criticized for being too slow to embrace advanced digital payment technologies.[191] The

---

[188] The definition of 'critical system' is further explained in 'Response to Feedback Received – Consultation Paper on the Notice on Technology Risk Management', The MAS, p 3, www.mas.gov.sg/-/media/MAS/News-and-Publications/Consultation-Papers/Response-to-Consultation-Paper_TRM-Guidelines.pdf.

[189] The MAS, 'FAQs – Payment Services Act 2019', pp 19–20, www.mas.gov.sg/regulation/faqs/faqs-on-payment-services-act-2019.

[190] Ibid.

[191] Robin Hui Huang, Cynthia Sze Wai Cheung and Christine Meng Lu Wang, 'The Risks of Mobile Payment and Regulatory Responses: A Hong Kong Perspective' (forthcoming) *Asian Journal of Law and Society*.

lukewarm attitude towards mobile payment in Hong Kong is partly due to the deep-rooted customer payment habits of using credit cards and the local Octopus card.

Mobile payment platforms or apps are normally within the category of multi-purpose stored value facility (SVF) under the Hong Kong regulatory regime. Apple Pay is not considered an SVF, as it does not perform any stored value function and users complete the transactions via the credit card.[192] Since the introduction of the Payment Systems and Stored Value Facilities Ordinance (SVF Ordinance)[193] in 2015, the SVF has been supervised and regulated by the HKMA which is the central bank as well as the banking regulator in Hong Kong. Under the SVF Ordinance, an SVF must obtain a licence unless falling within the exemption.[194] To obtain a licence, the applicant must satisfy several requirements: first, the principal business should be issuing SVF and not engaging in other irrelevant business without the approval of the HKMA.[195] Second, the applicant should own a paid-up capital not less than HKD 25 million or other equivalent convertible currency.[196] However, the HKMA might impose a higher amount in light of the risk and scale of the business of the particular applicant.[197]

Third, to ensure robust corporate governance, the SVF must implement appropriate risk-management policies and procedures, as well as sound and prudent operating rules.[198] As such, the appointment of the chief executive, director and controller of the applicant shall obtain prior consent from the HKMA.[199] Regarding the public concern over the safety of clients' funds particularly in the event of insolvency of the SVF, licensees are required to keep all funds for prescribed usage only and always maintain sufficient deposit to redeem the outstanding stored value.[200] Furthermore, the trust arrangement supported by legal opinion shall be put in place to guarantee the priority of the users if the SVF goes

---

[192] 'Insight – Part 1: Smart Tips on Using Stored Value Facilities', Hong Kong Monetary Authority, 23 August 2016, www.hkma.gov.hk/eng/news-and-media/insight/2016/08/20160823/.

[193] The Payment Systems and Stored Value Facilities Ordinance (Cap. 584), effective 12 November 2015.

[194] Ibid, section 8F.

[195] Ibid, part 2(1), sch. 3.

[196] Ibid, part 2(2), sch. 3.

[197] Ibid.

[198] Ibid, part 2(5), sch. 3.

[199] Ibid, part 2(2) & (3), sch. 3.

[200] Ibid, part 2(8), sch. 3.

bankrupt.[201] Fourth, the HKMA adopts a risk-based approach to address the global concern of money laundering, under which the applicant is required to take preventive measures and establish an AML/CFT monitoring system proportionate to the risks exposed.[202] The HKMA retains the power to revoke or suspend the licence as a penalty if the licensee fails to comply with the requirements.[203] Fifth, apart from the SVF Ordinance, the SVF must fully comply with the Personal Data (Privacy) Ordinance[204] in relation to privacy protection.

To address the issue of market fragmentation, on 17 September 2018, the HKMA launched the Faster Payment System (FPS), representing a watershed in the development of mobile payment in Hong Kong. The FPS removes the stumbling block to the popularization of e-wallets, enabling fund transfers to be made anytime and anywhere across the banks and the SVF via a phone number or email address.[205] Additionally, the HKMA and other interest parties, including the payment network operators, the bank industry, have worked on a common QR Code Standard for retail payment.[206]

5.5 Analysis and Suggestions

5.5.1 Overview

5.5.1.1 Strengths of the Chinese Law

The common goal for all jurisdictions in regulating mobile payment is to strike a proper balance between consumer protection and business development/technology innovation. As discussed above, similar to China, all our examined overseas jurisdictions have covered the four main regulatory elements, but each jurisdiction shows some distinctive features in their regulatory regimes.

---

[201] Ibid.

[202] 'Guidance Paper – Transaction Screening, Transaction Monitoring and Suspicious Transaction Reporting', Hong Kong Monetary Authority, revised May 2018, www.hkma.gov.hk/media/eng/doc/key-information/guidelines-and-circular/2018/20180510e3a1.pdf.

[203] SVF Ordinance, sch. 5.

[204] The Personal Data (Privacy) Ordinance (Cap. 486), effective 1 August 1996.

[205] Michael Yu, 'E-Wallets in Hong Kong', www.legco.gov.hk/research-publications/english/essentials-1718ise08-e-wallets-in-hong-kong.htm.

[206] 'Implementation Guideline (Effective from 17 September 2018) – Common QR Code for Retail Payments in Hong Kong', September 2018, www.hkma.gov.hk/media/eng/doc/key-functions/financial-infrastructure/infrastructure/retail-payment-initiatives/Implementation_Guideline_on_Common_QR_Code.pdf.

The United States, on the one hand, emphasizes minimum intervention by setting a relatively low entry requirement. On the other hand, the United States still emphasizes consumer protection via extending the coverage of the FDIC and insisting on limiting the liability of consumers for unauthorized payments. The United States also has a well-established legal framework in relation to the issues of AML, CFT and consumer protection. The United Kingdom puts much effort into strengthening consumer rights and protection via comprehensive and systematic regulations. Singapore emphasizes proportionality and flexibility by adopting a risk-based approach, while Hong Kong is dedicated to establishing a secure and suitable regime for mobile payment.

China largely took a hands-off approach in the early stage of mobile payment development, a decision that has proved one of the key drivers for the rapid growth of mobile payment in China. As the problems and risks associated with mobile payment gradually emerged, China responded quickly by establishing a comprehensive regulatory regime, including a licensing regime and a set of stringent requirements in relation to important issues such as clients' fund management and AML measures. By comparison with other jurisdictions, China sets a relatively higher entry threshold to screen out unqualified candidates at the entry stage. Furthermore, China seems to have paid more attention to the safety of clients' funds by establishing a centralized clearinghouse, which represents a significant development of the infrastructure used to operate the payment systems. In regard to the issues of AML and data protection, a large number of rules have been put in place by various regulators.

5.5.1.2 Weaknesses of the Chinese Law

Although the Chinese regulatory regime for mobile payment has many merits, there are some shortcomings that need to be properly addressed if China wishes to bring its mobile payment industry to a higher level.

Overall, China's mobile payment is governed by a patchwork of administrative rules issued over the past decade by various regulators in a piecemeal manner. This has made it difficult for market participants to understand and comply with the relevant rules, and also has led to gaps, overlaps and inconsistency in the regulatory framework.[207] In one

---

[207] Zhou Xue Dong Dai Biao: Ying Jin Kuai Chu Tai Fei Jin Rong Ji Gou Zhi Fu Fu Wu Guan Li Tiao Li (周学东代表：应尽快出台《非金融机构支付服务管理条例》) [The Call from Representative Zhou Dongxue: Regulations on Payment Services Provided by Non-Financial Institutions Should Be Promulgated), *CAIXIN* (财新网), 4 March 2015, http://topics.caixin.com/2015-03-04/100787732.html.

sense, the piecemeal approach is practical as it allows China to efficiently respond to emerging issues in a fast-changing setting like the mobile payment market. While it may be appropriate for the initial stage of market development, it can become problematic once the market has grown to a more advanced stage. China now has one of the largest markets of mobile payment in the world, which plays a very important role in the financial system. However, its current regulatory regime has evolved in an accretive way in response to problems, without any real focus on the overall mission in the long term.

The time has come for China to enact a unified law specifically for mobile payment to improve regulatory coherence, consistency and efficacy. The absence of such a law presents a threat to the sustainable development of mobile payment in China. In this regard, Singapore provides a good example to follow. As discussed earlier, Singapore streamlines its regulatory regime by incorporating and integrating all payment-related matters into one overarching piece of legislation and then specifying details through implementing rules. In doing so, the Singaporean regulator has absorbed public and industry opinions via public consultation from time to time, which helps ensure the suitability of the law to meet the market needs.[208]

With regard to its regulatory approach, China traditionally tends to apply regulatory requirements in a sweeping fashion, which can lead to the dangers of a 'one-size-fits-all' approach. Indeed, as exceptions are prone to abuse, Chinese regulators usually prefer the so-called one clean-cut (*yi dao qie*) approach. This may make it easy, and sometimes seemingly fair, to regulate the relevant entities, but it may come as a problematic Procrustean bed to the market. For example, China prescribes only one unitary standard of capital requirement for all third-party payment institutions, regardless of their size and risk level of the activities involved. Hence, the risk-based approach as adopted in Singapore and Hong Kong may be worthy of consideration for China in setting out specific regulatory requirements. Section 5.5.2 will conduct a more detailed discussion of the specific regulatory requirements and relevant suggestions.

5.5.2 *Improvement Suggestions*

5.5.2.1 Entry Threshold and Exit Mechanism

Controlling market access is one of the common regulatory measures in China. However, the licensing threshold in China may have chilling

---

[208] Ibid.

effects on the new entrants. It was predicted that at least half of the participants providing payment services have to leave the market since the promulgation of the 2010 Measures on Third-Party Payment Service.[209] The minimum capital requirement for getting a payment service licence in China[210] is around 37 times that of the United Kingdom[211] and 556 times that of the United States.[212] Given the high level of concentration in China's mobile payment market, in which Alipay and Tenpay together enjoy an effective monopoly in the payment market with more than 90 per cent of the market share.[213] The high entry threshold may reinforce market concentration and impede small participants from entering the market. This may eventually trap policymakers in the 'too big to fail' pitfall.[214]

Furthermore, the Chinese capital requirement is based on static registered capital, while the United States instead refers to dynamic corporate net worth. Registered capital cannot accurately reflect the asset of the company and thus may be insufficient to protect consumer interests.[215] Another problem with the Chinese law on market entry is illustrated by the validity term of the licence. Given the rapidly evolving landscape of the mobile payment market, the international practice to renew a licence in one year appears to be more pragmatic and effective. Last but not least, the way in which the licensing authority grants approval seems inconsistent and unpredictable, subject to heavy policy influence. This has caused much volatility and speculation in both the licensing price and the payment market itself. The suspension of granting of licence since 2016 led to scarcity, driving the market price of a licence in private

---

[209] Yingzhi Fang (方盈芝), Fei Jin Rong Ji Gou Zhi Fu Fu Wu Guan Li Ban Fa Jie Du Bao Gao (非金融机构支付服务管理办法》解读报告) [An Evaluation Report on Rules on the Administration of Payment Services Provided by Non-Financial Institutions], China E-Commerce Research Centre (中国电子商务研究中心), 26 June 2010, http://b2b .toocle.com/detail-5232440.html.

[210] See Section 5.3.1.

[211] See Section 5.4.2.

[212] See Section 5.4.1.

[213] 'Mobile Finance Got a Shrinking Share in China's Third-Party Mobile Payment Market', I Research, 12 March 2019, www.iresearchchina.com/content/details7_52849.html.

[214] Nicola Cetorelli and James Traina, 'Resolving "Too Big to Fail"', Federal Reserve Bank of New York Staff Reports, June 2018.

[215] Su Pan (苏盼), Mei Guo Di San Fang Zhi Fu Zhou Fa Jian Guan Zhi Du Shu Ping Ji Qi Shi (美国第三方支付州法监管制度述评及启示) [The Comment on the American Third-Party Payment State Regulation and the Lesson from It], (2016) Beijing University Financial Law 202–215, at 206.

transactions to more than RMB 1 billion in 2017,[216] before the price plunged by half in 2018 due to tightened regulation.[217]

As discussed before, the PBOC has the power to terminate a licence if there is any serious violation of the law, but there is no further detail on how the exit mechanism works.[218] This means that the insolvency or termination of payment institutions would be subject to the general law, including the *PRC Company Law*[219] and the *PRC Bankruptcy Law*.[220] However, payment institutions are different from ordinary companies, in that they usually involve a large amount of capital and a great number of customers. Therefore, there is a call for further guidance as to the exit of payment institutions, so as to minimize the negative impact on society. In this regard, lessons can be learned from the United Kingdom and the United States. For instance, setting up an insurance system similar to the FDIC to safeguard the customer interest upon the bankruptcy or insolvency of the payment institutions.

5.5.2.2 Management of Clients' Reserves

One of the most striking features of China's regulatory regime is the centralization of the settlement of clients' reserves and the 'no-interest' policy. It deals a blow to the small and medium payment service providers by cutting off a large source of revenue. And placing a great sum of money idle in the centralized settlement account might be a great waste of social resources.[221] It may threaten the survival of many small and medium payment institutions. Furthermore, it is not in line with international practice. It is also problematic, particularly after China has promised to open the payment market to foreign-invested

---

[216] Liao ShuMin, 'China's Internet Payment License Prices Are Geyser to USD92.3 Million', *YiCai Global*, 20 September 2017, www.yicaiglobal.com/news/china-internet-payment-license-prices-are-geyser-to-usd923-million.

[217] Emma Lee, 'Prices of China's Third-Party Payment Licenses Plunge by Half', 6 November 2018, https://technode.com/2018/11/06/payment-licenses/.

[218] See Section 5.3.1.

[219] Zhong Hua Ren Min Gong He Guo Gong Si Fa (中华人民共和国公司法) [Company Law of the People's Republic of China] (issued by the Standing Committee of the National People's Congress on 26 October 2018).

[220] Zhong Hua Ren Min Gong He Guo Qi Ye Po Chan Fa (中华人民共和国企业破产法) [Enterprise Bankruptcy Law of the People's Republic of China] (issued by the National People's Congress on 27 August 2006).

[221] ShuSong Ba (巴曙松) and Yang Biao (杨彪), Di San Fang Zhi Fu Guo Ji Jian Guan Yan Jiu Ji Jie Jian (第三方支付国际监管研究及借鉴) [The International Comparison over Third-Party Payment], (2012) 4 *Cai Zheng Yan Jiu* (财政研究) [*Financial Research*] 72–75, at 74.

enterprises.[222] In the United Kingdom and the United States, for example, payment institutions can invest clients' reserves in certain low-risk investments, allowing for a better balance between business efficiency and consumer protection.

Regarding the problem of dormant assets in payment accounts, the Singaporean approach provides a good example to follow. The PSA prescribes a maximum amount of funds that can be stored in an e-wallet,[223] and may therefore help to limit the total amount of dormant assets in a mobile payment platform. Furthermore, the PSA impliedly determines the ownership of dormant assets, in that payment platforms are not allowed to on-lend the user's money[224] and thus the ownership of the funds goes to the user. However, as Singapore does not provide details on returning the dormant asset to users, China is advised to further consider the US experience. Apart from setting a maximum amount of funds that can be stored in e-wallets, the US law requires that payment platforms shall transfer the funds in a dormant account to a designated agency if the user cannot be found within a certain period.[225]

5.5.2.3 AML Measures

AML is a global issue in the mobile payment sector. And China's AML regime is in line with international standards, thanks to the introduction of an array of AML measures. The most significant ones should be the full implementation of the 'real-name' system. However, there are still some remaining enforcement issues that should be addressed.

The major shortcoming is the decentralized supervision structure, under which enforcement is fragmented and the division of power amongst various regulators is not sufficiently clear. The FATF, a global watchdog for the AML and the CFT, has pointed out that China should make better use of financial intelligence in the AML investigation and

---

[222] Zhong Guo Ren Min Yin Hang Gong Gao (2018)Di Qi Hao ——Guan Yu Wai Shang Tou Zi Zhi Fu Ji Gou You Guan Shi Yi Gong Gao De Gong Gao (中国人民银行公告 (2018)第7号——关于外商投资支付机构有关事宜公告的公告) [Announcement No. 7 [2018] of the People's Bank of China – Announcement on Matters concerning Foreign-funded Payment Institutions] (issued on 19 March 2018).

[223] MAS, 'Frequently Asked Questions (FAQs) on the Payment Services Act (PS Act)', 13 April 2020, p 28, www.mas.gov.sg/-/media/MAS/Fintech/Payment-Services-Act /Payment-Services-Act-FAQ-13-April-2020.pdf.

[224] Ibid, p 27.

[225] Erin Fonte, '2017 US Regulatory Overview of Mobile Wallets and Mobile Payments' (2017) 17(4) *Wake Forest Journal of Business and Intellectual Property Law* 549, at 586.

enhance coordination between different agencies.[226] For instance, China may consider learning from the UK approach under which private sectors can also be involved to achieve self-discipline.[227] And the US approach that a single authority is responsible for the sharing of the investigatory information among different regulatory agencies, is also highly recommended.[228]

5.5.2.4 Consumer Protection

There are some important issues of consumer protection that China needs to address. For instance, data privacy and security challenges are faced by all countries when embracing the era of the data-driven economy. The United States and the United Kingdom have traditionally established a robust regime for data protection in the general setting. They further strengthened the protection in the specific context of mobile payment. In comparison, China has a lot of work to do both in terms of the rules and enforcement.[229] For instance, China introduces the 'minimal collection principle' for data collection, but payment institutions have discretion over the degree of 'minimum'.[230] By contrast, the US law entitles the users to refuse to give or share personal information, enabling the consumers to determine who can have access to their data.[231]

Another issue of consumer protection lies with unauthorized payments. It is onerous for consumers to bear the burden of proof in bringing an action against the payment institution because most of the evidence about the payment transaction is stored in the internal system of the payment institution.[232] And this is not in line with the international practice that consumers are protected unless there is gross negligence on their part.[233]

---

[226] Ben AuYeung and Yaqi Bao, 'FATF Report a Wake-Up Call for China on AML and Terrorist Financing', Wolters Kluwer, 24 June 2019, www.wolterskluwer com/en/expert-insights/fatf-report-a-wake-up-call-for-china-on-aml-and-terrorist-financing.

[227] See Section 5.4.2.

[228] See Section 5.4.1.

[229] For a more detailed discussion on the issue of protecting data privacy, see Chapter 6.

[230] See Section 5.3.4.

[231] See Section 5.4.1.

[232] Luo Pei-Xin (罗培新) and Wu Tao (吴韬), Fei Shou Quan Jiao Yi Zhong Di San Fang Zhi Fu Ji Gou De Fa Lu Ze Ren (非授权交易中第三方支付机构的法律责任) [The Legal Liability of the Third-Party Payment Institutions in Terms of Unauthorized Transaction], (2017) 20(3) Hua Dong Zheng Fa Da Xue Xue Bao (华东政法大学学报) [Journal of East China University of Political Science and Law] 83–89, at 86–87.

[233] Ibid, pp 86–87.

5.6 Conclusion

By allowing for payments via a mobile phone or device, mobile payment is a disruptive innovation in payment systems that has fundamentally changed the payments industry and the people's way of life. China, albeit not the originator of the mobile payment, has become a frontrunner in the global mobile payment markets, in terms of market volume, growth rate and innovation capability. This can be attributed to a number of enabling factors, including technological advancement in China such as the high penetration of smartphones and wide internet coverage, mobile payment's competitive advantages over the traditional payment in terms of convenience and flexibility, as well as the distinctive Chinese local context where the people are more receptive to the mobile payment due to a lack of credit card engagement and relative insensitivity to data protection issues.

While mobile payment brings important benefits to society, it does not come without risks. It is thus important to find an effective way to regulate mobile payment so that its benefits can be reaped while risks are contained. Over the past decade, China has made great efforts to gradually establish a regulatory framework for mobile payment. There are four main regulatory elements, namely controlling the market access through a licensing regime, imposing requirements on the management of clients' reserves, combating money laundering and terrorist financing, and strengthening consumer protection.

To better evaluate Chinese regulation, a comparative study is conducted on the regulation of mobile payment in several major jurisdictions, including the United States, the United Kingdom, Singapore and Hong Kong. From a comparative perspective, the Chinese regulatory regime has its distinctive features with both strengths and weaknesses. Drawing on international experiences, a number of suggestions are made for China to improve the efficacy of its regulatory regime for mobile payment. In general, China is advised to enact a unified law specifically for mobile payment, as its current regulatory regime has evolved in an accretive way in response to problems without any real focus on the overall mission in the long term. Furthermore, China should discard the 'one-size-fits-all' approach in favour of a more nuanced risk-based approach in setting out regulatory requirements.

More specifically, China sets a relatively higher entry threshold to control the market access, which may help screen out risky platforms from the market, but at the same time, intensify the problem of market monopoly. While China's establishment of a centralized clearinghouse represents a significant development of the infrastructure used to operate the payment systems, it may, coupled with the no-interest policy, raise fairness concerns and threaten the very survival of small or medium payment institutions. Despite strong AML measures, there are problems with the cooperation amongst various enforcement agencies and thus China needs to streamline the enforcement regime. Finally, there are important issues of consumer protection such as data protection and unauthorized payment, which need to be addressed by reforming relevant laws.

6

Data Privacy in Mobile Payment

6.1 Introduction

While there is no universal definition of mobile payment, it can be generally understood as payment 'for which the payment data and the payment instruction are initiated, transmitted or confirmed via a mobile phone or device'.[1] As a key component of Fintech, mobile payment offers a much more convenient means of payment than traditional ones, and can be classified into different types depending on the technologies used therein.[2] China's mobile payment industry has experienced explosive growth since 2013 and has played a significant role in the Chinese economy while increasing its influence in many overseas markets.

Mobile payment brings various benefits to consumers, such as flexibility, convenience and a well-integrated purchase experience. It is also beneficial to merchants in terms of its lower costs of record-keeping and accounting, higher operational efficiency and stronger digitizing marketing capacity.[3] Nevertheless, mobile payment is not without risks.[4] First, mobile payment is plagued by data privacy and security risks. Data privacy issues concern

---

[1] European Commission, 'Green Paper: Towards an Integrated European Market for Card, Internet and Mobile Payments', 2012, p 5, https://eur-lex.europa.eu/legal-content/EN/TXT/PDF/?uri=CELEX:52011DC0941&from=EN.

[2] For a more detailed discussion of the typology of mobile payment in China, see Robin Hui Huang et al, 'The Development and Regulation of Mobile Payment in China: Potential, Peril and Proposals', working paper.

[3] Asia Pacific Foundation of Canada, 'The Mobile Payment Revolution in China', p 4, www.asiapacific.ca/sites/default/files/publication-pdf/mobile_payment_report.pdf.

[4] For a comprehensive discussion of the risks of mobile payment in China, see Robin Hui Huang et al, 'The Development and Regulation of Mobile Payment in China: Potential, Peril and Proposals', working paper; OECD, 'Report on Consumer Protection in Online and Mobile Payments', 2012, p 22, www.oecd-ilibrary.org/docserver/5k9490gwp7f3-en.pdf?expires=1588255647&id=id&accname=guest&checksum=760D5A0FB4EBEC3EC084D715EC3EC084D715C7E6C3FF; Andrew James Lake, 'Risk Management in Mobile Money: Observed Risks and Proposed Mitigants for Mobile Money Operators', International Finance Corporation, www.ifc.org/wps/wcm/connect/e6ae6dd9-ad8c-4663-9c38-832c1d46a9f0/Tool+7.1.+Risk+Management.pdf?MOD=AJPERES&CVID=khAOg2B.

primarily unauthorized processing of data for commercial purposes, such as targeted advertisements. The data may also leak out mainly through an illegal data transaction or as a cybersecurity issue. Mobile devices are susceptible to viruses, worms and other malicious applications that could illegally track, steal and misuse users' sensitive financial information and pose a grave threat to the safety of their funds. Secondly, mobile payment users could be exposed to the risk of deceptive commercial practices involving inadequate or misleading disclosure. For example, consumers can be overcharged when the essential information about the actual cost of a transaction is hidden in the terms and conditions of the transaction. Thirdly, the liquidity risk of mobile payment may occur when a third-party payment service provider does not have sufficient liquid assets to meet its debts. Among the various risks of mobile payment, the data privacy risk is perhaps one of the most serious.[5] This chapter will thus focus on this issue, with the objective of critically evaluating the efficiency of data privacy protection in the context of mobile payment in China, and based on such evaluation, setting out improvement suggestions.

6.2 The Market Development and Data Privacy Risks

6.2.1 Overview

The development of the mobile payment market in China has not been a smooth curve. Before 2010, various groups of players, including telecommunication operators, commercial banks, domestic bank payment association UnionPay and third-party payment service providers attempted to explore their market shares in mobile payments.[6] Nevertheless, the development of mobile payment at that time was subject to some limitations, such as a lack of clear regulation of the market, incompatibility of mobile payment technology standards, low penetration rate of smart mobile devices, and poor mobile internet coverage.[7]

---

[5] On 2 November 2020, Mr Gang Yi (易刚), the President of the Chinese central bank, namely the People's Bank of China, attended a conference during the Hong Kong Fintech Week, stating that Fintech is a rule-changer in the financial markets and consumer privacy protection presents a huge challenge. Available at https://finance.sina.com.cn/china/gncj/2020-11-02/doc-iiznezxr9459573.shtml

[6] Guojia xinxi zhongxin (国家信息中心) [State Information Centre], 'Zhongguo yidong zhifu fazhan baogao' (中国移动支付发展报告) [China Mobile Payment Development Report], 2019, p 9, http://upload.xinhua08.com/2019/0508/1557302957552.pdf.

[7] Asia Pacific Foundation of Canada, 'The Mobile Payment Revolution in China', p 9, www.asiapacific.ca/sites/default/files/publication-pdf/mobile_payment_report.pdf.

To better regulate the mobile payment market, the PBOC, in 2010, issued 'The Measures of Administration of Non-financial Institution Payment Service Providers',[8] defining the entry barrier for non-financial institutions to engage in mobile payment. In 2011, the PBOC issued the first batch of licences to twenty-seven third-party payment service providers. The two giant payment service providers, Alipay and WeChat Pay, which were among the first group of licensed third-party mobile payment service providers, started to provide cheap payment services by mainly allowing merchants to make use of a simple printout of a QR code rather than an expensive card reader. Meanwhile, the rapid growth of the Online to Offline market in ride-hailing and food delivery created abundant small-ticket payment scenarios and further advanced the wide application of mobile payment.[9]

Against this backdrop, China's mobile payment market took off since 2013. By the end of June 2018, the number of mobile payment users in China reached about 890 million, and 2018's total value of mobile payment transactions reached CNY 277.39 trillion, compared to 202.93 trillion in 2017, 157.55 trillion in 2016, 108.22 trillion in 2015 and just 22.59 trillion in 2014.[10]

Alipay and WeChat Pay, the two largest digital payment platforms, have significantly transformed China's payment system. By integrating technologies and cooperating with other third-party service providers, Alipay and WeChat Pay have grown into multi-functional and all-in-one platforms, providing a whole range of features such as in-store payments, remote payments, peer-to-peer transfer, mobile top-up services, wealth management, insurance, microloans, travel booking, food delivery, online shopping, ride-hailing and so on. The innovation in mobile payment services has boosted private consumption and business development.

While mobile payment brings significant benefits to society, there are also severe issues of data protection. One high-profile case is the incident

---

[8] Feijinrong jigou zhifu fuwu guanli banfa (非金融机构支付服务管理办法) [The Measures of Administering Non-financial Institutions] (issued by the People's Bank of China on 14 June 2010, effective from 1 September 2010).

[9] Asia Pacific Foundation of Canada, 'The Mobile Payment Revolution in China', p 9, www.asiapacific.ca/sites/default/files/publication-pdf/mobile_payment_report.pdf; for more detailed discussion of the drivers behind the rapid growth of mobile payment in China see Robin Hui Huang et al, 'The Development and Regulation of Mobile Payment in China: Potential, Peril and Proposals', working paper.

[10] Guojia xinxi zhongxin (国家信息中心) [State Information Centre], 'Zhongguo yidong zhifu fazhan baogao' (中国移动支付发展报告) [China Mobile Payment Development Report], 2019, p 8, http://upload.xinhua08.com/2019/0508/1557302957552.pdf.

of Alipay's annual footprint report. On 3 January 2018, Ant Financial (an affiliate of Alibaba Group Holding Limited operating the Alipay mobile payment services of Alibaba's shopping platform) launched its Alipay Annual User Footprint Report within its Alipay mobile wallet application, allowing users to look up how often they had used Alipay over the previous year and for what purposes. However, the landing page of the report had a small box that was checked by default, which provided that 'I consent to the "Sesame Credit Service Agreement"'. Users who did not notice the checked box would have agreed to opt into this agreement under which Ant Financial can direct users' information to the third-party Sesame Credit, and the users were not allowed to revoke their consent. When Alipay's grasping terms of service came into light, many users started to express their concerns over their data privacy.

The Alipay case is by no means alone. In the same year, the Jiangsu Provincial Committee for the Protection of Consumers' Rights and Interests filed an action on behalf of consumers against Beijing Baidu Netcom Science Technology Co. Ltd over its violation of consumers' data privacy.[11] The committee believed that the two mobile applications developed by Baidu, 'Mobile Baidu' and 'Baidu Browser' hoovered up various types of personal information, including sensitive information such as users' location, their MMS messages and contact lists, from users without informing them of the privacy policy or obtaining their consent. Later on, Baidu approached the committee and offered to rectify the privacy issues of their mobile applications.

The above two cases involving China's giant internet companies are just the tip of the iceberg. The Security Research Institute of China Academy of Information and Communications, an affiliate of the Ministry of Industry and Information Technology (MIIT), investigated more than 200 mobile applications in 2019 and found a massive prevalence of data privacy issues – 67 per cent of mobile applications in the market contain no less than five data privacy risks, and 18.5 per cent of the mobile applications in the market carry at least ten data privacy risks.[12] These problems are

---

[11] Jiangsu sheng xiaofeizhe quanyi baohu weiyuanhui yu Beijing Baidu wangxun keji youxian gongsi qinquan zeren jiufenan (江苏省消费者权益保护委员会与北京百度网讯科技有限公司侵权责任纠纷案) [*Jiangsu Provincial Committee for the Protection of Consumers' Rights and Interests v. Beijing Baidu Netcom Science Technology Co. Ltd* (regarding the dispute on tort liabilities)] (Nanjing Intermediate People's Court of Jiangsu Province, Jiangsu (01) Civil (01) 2018).

[12] Zhongguo xinxi tongxin yanjiuyuan anquan yanjiusuo (中国信息通信研究院安全研究所) [Security Research Institute of China Academy of Information and Communications], 'Yidong yingyong shuju anquan yu geren xinxi baohu baipishu' (移动应用数据安全与个

playing out on different aspects, including but not limited to, non-transparent data privacy policies, unauthorized collection and sharing of personal information, and extensive harvesting of personal information.[1] Some mobile applications offering financial services hoover up more than fourteen types of personal information, which is way beyond the scope of data collection necessary for the provision of services.[14] These problems could potentially lead to identity theft, cyber fraud, pricing discrimination target advertising, pervasive monitoring and so forth. In sum, for mobile payment in China, how to protect data privacy has become a compelling and urgent issue.

6.2.2 Factors behind the Heightened Privacy Risk

When speaking of mobile payment, it is noted that the new and heightened privacy risks are mostly caused by the involvement of multiple players and the extensive collection of personal information used and generated in the course of mobile payment.

6.2.2.1 More Players in Mobile Payment

First, there are more players involved in mobile payment than in traditional payment services. In general, players of traditional payments include banks (including, in the case of card payments, the issuing bank, which provides the card to the consumer, and the acquiring bank, which is used by the merchant or seller), and payment processors who process payments by acting on behalf of acquiring or issuing banks.[15] Customers

---

人信息保护白皮书) [White Paper on Mobile Application Data Security and Personal Information Protection], December 2019, p 10, www.caict.ac.cn/kxyj/qwfb/bps/201912/P020191230332039577332.pdf.

[13] Zhongguo xinxi tongxin yanjiuyuan anquan yanjiusuo (中国信息通信研究院安全研究所) [Security Research Institute of China Academy of Information and Communications], 'Yidong yingyong shuju anquan yu geren xinxi baohu baipishu' (移动应用数据安全与个人信息保护白皮书) [White Paper on Mobile Application Data Security and Personal Information Protection], December 2019, p 10, www.caict.ac.cn/kxyj/qwfb/bps/201912/P020191230332039577332.pdf.

[14] Zhongguo xinxi tongxin yanjiuyuan anquan yanjiusuo (中国信息通信研究院安全研究所) [Security Research Institute of China Academy of Information and Communications], 'Yidong yingyong shuju anquan yu geren xinxi baohu baipishu' (移动应用数据安全与个人信息保护白皮书) [White Paper on Mobile Application Data Security and Personal Information Protection], December 2019, p 14, www.caict.ac.cn/kxyj/qwfb/bps/201912/P020191230332039577332.pdf.

[15] OECD, 'Report on Consumer Protection in Online and Mobile Payments', 2012, p 9, www.oecd-ilibrary.org/docserver/5k9490gwp7f3-en.pdf.

6.2 MARKET DEVELOPMENT AND DATA PRIVACY RISKS 183

can use their individual bank accounts through electronic channels by swiping their cards, which usually involves 'account-based electronic payment services'.[16] From a legal perspective, a simple and direct contractual relationship is established between licensed banks and customers under the traditional bank payment system.

By comparison, mobile payment uses mobile devices instead of physical plastic cards in a transaction, and thus many more actors are involved, including 'consumer facing' actors and 'behind the scenes' actors.[17] In addition to banks and payment processors, mobile payment services often involve new actors such as mobile payment service providers, mobile application developers, data analytics companies, e-commerce platform operators, hardware manufacturers and mobile network operators.[18] For example, when a transaction is initiated in a mobile wallet application, communication is made between the consumer and the mobile payment service provider. After the consumer's transaction request is received and authenticated, the mobile payment service provider would transfer the funds from the consumer's account to the merchant's account. The merchant can then request to transfer the funds to his bank account which has been pre-registered in the mobile wallet application. From a legal perspective, there could be two separate contractual relationships, one is between customers and non-bank entities, the other between banks and non-bank entities.[19] With so many parties involved in the process of mobile payment, the risk of data leakage and abuse will become significantly higher.

6.2.2.2 More Extensive Collection of Data

The privacy risk is further amplified by the extensive collection of personal data. In a typical credit card transaction, parties to the transaction have a limited understanding of the sales. Merchants may know the names of customers and the products that the customers purchase. The traditional

---

[16] Khiaonarong Tanai, 'Oversight Issues in Mobile Payments', *IMF Working Paper No.* WP/14/123, 2014, p 7.

[17] Edith Ramirez, Opening Remarks at FTC Privacy Conference', FTC Privacy Conference, 2017, pp 2–3, www.ftc.gov/system/files/documents/public_statements/1049653/ramirez_-_privacycon_remarks_1-12-17.pdf.

[18] OECD, 'Consumer Policy Guidance on Mobile and Online Payments', 2014, p 10, www.caa.go.jp/policies/policy/consumer_policy/international_affairs/pdf/150415adjustments_2.pdf.

[19] Congdon Stephen, 'What's in Your Wallet: Addressing the Regulatory Grey Area Surrounding Mobile Payments' (2016) 7 *Case Western Reserve Journal of Law, Technology and the Internet* 95, 99.

payment networks receive limited information from transactions, such as the account numbers, the amounts of fees and the identities of merchants. The banks usually only receive information on the total amount of purchases and, the places of purchase. The issuing banks will also know the identities of consumers.[20]

However, the nature of mobile devices makes mobile payment users susceptible to data harvesting. As mobile devices contain multiple sensors (such as cameras, microphones, movement sensors, GPS and Wi-Fi capabilities), it can generate various sensitive personal data, such as facial images, voices and information of geographical locations.[21] Mobile devices can also be 'physically tracked via their wireless interfaces by third-parties' or 'tracked by third-parties on the internet',[22] and data brokers could easily track our IP address, location, behavioural habits, purchase habits and other online activities. Moreover, as mobile devices are always turned on, connected to the internet and carried around by the users, it means that data brokers could continuously and pervasively monitor us.[23]

The extensive data harvesting is one of the key defining features of big data, a powerful technique 'that aids in the collection and mathematical analysis of data, using traditional statistical methods as well as more innovative analytical tools'.[24] Many internet companies, such as Google, Facebook and Amazon, have engaged in big data and monetized data. They harvest large amounts of personal data, exploiting them for target advertising and training 'its search algorithms, and develop new data-intensive services such as voice recognition, translation, and location-based services'.[25] These services can generate new revenue. The technique of profiling comes along with big data. It is 'a computerized method involving data mining from data warehouses',[26] which is 'similar

---

[20] Chris Jay Hoofnagle, Jennifer M. Urban, and Su Li, 'Mobile Payments: Consumer Benefits & New Privacy Concerns', 24 April 2012, p 6, https://ssrn.com/abstract=2045580.

[21] European Union Agency for Network and Information Security (ENISA), 'Privacy and Data Protection in Mobile Applications: A Study on the App Development Ecosystem and the Technical Implementation of GDPR', p 11.

[22] Ibid, p 12.

[23] Ibid, p 11.

[24] Viktor Mayer-Schonberger and Yann Padova, 'Regime Change: Enabling Big Data through Europe's New Data Protection Regulation' (2016) 17 *Columbia Science & Technology Law Review* 315, 318; as to the feature of big data, see Ira S. Rubinstein, 'Big Data: The End of Privacy or a New Beginning?' (2013) 3(2) *International Data Privacy Law*, 74, 77.

[25] Ira S. Rubinstein, 'Big Data: The End of Privacy or a New Beginning?' (2013) 3(2) *International Data Privacy Law* 74, 76.

[26] Dinant et al., 'Consultative Committee of the Convention for the Protection of Individuals with Regard to Automatic Processing of Personal Data: Application of Convention 108 to the

6.2 MARKET DEVELOPMENT AND DATA PRIVACY RISKS   185

to behavioral analysis since the aim is ... to establish a strong mathematical correlation between certain characteristics that the individual shares with other "similar" individuals and a given behaviour which one wishes to predict or influence'.[27] For instance, it allows advertisers to use the information to create detailed profiles of individual consumers and direct tailored advertisements to consumers based on the data collected.[28]

Although the technology of profiling could provide consumers with advertisements customized to their taste and preference, it has caused a series of significant problems. Firstly, data profiling often takes the form of 'pervasive and non-transparent commercial observation' of consumer online behaviour.[29] Consumers are not aware of which types of data will be collected and how the data will be used and processed. It is a direct interference with consumers' rights to personal data protection. Secondly, by aggregating discrete or de-identified data sets, data profiling can generate personally identifiable information that is ultimately linked to individual users. One possibility is that profiling can 'generate a predictive model of what has a high probability of being [personally identifiable information]'.[30] For example, in 2012, *New York Times* published an article, criticizing the retailer Target for using data mining techniques to analyse their customers' purchase history and predict pregnant female customers.[31] After inferential analysis, Target disclosed relevant information to marketers who then directed relevant advertisements to those pregnant women. The data analytics thus resulted in the unauthorized disclosure of sensitive personal information and the direct invasion of consumers' privacy.

Thirdly, based on the aggregation of consumers' purchase history, profiling enables merchants to use unfair commercial practices, such as price

---

Profiling Mechanism – Some Ideas for the Future Work of the Consultative Committee', 2008, p 5, www.statewatch.org/news/2008/aug/coe-profilingpaper.pdf.

[27] Ibid.

[28] Charles Gibney, Steve Trites, Nicole Ufoegbune, and Bruno Lévesque, 'International Review: Mobile Payments and Consumer Protection,' Research Division, Financial Consumer Agency of Canada, 2015, p iv, www.canada.ca/content/dam/canada/financial-consumer-agency/migration/eng/resources/researchsurveys/documents/internationalre viewmobilepaymentsandconsumerprotection.pdf.

[29] N. J. King and P. W. Jessen, 'Profiling the Mobile Customer – Privacy Concerns When Behavioural Advertisers Target Mobile Phones Part I' (2010) 26 *Computer Law and Security Review* 455, 459.

[30] Kate Crawford and Jason Schultz, 'Big Data and Due Process: Toward a Framework to Redress Predictive Privacy Harms' (2014) 55 *Boston College Law Review* 93, 94.

[31] Charles Duhigg, 'Psst, You in Aisle 5', *New York Times*, 19 February 2012.

discrimination between different groups of consumers.[32] Fourthly, target advertising may infringe consumers' liberty and autonomy as consumers who are unaware of the profiling are likely to be manipulated by marketers.[33] This risk is acute in the group of vulnerable people targeted by promotions of unhealthy food, medication or high-interest consumer loans.[34] Profiling can even be used in politics to manipulate voters. In March 2018, *The Times, The Observer* and *The Guardian* published a joint investigation into how the consulting firm Cambridge Analytica collected data from more than 50 million Facebook users, without their consent, to build their profiles and make tailored political advertisements to potential voters so as to influence their voting.[35] It quickly aroused worldwide outrage. The Federal Trade Commission (FTC) filed a complaint against Facebook, alleging that Facebook violated the FTC's 2012 order by misrepresenting the control that the users had over their personal information, failing to institute and maintain a reasonable programme to ensure consumers' privacy, and deceptively failing to disclose that it would use the users' phone numbers for target advertising.[36] The FTC eventually settled with Facebook and imposed a record-breaking USD 5 billion penalty on Facebook.

In summary, the data-driven economy incentivizes extensive data harvesting and relentless data profiling. The balancing of the need to protect consumer privacy and financial and technological innovation has become extremely challenging. In Section 6.3, we will discuss China's regulatory framework of data protection and its evolution.

6.3 China's Regulatory Framework of Data Protection

6.3.1 The Evolution of the Regulatory Framework

In China, data privacy of mobile payments is generally regulated under a broad framework of data protection. This framework has undergone

---

[32] Nancy J. King and Pernille Wegener Jessen, 'Profiling the Mobile Customer – Privacy Concerns When Behavioural Advertisers Target Mobile Phones Part I' (2010) 26 *Computer Law and Security Review* 455, 459.

[33] Karen Yeung, 'Five Fears about Mass Predictive Personalization in an Age of Surveillance Capitalism' (2018) 8(3) *International Data Protection Law* 258, 262–63.

[34] Nancy J. King and Pernille Wegener Jessen, 'Profiling the Mobile Customer – Privacy Concerns When Behavioural Advertisers Target Mobile Phones Part I' (2010) 26 *Computer Law and Security Review* 455, 461; for a comprehensive discussion, see Ryan Calo, 'Digital Market Manipulation' (2014) 82 *George Washington Law Review* 996.

[35] Matthew Rosenberg, Nicholas Confessore, and Carole Cadwalladr, 'How Trump Consultants Exploited the Facebook Data of Millions', *New York Times*, 17 March 2018.

[36] *United States of America v. Facebook, Inc* (Case No. 19-cv-2184).

6.3 CHINA'S REGULATORY FRAMEWORK OF DATA PROTECTION   187

a structural evolution from a traditional and piecemeal approach to a principles-based approach by consolidating the fragmented data protection-related provisions and systematizing the data protection regime.

6.3.1.1 Before 2016: A Traditional and Piecemeal Approach

Before 2016, there was no general data protection law, but traces of data protection could be found in different laws. The Constitution of the PRC[37] (Constitution) makes reference to privacy once, stating that citizens' privacy of correspondences is protected, and no organization or individual may, on any ground, infringe upon the freedom and privacy of citizens' correspondence, except in cases to meet the needs of the state security or of the investigation into criminal offences, public security and so forth.[38] Article 38 also states that citizens' personal dignity is inviolable.[39] However, these constitutional rights may not be directly relevant to data protection since the Constitution in China cannot directly serve as the legal ground for a judicial decision.[40]

China's civil and criminal laws protect the individuals' right to privacy. The Tort Liability Law of the PRC[41] (Tort Liability Law) which came into effect in July 2010 recognizes the right to privacy as independent civil right.[42] Article 36 protects individuals' civil rights and interests from online infringement.[43] Individuals thus have a cause of action in tort if their right to privacy is infringed. The Ninth Amendment to the Criminal Law of the PRC (Criminal Law)[44] contains several important provisions

---

[37] Zhonghua renmin gongheguo xianfa (中华人民共和国宪法) [Constitution of the People's Republic of China] (promulgated by the National People's Congress on 4 December 1982, effective from 4 December 1982; amended in 1988, 1993, 1999, 2004 and 2018).

[38] Constitution, art. 40.

[39] Ibid, art. 38.

[40] Tong Zhiwei, 'A Comment on the Rise and Fall of the Supreme People's Court's Reply to Qi Yuling's case' (2010) 43 *Suffolk University Law Review* 669, 678 (pointing out that 'China is a state of statutory laws and any provision of constitutional rights must be implemented through laws made by legislative bodies; otherwise, the constitutionally recognized rights cannot be practically protected').

[41] Zhonghua renmin gongheguo qinquan zerenfa (中华人民共和国侵权责任法) [Tort Liability Law of the People's Republic of China] (promulgated by the Standing Committee of the National People's Congress on 26 December 2009, effective from 1 July 2010).

[42] Tort Liability Law, art. 2.

[43] Ibid, art. 36.

[44] Zhonghua Renmin Gongheguo Xingfa Xiuzhengan (9) (中华人民共和国刑法修正案九) [The Ninth Amendment to the Criminal Law of the PRC] (promulgated by the Standing Committee of the National People's Congress on 29 August 2015, effective from 1 November 2015).

relating to data protection. Particularly, it imposes severe punishment for the illegal activities of (1) selling or providing citizens' personal information to third parties and (2) selling or providing to third parties citizens' personal information obtained during the course of performing duties or providing services.[45] Network service providers may face criminal liability if they fail to fulfil 'information network security administration duties prescribed by laws or administrative regulations' and take remedial action.[46][47]

In December 2012, the Standing Committee of the National People's Congress (NPCSC) promulgated 'The Decision on Strengthening Online Information Protection' (2012 NPSCS Decision).[48] Despite its title as a decision, the instrument was, until 2016, the highest-level law specifically dealing with data protection. It sets out several basic principles or data protection and acts as the primary baseline for the subsequent privacy regulation in China.[49] In particular, Article 2 of the 2012 NPCSC Decision specifies that network service providers shall 'abide by the principles of legality, legitimacy and necessity, clearly indicate the objective, methods and scope for collection and use of information and obtain consent from the person whose data is collected.'[50] Following this decision, China makes continuous efforts in developing the regime of personal data protection through making or amending laws and regulations in various sectors. China also updated the Law on the Protection of Consumer Rights and Interests (Consumer Protection Law) in 2013.[51]

In addition to general laws, China's central bank, the People's Bank of China (PBOC), paid close attention to the issue of data privacy in the financial industry. In 2011, the PBOC issued a circular to the banking industry on the issue of protecting personal financial information.[52] This

---

[45] Criminal Law, art. 17.

[46] Ibid, art. 28.

[47] 2012 NPSCS Decision, art. 2.

[48] 'Guanyu jiaqiang wangluo xinxi baohu de guiding' (关于加强网络信息保护的决定) [The Decision on Strengthening Online Information Protection] (promulgated by the NPSCS on 28 December 2012, effective from 28 December 2012).

[49] Graham Greenleaf, *Asian Data Privacy Laws: Trade & Human Rights Perspectives* (Oxford: Oxford University Press, 2014), 204.

[50] 2012 NPSCS Decision, Article 2.

[51] Zhonghua renmin gongheguo xiaofeizhe quanyibaohufa (中华人民共和国消费者权益保护法) [Law of the People's Republic of China on the Protection of Consumer Rights and Interests] (promulgated by the NPCSC on 31 October 1993, effective from 1 January 1994; amended in 2009 and 2013).

[52] 'Guanyu yinhangye jinrong jigou zuohao geren jinrong xinxi baohu gongzuo de tongzhi' (关于银行业金融机构做好个人金融信息保护工作的通知) [Circular of the People's

6.3 CHINA'S REGULATORY FRAMEWORK OF DATA PROTECTION   189

circular laid down a foundation for the PBOC's future regulation in the area of data privacy protection. For example, it requires that banks must establish internal control systems to ensure their confidentiality of personal financial information and should not collect information irrelevant to their services. In March 2012, the PBOC issued another circular requiring the banks to strengthen the protection of data privacy in accordance with laws and regulations.[53]

The above circulars were only applicable to banks.[54] In December 2015, the PBOC further issued a regulation on mobile payment service providers.[55] In relation to data privacy protection, this regulation lays out several requirements. First, non-bank payment institutions must establish an internal data management and risk control system.[56] Second, the payment institutions must not store certain sensitive information, such as magnetic track information and chip information of bank cards, account passwords and card verification codes. Third, without consent of clients and banks, they must not store the expiration date of bank cards. They must not provide other organisations with clients' information unless otherwise authorised by the laws or approved by the clients.[57] Last but not least, they should comply with the principles of minimization when collecting and processing the clients' information and should also inform clients of the scope and purpose of data collection and processing.

6.3.1.2   After 2016: A Comprehensive and Proactive Regime

The Cybersecurity Law of the PRC (Cybersecurity Law), enacted in November 2016, is thus far the most important and comprehensive law

---

Bank of China on the Protection of personal Financial Information by Bank and Financial Institutions] (issued by the People's Bank of China on 21 January 2011, effective from 1 May 2011).

[53] Guanyu yinhangye jinrong jigou jinyibu zuohao geren jinrong xinxi baohu gongzuo de tongzhi (关于银行业金融机构进一步做好个人金融信息保护工作的通知) [Circular of the People's Bank of China on the Further Protection of personal Financial Information by Bank and Financial Institutions] (issued by the People's Bank of China on 27 March 2012, effective from 27 March 2012).

[54] Zhonghua renmin gongheguo xiaofeizhe quanyibaohufa (中华人民共和国消费者权益保护法) [Law of the People's Republic of China on the Protection of Consumer Rights and Interests] (promulgated by the NPCSC on 31 October 1993, effective from 1 January 1994; amended in 2009 and 2013).

[55] 'Feiyinhang Zhifu Jigou Wangluo zhifu yewu guanli banfa' (非银行支付机构网络支付业务管理办法) [The Management Measures of the Mobile Payment Business of the Non-bank Payment Institutions] (issued by the People's Bank of China on 28 December 2015, effective from 28 December 2015).

[56] Ibid., Article 20.

[57] Ibid., Article 20.

relating to data protection.[58] Although the major purpose of this law is to reduce the risk of cyberattacks and safeguard national security, it reiterates the basic requirements in the 2012 NPCSC Decision, articulates a set of data protection principles, specifies the data subject's rights, and stipulates penalties for violations of the law. For instance, Article 41 provides that network operators shall follow the principles of legality, propriety and necessity, disclose the rules of collection and use of personal information, clearly state the purpose, method and scope of the collection and use of information, and shall obtain data subjects' consent.[59]

The Cybersecurity Law is accompanied by the Personal Information Security Specification (2018 Specification), a comprehensive guide setting out the compliance requirements of data protection.[60] The 2018 Specification is a nationally recommended standard. Under Article 2 of the Standardization Law of the PRC, the national standards are divided into mandatory standards and recommended standards; while mandatory standards must be implemented, recommended standards are recommended for implementation.[61] As such, the 2018 Specification is not mandatory. However, it can act as a regulatory baseline for judicial and law enforcement authorities as well as companies to determine compliance with the requirements of data protection.[62] In addition, it may reflect the direction of future legislation on data protection.

Following the enactment of the Cybersecurity Law, the PBOC issued an implementing rule for the financial industry, titled 'Measures for the Protection of the Rights and Interests of Financial Consumers'.[63] It

---

[58] Zhonghua renmin gongheguo wangluo anquan fa (中华人民共和国网络安全法) [Cybersecurity Law of the People's Republic of China] (promulgated by the NPCSC on 7 November 2016, effective from 1 June 2017).

[59] Cybersecurity Law, art. 41.

[60] Xinxi anquan jishu – Geren xinxi anquan guifan (信息安全技术 – – 个人信息安全规范) [Information Security Technology – Personal Information Security Specification] (issued by State Administration of Market Supervision and Administration and National Standardisation Management Committee on 29 December 2017, effective from 1 May 2018; amended in 2019 and 2020).

[61] Zhonghua renmin gongheguo biaozhunhua fa (中华人民共和国标准化法) [Standardisation Law of the People's Republic of China] (promulgated by the NPCSC on 29 December 1988, effective from 1 April 1989; amended in 2017), art. 2.

[62] 2018 Specification, section 1.

[63] Zhongguo renmin yinhang jinrong xiaofeizhe quanyi baohu shishi banfa (中国人民银行金融消费者权益保护实施办法) [Measures of the People's Bank of China for the Protection of the Rights and Interests of Financial Consumers] (issued by the People's Bank of China on 14 December 2016, effective from 14 December 2016).

6.3 CHINA'S REGULATORY FRAMEWORK OF DATA PROTECTION 191

imposes the obligations of data privacy protection on financial institutions. According to Article 2, financial institutions include banks and, other financial institutions providing cross-market and cross-industry financial products and services, as well as non-bank payment institutions.[64] In other words, mobile payment service providers are required to comply with this rule. Chapter 3 of this rule specifically deals with the issue of data privacy protection. It defines 'personal financial information' as 'the personal information obtained, processed and preserved by financial institutions in the course of ordinary business or through other channels, which includes the information of personal identity, asset, account, credit, transaction and other information that can reflect certain situations of individuals.'[65] It reiterates the key principles for data protection laid out in the Cybersecurity Law. For instance, Article 28 requires that when collecting personal financial information, financial institutions follow the principles of legality, reasonableness and necessity, collect personal financial information in accordance with the requirements of laws and regulations and business needs, and shall not collect information which is irrelevant to business, collect information in an improper manner, or illegally store personal financial information.[66]

In line with the 2018 Specification, the PBOC issued 'Personal Financial Information Protection Technical Specification' (2020 Specification) in February 2020.[67] Similar to the role of the 2018 Specification, the 2020 Specification sets out the best practice for data privacy protection.[68] It classifies personal financial information and sets forth various requirements governing the different categories of the data. As the 2020 Specification basically incorporates the framework of the 2018 Specification, the 2020 Specification will be discussed only to the extent necessary to avoid repetition.

---

[64] Ibid., Article 2.

[65] Ibid., Article 27.

[66] Ibid., Article 28.

[67] 'Geren jinrong xinxi baohu jishu guifan' (个人金融信息保护技术规范) [Personal Financial Information Protection Technical Specification] (issued by the People's Bank of China on 13 February 2020).

[68] The financial institutions refer to the licensed financial institutions regulated by the state financial regulatory departments as well as the relevant institutions involved in the processing of personal financial information (2020 Specification, Section 3.1). The licensed financial institutions include banks, non-bank payment institutions, and the licensed financial service companies. The relevant institutions involving in the processing of financial information include the telecommunication service providers, information technology providers and marketing service providers.

In September 2020, the PBOC also updated 'Measures for the Protection of the Rights and Interests of Financial Consumers' in accordance with the Cybersecurity Law and the 2020 Specification.[69] It adds the requirements of disclosure, data breach notification and data classification.

In addition to the various rule-making efforts, the PBOC also endeavoured to improve the financial infrastructure to provide adequate technical support for data protection. In 2017, the PBOC instructed the Payment and Clearing Association of China to establish a unified payment clearing platform for non-bank payment institutions.[70] By doing so, the PBOC can monitor information on mobile payment transactions, regulate relevant financial activities, and deal with the risks of money-laundering.

6.3.2 Main Elements of Current Regulatory Regime

6.3.2.1 Concept of Personal Information

In general, there are two groups of payment data collected and processed in mobile payment, namely essential payment data and ancillary data.[71] The essential payment data refers to the information in relation to the identity of payers (e.g. names, telephone numbers, ID card numbers), account numbers of both payers and payees, data and time of payments, and primary authorisation numbers for card transactions.[72] The ancillary data refers to the information in relation to the location where payments were made, device information, IP addresses, search and browsing histories, etc.[73]

---

[69] 'Zhongguo renmin yinhang jinrong xiaofeizhe quanyi baohu shishi banfa' (中国人民银行金融消费者权益保护实施办法) [Measures for the Protection of the Rights and Interests of Financial Consumers of the People's Bank of China] (issued by the People's Bank of China on 15 September 2020, effective from 1 November 2020).

[70] 'Zhongguo renmin yinhang zhifujiesuan si guanyu jiang feiyinhang zhifu jigou wangluo zhifu yewu you zhilian moshi qianyi zhi wanglian pingtai chuli de tongzhi' (中国人民银行支付结算司关于将非银行支付机构网络支付业务由直连模式迁移至网联平台处理的通知) [Notice on Migrating the Online Payment Business of Non-bank Payment Institutions from Direct Connection Mode to Network Platform Processing] (issued by the People's Bank of China on 4 Aug 2017).

[71] Payment System Regulator (UK), 'Data in the Payments Industry' (2018), p. 17, available at https://www.psr.org.uk/sites/default/files/media/PDF/PSR-Discussion-paper-Data-in-the-payments-industry-June-2018.pdf

[72] Payment System Regulator (UK), 'Data in the Payments Industry' (2018), p. 17, available at https://www.psr.org.uk/sites/default/files/media/PDF/PSR-Discussion-paper-Data-in-the-payments-industry-June-2018.pdfhttps://www.psr.org.uk/sites/default/files/media/PDF/PSR-Discussion-paper-Data-in-the-payments-industry-June-2018.pdf.

[73] Payment System Regulator (UK), 'Data in the Payments Industry' (2018), p. 17, available at https://www.psr.org.uk/sites/default/files/media/PDF/PSR-Discussion-paper-Data-in-

6.3 CHINA'S REGULATORY FRAMEWORK OF DATA PROTECTION   193

Therefore, the starting point of considering China's current regulatory regime in the area of mobile payment is the concept of personal information. In other words, the first question is which kinds of personal information are protected under the regulatory regime. Under the Cybersecurity Law, personal information refers to 'all kinds of information, recorded electronically or through other means, that taken alone or together with other information, is sufficient to identify a natural person's identity, including, but not limited to, natural persons' full names, birth dates, identification numbers, personal biometric information, addresses, telephone numbers, and so forth'.[74] The 2018 Specification expressly expands the scope of personal information, referring to 'any information that is recorded, electronically or otherwise, can be used solely or in combination with other information to identify the identity of a natural person or reflect the activities of a natural person'.[75] Arguably, this definition may extend to cover 'the information that may reflect a specific person (without necessarily identifying) them'.[76] If this is the case, the 2018 Specification would not only apply to the personally identifiable information but also to the information 'which gives an organisation the capacity to interact with a person on an individuated basis (such as behavioural target marketing using data) which does not enable the [data controller] to identify the data subject'.[77]

The 2020 Specification applies to the personal financial information, which is defined as 'personal information collected, processed and stored through the financial products and services by the financial institutions.'[78] This essentially incorporates the concept of personal information set out in the 2018 Specification. Additionally, the 2020 Specification grades the personal financial information into three categories, namely C1, C2 and C3. C3 refers to all kinds of user authentication information, such as bank card magnetic track data, expiration dates, pin codes of bank cards, personal biometric information, etc. C2 refers to the information that

---

the-payments-industry-June-2018.pdfhttps://www.psr.org.uk/sites/default/files/media/
PDF/PSR-Discussion-paper-Data-in-the-payments-industry-June-2018.pdf.

[74] Cybersecurity Law, art. 76(5).

[75] 2018 Specification, section 3.1.

[76] Greenleaf Graham and Livingston Scott, 'China's Personal Information Standard: The Long March to a Privacy Law' (2017) 150 *Privacy Laws & Business International Report* 25, 26.

[77] Greenleaf Graham and Livingston Scott, 'China's Personal Information Standard: The Long March to a Privacy Law' (2017) 150 *Privacy Laws & Business International Report* 25, 26.

[78] 2020 Specification, Section 3.2.

indicates the identity and financial status of a specific data subject, and the information to be used for financial products and services. It includes identity card information, account usernames, SMS passwords, KYC information, transaction details and other personal details (such as home addresses). C1 refers to the information for internal use by the financial institutions, such as account opening dates, the account-opening bank and a customer's payment token. It also includes any non-C3 and non-C2 personal financial information.

The 2018 Specification draws a distinction between general personal data and sensitive personal data. Sensitive personal data is defined as 'personal data that, if disclosed or illegally processed, might endanger personal and property security, damage personal reputation, or physical or psychological health, or lead to discriminatory treatment and so forth'.[79] Appendix B of the 2018 Specification has listed some examples of sensitive information, such as bank account, authentication information, payment records, credit information, payment records, personal identity information, browsing history and geographical location.[80] In this respect, C2 and C3 fall into the category of sensitive personal data.

Accordingly, the enhanced protective mechanisms for sensitive information under the 2018 Specification should also be applied, such as explicit consent from data subjects before collection,[81] encryption storage and transmission of sensitive information,[82] and special controls of accessing sensitive information.[83]

6.3.2.2 Data Controllers and Data Processors

As discussed above, the 2020 Specification imposes upon financial institutions the obligations of protecting data privacy and cybersecurity. The term 'financial institutions' refers to licensed financial institutions regulated by the authorities and the relevant institutions involved in the processing of personal financial information.[84] The licensed financial institutions include banks, non-bank payment institutions, and licensed financial service companies. The relevant institutions involved in the processing of financial information may include telecommunication service providers, information technology providers and marketing

---

[79] 2018 Specification, section 3.2.
[80] Ibid, Appendix B.
[81] 2018 Specification, section 5.4(b).
[82] Ibid, section 6.3(a).
[83] Ibid, section 7.1(e).
[84] 2020 Specification, Section 3.1.

service providers. For the ease of analysis, the relevant financial institutions here can be categorized into two types: data controllers and data processors.

The Cybersecurity Law imposes upon the network operators the legal responsibility for complying with the respective data protection obligations. Network operators refer to the owners and administrators of networks as well as network service providers.[85] This loosely defined term would encompass almost all the business that owns or administrates networks. The 2018 Specification provides a more specific concept 'data controller'. Data controller means 'any organization or person that has the power to decide the purpose and method of processing personal information'.[86] It is the data controller who has the obligation to comply with the respective requirements. In light of the increasingly important role of the data outsourcing services, the 2018 Specification also makes a distinction between a data controller and a third-party data processor. The delegation of data processing by the data controller to the data processor should be within the data subject's authorization.[37] The data processor should strictly follow the data controller's instructions.[88]

In the context of mobile payment, a merchant can be seen as a data controller of the purchase data that he processes for a sales agreement. A bank is also a data controller of its customers' financial information. A payment processor is likely to be a processor as it operates on behalf of the issuing or acquiring bank to evaluate whether transactions are valid. A mobile payment application developer can act in both capacities. It can be a processor if the mobile application is developed at the request and on behalf of a bank or financial institution to facilitate contactless payments. On the other hand, if the developer retains access to personal data to provide additional services, such as tailored advertisements, it qualifies as a controller as well. Both e-commerce platform providers and mobile payment service providers are, by definition, data controllers, and a third-party service provider for authentication of users or personalized advertisement is a data processor dealing with data on behalf of the data controller. In summary, in mobile payments, data controllers may include merchants, banks, and non-bank payment service providers, mobile payment application developers and, e-commerce platform

---

[85] Cybersecurity Law, art. 76(3).
[86] 2018 Specification, section 3.4.
[87] Ibid, section 9.1(a).
[88] Ibid, section 9.1(c).

providers. Data processors may include payment processors, mobile payment application developers, third-party service providers.

Before engaging a third party as the data processor, the data controller should carry out a personal information security impact assessment ensuring that the data processor has sufficient data security capabilities and provides sufficient security safeguards.[89] The data controller should also supervise the data processor and record the processor's activities.[90] In addition to the general requirements, the financial institutions are not allowed to authorize a non-financial institution to collect C2 or C3-level personal financial information.[91] They may not authorize a third-party to process any C2 or C3-level personal financial information that supports user authentication (e.g. one-time password or a SMS code).[92] The information to be outsourced should be de-identified.[93] The data processor has a number of direct obligations, including strictly following the data controller's instructions, obtaining its authorization before engaging a sub-processor and deleting all personal data at the end of the engagement.[94]

6.3.2.3 Principles of Fair Information Practices

The fundamental principles of data protection under the Cybersecurity Law and the 2018 Specification are based on the Fair Information Practices (FIPs). The 2020 Specification reiterates these principles. The FIPs originated from a 1973 report by the US Department of Health, Education and Welfare, and it became extremely influential in shaping privacy law in the United States and around the world.[95] The Cybersecurity Law incorporated several key principles of the FIPs, including principles of lawfulness, fairness and transparency, integrity and confidentiality, data minimization and data subjects' participation. The 2018 Specification further introduces principles of purpose limitation, accuracy and storage limitation.

---

[89] 2018 Specification, section 9.1(b).
[90] Ibid, section 9.1(d).
[91] 2020 Specification, Section 6.1.1(a).
[92] 2020 Specification, Section 6.1.4.4 (b).
[93] 2020 Specification, Section 6.1.4.4 (c).
[94] Ibid, section 9.1(c).
[95] For a history of the FIPs, see Robert Gellman, 'Fair Information Practices: A Basic History', 7 October 2019, https://ssrn.com/abstract=2415020; Paul M. Schwartz, 'The EU–US Privacy Collision: A Turn to Institutions and Procedures' (2013) 126 *Harvard Law Review* 1966.

6.3 CHINA'S REGULATORY FRAMEWORK OF DATA PROTECTION 197

The Cybersecurity Law states that the network operators should abide by the principles of lawfulness, propriety and necessity.[96] Under the 2018 Specification, the principle of lawfulness means that data controllers shall not deceive, trick or coerce data subjects to provide personal information, or conceal the data collection functions of their products or services, or obtain data from illegal channels.[97] The principle of necessity is closely connected with the principle of data minimization. Under the Cybersecurity Law, 'network operators must not collect personal information unrelated to the services they provide'.[98] The 2018 Specification modifies this with a stricter approach, requiring that 'the type of personal information collected should be directly related to the business function of the product or service; it means that the function of the product or service cannot be realized without the participation of the above personal information'.[99] In addition, 'the frequency of automatic collection of personal information should be the minimum frequency necessary to realize the business function of the product or service',[100] and 'the amount of indirect acquisition of personal information should be the minimum necessary to realize the business function of the product or service'.[101]

Furthermore, the Cybersecurity Law requires network operators to 'make public rules for collection and use, explicitly stating the purposes, means and scope for collecting or using information, and obtaining the consent of the person whose data is gathered'.[102] This principle of transparency aims to keep data subjects informed of how their data are being used and offset information asymmetry between the data controllers and data subjects. The 2018 Specification further requires that the scope, purposes, and rules of data processing should be open to the public in an explicit, intelligible, reasonable and accessible manner.[103] The 2018 Specification also spreads out the particular consent requirements. It prohibits the seeking of bundle consent and forced consent.[104] An individual's express consent through opt-in or other affirmative action is required

---

[96] Cybersecurity Law, art. 41.
[97] 2018 Specification, section 5.1.
[98] Cybersecurity Law, art. 41.
[99] 2018 Specification, section 5.2(a).
[100] Ibid, section 5.2(b).
[101] Ibid, section 5.2(c).
[102] Cybersecurity Law, art. 41.
[103] 2018 Specification, sections 5.5(b)–(d).
[104] Ibid, section 5.3(a).

198 DATA PRIVACY IN MOBILE PAYMENT

to collect sensitive personal data, and such consent must be fully informed and involve a clear and definitive expression of intent.[105]

The Cybersecurity Law does not contain the principle of purpose limitation. The 2018 Specification introduces this principle, stipulating that 'the use of personal information should not exceed the scope that is directly or reasonably related to the purpose claimed at the time of the collection of personal information'.[106] The 2018 Specification also introduces the requirement of storage limitation, stating that 'the storage period of personal information should be the minimum time necessary to achieve the purpose authorized by the data subject',[107] and the data must be erased or anonymized when those purposes have been served.[108]

The Cybersecurity Law requires that 'network operators shall strictly maintain the confidentiality of user information they collect, and establish and complete user information protection systems'.[109] It further requires that network operators shall adopt technical measures and other necessary measures to ensure the security of personal information.[110] In the case of data breaches, remedial measures shall be immediately taken, and network operators shall promptly inform the users and to make a report to the competent departments in accordance with regulations.[111,112] The 2013 Specification also requires that an incident notification must explain the nature and the impact of the incident, the measures taken or to be taken in response, the practical recommendations for data subjects to minimize the impact of the incident, and the data subjects' rights and remedies.[113]

The 2018 Specification requires organisations to employ enhanced security measures, such as de-identification of personal information and encryption of sensitive personal data.[114] Likewise, under the 2020 Specification, financial institutions should use de-identification, anonymisation or encryption where necessary to protect personal financial information after collection.[115] The 2020 Specification further specifies

---

[105] Ibid, section 5.4(b).
[106] Ibid, section 7.3.
[107] Ibid, section 6.1(a).
[108] Ibid, section 6.1(b).
[109] Cybersecurity Law, art. 40.
[110] Ibid, art. 42.
[111] Ibid, art. 42.
[112] 2018 Specification, sections 6.2 and 6.3.
[113] Ibid, sections 10.1 and 10.2.
[114] 2018 Specification, Sections 6.2 & 6.3.
[115] 2020 Specification, Section 6.1.

6.3 CHINA'S REGULATORY FRAMEWORK OF DATA PROTECTION 199

that the transmission of information in C2 or C3 categories through a public network should be conducted through encrypted channels.[116]

Network operators are obligated to allocate persons responsible for network security as part of their internal security management systems.[117] The 2018 Specification and the 2020 Specification stipulate controllers' duties of responsibility and accountability.[118] Financial institutions should establish a specific unit responsible for protecting financial information,[119] and exercise necessary supervision of the responsible personnel.[120] For other entities acting as data controllers, they are expected to designate a person or agent to manage personal data. If an organization has more than 200 personnel and its main business involves processing personal data, or if the organization is expected to handle the personal data of more than 1 million people over the next twelve months, then it should establish a department with dedicated staff to handle personal data security.[121]

Under the Cybersecurity Law, data subjects can request network operators to delete their personal information if individuals discover that network operators have violated the provisions of laws, administrative regulations or agreements between the parties to gather or use their personal information.[122] The 2018 Specification gives more control to the data subjects. For instance, the data subject has the right to access his information collected by the data controllers[123] and the right to rectify inaccurate information.[124] Data subjects can revoke consent to data processing, after which the data controller is not allowed to further process the data.[125] The 2018 Specification also reiterates data subjects' rights of deletion in the case where the data controller has breached its legal obligations or an agreement with the data subject. The same right extends to information in the possession of data processors.[126] Personal data should also be deleted or anonymized when users close down accounts.[127]

---

[116] 2020 Specification, Section 6.1.3.
[117] Cybersecurity Law, art. 21.
[118] 2018 Specification, Section 11; 2020 Specification, Section 7.2.
[119] 2020 Specification, Section 7.2.2.
[120] 2020 Specification, Section 7.2.3.
[121] Ibid, section 11.
[122] Cybersecurity Law, art. 43.
[123] 2018 Specification, section 8.1.
[124] Ibid, section 8.2.
[125] Ibid, section 8.4(a).
[126] Ibid, section 8.3.
[127] Ibid, section 8.5.

6.3.2.4 Enforcement

Under the Cybersecurity Law, the Cyberspace Administration of China is responsible for the overall planning and coordination of cybersecurity work and related supervision and management work.[128] The implementation of the Cybersecurity Law is left to the Public Security Bureau and the MIIT.[129] While the Public Security Bureau is mainly responsible for the investigation of criminal offences, the MIIT, as the chief internet and telecommunication regulator, is responsible for dealing with privacy-related complaints.

Apart from the general agencies for data protection, attention also needs to be paid to the specialist financial regulators, particularly because mobile payment represents a form of financial service. The current financial regulatory structure in China has the defining feature of being sector-based.[130] As the central bank, the PBOC assumes responsibility for monetary policies and the stability of the national financial system generally. The China Banking and Insurance Regulatory Commission (CBIRC) and the China Securities Regulatory Commission are the authorities responsible for regulating the banking and insurance sectors and the securities sector respectively. The banking sector is broadly defined to cover commercial banks, non-bank financial institutions and trust companies.[131] Hence, as non-bank financial institutions, mobile payment platforms are subject to the regulations of both the PBOC and the CBIRC.

Individuals and organizations have the right to report conducts endangering cybersecurity to relevant departments.[132] Cybersecurity refers to the 'capacity for network data to be complete, confidential and usable as well as protecting them from attack'.[133] The relevant competent departments may order the organizations to make corrections, and can, according to the circumstances, confiscate any illegal income made and impose a fine of not less than one time and not more than ten times the illegal gains. If there are no illegal gains, a fine of not more than CNY 1 million shall be imposed, and the person in charge and other persons directly responsible shall be

---

[128] Cybersecurity Law, art. 8.

[129] Ibid, art. 8.

[130] Robin Hui Huang, *Securities and Capital Markets Law in China* (Oxford University Press, 2014), 24-35.

[131] Robin Hui Huang, *Securities and Capital Markets Law in China* (Oxford University Press, 2014), 27-29; Robin Hui Huang, 'The Logics and Path of the Reform of China's Financial Regulatory Structure: International Experiences and Local Choice' 2019(3) *Faxue Jia [Renmin University Law Journal]* 124-137 (discussing the development and function of the CBIRC).

[132] Ibid, art. 14.

[133] Ibid, art. 76.

fined not less than CNY 10,000 but not more than CNY 100,000. If the circumstances are serious, the relevant departments can suspend the organizations' relevant business and revoke their business licences.[134]

In addition to administrative fines, private action is available for individuals whose rights have been harmed.[135] An individual may file a claim in tort if his right or interest has been infringed.[136] Network users and network service providers may be required to make apologies and restore the claimants' reputation.[137] Where their violations cause 'financial loss or grave psychological harm', the claimants can request compensation.[138] Where the loss or harm is not ascertainable, the courts may order damages up to CNY 500,000.[139]

The Cybersecurity Law states that where any breaches of the law constitute a crime, criminal responsibility will apply to the wrongdoers.[140] The Criminal Law which has been discussed above would apply.

6.4 International Experiences

The internet landscape has changed profoundly over the past decades. In the international arena, many jurisdictions are evaluating or reforming their regulatory frameworks to protect consumers and respond to technological innovation. In this section, we will examine the regulatory frameworks of some major jurisdictions, including the United States, the EU, Singapore and Hong Kong.

6.4.1 The United States

The United States deals with data privacy on a sectoral basis. There is no omnibus records of federal privacy statutes, and the method of protecting

---

[134] Ibid, art. 64.
[135] Ibid, art. 74.
[136] Civil Code, art. 120 and 1194.
[137] Zuigao renmin fayuan guanyu shenli liyong xinxi wangluo qinhai renshenquanyi minshi jiufen anjian shiyong falv ruogan wenti de guiding (最高人民法院关于审理利用信息网络侵害人身权益民事纠纷案件适用法律若干问题的规定) [Provisions of the Supreme People's Court on Several Issues Concerning the Application of Law in the Trial of Civil Disputes over the Use of Information Network to Infringe upon Personal Rights and Interests] (issued by Supreme People's Court on 23 June 2014, effective from 10 October 2014), art. 16.
[138] Ibid, art. 17.
[139] Ibid, art. 18.
[140] Cybersecurity Law, art. 74.

202   DATA PRIVACY IN MOBILE PAYMENT

personal information depends on the specific category of the information involved.

The categories covered under the federal laws include, among others, health care data (under the Health Insurance Portability and Accountability Act),[141] financial data (under the Gramm–Leach–Bliley Act),[142] children's information (under the Children's Online Privacy Protection Act),[143] consumer credit data (under the Fair Credit Reporting Act),[144] electronic communication data (under the Electronic Communications Privacy Act).[145] The FTC, which is the main regulatory body addressing privacy breaches,[146] 'fills in some of the statutory gaps' by taking actions against unfair and deceptive data protection practices.[147]

The pertinent laws for mobile payment privacy protection include the Gramm–Leach–Bliley Act and the FTC Act.[148] The Gramm–Leach–Bliley Act imposes several obligations of protecting consumers' non-public personal information from financial institutions engaging in financial activities. Financial institutions must provide consumers with 'clear and conspicuous' notice describing their privacy policies.[149] Financial institutions are generally not allowed to share non-public personal information with non-affiliated third parties unless they provide consumers with notice and an option to opt out,[150] nor can they share consumers' financial information to third parties for direct marketing.[151] Federal banking regulators are responsible for supervising depository institutions, and the FTC regulates all non-depository institutions.[152] Wrongdoers who 'knowingly and intentionally' obtain or disclose 'customer information

---

[141] 42 USC 1320d.

[142] 15 USC 6801–6809.

[143] 15 USC 6501 et Seq.

[144] 15 USC 1681–81t.

[145] 18 USC 2510–2522, 2701–2711, 3121–3126.

[146] FTC, 'Division of Privacy and Identity Protection', www.ftc.gov/about-ftc/bureaus-offices/bureau-consumer-protection/our-divisions/division-privacy-and-identity.

[147] FTC, 'Privacy and Security Enforcement,' www.ftc.gov/news-events/media-resources/protecting-consumer-privacy/privacy-security-enforcement; Daniel Solove and Woodrow Hartzog, 'The FTC and the New Common Law of Privacy' (2014) 114 *Columbia Law Review* 583, 587.

[148] 15 USC 41 et. seq.

[149] 15 USC § 6803(a); 12 C.F.R. §§ 1016.4–1016.6.

[150] 15 USC § 6802; 12 C.F.R. § 1016.10(a).

[151] 15 USC § 6802(d); 16 C.F.R. § 313.12(a).

[152] 15 USC § 6805(a)(1)–(7).

through false or fraudulent statements or representations will face criminal liability.[153]

The FTC Act gives the FTC authority to take actions against unfair and deceptive data protection practices. Generally speaking, an act or practice is unfair only if it 'causes or is likely to cause substantial injury to consumers which is not reasonably avoidable by consumers themselves and not outweighed by countervailing benefits to consumers or to competition'.[154] As for the concept 'deceptive', the FTC has clarified that an act or practice is to be considered deceptive if it involves a material 'representation, omission, or practice that is likely to mislead [a] consumer' who is 'acting reasonably in the circumstances'.[155]

Some scholars have pointed out that the FTC's enforcement approach is based on the principle of 'common law of privacy'.[156] Crucial to this principle is the idea of 'notice and choice' where companies are required to disclose their privacy policy enabling their users to make an informed choice.[157] Companies are bound by their data privacy and data security promises.[158] Companies act deceptively if they make false representations in order to induce disclosure of personal information,[159] or provide insufficient notice to their privacy practices.[160] Ultimately, the FTC has discretion in deciding whether a privacy practice is unfair or deceptive. The FTC can either bring administrative proceedings or civil proceedings. In an administrative proceeding, an administrative law judge may issue a cease and desist order prohibiting the wrongdoing company from engaging in any wrongful conduct.[161] In civil proceedings, the FTC can seek equitable relief or seek civil penalties if the party has violated a cease and desist order or consent decree.[162] The FTC Act does not provide a right to private action, nor does it provide a criminal sanction.

---

[153] 15 USC §§ 6821, 6823.

[154] 15 USC § 45(n).

[155] FTC, 'Policy Statement on Deception', 14 October, 1983, pp 1–2.

[156] Daniel Solove and Woodrow Hartzog, 'The FTC and the New Common Law of Privacy' (2014) 114 Columbia Law Review 583, 619.

[157] FTC, 'Protecting Consumer Privacy in an Era of Rapid Change', 2010, p 40, www.ftc.gov/ sites/default/files/documents/reports/federal-trade-commission-bureau-consumer-protec tion-preliminary-ftc-staff-report-protecting-consumer/101201privacyreport.pdf.

[158] Daniel Solove and Woodrow Hartzog, 'The FTC and the New Common Law of Privacy' (2014) 114 Columbia Law Review 583, 628.

[159] Ibid, p 630.

[160] Complaint, In the Matter of Sears Holdings Management Co., No. C-4264 (FTC, 31 August 2009).

[161] 15 USC §§ 45(a)(2), 45(b).

[162] 15 USC §§ 45(l)–(m).

In addition, all fifty states have enacted data breach notification statutes following the California Security Breach Notification Law with effect from 1 July 2003 to establish data breach notification mechanisms.[163]

6.4.2 The European Union

The right to data protection is one of the fundamental rights in the EU. This right is believed to be grounded in the concept of human dignity.[164] The stand-alone right to data protection marks one of the major differences between the United States and the EU in protecting personal data.[165]

The early history of the EU data protection law begins within individual European countries, such as Sweden (1973), the Federal Republic of Germany (1977), Austria (1978), Denmark (1978), France (1978) and Norway (1978).[166] In 1995, the EU started to harmonize the data privacy law and adopted the 95 Directive to protect the collection, use, process and exchange of personal data based on the recommendation proposed by the OECD.[167] The 95 Directive was replaced by the GDPR in 2018.[168]

Key principles of data protection in the GDPR are specified in Article 5, including the principles of lawfulness, fairness, transparency, purpose limitation, data minimization, accuracy, storage limitation, integrity and confidentiality and accountability. The GDPR requires data controllers and processors to have a lawful basis for processing personal data. These legal bases include consent, performance of the contracts, compliance with legal obligations, protection of vital interests of the data subject or another individual, tasks carried out in the public interest, and legitimate interests of the controllers or

---

[163] National Conference of State Legislatures, 'Security Breach Notification Laws', 2013, www.ncsl.org/research/telecommunications-and-information-technology/security-breach-notification-laws.aspx.

[164] Orla Lynskey, *The Foundations of EU Data Protection Law* (Oxford University Press, 2015), p 242.

[165] James Q. Whitman, 'The Two Western Cultures of Privacy: Dignity versus Liberty' (2004) 113 *Yale Law Review* 1151; Paul M. Schwartz, 'The EU–US Privacy Collision: A Turn to Institutions and Procedures' (2013) 126 *Harvard Law Review* 1966.

[166] Colin J. Bennett and Charles D. Raab, *The Governance of Privacy: Policy Instrument in Global Perspective* (MIT Press, 2006), p 127.

[167] Summaries of EU Legislation, 'Protection of Personal Data', https://eur-lex.europa.eu/legal-content/EN/TXT/?uri=LEGISSUM%3Al14012.

[168] Regulation (EU) 2016/679 of the European Parliament and of the Council of 27 April 2016 on the protection of natural persons with regard to the processing of personal data and on the free movement of such data, and repealing Directive 95/46/EC (General Data Protection Regulation) [2016] OJ L 119/1.

a third party.[169] The individuals have the right to be informed, right of access, right to rectification, right to be forgotten, right to restrict processing and right to data portability.[170] Data controllers are required to implement a range of measures designed to ensure the compliance with the GDPR, such as establishing GDPR-conforming contracts with data processors,[171] maintaining records of processing activities,[172] conducting impact assessments on personal data use,[173] and appointing a data protection officer.[174]

In the event of a personal data breach, the GDPR requires data controllers to notify the relevant authorities of any breach within seventy-two hours of discovering it.[175] The GDPR allows European data protection authorities to fine companies up to the higher of EUR 20 million or 4 per cent of their global turnover for the most severe category of data protection violations.[176] Individuals also have the right to lodge a complaint with regulatory authorities.[177] They can seek an effective judicial remedy against data controllers and processors, and obtain compensation for their damages suffered.[178]

The Payment Service Directive 2 (PSD2)[179] came into force on 12 January 2016, and the EU Member States were required to legislate it into national law by 13 January 2018.[180] The European Commission considered the PSD2 to be necessary to address the potential gaps in the regulatory regime for payment services. In terms of data protection, there are considerable overlaps between the PSD2 and the GDPR. The PSD2 reiterates the application of the 'principles of necessity, proportionality, purpose limitation and proportionate data retention period' to payment service providers.[181]

---

[169] Ibid, art. 6.
[170] Ibid, art. 12–23.
[171] Ibid, art. 28(3).
[172] Ibid, art. 30.
[173] Ibid, art. 35.
[174] Ibid, art. 37–39
[175] Ibid, art. 33.
[176] Ibid, art. 83(5)–(6).
[177] Ibid, art. 77.
[178] Ibid, art. 79 and 82.
[179] Directive (EU) 2015/2366 of the European Parliament and of the Council of 25 November 2015 on payment services in the internal market, amending Directives 2002/65/EC, 2009/110/EC and 2013/36/EU and Regulation (EU) No 1093/2010, and repealing Directive 2007/64/EC [2015] OJ L 337/35.
[180] PSD2, art. 115(2).
[181] Ibid, recital 89.

It is worth noting that the PSD2 lays out stricter obligations of data protection on third-party payment providers (including payment initiation service providers and account information service providers). Under the GDPR, personal data can only be collected for 'specified, explicit and legitimate purposes'.[182] By comparison, the PSD2 states that third-party payment providers can only access, process and retain personal data necessary for the provision of their payment services, with the explicit consent of the payment service user.[183] They are not allowed to 'use, access or store any data for purposes other than for performing their service explicitly requested by the customer'.[184] It essentially prohibits third-party payment providers from collecting ancillary information, which is not necessary for the service of payment or using the information for additional marketing purposes.

Under the PSD2, payment service providers are required to notify their home competent authority in the case of a 'major operational or security incident'.[185] Where the incident may have an impact on the financial interests of payment service users, payment service providers must also inform payment service users of the incident and requisite mitigation measures without undue delay.[186]

Additionally, the E-Privacy Directive[187] gives individuals specific protections in relation to online tracking issues, and it can be summarized as follows. First, unsolicited marketing by phone, email or other electronic messages may only be allowed if consumers have given their prior consent.[188] Secondly, service providers must obtain users' active and clear consent before setting cookies.[189] Thirdly, service providers must take appropriate measures to safeguard the security of their service, and they are obligated to notify the relevant authorities and consumers in the

---

[182] Ibid, art. 5(1)(b).

[183] Ibid, art. 94(2).

[184] Ibid, art. 66 and 67.

[185] Ibid, art. 96(1).

[186] Ibid, art. 96(1).

[187] Directive 2002/58/EC of the European Parliament and of the Council of 12 July 2002 concerning the processing of personal data and the protection of privacy in the electronic communications sector (Directive on privacy and electronic communications) [2002] OJ L 201/37.

[188] E-Privacy Directive, art. 13.

[189] Ibid, art. 5(3) and recital 24; European Commission, 'Cookie Policy' (explaining that a cookie is a small text file that a website stores on the user's computers or other devices when the user visits the site which allows the service providers to recognize that user's device and store some information about the user's preferences or past actions), https://ec.europa.eu/info/cookies_en.

6.4 INTERNATIONAL EXPERIENCES

case of a data breach.[190] Fourthly, subject to several exemptions,[191] service providers are obligated to erase or anonymize the data processed when no longer needed.[192]

6.4.3 Singapore

Singapore's key data protection law is the Personal Data Protection Act (PDPA)[193] which is structured around the fundamental principles of FIPs. These principles are very similar to those in the 2018 Specification and the GDPR and thus will not be discussed again here. The PDPA is enforced by the Personal Data Protection Commission who has the power to make orders to an organization to ensure its compliance with the PDPA and impose penalties not exceeding SGD 1 million.[194] Criminal penalties may also be imposed on organizations or individuals that obstruct the commission or its authorized delegate in the performance of its duties or powers under the PDPA.[195]

The PDPA provides several rights to individuals. They can give notice to the relevant organizations to withdraw their consent given or deemed to have been given in respect of collection, use or disclosure of their personal data.[196] Individuals have rights to access personal data[197] and to make corrections.[198] Besides, the PDPA provides for the right of an individual to take civil action against an organization if that individual suffers loss or damage as a result of a contravention of the PDPA.[199] The possible remedies include injunction, declaration, damages or other relief as the court thinks fit. The PDPA imposes very limited obligations on data processors. These obligations are restricted to the areas of data security[200] and data retention.[201]

The PDPA also establishes the Do Not Call Registry (DNCR) scheme, which allows individuals to opt out of receiving certain direct marketing

---

[190] Ibid, art. 4.
[191] Ibid, art. 15.
[192] Ibid, art. 6.
[193] Personal Data Protection Act (2012) (Singapore).
[194] Ibid, section 29.
[195] Ibid, part X.
[196] Ibid, section 16.
[197] Ibid, section 21.
[198] Ibid, section 22.
[199] Ibid, section 32.
[200] Ibid, section 24.
[201] Ibid, section 25.

messages. Section 40 of the PDPA states that 'a subscriber may apply to the commission, in the form and manner prescribed to add his Singapore telephone number to a register'.[202] The PDPA prohibits any person or organization from sending marketing messages to a number that is listed on the DNCR.[203] Fines of up to SGD 10,000 may be imposed on the failure to comply with the DNCR obligations.[204]

There are a very wide range of circumstances allowing for the collection, use, or disclosure of personal information without obtaining consent from data subjects (or allowing collection from third parties).[205] Many exemptions are phrased in very broad terms, which could give rise to significant legal uncertainty and undermine the effectiveness of such protection.

Unlike the EU or China, Singapore does not distinguish between general personal information and sensitive personal information. Therefore, there is no enhanced protection on sensitive personal information. Currently, under the PDPA there is no mandatory requirement for data users to notify authorities or data subjects about data breaches.

6.4.4 Hong Kong

The Personal Data (Privacy) Ordinance (PDPO) establishes Hong Kong's data protection legal framework.[206] All organizations that collect, hold process or use personal data must comply with the PDPO. Similar to the EU's approach, Hong Kong basically structures the PDPO around the FIPs.

Hong Kong has strengthened its regulation on direct marketing by adding relevant provisions into the PDPO, effective from 1 April 2013 Data users must obtain subjects' express consent before they use or transfer the data subjects' personal data for marketing purposes.[207] Non-compliance with the direct marketing provisions is an offence, and the highest penalties are a fine of HKD 500,000 and imprisonment for three years.[208] Under the PDPO, there is no mandatory requirement of data breach notification or the appointment of data protection officers. The

---

[202] Ibid, section 40.
[203] Ibid, section 43.
[204] Ibid, section 43.
[205] Ibid, section 17 and second to fourth schedules.
[206] Personal Data (Privacy) Ordinance (Hong Kong) (Cap. 486).
[207] Ibid, section 35E.
[208] Ibid, section 35E(4).

PDPO also fails to regulate data processors appointed by data users for the data process.

The sanctions under the PDPO are very limited. A contravention of the data protection principles does not in itself constitute a crime or result in any punishment. The Privacy Commissioner for Data Protection has the power to issue notices requiring data users to take steps to make corrections or prevent further violations.[209] Data users will only commit an offence if they fail to comply with the enforcement notice or violate the requirement again. In that case, the maximum fine is HKD 50,000 and imprisonment for two years.[210] If a data user contravenes more than one notice, the maximum penalty is a fine of HKD 500,000 and imprisonment for three years.[211]

6.5 Evaluation and Recommendations

6.5.1 Comparative Insights and Merits of the Chinese Law

The above examination of some major jurisdictions' data protection regimes shows that both the United States and the EU have well-established regulatory frameworks, but the EU's model is proven to be more influential in shaping other jurisdictions' data protection laws, such as those of Singapore and Hong Kong. We also note that the effectiveness of Singapore's data protection law is partially undermined by its wide exemption, while the sanctions under Hong Kong's data protection law are inadequate.

In the EU, the right to data protection is a fundamental right[212] and protected by a comprehensive set of legal rules. The GDPR has a wide scope of application, covering all natural or legal persons collecting and processing personal data. By comparison, in the United States, there is no unified data protection law and the respective data protection provisions are scattered among many laws that regulate different sectors. While the EU's data protection law is structured around data subjects' right to data protection, the United States' philosophy of data protection is based on the idea that consumers' interests should be protected against deception or unfairness.[213] Despite their different approaches, data protection laws

---

[209] Ibid, section 50.
[210] Ibid, section 50A.
[211] Ibid, section 50B.
[212] The Charter of Fundamental Rights of the European Union, art. 8.
[213] Paul M. Schwartz and Karl-Nikolaus Peifer, 'Transatlantic Data Privacy Law' (2017) 106 *Georgetown Law Journal* 115, 119.

on both sides are informed by the FIPs and share the core principles of fairness, lawfulness, transparency, data minimization, purpose limitation and so forth. But some principles in the United States are less stringent than those in the EU. One classic example is that data subjects in the United States are generally required to opt out to stop sharing their personal data with third parties rather than opt into the service. The underlying reason behind the less stringent requirements seems that the United States is trying to strike a balance between the internet economy innovation and the consumer protection.[214]

By comparing China's regulatory approach with other jurisdictions', we find that China started with a piecemeal approach resembling the US model but is now moving towards the EU's principle-based approach.[215] The 2018 Specification, as a comprehensive guide of data protection, substantially follows the GDPR's approach. Significantly, the Cybersecurity Law and the 2018 Specification widen the application scope, covering all organizations that collect and process personal data, and impose strict obligations of data protection on them.

In the context of mobile payment, the laws and regulations address the privacy risks of mobile payment, such as target advertising. For instance, 'the information that may reflect a specific person (without necessarily identifying) them'[216] now falls within personal information so that the collection and processing of personal data will be subject to the data protection requirements under the 2018 Specification. It would help to deal with target marketing, one of the major threats to the data privacy of mobile payments, particularly in the case where target marketing does not directly use the personally identifiable information but often uses software to build personal profiles excluding necessary identifiable information.[217]

The 2018 Specification deals with online tracking problems that are often considered intrusive and threatening to personal data privacy.

---

[214] Gina Stevens, 'Privacy Protections for Personal Information Online', 2011, Congressional Research Service, p 2.

[215] For a comprehensive discussion, see Emmanuel Pernot-Leplay, 'China's Approach on Data Privacy Law: A Third Way between the US and the EU?' (2020) 8 *Penn State Journal of Law & International Affairs* 49.

[216] Greenleaf Graham and Livingston Scott, 'China's Personal Information Standard: The Long March to a Privacy Law' (2017) 150 *Privacy Laws & Business International Report* 25, 26.

[217] Paul M. Schwartz and Daniel J. Solove, 'The PII Problem: Privacy and a New Concept of Personally Identifiable Information' (2011) 86 *New York University Law Review* 1814, 1854–1855.

6.5 EVALUATION AND RECOMMENDATIONS

Many online platform service providers would place cookies or similar tracking devices on users' equipment without their knowledge to track their online behaviour and usage patterns in order to develop a specific profile and provide consumers with tailored advertisements.[218] The 2018 Specification regards the information of online activities as sensitive information and requires service providers to obtain the users' opt-in consent before collecting such information.[219]

The 2018 Specification also makes a distinction between anonymized data and de-identified data.[220] It does not exclude the de-identified data from the scope of personal information as this type of datum may still be identified with the help of additional information.[221] The special mechanisms of protecting sensitive personal information are introduced, such as explicit consent from data subjects before collection,[222] encryption storage and transmission of sensitive information,[223] as well as special controls of accessing sensitive information.[224] Likewise, under the 2020 Specification, financial institutions should use de-identification, anonymization or encryption where necessary to protect the personal financial information after collection.[225]

In relation to the consent requirement, the 2018 Specification prohibits the bundle or forced consent.[226] Opt-in consent is required before the collection of sensitive information is allowed.[227] The principle of transparency is also strengthened. The disclosure statements are required to be presented in a concise, meaningful, timely and accessible manner.[228] A standardized short-form notice is introduced to allow users to digest privacy policies more easily.[229]

As discussed before, the PBOC has played a proactive role in strengthening data privacy protection for the financial industry. The 2020

---

[218] Ira S. Rubinstein, Ronald D. Lee and Paul M. Schwartz, 'Data Mining and Internet Profiling: Emerging Regulatory and Technological Approaches' (2008) 75 *University of Chicago Law Review* 261, 271.

[219] 2018 Specification, section 5.4(b).

[220] Ibid, sections 3.14 and 3.15.

[221] Paul Ohm, 'Broken Promise of Privacy: Responding to the Surprising Failure of Anonymization' (2010) 57 *UCLA Law Review*, 1701, 1716–1727.

[222] 2018 Specification, section 5.4(b).

[223] Ibid, section 6.3(a).

[224] Ibid, section 7.1(e).

[225] 2020 Specification, Section 6.1.

[226] Ibid, section 5.3(a).

[227] Ibid, section 5.4(o).

[228] Ibid, sections 5.5(b) and (c).

[229] Ibid, appendix D.

Specification represents the PBOC's more recent effort in this regard. It adds some industry-specific parameters by grading the personal financial information into three categories, which in turn require different protective measures. By doing so, it provides clearer guidance on data protection for the relevant institutions, including banks and non-bank payment institutions. In general, the 2020 Specification largely aligns with the 2018 Specification on the FIPs and specific technical requirements, such as de-identification, anonymization and encryption.

Overall, in relation to data privacy protection, the rules issued by the PBOC[230] are essentially intended to embody and specify the general regulatory requirements of data protection for the financial markets, and do not really introduce many new regulations. While the general regulatory regime can be used to deal with many privacy risks in mobile payment, some risks are much more acute for mobile payment users. Accordingly, it is important for the regulators to make specific rules to facilitate compliance and enforcement regarding the privacy issue in mobile payment.

6.5.2 Remaining Problems and Recommendations

6.5.2.1 Improving Certain Regulatory Requirements and Principles

For mobile payment, there are some remaining problems with the regulation, the chief among which is the ineffective requirements of consent and disclosure, the ambiguous principle of purpose limitation, and the limited applicability of the principle of data minimization. These problems need to be addressed in order to improve the efficacy of the regulation.

To begin with, while the disclosure requirement is crucial to data protection, the effectiveness of disclosure is undermined in the context of mobile payment. One major reason is that privacy policies are often provided in scrolling text boxes present on mobile phones' small

---

[230] For example, 'Feiyinhang Zhifu Jigou Wangluo zhifu yewu guanli banfa' (非银行支付机构网络支付业务管理办法) [The Management Measures of the Mobile Payment Business of the Non-bank Payment Institutions] (issued by the People's Bank of China on 28 December 2015, effective from 28 December 2015); 'Zhongguo renmin yinhang jinrong xiaofeizhe quanyi baohu shishi banfa (中国人民银行金融消费者权益保护实施办法) [Measures for the Protection of the Rights and Interests of Financial Consumers of the People's Bank of China] (issued by the People's Bank of China on 15 September 2020, effective from 1 November 2020).

6.5 EVALUATION AND RECOMMENDATIONS   213

screens.[231] They are often several pages long, and users usually would not spend considerable time reading the policies which are full of complex and technical terms before using a particular service. The inefficiency of the disclosure requirement further undermines the effectiveness of the consent requirement.[232] Although the 2018 Specification requires consumers' affirmative consent, many consumers may simply tick consent boxes without reading or understanding the policies.[233] The prohibition on bundle consent is mainly theoretical with little practical meaning, as a single collection request for its major mobile payment service will allow the mobile payment service providers to collect all the necessary information. If consumers refuse to accept the privacy policy, their access to the platform will be denied.

Inspired by the EU's approach, this chapter makes two recommendations to solve this issue. First, a multi-layered notice mechanism can be used. Specifically speaking, the essential information in relation to the data collection and processing should be presented in the initial notice to the consumers in a concise and readable manner.[234] It can be combined with the use of icons, images or videos. Further detailed information can be made available through hyperlinks.[235] The primary purpose of this approach is to allow consumers to quickly grasp the key information on the privacy policies. Secondly, we note that the mobile payment service providers usually make their service contingent upon consumers' acceptance of their privacy policy practices of extensively collecting their personal information (both financial and ancillary information). The problem with this 'take-it-or-leave-it' approach is, however, particularly unfair to the consumers in China where the mobile payment market is dominated by two giants – Alipay and WeChat Pay, and consumers do not have alternative choice but to accept their privacy policies. Therefore,

---

[231] Marla Blow, 'Statement for the Record of Marla Blow before the House Financial Services Subcommittee on Financial Institutions and Consumer Credit', 2012, House Financial Services Subcommittee, p 2, https://financialservices.house.gov/uploadedfiles/hhrg-112-ba15-wstate-cfpb-20120629.pdf.

[232] Bert-Jaap Koops, 'The Trouble with European Data Protection Law' (2014) 4(4) *International Data Protection Law* 250, 251.

[233] Marla Blow, 'Statement for the Record of Marla Blow before the House Financial Services Subcommittee on Financial Institutions and Consumer Credit', 2012, House Financial Services Subcommittee, p 2, https://financialservices.house.gov/uploadedfiles/hhrg-112-ba15-wstate-cfpb-20120629.pdf.

[234] Data Protection Working Party, 'Opinion 02/2013 on Apps on Smart Devices', art. 29, p 24, https://ec.europa.eu/justice/article-29/documentation/opinion-recommmendation/files/2013/wp202_en.pdf.

[235] Ibid.

like the requirement of the PSD2 in the EU, the data controllers should only collect and process personal data necessary for the provision of their payment services. Even if they intend to collect ancillary data for additional purposes (such as marketing purpose), a separate consent from consumers must be obtained.

Furthermore, the Cybersecurity Law does not contain the principle of purpose limitation. The 2018 Specification also fails to give a detailed definition of this principle except a simple statement that 'the use of personal information should not exceed the scope that is directly or reasonably related to the purpose claimed at the time of the collection of personal information'.[236] The issue is how to determine whether the purpose for which the data are originally collected and processed is directly or reasonably related to the purpose of further processing. For example, one privacy concern arising in mobile payment is target advertising. If we have booked a flight on an online platform, we may find that this platform will keep recommending advertisements on hotels after the booking. Would we say that this advertising is directly or reasonably relevant to the original purpose of collecting information which is supposed to be the execution of payment?

The EU's Article 29 Data Protection Working Party has provided a systematic approach to deal with this issue. When examining whether the additional purpose of processing data is directly or reasonably related to the original purpose, the following factors could be taken into consideration: whether the new purpose was already implied or a logical next step in the processing, whether the consumers expressly consented to the further processing, whether the processing involved sensitive personal information, and whether the controllers have adopted safeguards 'to ensure fair processing and to prevent any undue impact on the data subjects (e.g. anonymization, increased transparency, a possibility to object)'.[237] Another practical approach to deal with this problem is that a data controller could list the original purpose and the additional purposes of collecting and processing data, allowing consumers to opt in for the acceptable ones.

Last but not least, under the 2018 Specification, the principle of data minimization only applies to the stage of data collection.[238] By comparison,

---

[236] 2018 Specification, section 7.3.

[237] Data Protection Working Party, 'Opinion 03/2013 on Purpose Limitation', art. 29, p 2, https://ec.europa.eu/justice/article-29/documentation/opinion-recommendation/files/2013/wp203_en.pdf.

[238] 2018 Specification, section 5.2.

under the GDPR, the principle of data minimization does not only apply to data collection but applies to all types of data processing.[239] It is possible for information that is initially collected in a lawful manner under this principle to be illegally processed later. Therefore, it is important to ensure that all stages of data processing should comply with the principle of data minimization.

6.5.2.2 Establishing a Unified Data Protection Law and a Unified Enforcement Agency

Although China is moving towards a coherent legal structure on data protection, the relevant laws and regulations are still broad-brush and repetitive. The 2018 Specification and the 2020 Specification are not mandatory. No direct penalties would be applied for contravention of these two specifications. Although it can act as a reference for law enforcement authorities to decide compliance with various data protection rules, the authorities have latitude in their enforcement and this can create significant legal uncertainty. We can find that a unified data protection law is a global common practice. It is submitted that China should incorporate the basic principles and specific requirements of data protection into one unified law to reduce fragmentation of laws, strengthen consistency in enforcement, simplify the regulatory environment and reduce unnecessary costs and administrative burden. In light of our analysis of the efficiency of China's current data privacy protection regime, it is recommended that future legislation could be structured around two well-recognized axes.[240] The first one is privacy by design, where companies are obligated to comply with the data protection requirements at every stage of the development of products and services. The second axis is privacy by default where the data controllers make pre-existing choices on behalf of the data subjects regarding the data processing option, and in doing so, they must ensure that only the personal data that are necessary to achieve the purpose of the processing are enabled.

Apart from a unified data protection law, there is also a need for a unified enforcement agency, which is more efficiently structured to facilitate the enforcement of the law. Under China's current regulatory regime, there are multiple enforcement agencies responsible for enforcing the myriad statutory protections, including but not limited to, the

---

[239] GDPR, art. 5.

[240] Ibid, art. 25; as to the problems with art. 25, see Ira S. Rubinstein and Nathaniel Good, 'The Trouble with Article 25 (and How to Fix It): The Future of Data Protection by Design and Default' (2020) 10(1) *International Data Privacy Law* 37.

Cyberspace Administration of China, the Public Security Bureau and the MIIT. In addition, as non-bank financial institutions, mobile payment service providers are also subject to the regulation of both the PBOC and the CBIRC. The State Administration for Industry and Commerce has the responsibility to protect consumers' rights, including the right to data protection.

By examining the experiences of those overseas jurisdictions, we note that a unified law enforcement agency is a common practice in data privacy protection. However, in China, the enforcement could be hampered by the existence of multiple enforcement agencies authorized by different laws. This is illustrated by Alipay case which has been introduced above. As Ant Financial is subject to the regulation of multiple authorities, including the Cyberspace Administration of China, the MIIT and the PBOC, these authorities have taken different actions against the company. On 6 January 2018, the Security and Coordination Office of the Cyberspace Administration of China made inquiries into Ant Financial and Sesame Credit, concluding that Ant Financial failed to meet the data protection requirements set out in the 2018 Specification. On 11 January 2018, the Communication Management Office of the MIIT inquired into three technology companies – Alibaba Group, Baidu and ByteDance and reprimanded these companies for not giving sufficient notification to users on their privacy policies. These companies were requested to immediately rectify and improve their privacy policy to protect the users' rights and interests. On 22 March 2018, the Hangzhou Central Branch of the PBOC imposed an administrative fine of CNY 180,000 on Ant Financial on the basis that the data practice of Ant Financial failed to provide adequate protection for financial consumers' right to know and right to choose.

In sum, the lack of a single privacy law enforcement agency has caused conflict and friction between different authorities, leading to fragmented and incoherent decision-making. Different authorities may also bring actions for the same violation, which will not only result in a waste of regulatory and judicial resources but will also give rise to the issue of inconsistent judgements. Therefore, China should consider establishing a unified agency responsible for the enforcement of a unified data protection law.

6.5.2.3 Enhancing Both Public and Private Enforcement

As with any other areas of law, the effectiveness of the data protection regime depends on both substantive rules and enforcement strategies. In general, law enforcement strategies can be broadly divided into two modes, including public enforcement and private enforcement. Public enforcement is initiated by a state official such as a regulator or a prosecutor, while private enforcement is done so by a private party in the form of civil actions for compensation or rescission. These two modes of law enforcement have their own strengths and weaknesses. For instance, public enforcement has advantages vis-à-vis private enforcement in terms of the power to investigate and impose severe penalties. Private enforcement, however, has its own strengths. First, while the function of deterring misconduct is common to both public and private enforcement, private enforcement also has the important function of compensating victims that public enforcement usually cannot perform. Second, the efficacy of public enforcement depends highly on the organizational capacity and resources of the regulator. As discussed above, there is a need for China to establish a uniform regulator for data protection. Hence, China is advised to pursue both enforcement strategies in relation to the data protection law.

On the one hand, the private enforcement in the form of civil litigation is often sought on the basis of tort law, but a claimant may face many difficulties in pursuing the action. First, there can be an enormous imbalance of economic power and informational asymmetry between the aggrieved individuals and the organizational data controllers, which makes it difficult for the claimants to produce evidence and prove the tortious act. This problem may become particularly acute where the data controllers exclusively possess the impugned information. For instance, in the case of *Lin Nianping v. Sichuan Airlines Co., Ltd*, a passenger named Lin Nianping sued Sichuan Airlines for disclosing his personal information (including his name, phone number and flight information) to a third party who subsequently misled Lin Nianping to buy another air ticket.[241] The court found that Lin Nianping was an ordinary consumer who did not possess material evidence to prove the respondent's actual negligence of failing to protect personal data, whereas Sichuan Airlines Co Ltd was in a favourable position to provide the necessary evidence to prove otherwise. Lin Nianping had already proven a strong likelihood that the company disclosed the passenger's information, and it would be unfair to require him to further prove that Sichuan Airline Co Ltd was actually negligent. The reversal of the evidential burden has also been

---

[241] Lin Nianping yu Sichuan hangkong gufen youxian gongsi qinquan zeren jiufenan (林念平与四川航空股份有限公司侵权责任纠纷案)[*Lin Nianping v. Sichuan Airlines Co., Ltd* (regarding the dispute on tort liabilities)] (Chengdu Intermediate People's Court of Sichuan Province, civil (1634) 2015).

confirmed in *Pang Lipeng v. China Eastern Airlines Co., Ltd. and Beijing Qunar Information Technology Co., Ltd* [242] which was later compiled by the Supreme People's Court into the list 'The First Batch of Typical Cases Related to the Internet'.[243] The Supreme Court remarked that the claimant as an ordinary passenger did not have the ability to prove the respondents' negligence of failing to protect personal data, and the court cannot and should not require the claimant to prove that the respondent must have leaked the passenger's personal information. It was for the respondent to prove otherwise.

The second difficulty lies in the problem of proving concrete harm or loss suffered by the aggrieved party as 'the risk accompanying the collection, use, and dissemination of personal data is accumulative'.[244] Thirdly, even though the claimants could succeed in their claims, the courts may only award a small amount of damages. For example, in *Lin Nianping*, the court eventually ordered Sichuan Airline Co Ltd to make an apology and compensate Lin Nanping with CNY 5,648 (about USD 806).[245] In *Pang Lipeng*, the court only ordered an apology to be made.[246] It may discourage the aggrieved party from bringing private actions. Fourthly, many data practices, such as data harvesting and profiling, often take place in a nontransparent manner. Without the knowledge of how their data are misused, individuals cannot effectively protect their personal data on their own.

On the other hand, under the mode of public enforcement, the relevant competent departments may order the organizations to make

---

[242] Pang Lipeng su zhongguo dongfang hangkong gufen youxian gongsi, Beijing quna xinxi jishu youxian gongsi yinsiquan jiufenan (庞理鹏诉中国东方航空股份有限公司、北京趣拿信息技术有限公司隐私权纠纷案) [*Pang Lipeng v. China Eastern Airlines Co., Ltd. and Beijing Qunar Information Technology Co., Ltd* (regarding the dispute on right of privacy)] (The First Intermediate People's Court of Beijing, civil (509) 2017).

[243] 'Diyipi she hulianwang dianxing anli' (第一批涉互联网典型案例) [The First Batch of Typical Cases Related to the Internet] (issued by the Supreme People's Court of the PRC on 16 August 2018).

[244] Ding Xiaodong, 'Personal Data Protection: Rethinking the Reasons, Nature, and Legal Framework' (2018) 13 *Frontiers of Law in China* 380, 387.

[245] Lin Nianping yu Sichuan hangkong gufen youxian gongsi qinquan zeren jiufenan (林念平与四川航空股份有限公司侵权责任纠纷案)[*Lin Nianping v. Sichuan Airlines Co., Ltd* (regarding the dispute on tort liabilities)] (Chengdu Intermediate People's Court of Sichuan Province, civil (1634) 2015).

[246] Pang Lipeng su zhongguo dongfang hangkong gufen youxian gongsi, Beijing quna xinxi jishu youxian gongsi yinsiquan jiufenan (庞理鹏诉中国东方航空股份有限公司、北京趣拿信息技术有限公司隐私权纠纷案) [*Pang Lipeng v. China Eastern Airlines Co., Ltd. and Beijing Qunar Information Technology Co., Ltd* (regarding the dispute on right of privacy)] (The First Intermediate People's Court of Beijing, civil (509) 2017).

6.5 EVALUATION AND RECOMMENDATIONS

corrections, and can, according to the circumstances, confiscate any illegal income, and impose a fine of not less than one time and not more than ten times the illegal gains. If there are no illegal gains, a fine of not more than CNY 1 million shall be imposed, and the person in charge and other persons directly responsible shall be fined not less than CNY 10,000 but not more than CNY 100,000.[247] However, there are two issues with administrative fines. First, it may be easy to calculate the gains from the illegal trade in data but it would prove difficult to assess the unlawful gains made by internet companies. As discussed above, many internet companies, like Google and Facebook, do not trade in the personal data but use the data for target advertising and supply the data to develop their AI services, which can in turn generate new sources of profits. Assuming the data used in the development of AI services are illegally collected or processed, should we take into account the remote gains derived from the development of new technology? Secondly, the current level of fines in China is inadequate to act as a deterrent. In the Alipay case, Alipay was only fined CNY 180,000 (about USD 25,700) by the PBOC, which was negligible compared with this technology giant's annual revenue. By comparison, the GDPR allows European data protection authorities to fine companies up to the higher of EUR 20 million or 4 per cent of their global turnover for the most serious category of data protection violations.[248]

With the above observations, this chapter makes the following suggestions. First, given the massive asymmetry of information and evidential difficulties which limit the utility of private enforcement, this chapter suggests that a 'piggyback' mechanism be introduced whereby the private action follows and thus can piggyback on the public enforcement in relation to threshold questions, such as the occurrence of infringements and the guilt of relevant people.[249] Second, as most data privacy infringements are motivated by the pursuit of profits, substantial fines can be introduced to deter illegal uses of personal data.[250] To incentivize data controllers and data processors to comply with the requirements of data

---

[247] Cybersecurity Law, art. 64.

[248] GDPR, art. 83(5)–(6).

[249] A piggyback mechanism of this kind has been employed for the bringing of private securities litigation in China. For a detailed discussion of this mechanism, see Robin Hui Huang, 'Private Enforcement of Securities Law in China: A Ten-year Retrospective and Empirical Assessment' (2013) 61 *American Journal of Comparative Law* 757.

[250] Paul Nemitz, 'Fines under the GDPR', 2017, *CPDP 2017 Conference Book*, https://ssrn.com/abstract=3270535.

protection, future legislation should develop a system to determine fines for wrongdoers by taking into consideration economic and informational power of data controllers and processors, past acts of non-compliance and the risks to which personal data are exposed as a result of their illegal practices. Similarly, in the private enforcement, the compensation awarded to the victims could be calculated by reference to the extent to which the personal data are illegally collected and the risk to which the personal data are exposed in the illegal data practices.

6.6 Conclusion

Mobile payment has transformed the Chinese economy. While consumers are enjoying the great benefits provided by mobile payment, they are also plagued by the serious issue of data privacy risks. This chapter first examined the development of mobile payment in China, and the factors responsible for the heightened privacy risks of mobile payment. It found that the involvement of multiple players in mobile payment and extensive data harvesting contribute to these privacy risks. This chapter then discussed the transformation process of China's data protection regime, under which China started with a piecemeal approach and is now moving towards a principle-based framework. At present, China's data protection regime mainly comprises the Cybersecurity Law and relevant regulatory rules such as the 2020 Specification, which together set out the key regulatory elements such as the concept of personal information, the obligations for data controllers and processors, as well as the principles of the FIPs.

By examining the experiences of some overseas jurisdictions, including the United States, the EU, Singapore and Hong Kong, this chapter found that China's current regulatory approach bears more resemblance to that of the EU. The 2018 Specification, as a comprehensive guide to personal data security and privacy, substantially follows the GDPR's regulatory structure. China's current regulatory regime strengthens the standard of privacy protection and addresses a series of privacy issues arising from mobile payment, such as target advertising and online tracking. Despite China's efforts to enhance data privacy protection in the digital age, more needs to be done. This chapter made the following observations and suggestions. Firstly, there are some remaining issues, including, among others, the ineffective requirements of consent and disclosure, the ambiguous principle of purpose limitation, and the limited applicability of the principle of data minimization. Secondly, a unified law and a unified enforcement agency should be established to reduce the fragmentation of laws, strengthen consistency in enforcement, simplify the regulatory environment and reduce unnecessary costs and administrative burden. Finally, both private enforcement and public enforcement should be strengthened to compel data controllers to comply with the regulatory requirements.

7

Robo-Advisors

7.1 Introduction

'Fintech' has created new business models, including the fastest-growing robo-advisors.[1] Since 'Betterment', the first robo-advisor company, was founded in New York in 2010, various robo-advisor companies have proliferated to provide automated investment services. 'Robo-advisor', also known as the digital advisor or automated advisor, refers to 'the provision of financial advice in an online environment using algorithms and other technology tools'.[2] It is an AI-driven virtual financial advisor that uses algorithms, data-driven strategies and technology to provide financial services based on investors' risk tolerance.[3] As a more electronic and less 'hands-on' style of investing, robo-advisors have become a new trend in investment advisory and wealth management industries. Compared with human advisors, robo-advisors enjoy several important advantages, such as reducing costs by implementing a passive investment strategy, avoiding conflicts of interest and behavioural biases through algorithm analysis and providing services 24/7 for clients anywhere.[4]

---

[1] Kapronasia, 'Robo-Advisors in China', 2017, www.kapronasia.com/research/reports/robo-advisors-in-china.html.

[2] Hong Kong Securities and Futures Commission, Guidelines on Online Distribution and Advisory Platforms, 2019, p 14, www.sfc.hk/web/EN/assets/components/codes/files-current/web/guidelines/guidelines-on-online-distribution-and-advisory-platforms/guidelines-on-online-distribution-and-advisory-platforms.pdf.

[3] See Research Office of Legislative Council Secretariat, Regulation of Financial Technology in Selected Places, IN14/18–19, www.legco.gov.hk/research-publications/english/1819in14-regulation-of-financial-technology-in-selected-places-20190528-e.pdf; McCarthy Tétrault LLP, 'Regulation of Online Advisors: An International Overview', CyberLex, Lexology, 2019, www.lexology.com/library/detail.aspx?g=1da97f3a-ce71-4534-8b5a-13213e85f4c1.

[4] Chase T. Rourke, 'Leveraging the Competition: How Wealth Managers Can Use Robo-Advisors to their Advantage', *The University of Iowa's Institutional Repository*, Iowa Research Online, 2019, https://ir.uiowa.edu/honors_theses/308/.

7.1 INTRODUCTION

However, robo-advisors also bring risks because of their high dependence on technology and big data application. In the case of *Lowe v. SEC* in 1985, the US Supreme Court said that investment consulting organizations could not completely perform their basic functions unless all conflicts of interest were removed.[5] Hence, there is a need to strike a balance between promoting innovation and protecting investors. When regulation is effective in ensuring the independence of financial consulting companies, robo-advisors are advantageous in their ability to act without bias, emotions and conflicts of interest when furnishing advice for their clients.

The investment advisor regulatory regime in China's Securities Law[6] and other statutes were transplanted from overseas jurisdictions to regulate securities advising activities by relevant securities companies among others. On 8 July 2017, the 'New Generation of AI Development Plan' (*Xinyidai Rengong Zhineng Fazhan Guihua*, or 新一代人工智能发展规划 in Mandarin) was issued and implemented by the State Council, which aims to develop intelligence finance as one of its critical tasks. In the robo-advisory industry, China has certain advantages, such as strong consumer demand; but it also has many disadvantages, such as more serious regulatory risks.

This chapter aims to analyse the issues of the current regulation of robo-advisors in China and give suggestions for future developments. It recommends establishing a uniform piece of legislation for both human and AI investment advisors, which would contain additional requirements for robo-advisors by applying consistent standards as human advisors. The purpose is to establish a relationship of trust and confidence between investors and investment advisors. This research also recommends that regulations of the investment advisory business and asset management business be unified to facilitate the development and evolution of investment advisors and robo-advisors in the financial market. This chapter only focuses on robo-advisors that provide investment services directly to clients. Other types of robo-advisors that provide data analysis to human advisors or publish analyses to the public are not covered.

---

[5] *Lowe v. SEC*, 472 US 181 (1985).

[6] Zhonghua Renmin Gongheguo Zhengquan Fa (中华人民共和国证券法) [Securities Law of the People's Republic of China] (promulgated by the Nat'l People's Cong., 29 December 1998 effective 1 July 1999, amended in 2004, 2005, 2013, 2014 and 2019) [hereinafter Securities Law]. The revisions of the Securities Law in 2005 and 2019 were comprehensive overhauls.

7.2 Background: Concept and Market Development

7.2.1 Market Development

The robo-advisory industry has been growing rapidly in the past ten years. When the two pioneer companies, Betterment and Wealthfront, were established in 2008,[7] the United States became the first country to have robo-advisors. This was a response to the loss of trust of investors in financial institutions in the aftermath of the 2008 global financial crisis. Since then, traditional institutions started to enter the robo-advisory market, e.g. Fidelity, Blackrock and Credit Swiss. The total assets under management have surpassed USD 1 trillion in 2020, compared with USD 250 billion in 2017, and the number is expected to reach USD 2.7 trillion by 2024, with 430 million users. The value of assets under management by robo-advisors in the United States has reached a total amount of USD 1.05 trillion in 2020, followed by China (USD 312 billion) and the United Kingdom (USD 24 billion).[8]

According to Deloitte, there are four phases in the evolution of robo-advisors.[9] Robo-advisors available in the market nowadays belong to the fourth phase, which is named 'robo-advisor 4.0'. The distinctive feature of robo-advisor 4.0 is that the machine is equipped with self-learning AI, enabling the machine to automatically adjust clients' investment portfolios according to changing market conditions.

Since the first robo-advisor platform was launched in 2015, there are currently more than thirty robo-advisor platforms in China, such as Capricorn Intelligent Investment (Mojie Zhitou or 摩羯智投 in Mandarin).[10] In 2016, there were more than 300 million internet financial customers in China. With low costs and the ability to disperse risks, robo-

---

[7] L. Reiners, 'Regulation of Robo-advisory Services', in Jelena Madir (ed), *FinTech: Law and Regulation* (Edward Elgar, 2019), p 355.

[8] Statista, 'Robo-Advisers Worldwide', 2020, www.statista.com/outlook/337/100/robo-advisors/worldwide.

[9] Deloitte classifies the evolution of robo-advisors into four stages: at stage 1.0, the robo-advisors provides product or portfolio investment proposal based on online questionnaire; stage 2.0 involves fund management, risk-based portfolio allocation, managed adjustments and rebalancing; stage 3.0 includes pre-defined investment rule-sets, and stage 4.0 includes fully automated investments, self-learning algorithms and automatic asset shifts. See Deloitte, 'The Expansion of Robo-Advisory in Wealth Management', 2016, www2.deloitte.com/content/dam/Deloitte/de/Documents/financial-services/Deloitte-Robo-safe.pdf.

[10] Zheng Jianing (郑佳宁), 'Lun Zhineng Tougu Yunyingzhe De Minshi Zeren' (论智能投顾运营者的民事责任) [On the Civil Liability of Robo-Advisor Operators: An Expansion Centering on Fiduciary Duties], (2018) 39(010) *Faxue Zazhi* (法学杂志) [Law Science Magazine] 62.

advisors can meet financial needs of the public. At present, commercial banks increasingly begin to enter this business.[11] Assets under the management of robo-advisors are estimated to reach USD 74,000 million in 2020 and show an annual growth rate of 15.2 per cent from 2020 to 2024.[12] On 8 July 2017, the 'New Generation of AI Development Plan' was issued and implemented by the State Council, with the development of intelligent finance as one of its key tasks. It requires China's financial industry to gradually build big data systems, innovate intelligent products and services, and improve early warning mechanisms with the help of AI technology.[13] The plan implies a new era of AI and robo-advisor development in China.

7.2.2 The Workings of Robo-Advisors

To formulate investment decisions and manage clients' assets, robo-advisors typically work through several stages.[14] These stages include the following aspects. The first stage is completing an online questionnaire. Clients are usually required to complete a standard online questionnaire designed to collect relevant information such as their investment goals and capacity to tolerate risks. For instance, they may be asked about their reaction to market fluctuations and the time required for return. The second stage is making recommendations. Upon receiving replies to the questions, the algorithms will make recommendations on the allocation of funds accordingly based on the modern portfolio theory. The portfolio's optimization is adjusted by considering investment goals and the desired risk level. The third stage is transferring funds. The investors transfer their funds into an account owned by the platform, which will be further transferred to a bank or a third-party payment institution for custody. The fourth stage is rebalancing the portfolios. The platform monitors the asset status in

---

[11] Zhongguo Chanye Xinxi Wang (中国产业信息网) [China Industrial Information Network], 'Zhongguo Zhineng Tougu Hangye Fazhan Gaikuang Guanli Zichan Guimo Ji Hangye Fazhan Qianjing Fenxi Yuce' (中国智能投顾行业发展概况、管理资产规模及行业发展前景分析预测) [Analysis and Forecast on the Development Situation, Management Assets Scale and Industry Development Prospect of China's Intelligent Investment Consulting Industry], 2019, www.chyxx.com/industry/201905/735150.html.

[12] Statista, 'Robo-Advisors', 2020, www.statista.com/outlook/337/117/robo-advisors/china.

[13] Guowuyuan (国务院) [The State Council], Guowuyuan Guanyu Yinfa Xinyidai Rengong Zhineng Fazhan Guihua De Tongzhi (国务院关于印发新一代人工智能发展规划的通知) [The State Council Issued the Notice on Development Plan of New Generation Artificial Intelligence], 2020, www.gov.cn/zhengce/content/2017-07/20/content_5211996.htm.

[14] Abraham Facundo et al, 'Robo-Advisors: Investing through Machines' (2019) 21 Research & Policy Briefs World Bank Group 1.

real-time in light of changing market situations, adjusts the asset portfolio according to the risk profile of investors in a timely manner, and automatically balances the asset allocation on a continuous basis.

In the process above, algorithms are used to create and refine clients' portfolios to satisfy pre-defined investment strategies which are subject to changes by sophisticated AI learning processes. Human advisors and programmers play a supervising role in overseeing such algorithms. The extent to which human factors are involved varies greatly from robo-advisor to robo-advisor. Some conventional human advisors use robo-advisors for data analyses only (i.e., hybrid-robo-advice) while other robo-advisors operate independently. Nonetheless, the ultimate aim is to minimize human interaction so that both investors and human advisors can adopt a hands-free approach without the need to closely monitor the market.

Specifically, the robo-advisory services available in the market could be broadly categorized into three groups: (1) full automation (advice given with zero human intervention), (2) advisor-assisted (clients could opt to contact an advisor when needed), and (3) guided advice (human advisor provides investment advice with the assistance of the technology tool).[15] Based on whether the robo-advisor offers automatic account management and the category of products the robo-advisor can recommend, Chinese robo-advisors can be categorized into three models: (1) the 'classic model', under which robo-advisors have to work in conjunction with overseas firms to provide auto-account management; (2) the 'asset allocation advisory model' or 'portfolio recommendation model', which focuses on open-end mutual funds but does not provide auto-account management services to clients; (3) the 'specific stock recommendation model', which focuses on equity investment but does not provide auto-account management services to clients.[16]

Furthermore, according to the operational model, China's robo-advisor platforms can be generally divided into three categories: (1) robo-advisor platforms that rely on traditional financial companies, such as Capricorn Intelligent Investment which is affiliated with China Merchants Bank (Zhaoshang Yinhang or 招商银行 in Mandarin); (2) robo-advisor platforms that rely on internet financial

---

[15] Hong Kong Securities and Futures Commission, Guidelines on Online Distribution and Advisory Platforms, 2019, p. 14, www.sfc.hk/web/EN/assets/components/codes/files-current/web/guidelines/guidelines-on-online-distribution-and-advisory-platforms/guidelines-on-online-distribution-and-advisory-platforms.pdf.

[16] Li Guo, 'Regulating Investment Robo-Advisors in China: Problems and Prospects', (2020) 21 *European Business Organization Law Review* 69.

7.2 BACKGROUND

Table 7.1 *A comparison of robo-advisory services between China and the United States*

	United States	China
Characteristics and habits of financial customers	Institutional investors, long-term investment	Retail investors, speculative short-term investment
Maturity of the financial market	More categories of products and robust market	Fewer categories of products and immature market
Taxation system	Multiple systems of taxation	No basis of tax plans
Policy regulation	Unified regulation of asset management and investment consulting businesses	Segregated regulation of asset management and investment consulting businesses

Note: From Mo Tao (莫涛), Shendu Zhineng Tougu De Fazhan Xianzhuang He Weilai Fazhan Qushi (深度：智能投顾的发展现状和未来发展趋势) [Depth: Development Status and Future Development Trend of Intelligent Investment Consulting], (2017), www.sohu.com/a/128152366_454523.

companies or wealth management companies, such as Tonghuashun IFind Intelligent Investment Consultants (Tonghuashun IFind Zhineng Touzi Guwen or 同花顺iFind智能投资顾问 in Mandarin); (3) independent robo-advisor platforms, such as financial manager Rubik's cube (Licai Mofang or 理财魔方 in Mandarin).[17]

In practice, there are certain unique characteristics about China's robo-advisory service users. For example, investors generally lack the habit of long-term investment and asset allocation and are accustomed to retail investors' operation modes in financial asset investment. They are generally unwilling to provide real asset information, so the effectiveness of the platform's risk testing is weakened. The available investment amount from the investors' funds is usually low (Table 7.1)[18]

---

[17] Gao Simin (高丝敏), 'Zhineng Touzi Guwen Moshi Zhong De Zhuti Shibie He Yiwu Sheding' (智能投资顾问模式中的主体识别和义务设定) [Subject Identification and Obligation Setting in the Mode of Intelligent Investment Consultant], (2018) 040(005) *Faxue Yanjiu* (法学研究) [Chinese Journal of Law] 40.

[18] Zhongguo Chanye Xinxi (中国产业信息), 'Erlingyiba Nian Zhongguo Zhineng Tougu De Fazhan Xianzhuang Ji Weilai Fazhan Qushi Fenxi' (2018年中国智能投顾的发展现

7.2.3 Benefits and Risks

Automated investment advice firms have brought significant benefits by improving the delivery of high-quality and less-biased financial advice, as well as accelerating changes in the asset management industry.[19] Robo-advisors can deliver financial advice at a fraction of the cost associated with traditional financial services, which would be a viable option for retail investors.[20]

Robo-advisors in China have great potential benefits in facilitating financial market development. First, the investment threshold is relatively low, and target clients are widespread. By contrast, traditional investment consultants only serve high-net-wealth individuals. Second, service fees are relatively low. Most robo-advisors in China adopt free marketing strategies, which can benefit most financial customers. Third, robo-advisors in China are more rational and professional than traditional advisors. They can eliminate the influences of human nature and emotion on investment and effectively avoid moral hazards.[21]

China has certain advantages in robo-advisory services, including strong consumer demands, a rapidly rising middle class, and a shift towards investment products outside of deposits. Chinese investors are generally very open to AI investment services because AI has already been an integral part of Chinese people's everyday life. Some surveys show that more than half of Chinese investors have expressed their willingness to try new products and new business models. The proportion of Chinese investors who have tried robo-advisory investment services is over 30 per cent.[22] These attributes of the Chinese market make robo-advisors more useful and beneficial in the near future.

状及未来发展趋势分析) [Analysis on the Development Status and Future Development Trend of China's Intelligent Investment Consulting in 2018], 2018, www.chyxx.com /industry/201801/606479.html.

[19] Benjamin P. Edwards, 'The Rise of Automated Investment Advice: Can Robo-Advisers: Can Robo-Advisers Rescue the Retail Market' (2018) 93 *Chicago-Kent Law Review* 97

[20] Philipp Maume, 'Regulating Robo-Advisory', (2019) 55 *Texas International Law Journal* 49.

[21] Xue Zhisheng (薛智耘) and Wang Ting (王婷), 'Woguo Zhineng Tougu De Fazhan Tiaozhan Jiqi Jianguan Huiying' (我国智能投顾的发展、挑战及其监管回应) [The Development, Challenge and Regulatory Response of Intelligent Investment Advisors in China], (2019) 10(1) *Jinrong Fuwu Fa Pinglun* (金融服务法评论) [Comments on Financial Services Law].

[22] GlobalData Financial Services, 'China's Robo-advice Space Leads the Way', 2019, www .verdict.co.uk/private-banker-international/comments/china-robo-advisors-lead-way/

Despite potential benefits, there are also serious concerns over robo-advisors' automated investment practice. Even if the algorithm is not flawed, its reliability in a bear market is doubtful. In addition to potential conflicts of interests between robo-advisory firms and their clients, inexperienced customers might misunderstand the software's queries or misinterpret its advice.[23] Robo-advisors in China have a relatively low level of service quality and their development faces many serious problems, such as weakened wealth management function, inadequate risk assessment and insufficient information disclosure.[24] First, China's securities investment consultants only provide investment advice and cannot obtain authorization to entrust clients' accounts. According to the Securities Law, securities investment consulting institutions shall not make investment decisions on behalf of their clients.[25] Second, some robo-advisors in China have certain deficiencies in forming a comprehensive, accurate and objective understanding of customers' risk status, which are mainly reflected in the customers' financial status and know-your-product requirement. Third, at present, the information disclosure system for robo-advisors in China is still immature, which results in more conflicts of interest and algorithm risks.[26] In terms of investor protection and financial market regulation, China only sets out principle-based requirements for investment consultants in relation to client eligibility criteria. There are no unified, nor specific standards in terms of investor classification, product classification or the need for a comprehensive understanding of customer obligations. The Chinese law also does not mention the special provisions on the suitability requirements for robo-advisors.[27]

[23] Philipp Maume, 'Regulating Robo-Advisory', (2019) 55 *Texas International Law Journal* 49.

[24] Guo Li (郭雳), 'Zhineng Tougu Kaizhan De Zhidu Quzhang Yu Falv Zhutui' (智能投顾开展的制度去障与法律助推) [To Boost the Robo-advisor in China: Removing Institutional Obstacles and Ameliorating Legal Conditions], (2019) 037(C03) *Zhengfa Luntan* (政法论坛) 184.

[25] 2020 Securities Law, art. 161.

[26] Guo Li (郭雳), 'Zhineng Tougu Kaizhan De Zhidu Quzhang Yu Falv Zhutui' (智能投顾开展的制度去障与法律助推) [To Boost the Robo-advisor in China: Removing Institutional Obstacles and Ameliorating Legal Conditions], (2019) 037(C03) *Zhengfa Luntan* (政法论坛) 184. Although not enough, there have been requirements of disclosing conflicts of interests over robo-advisors in the United States. It is argued that the SEC should shift its focus from advice quality to conflict of interest issues. See Megan Ji, 'Are Robots Good Fiduciaries: Regulating Robo-Advisors under the Investment Advisers Act of 1940' (2017) 117 *Colum. L. Rev.* 1543.

[27] Guo Li (郭雳), 'Zhineng Tougu Kaizhan De Zhidu Quzhang Yu Falv Zhutui' (智能投顾开展的制度去障与法律助推) [To Boost the Robo-advisor in China: Removing

7.3 Regulatory Framework

7.3.1 Overview

The New Generation of AI Development Plan clearly defines the development goals and strategies of AI in Mainland China. To improve the efficacy of the investment advisory regime, reform efforts in China have been made over the years to facilitate the prosperity of robo-advisors against the background of AI development. In principle, robo-advisors are regulated under the same legislative framework and by comparable standards as human advisors, because the law is technology-neutral.[28] The US SEC defined robo-advisors as 'typically registered investment advisors' registerable under the Investment Advisor Act of 1940.[29] In China, there is no legal definition of 'robo-advisor' under the existing law. The CSRC, the Chinese securities market's watchdog, stated in its official website that 'robo-advisors' providing services related to securities and futures are deemed to engage in securities investment consulting businesses and should obtain securities and futures business permits from the CSRC.[30] Article 160 of the Securities Law requires that whoever provides securities investment consulting services shall be subject to the approval of the CSRC.[31]

To enforce the Securities Law, the CSRC and other relevant government departments have separately and jointly issued several statutes to regulate investment consultants. Specifically, the traditional main statutes regulating advisors are 'the Interim Measures for the Administration of Securities and Futures Investment Consultation' (the 1998 Investment Consultation Measures)[32] and 'the Interim Provisions on Securities Investment Advisor

---

Institutional Obstacles and Ameliorating Legal Conditions], (2019) 037(003) *Zhengfa Luntan* (政法论坛) 184.

[28] Tom Baker and Benedict G. C. Dellaert, 'Regulating Robo Advice across the Financial Services Industry' (2018) 103 *Iowa Law Review* 713.

[29] The US Securities and Exchange Commission Division of Investment Management, IM Guidance Update No. 2017-02, 2017, www.sec.gov/investment/im-guidance-2017-02 .pdf.

[30] CSRC, 'Jingti Zhineng Tougu Feifa Touzi Zixun Xianjing' (警惕'智能投顾'非法投资咨询陷阱') [Be Wary of the Illegal Investment Advisory Traps of Robo-Advisors], 2015, www.csrc.gov.cn/pub/shanxidong/ztzl/djffzqhd/201608/t20160801_301505.htm.

[31] 2020 Securities Law, art. 160.

[32] Zhengquan Qihuo Touzi Zixun Guanli Zanxing Banfa (证券、期货投资咨询管理暂行办法) [Interim Procedures on Administration of Securities and Futures Investment Consultancy] (promulgated by the Securities Commission of the State Council, 25 December 1997, effective 1 April 1998) [hereinafter Investment Consultation Measures]. The Securities Commission of the State Council was a predecessor of the CSRC.

Business' (the 2020 Investment Advisor Provisions).[33] In the new era of AI, the robo-advisor's regulatory statute is 'the Interim Provisions on Strengthening the Supervision over Securities Investment Consulting Services Using Stock Picking Software' (the 2020 Stock Picking Software Provisions).[34] To further improve the regulation of advisors' asset management functions, several ministry-level governmental departments jointly issued 'the Guiding Opinions on Regulating the Asset Management Business of Financial Institutions' (the 2018 Asset Management Guiding Opinions).[35]

To a lesser extent, some other statutes are relevant to robo-advisors as well, including the Regulation on the Supervision and Administration of Securities Companies ('the 2014 Securities Companies Regulation'),[36] the Interim Provisions on the Release of Securities Research Reports (the 2020 Release of Reports Provisions),[37] and 'the Standards of Practice for Securities Investment Consulting Institutions (for Trial Implementation)' issued by the Securities Association of China (the 2019 Notice of Standards).[38]

---

[33] Zhengquan Touzi Guwen Yewu Zanxing Guiding (证券投资顾问业务暂行规定) [Interim Provisions on the Securities Investment Advisor Business] (promulgated by the China Securities Regulatory Commission, 12 October 2010, effective 1 January 2011, amended 20 March 2020) [hereinafter Investment Advisor Provisions].

[34] Guanyu Jiaqiang Dui Liyong Jiangu Ruanjian Congshi Zhengquan Touzi Zixun Yewu Jianguan De Zanxing Guiding (关于加强对利用'荐股软件'从事证券投资咨询业务监管的暂行规定) [Interim Provisions on Strengthening the Supervision over Securities Investment Consulting Services Using 'Stock Picking Software'] (promulgated by the China Securities Regulatory Commission, 5 December 2012, effective 1 January 2013, amended 20 March 2020) [hereinafter Stock Picking Software Provisions].

[35] Guanyu Guifan Jinrong Jigou Zichan Guanli Yewu De Zanxing Guiding (关于规范金融机构资产管理业务的指导意见) [Guiding Opinions on Regulating the Asset Management Business of Financial Institutions] (promulgated by the People's Bank of China, the China Banking and Insurance Regulatory Commission, the China Securities Regulatory Commission, and the State Administration of Foreign Exchange, 27 April 2018, effective 27 April 2018) [hereinafter Asset Management Guiding Opinions].

[36] Zhengquan Gongsi Jiandu Guanli Tiaoli (证券公司监督管理条例) [The Regulations on the Supervision and Administration of Securities Companies] (promulgated by the the State Council, 23 April 2008, effective 1 June 2008, amended 29 July 2014) [hereinafter Securities Companies Regulation].

[37] Fabu Zhengquan Yanjiu Baogao Zanxing Guiding (发布证券研究报告暂行规定) [The Interim Provisions on the Release of Securities Research Reports] (promulgated by the China Securities Regulatory Commission, 12 October 2010, effective 1 January 2011, amended 20 March 2020) [hereinafter Release of Reports Provisions].

[38] Zhengquan Touzi Zixun Jigou Zhiye Guifan (Shixing) De Tongzhi (证券投资咨询机构执业规范(试行)) [The Standards of Practice for Securities Investment Consulting Institutions (for Trial Implementation)] (promulgated by the Securities Association of China, 3 June 2019, effective 3 June 2019).

The CSRC and its locally dispatched offices are the public enforcers of the above Chinese laws and the supervisors and administrators of the advisor business in China. They may take regulatory measures when an investment advisor or its personnel violates relevant legal provisions. The available punishment tools stipulated by the laws include 'correction', 'regulatory talk', 'letter of warning', 'submission of a compliance inspection report', 'disciplinary action against the relevant person' and so on.[39]

Other relevant financial regulatory authorities can also enforce relevant rules in their own capacity, such as the PBOC, the CBIRC and the State Administration of Foreign Exchange (SAFE). These ministry-level governmental departments under the State Council jointly issued the 2018 Asset Management Guiding Opinions together with the CSRC and have separate regulatory powers in the current sector-based Chinese financial regulatory structure.[40] As a self-disciplinary industry association, the Securities Association of China (SAC) is required to conduct self-disciplinary management of the advisor business by law.[41]

7.3.1.1 The Regulation of Traditional Advisors

The Securities Law requires that whoever provides securities investment consulting services shall be subject to the approval of the CSRC.[42] A securities investment consulting institution and its employees that provide securities trading services shall not make securities investment as an agent on behalf of the client. Otherwise, the service provider shall assume compensatory liability under the law for losses of investors.[43]

The 1998 Investment Consultation Measures is the first such instrument that regulates the securities consultancy business in China. 'Securities and futures investment consultancy' means direct or indirect paid consultancy services such as securities and futures investment analyses, forecasts, or suggestions given by institutions engaged in securities and futures investment consultancy and their consultants to securities and futures investors or clients.[44] The scope of applicable products is

---

[39] 2020 Investment Advisor Provisions, art. 33.

[40] Huang Hui (黄辉), 'Zhongguo Jinrong Jianguan Tizhi Gaige De Luoji Yu Lujing Guoi Jingyan Yu Bentu Xuanze' (中国金融监管体制改革的逻辑与路径：国际经验与本土选择) [The Logics and Path of China's Financial Regulatory Structure: International Experiences and Local Choice], (2019) 2019(3) *Faxuejia* (法学家) [Jurist] 124.

[41] 2020 Investment Advisor Provisions, art. 6.

[42] 2020 Securities Law, art. 160.

[43] Ibid, art. 161.

[44] 1998 Investment Consultation Measures, art. 2. The business can be conducted through the following means: (1) commissioned by investors or clients to provide investment

limited to 'securities and futures', which is relatively narrower than 'financial products'. It indicates that the legislators at that time were more cautious and conservative in regulating investment consultants. Despite the historical confinement, this provision is broad enough to cover various forms of robo-advisors in the securities and futures investment consultancy business.

To provide detailed rules for securities investment advisors, the Investment Advisor Provisions was issued and revised. The 'securities investment advisor business' is viewed as a basic form of the securities investment consulting business, which is under the regulation of the 1998 Investment Consultation Measures. 'Securities investment advisor business' means that a securities company or securities investment consulting agency provides investment advisor services involving securities and securities-related products to clients to assist them in making investment decisions and obtain economic benefits directly or indirectly. The advisor services mainly include three categories: the provision of advice on investment product selection, investment portfolio and wealth management plans.[45]

Compared with the 1998 Investment Consultation Measures, the regulatory scope of the 2020 Investment Advisor Provisions is focused on 'securities'. The providers of such services are limited to securities companies or securities investment consulting agencies. The services provided involve securities and securities-related products. Thus, the 2020 Provisions are narrower than the 1998 Investment Consultation Measures, because the latter regulates the provision of consultancy for futures transactions as well as securities transactions.

7.3.1.2 The Stock Picking Software Provisions

The CSRC stated in its official website that the Stock Picking Software Provisions are the primary regulatory tool for robo-advisors,[46] which were issued in 2013 and revised in 2020 as an official regulatory response

---

consultancy services; (2) undertaking lectures, seminars and analysing meetings in respect of investment consultancy; (3) publishing articles, commentaries and reports in newspapers and magazines, or providing investment consultancy services through radio stations, television stations and other media; (4) providing investment consultancy services through telephone, facsimile, computer networks and other telecommunications systems; (5) other means as determined by the CSRC.

[45] 2020 Investment Advisor Provisions, art. 2.

[46] CSRC, 'Jingti Zhineng Tougu Feifa Touzi Zixun Xianjing' (警惕'智能投顾'非法投资咨询陷阱) [Be Wary of the Illegal Investment Advisory Traps of Robo-Advisors], 2016, www.csrc.gov.cn/pub/shanxidong/ztzl/djffzqhd/201608/t20160801_301505.htm.

to the rapid development of robo-advisors in China. Accordingly, the term 'stock picking software' means software products, software tools, or terminal units with one or more securities investment consulting service functions which means the provision of the following types of information: (1) investment analysis opinions regarding specific securities investment varieties or predicting the price trend of specific securities investment varieties; (2) suggestions on the selection of specific securities investment varieties; (3) suggestions on the trading opportunities for specific securities investment varieties; (4) any other securities investment analysis, predictions or suggestions.[47]

The 2020 Stock Picking Software Provisions clarify that selling or providing the 'stock picking software' falls under the securities investment consulting business. Where the Stock Picking Software Provisions do not provide specific rules, the service providers must abide by the Securities Law, the Investment Consultation Measures, the Investment Advisor Provisions and other relevant rules of the CSRC.[48] No institution or individual without the qualification for engaging in the investment consulting business may engage in businesses using a 'stock picking software'.[49]

The 2020 Stock Picking Software Provisions also provide detailed rules on the fiduciary duties and information disclosure duties of robo-advisors. The service providers using 'stock picking software' shall adhere to the principles of objectiveness, impartiality and good faith, and shall not mislead or defraud clients or infringe upon clients' interests.[50] The necessary information shall be publicized on the company's business premises.[51] The clients should be informed of the most important software issues, such as the software's role and limitations, the dispute settlement methods and the potential risks and hazards in an objective and accurate manner.[52]

7.3.1.3 The Asset Management Guiding Opinions

It is a great pity that the 1998 Investment Consultation Measures exclude asset management businesses from the investment consulting business.

---

[47] Software products gathering securities information or statistics on historical data without the functions of providing securities investment analysis, predictions or suggestions are excluded from 'stock picking software'. See 2020 Stock Picking Software Provisions, art. 1.

[48] Ibid, art. 4.

[49] Ibid, art. 2.

[50] Ibid, art. 3.

[51] Ibid, art. 4.

[52] Ibid, art. 5.

To facilitate the development of asset management businesses and to allow the robo-advisor industry to boom, the Asset Management Guiding Opinions were issued jointly by the PBOC, the CBIRC, the CSRC and the SAFE, allowing robo-advisors to conduct asset management business in China.

Under the 2013 Asset Management Guiding Opinions, 'asset management business' means financial services provided by a financial institution to invest and manage its clients' entrusted assets.[53] The asset management business is the off-balance-sheet business of financial institutions. To deal with the problem of rigid repayment, no financial institution in the asset management business shall undertake to guarantee principal and returns.[54] Asset management products shall either be publicly offered to the general public or privately offered to qualified investors.[55] Investors shall be divided into the general public and qualified investors. 'Qualified investor' means a person or an organization capable of identifying and assuming risks and make an investment not less than a certain amount in an asset management product and meets certain financial and experience requirements.[56]

In the robo-advisor business, the investment advisor qualification shall be obtained in order to use AI technology for the investment advisory business. In this aspect, the Asset Management Guiding Opinions makes distinctions between financial and non-financial institutions. Only financial institutions can use AI technology for their asset management business, in which the rules of client eligibility, investment scope, information disclosure and risk isolation must be observed. Non-financial institutions are excluded from conducting an asset management business, which may hinder the development of robo-advisor companies without any financial licence.

The service provider shall not use AI to mislead investors and exaggerate asset management products. To prevent black-box operations of

---

[53] The financial institution can be banking, trust, securities, fund, futures, or insurance asset management institution, financial asset investment company or any other financial institution.

[54] 2018 Asset Management Guiding Opinions, art. 2.

[55] Ibid, art. 4.

[56] Ibid, art. 5. The qualified investor should have an investment experience of not less than two years and satisfy any of the following conditions: (1) family financial net assets are not less than CNY 3 million; family financial assets are not less than CNY 5 million; or the average annual income of the person in the immediate preceding three years is not less than CNY 400,000; (2) a corporate entity whose net assets at the end of the immediate preceding year are not less than CNY 10 million; (3) investors otherwise deemed qualified by financial authorities.

AI technology, the service providers are imposed with enhanced information disclosure duties. They are required to file the main parameters of their AI model and the main logic of asset allocation algorithms within the financial regulatory authority.[57] The Asset Management Guiding Opinions enable investors to seek remedies from the service provider. The financial institution shall be liable for any damages caused to investors by its illegal acts or improper management.[58]

7.3.2 Key Elements

7.3.2.1 The Entry Threshold

The Securities Law does not restrict financial consulting services that are provided by humans. The Asset Management Guiding Opinions provide that a robo-advisor using AI technology for investment advisory businesses shall obtain an investment advisor qualification. Thus, the registration requirements for investment advisors under the Securities Law apply to robo-advisors. If a securities company or a securities consulting company directly or indirectly obtains economic benefits by using robo-advisors to provide clients investment advice and assist them in making investment decisions, such a company should be deemed as engaging in the 'securities investment advisor business' and subject to the approval of the CSRC. No institution or individual without the qualification of engaging in the consulting business may engage in such business using stock picking software.[59] Robo-advisor service providers should independently conduct service processes and not employ any institution or individual without the qualification of engaging in the consulting business.[60]

To apply for the qualification in the consultancy business, the consultancy service providers should meet several requirements in terms of corporate governance under the Investment Consultation Measures, including (1) for institutions engaged in securities investment consultancy services or futures investment consultancy services separately, more

---

[57] The financial regulatory authority means the People's Bank of China, the banking and insurance regulatory institution of the State Council, the securities regulatory institution of the State Council, or the State Administration of Foreign Exchange. See 2018 Asset Management Guiding Opinions, art. 31.

[58] Where defects in algorithm models or system malfunctions cause the herd effect and affect the stable operation of the financial market, the financial institution shall take manual intervention measures in a timely manner and forcibly adjust or terminate AI business. See ibid, art. 23.

[59] 2020 Stock Picking Software Provisions, art. 2.

[60] Ibid, art. 4.

than five full-time employees with professional qualifications should be accommodated; for institutions engaged in both services, more than ten full-time employees should be accommodated; at least one of their high-ranking managers has acquired qualifications ; (2) having more than CNY 1 million in registered capital; (3) possessing a fixed business site and necessary business communications facilities; (4) having formulated articles of association for the company; (5) having sound internal management mechanisms; (6) meeting other conditions as required by the CSRC.[61]

Individual investment consultants applying for the qualification of engagement in the investment consultancy business shall meet several requirements in terms of professional certificates: (1) Chinese citizenship; (2) full capacity for civil conduct; (3) good integrity and work ethic; (4) no record of criminal sanction or significant violations in the business; (5) educational background of the level of college or above; (6) over two years of experience in conducting business; (7) a record of passed examinations for qualification organized by the CSRC; (8) other requirements as stipulated by the CSRC.[62]

These qualifications and requirements are designed to regulate institutional consultants as well as their natural-person personnel. It is not clear whether the same requirements apply to the robo-advisors, which need more detailed and technical regulations. For instance, the registration and qualification requirements of investment consultants in the Investment Consultation Measures do not apply to robo-advisors, because Article 13 requires such consultants to have full capacity for civil conduct and possess the citizenship of the PRC. For robo-advisors, there are no individual consultants offering suggestions to investors. A possible interpretation is that natural-person operators and developers of the algorisms in robo-advisors should be regulated in the same way as traditional individual consultants. Also, the qualification requirements contained in chapter 2 of the Investment Consultation Measures relating to a company's qualification to engage in securities and futures investment consultancy businesses should be considered applicable to robo-advisor companies.

7.3.2.2 The Power of Attorney

Robo-advisors, including the 'stock picking software', fall under the securities investment consulting and advisory businesses. The scope of

---

[61] 1998 Investment Consultation Measures, art. 6.
[62] Ibid, art. 13.

applicable products for robo-advisors is limited to 'securities', which is relatively narrower than the concept 'financial products'.

Robo-advisors can conduct business in the securities consultancy business. The CSRC makes distinctions between 'asset management' and 'investment consulting' as two categories of businesses that are subject to different registration requirements. According to the relevant provisions, investment consultants cannot buy or sell securities and futures on behalf of investors,[63] securities investment advisors cannot make any investment decision on behalf of a client,[64] and a securities investment consulting institution and its employees that provide securities trading services cannot make securities investments as an agent on behalf of a client.[65]

Each of the traditional statutes has clear provisions that prohibit service providers from conducting asset management businesses. Specifically, the 1998 Investment Consultation Measures aim to regulate the business activities of institutions and their personnel to protect investors' interests. Consultancy institutions are not allowed to provide investors with investment suggestions based on false information, market talks or inside information.[66] They are prohibited from buying and selling securities and futures on behalf of investors.[67] Similarly, Article 12 of the 2020 Investment Advisor Provisions stipulates that any investment decision made and any investment risks shall be assumed by the client, and a securities investment advisor shall not make any investment decision on behalf of a client. When these bans are violated, the local branches of the CSRC will give the violator a warning, confiscate their illegal income, or impose an administrative fine (CNY 10,000–50,000 for institutions and CNY 10,000–30,000 for personnel). If the violations are severe, the CSRC can suspend or revoke the institutions' business qualifications.[68]

These limits on investment consultants' full power of attorney disable robo-advisors from conducting asset management business for investors, especially inexperienced market players. The prohibition of asset management businesses hinders the healthy development of the robo-advisors in China, which indicates that Chinese legislators are adopting an overly cautious approach of regulation.

[63] 1998 Investment Consultation Measures, art. 24.
[64] 2020 Investment Advisor Provisions, art. 12 (5).
[65] 2020 Securities Law, art. 161.
[66] 1998 Investment Consultation Measures, art. 21.
[67] Ibid, art. 24.
[68] Ibid, art. 34 and 36.

7.3.2.3 The Fiduciary Duties

Fiduciary duties are generally imposed on investment advisory service providers, which prevent conflicts of interest and effectively protect the legitimate interests of clients. When providing advisory services, service provider and their personnel should be loyal to their clients' interests; they also owe their clients a duty of care and a duty to diligently and prudently provide investment advisory services.

Specifically, the 2020 Investment Advisor Provisions imposes fiduciary duties on service providers, which aims to strengthen compliance management, improve internal controls, prevent conflicts of interest and effectively protect clients' legitimate interests.[69] Accordingly, the duty of care requires the service provider and their personnel to notify a client of the investment's basic information;[70] when providing services, they cannot damage their clients' interests for the benefit of other parties (including for the benefit of the company or its affiliates, securities investment advisors or any other party, and other clients).[71] Also, the duty of care requires them to adhere to the principle of honesty and good faith, and to diligently and prudently provide investment advisory services for clients.[72]

The 2020 Stock Picking Software Provisions provide that the service provider's conduct should follow certain fiduciary standards. The service providers that use 'stock picking software' should adhere to the principles of objectiveness, impartiality and good faith, and cannot mislead or defraud clients or infringe upon clients' interests.[73] Clients should be fairly treated in that different clients should not be sold the same products at varying prices.[74]

The 2018 Asset Management Guiding Opinions provide similar requirements. A financial institution bears the obligations of good faith, diligence, and dutifulness for their principals' interests, and a principal shall invest at its own risk and acquire returns.[75] The rules for prudential business should be observed to develop a scientific and reasonable investment strategy and risk-management system to prevent risks effectively. Otherwise, the service provider would be liable for damages caused to the

---

[69] 2020 Investment Advisor Provisions, art. 3.
[70] Ibid, art. 12.
[71] Ibid, art. 16.
[72] Ibid, art. 4.
[73] 2020 Stock Picking Software Provisions, art. 3.
[74] Ibid, art. 4.
[75] 2018 Asset Management Guiding Opinions, art. 2.

investors by its failure to practically fulfil the duty of commissioned management according to the principles of good faith, diligence and dutifulness.[76] To mitigate risks, the service provider is forbidden to invest in certain businesses, such as credit assets of commercial banks.[77]

Several statutes have emphasized the 'client eligibility principle'. The 2020 Investment Advisor Provisions require service providers to evaluate the appropriateness of their investors. They should first gather information on the clients' identity, property and income status, securities investment experience, investment demand and risk appetite, then evaluate their risk tolerance and keep a record in written or electronic form.[78] Then, according to such information, the advisor provides appropriate investment advice based on the evaluation of the client's risk tolerance and service needs;[79] such advice must be reasonably founded.[80] Additionally, the 2020 Stock Picking Software Provisions require the service provider to formulate rules and procedures for evaluating clients, classifying and grading software products, disclosing product features and risks, and selling only appropriate products to eligible clients.[81] The 2018 Asset Management Guiding Opinions require financial institutions to understand their products and clients, strengthen the eligibility management of investors, and sell products commensurate with investors' capability to identify and assume risks when offered asset management products.[82]

7.3.2.4 The Information Disclosure Duties

The Chinese laws provide that when advising customers on investment or asset allocation, advisors are required to warn them of the risks and cannot promise or guarantee them investment income.[83] If investment advisors use software tools and terminal equipment as carriers, they should reveal the inherent defects, user risks and functional limitations of such carriers.[84] Securities companies are required to provide clients

---

[76] Ibid, art. 8.

[77] Ibid, art. 11. A publicly offered product shall mainly invest in standard debt assets and publicly traded stock and abstain from investing in the shares in unlisted enterprises. See ibid, art. 10.

[78] 2020 Investment Advisor Provisions, art. 11.

[79] Ibid, art. 15.

[80] The basis of investment advice shall include securities research reports, investment analysis opinions, theoretical models and analysing methods.

[81] Ibid, art. 4.

[82] 2018 Asset Management Guiding Opinions, art. 6.

[83] 2019 Notice of Standards, art. 16; Investment Advisor Provisions, art. 19.

[84] Investment Advisor Provisions, art. 27.

with a risk disclosure statement of which the content and format are determined by the SAC.[85]

The 2020 Stock Picking Software Provisions require necessary information to be publicized on the company's business premises, website and the website of the SAC. Such key information includes but is not limited to the company name, domicile, contact information, number of advisory business permits, product categories, specific functions and service fee rates. Besides, the provider shall file for recordation the necessary materials with the CSRC and the SAC. Where the robo-advisor services are provided online, clients should be informed of the company's contact information. The service provider shall not conduct false, untruthful, exaggerated or misleading sales promotion about product functions and service performances.[86] Clients should receive investor education, be informed of the stock picking software's role and limitations, dispute settlement methods and the risks and hazards in an objective and accurate manner.[87]

The 2018 Asset Management Guiding Opinions require a financial institution to expressly explain the type of asset management product to investors and make investments based on the nature of the product. The type of product may not be changed without authorization.[88] Besides, investors are entitled to full disclosure on several important items of the product. For instance, a financial institution shall disclose offering information, investment direction, leverage, yield distribution, custodian arrangements, information of investment accounts, major investment risks and other relevant content of asset management products to investors voluntarily, authentically, accurately, completely and promptly, except otherwise provided by the laws and regulations issued by the state.[89]

7.4 Evaluation: Strengths and Weaknesses

7.4.1 Strengths

Chinese law stipulates specific professional qualifications and entry requirements designed to regulate institutional consultants and their

---

[85] Ibid, art. 13.
[86] 2020 Stock Picking Software Provisions, art. 4.
[87] Ibid, art. 5.
[88] 2018 Asset Management Guiding Opinions, art. 4.
[89] See ibid, art. 12.

natural-person personnel. The entry threshold is set high to provide enhanced protection for retail investors who constitute the absolute majority of investors in China and are usually poorly equipped with the basic knowledge to understand market conditions. Considering the failure of peer-to-peer investment in the financial market, the irrationality of Chinese retail investors is a major concern for the regulation of the robo-advisor market.[90] Financial permits are usually granted to financial companies that can satisfy certain hardware and software conditions. To some extent, the harsh market entry threshold along with the restriction on robo-advisors' asset management power can exclude unqualified applicants from disturbing the market and harming investors' interests.

To facilitate the protection of investors' interests, Chinese law imposes fiduciary duties on service providers, including the duty of loyalty and the duty of care. Accordingly, the service providers should strengthen compliance management, improve internal controls, prevent conflicts of interest to effectively protect clients' legitimate interests;[91] they should also diligently and prudently provide services to clients;[92] they should abide by information disclosure duties and conduct standards, and should not defraud clients or infringe upon clients' interests.[93] Although not perfect nor detailed, the fiduciary duties and information disclosure requirements indicate that Chinese policymakers are aware of the potential benefits and risks brought about by robo-advisors. The emphasis on fiduciary duties and market transparency can boost investors' confidence and trust in robo-advisors' services and facilitate the AI development in China.

The legal consequences provided by the Chinese law allow for both public and private enforcement to deter operators of robo-advisors from defrauding clients. The CSRC, the Chinese securities market's watchdog, is responsible for supervising the robo-advisor business. Investors that suffer losses are entitled to seek compensation from robo-advisor companies. In the Chinese securities market, a centralized public enforcement regime is usually more efficient in enforcing legal rules than investors' private enforcement in court, because the administrative regulator is better equipped than the courts to deal with highly professional

---

[90] For more information on the Chinese P2P market development, see Robin Hui Huang, 'Online P2P Lending and Regulatory Responses in China: Opportunities and Challenges' (2018) 19 *European Business Organization Law Review* 63.

[91] 2020 Investment Advisor Provisions, art. 3.

[92] Ibid, art. 4.

[93] Ibid, art. 3.

and technical securities cases.[94] The regulatory measures of the CSRC include corrections, regulatory talks, letters of warning, submission of compliance inspection reports, disciplinary action against relevant persons and so on.[95] These measures are usually more efficient in deterring violators and useful in protecting investors than time-consuming civil litigations.[96] Also, the SAC as an industry association shall conduct self-disciplinary management of robo-advisors.[97] It can greatly influence member securities companies, who are the major operators of the robo-advisor business.

7.4.2 Weaknesses

7.4.2.1 Harsh Entry Threshold and Less Service Functions

In China, a financial institution may use robo-advisors for both the consulting business and asset management business if the institution satisfies the registration requirements for both. In practice, only a very small number of financial institutions can obtain both investment advisor and asset management licences because the registration threshold is set very high.

Although having its strengths and merits, the market entry threshold in China has been overly high, which undermines the development of robo-advisors in their full capacities. The harsh requirements deprive investors of the opportunity to seek professional advice from different robo-advisors and the chance to enjoy all the functions robo-advisory services can offer. Currently, in the Chinese financial market, the main function of robo-advisors is to promote financial products. Institutions such as JD Finance, Pingan Insurance and China Merchants Bank use robo-advisors as sales agents rather than professional consultants.[98]

---

[94] For more information on the public and private enforcement of the securities law in China, see Robin Hui Huang, 'Private Enforcement of Securities Law in China: A Ten-Year Retrospective and Empirical Assessment' (2013) 61 *American Journal of Comparative Law* 757.

[95] 2020 Investment Advisor Provisions, art. 33.

[96] Research shows that the CSRC has played an essential role in enforcing the regulatory rules in the securities market. See Robin Hui Huang and Charles Chao Wang, 'The Mandatory Bid Rule Under China's Takeover Law: A Comparative and Empirical Perspective' (2020) 53(2) *The International Lawyer*.

[97] 2020 Investment Advisor Provisions, art. 6.

[98] HCR Co, 'Zhongguo Zhineng Tougu Shichang Fazhan Qushi Yanjiu Baogao' (中国智能投顾市场发展趋势研究报告) [Analysis Report of the Market Development Trend of Robo-Advisors in China], 2017, p 7, http://ftp.shujuju.cn/platform/file/2017-02-16/2a6103219f6b4395a3aa2dc1a95ad2ef.pdf.

According to the 2018 Report of Individual Investors, only 6.3 per cent of investors made their decisions with professional investment advisors, 1.4 per cent of investors obtained financial information from professional advisors, and 58.8 per cent of the investors think they need investment advisors but have no need for asset management services.[99] On the other hand, these three statistics have increased compared to the 2017 report. Using robo-advisors to promote financial products as a main function impacts the quality of the advisory service provided, causing potential conflicts of interest and misrepresentations. That's why individual investors have shown a lower level of interaction with robo-advisors.[100]

Besides, the harsh entry threshold means that robo-advisors face potentially serious legal risks. Under the 'classic model', robo-advisors in China usually cooperate with overseas securities companies to provide autonomous account management service to clients in Mainland China. Although this has the effect of lowering the entry threshold for robo-advisors in China, the robo-advisors may face serious legal risks. Article 95 of the Securities Companies Regulation requires overseas securities institutions operating their business in China to obtain the approval from the regulator. Hence, these robo-advisors may be deemed as operating illegal securities business without a licence, and domestic clients may not be well protected.[101]

7.4.2.2   Insufficient and Inconsistent Asset Management Power

The concept of 'securities investment consulting', also known as 'investment consulting business' in China is narrower than that in the United States. It refers to the investment advisory services of securities-related products provided by operators to customers, which is limited to 'investment consultation' (Touzi Zixun or 投资咨询 in Mandarin) and excludes 'asset management' (Zichan Guanli or 资产管理 in Mandarin). The concept 'investment consultant' (Touzi Guwen or 投资顾问 in Mandarin) in

---

[99] Zhongguo Zhengquan Touzi Jijinye Xihui (中国证券投资基金业协会) [Asset Management Association of China], 'Jijin Geren Touzizhe Touzi Qingkuang Diaocha Wenjuan Fenxi Baogao Erling Yiba Niandu' (基金个人投资者投资情况调查问卷分析报告（2018年度）) [The 2018 Analysis Report of Questionnaires by Individual Fund Investors], 2018, p 18, www.amac.org.cn/researchstatistics/report/tzzbg/202001. P020200106520189708039.pdf.

[100] Possible reasons include that investment advisors as a profession is not common in the Chinese financial market and that many advisors are previous salespersons in financial companies, and thus investors generally have doubts on their relevant expertise.

[101] Li Guo, 'Regulating Investment Robo-Advisors in China: Problems and Prospects' (2020) 21 *European Business Organization Law Review* 69.

China is often confused with 'securities analysts', 'securities brokers' and 'financial advisors'.

There are historical reasons to explain why investors are forbidden to entrust investment consultants with the task of conducting asset management businesses. The ban was aimed at preventing employees of securities investment consulting institutions from committing insider dealing and market manipulation. It was expected to ensure that the personnel of consulting institutions serve their clients with due diligence.[102] There are legitimate concerns that licensed companies may abuse their discretionary power to invest in high-risk securities in the name of its clients' accounts, causing damages to individual or average-sized institutional investors.[103]

In the AI and big data era, this ban hinders the development of traditional securities investment consulting companies by weakening the wealth management functions of robo-advisors and making it difficult for them to earn profits.[104] Restrictions on the advisor licence in general and on non-financial companies to use robo-advisors in asset management impede the development of robo-advisors, which in turn limit their functions to stage 1.0. It is impossible to find an all-in-one wealth management company in China like Betterment or Wealthfront where investors can plan, save, invest or supervise their money in one place. This can cause the development of robo-advisors in China to lag behind other countries and prevent the financial market from entering into an era of automation. The full potential of robo-advisors cannot be realized because of the lack of a supportive regulatory framework in China.[105] It has been argued that China should broaden the definition of the investment consulting business to cover the asset management business.[106]

---

[102] Guo Li (郭雳), 'Zhineng Tougu Kaizhan De Zhidu Quzhang Yu Falv Zhutui' (智能投顾开展的制度去障与法律助推) [To Boost the Robo-advisor in China: Removing Institutional Obstacles and Ameliorating Legal Conditions], (2019) 037(003) *Zhengfa Luntan* (政法论坛) 184.

[103] Zhengquanfa Shiyi Bianxiezu (《证券法释义》编写组) [Editors Board of the <Interpretation of Securities Law>], *Zhonghua Renmin Gongheguo Zhengquanfa Shiyi* (中华人民共和国证券法释义) [The Interpretation of the Securities Law of the People's Republic of China] (China Legal Publishing House, 2005), p 225.

[104] Guo Li (郭雳), 'Zhineng Tougu Kaizhan De Zhidu Quzhang Yu Falv Zhutui' (智能投顾开展的制度去障与法律助推) [To Boost the Robo-advisor in China: Removing Institutional Obstacles and Ameliorating Legal Conditions], (2019) 037(003) *Zhengfa Luntan* (政法论坛) 184.

[105] Ibid.

[106] Wu Ye (吴烨) and Ye Lin (叶林), 'Zhineng Tougu De Benzhi Ji Guizhi Lujing' ('智能投顾'的本质及规制路径) [A Study on the Legal Regulation of 'Robo-advisers'], (2018) 039(005) *Faxue Zazhi* (法学杂志) [Law Science Magazine] 16.

China's regulatory agencies came to realize this problem and gradually adjusted their policies accordingly. On 17 November 2017, five governmental ministries[107] jointly issued the Asset Management Guidance in which 'asset management business' refers to the financial services that banks, trusts, securities, funds, futures, insurance asset management institutions and other financial institutions provide to invest and manage the investors' entrusted property. Financial institutions provide investment and management financial services for clients and charge fees, while clients bear the risks. Most importantly, the Asset Management Guidance states that financial institutions using AI technology and robot investment consultants to carry out asset management businesses shall obtain the approval of the financial supervision and regulation department, obtain the corresponding investment consultant qualification, fully disclose information, and report the main parameters of the intelligent investment advisory model and the main logic of asset allocation.[108]

The release of this instrument shows that China's regulatory authorities have become more inclined towards supporting the prosperity of the asset management business of robo-advisors, which creates conditions for the amendment of the Securities Law and creates a streamlined regulatory framework for the future. However, the inconsistent treatment of financial and non-financial institutions may cause unfair competition. In China, a robo-advisor operated by a financial institution can conduct both consulting businesses and asset management businesses if the financial institution satisfies the registration requirements for both. By contrast, a robo-advisor operated by a non-financial institution can only have advisory powers.

7.4.2.3   Weak Fiduciary Duties and KYC Practice

Current laws in China have not provided detailed rules to enforce directors' fiduciary duties. In practice, fiduciary duties and derivative litigations have been applied solely to limited liability companies in China.[109] Many of the securities companies who are major operators of robo-advisors are joint-stock companies or public companies in China. They are under much less scrutiny by the courts.

---

[107] These include the people's Bank of China, China Banking Regulatory Commission, China Securities Regulatory Commission, China Insurance Regulatory Commission and foreign exchange administration.

[108] Asset Management Guidance, art. 22.

[109] Hui Huang, 'Shareholder Derivative Litigation in China: Empirical Findings and Comparative Analysis' (2012) 27 *Banking and Finance Law Review* 619.

In the scenario of robo-advisor regulation, the Chinese law fails to provide detailed and workable rules requiring financial consulting companies or investment advisors to act in the best interests of their clients. Relevant provisions only require them to be 'loyal to the interests of clients',[110] to 'maintain the lawful rights and interests of investors'[111] and provide 'appropriate advice' to clients. In comparison, the US Investment Advisor Act and relevant laws provide detailed rules to ensure that an investment advisor has a fiduciary duty to act 'in the best interests of its client'[112] and provide 'only suitable investment advice'. Similarly, the Hong Kong SFC requires any licensed person to act 'in the best interests of its client' and provide 'suitable advice in all the circumstances'.[113] Compared to those in the United States and Hong Kong, investment advisors in China are subject to a lower standard of fiduciary duties when acting for their clients. This can lead to problems like robo-advisors providing a beneficial portfolio that is not in the best interests of their clients.

The know-your-client (KYC) process does not function well in China due to many local factors. The law requires a securities investment advisor to provide appropriate investment advice to clients according to the client's information learned during the KYC process.[114] A reasonable basis for such appropriate advice includes clients' financial position and investment objects. Robo-advisors rely on data collected from both financial products suppliers and clients to rank and match them. However, product suppliers may fail to provide sufficient data for the algorithm to apply rules effectively for many reasons, such as that the suppliers do not retain an electronic form of certain data or that some data are not legally available to the public. Clients' data can be collected directly by answering questionnaires or from a third party, such as banks or insurance companies. Clients may not be willing to reveal their total assets and risk-tolerance levels. Such a third party may also fail to provide sufficient data due to legal restraints or other reasons.

---

[110] 2020 Release of Reports Provisions, art. 5.

[111] 2019 Notice of Standards, art. 2.

[112] The US Securities and Exchange Commission Division of Investment Management, IM Guidance Update No. 2017-02, 2017, p 6, www.sec.gov/investment/im-gu-dance-2017-02.pdf.

[113] Code of Conduct for Persons Licensed by or Registered with the Securities and Futures Commission, GP1, sections 5.1A, 5.2 and 5.5.

[114] 2019 Notice of Standards, art. 15.

7.4.2.4 Inadequate Information Disclosure Duties

In Chinese law, robo-advisors should advise customers on securities investment based on a reasonable basis but are not required to disclose such a basis in detail. Article 14 of the 2019 Notice of Standards and Article 16 of the Investment Advisor Provisions provide that securities investment consulting institutions or investment advisors shall advise customers on securities investment on a reasonable basis. The bases for investment advice include research reports and securities research reports from securities investment consulting institutions and investment analysis opinions based on securities research reports, theoretical models, algorithm models and analysis methods.[115] These requirements are rigid and not enough to inform investors of the highly technical decision-making mechanism of algorisms. Investors may never read the reports or understand the ambiguous nature of the robots that advise them. Besides, the current risk disclosure statement does not contain risks that are unique to robo-advisors. Disclosure by robo-advisors may be made solely electronically, including via email, websites and messages etc. An investor's ability to understand the disclosed information varies with one's education level and investment experience. In principle, human and AI investment advisors should have a duty all the same to disclose all material facts to clients.

In practice, the information asymmetry problem between clients and robots can hardly be handled appropriately in China. When dealing with robo-advisors, clients usually have limited access to human assistants or advisors, meaning that they may not have the opportunities to ask questions, and it is difficult for a robot to ensure that their clients are reasonably informed. In the 2018 Report of Individual Investors, it was found that 27.8 per cent of the investors in China never read prospectus before making decisions to invest, among which 6.5 per cent reported that they do not understand the content, and other 21.3 per cent reported that they do not know what content is important to them. 46.3 per cent of these investors said that they might read the prospectuses, but do not know what content is important to them as well.[116] This means that

---

[115] Ibid, art. 14; Investment Advisor Provisions, art. 16.

[116] Zhongguo Zhengquan Touzi Jijinye Xihui (中国证券投资基金业协会) [Asset Management Association of China], Jijin Geren Touzizhe Touzi Qingkuang Diaocha Wenjuan Fenxi Baogao Erling Yiba Niandu (基金个人投资者投资情况调查问卷分析报告 (2018 年度)) [The 2018 Analysis Report of Questionnaires by Individual Fund Investors], 2018, p 31, www.amac.org.cn/researchstatistics/report/tzzbg/20200 / P020200106520189708039.pdf.

consulting companies should find a more effective way to make disclosures, and legislators should require such disclosure to be made in a plain
manner for clients' understanding.

7.5 Reform Suggestions

To establish a relationship of trust and confidence between investors and
robo-advisors in China, scholars have put forward many reform proposals, such as lowering the regulatory threshold and allowing investment advisors to engage in the asset management business.[117] To
facilitate the evolution of automation in the Chinese financial market,
this research argues that several suggestions should be adopted by
Chinese policymakers and market players.

7.5.1 Relaxing and Refining the Entry Threshold of Robo-Advisors

This research argues that the traditional harsh entry threshold should
be relaxed to boost the market development of robo-advisors in China.
On the other hand, technology-unique requirements should be
imposed on robo-advisors in a more scientific way to enable more
service functions. In achieving this objective, the requirements for the
standards of algorism design should be considered. One of the legal
challenges is how to decide whether a robo-advisor is well-designed
enough to provide financial advice. Two key factors are related to the
standards of being 'well designed': its professional competence and the
system's stability.

In terms of assessing professional competence, Article 13 of the
Investment Consultation Measures require an investment consultant to
pass the CSRC examinations in order to be qualified. These examinations
may not be suitable for robo-advisors. In Hong Kong, the SFC requires
robo-advisors to have a 'suitably-qualified person' to test, review and
ensure the reasonableness of advice provided on the platform.[118] Thus, in

---

[117] Guo Li (郭雳) and Zhao Jiyao (赵继尧), 'Zhineng Tougu Fazhan De Falv Tiaozhan Jiqi
Yingdui' (智能投顾发展的法律挑战及其应对) [The Legal Challenges and Responses
to the Development of Robo-Advisors], (2018) 311(06) *Zhengquan Shichang Daobao* (证
券市场导报) [Securities Market Herald] 73; Li Wenli (李文莉) and Yang Mingjie (杨明
捷), 'Zhineng Tougu De Falv Fengxian Ji Jianguan Jianyi' (智能投顾的法律风险及监管
建议) [The Legal Risk and Regulatory Advise for Robo-Advisors], (2017) 8 *Faxue* (法学)
[Law Science] 15.

[118] Hong Kong Securities and Futures Commission, Guidelines on Online Distribution and
Advisory Platforms, 2019, p 14, www.sfc.hk/web/EN/assets/components/codes/files-

regard to the professional competence assessment, regulators should consider requirements such as: the designers' explanation of the algorithm, including the factors taken into account when designing strategies and portfolios; the designers' explanation of the outcomes that the algorithms are seeking,[119] such as to provide more return and income in order, to maintain diversification and low costs or to limit exposure to stock market volatility.

In terms of assessing system stability, regulators should require robo-advisors providers to establish a testing and backtesting mechanism, pass a well-designed system test and make sure that they have the capabilities to maintain, update and repair the programmes or systems from time to time, particularly in case of system failure emergencies.

The distinction between brokers and investment advisors should be emphasized. Regulators in China should clarify the distinction between brokers and investment advisors in order to regulate them unambiguously. The relevant considerations include their duties, scope of services and fee models. In practice, clients have a transaction-based relationship with their brokers who charge fees on a transactional basis, and a fee-based relationship with their investment advisors who may charge fees based on a percentage of the assets in the account or based on subscription plans. Brokers may advise on particular transactions while investment advisors also advise on general investment strategies and continuously monitor portfolios. Advisors also have a higher standard of fiduciary duty to act in the best interest of investors while brokers only provide suitable recommendations on particular transactions.[120]

7.5.2 Encouraging Fair Competition in Robo-Advisors' Asset Management Business

The US Investment Advisors Act of 1940 stipulates that investment advisors can conduct businesses, including both investment consulting and asset management. It is a broad version of the term 'investment advisor'. Because the Advisers Act was devised primarily to regulate human behaviour, the regulators have to determine how robo-advisors

---

current/web/guidelines/guidelines-on-online-distribution-and-advisory-platforms/guidelines-on-online-distribution-and-advisory-platforms.pdf.

[119] Tom Baker and Benedict G. C. Dellaert, 'Regulating Robo Advice across the Financial Services Industry' (2018) 103 *Iowa Law Review* 713.

[120] Christine Lazaro, 'The Future of Financial Advice: Eliminating the False Distinction Between Brokers and Investment Advisers' (2013) 87(2) *St. John's Law Review*.

fit into its framework.[121] In *Lowe v. SEC*, the US Supreme Court stated that the powers of investment counsel firms concerning the management of the funds of their investment company clients were either discretionary or advisory.[122] Thus, investment advice and asset management are the two major functions of robo-advisors. Particularly, automated portfolio rebalancing as a critical method to manage assets is the key advantage that robo-advisors possess over human advisors, for it ensures that the investors' portfolios can react to market fluctuations instantly without wasting time in human analysis and communication, and thus maintaining the asset allocation in line with customized financial needs and goals of the investors. Besides, many financial institutions and innovative start-ups such as Bridgewater, Blackrock and Wealthfront have started to work either independently or in partnership to develop a fully automated AI investment system.

The empowerment of robo-advisors in the asset management business has gained momentum worldwide. Currently, 80 per cent of German, EU, UK and US robo-advisors have 3.0 capabilities with a trend of moving towards 4.0.[123] For instance, Betterment, one of the leading robo-advisor companies, creates portfolios from clients' risk tolerance and then manages their clients' accounts with asset allocation of exchange-traded funds that match the tolerance recorded. It provides various portfolio strategies for clients to select from while allowing personalized adjustments. Its SmartDeposit, an automated cash investment tool, enables clients to invest automatically without involving the actual process. Regulations in Hong Kong, Singapore and Australia all recognize that robo-advisors may provide portfolio or asset management services to clients.[124]

---

[121] Megan Ji, 'Are Robots Good Fiduciaries: Regulating Robo-Advisors under the Investment Advisers Act of 1940' (2017) 117 *Columbia Law Review* 1543.

[122] Discretionary powers imply the vesting with an investment counsel firm control over the client's funds, with the power to make the ultimate determination with respect to the sale and purchase of securities for the client's portfolio. In contrast, vesting advisory powers with an investment counsel firm merely means that the firm may make recommendations to its client with whom rests the ultimate power to accept or reject such recommendations. See *Lowe v. SEC*, 472 US 181 (1985), p 27.

[123] Deloitte, 'The Expansion of Robo-Advisory in Wealth Management', 2016, www2.deloitte .com/content/dam/Deloitte/de/Documents/financial-services/Deloitte-Robo-safe.pdf.

[124] For more information on the data, see Hong Kong Securities and Futures Commission, Guidelines on Online Distribution and Advisory Platforms, 2019, www.sfc.hk/web/EN/ assets/components/codes/files-current/web/guidelines/guidelines-on-online-distribu tion-and-advisory-platforms/guidelines-on-online-distribution-and-advisory-plat forms.pdf; Monetary Authority of Singapore, Guidelines on Provision of Digital Advisory Services, CMG-G02, 2018, www.mas.gov.sg/regulation/guidelines/guidelines-

Discretionary management relies on a trust-based consumer decision-making model.[125] However, between advisory services and asset management there lies a huge gap. Radical changes in legislation may lead to market turmoil and serious compliance issues. Since the prohibition of discretionary power prevents robo-advisors from providing comprehensive service to clients and the Chinese financial market is not prepared to welcome full discretionary management, this research suggests that Chinese legislators and policymakers allow robo-advisors to provide limited discretionary management where investors and regulators together set a list of restrictions for the former. For example, investors may require a set ratio of bonds to stocks, a predefined asset class to invest, or rules that certain investments must be avoided.[126] Legislators and policymakers should do that to facilitate the development and evolution of automation in the financial market. This enables an all-in-one financial company that provides comprehensive wealth management services to clients, enables investors to plan long-term investment strategies while flexibly making adjustments from time to time and tracking their investments in one place.

As discussed, a financial institution may use robo-advisors for both consulting and asset management if the institution satisfies the registration requirements for both. By contrast, a robo-advisor of a non-financial institution usually has advisory powers only. The inconsistent treatment for financial and non-financial companies hinders the robo-advisor market's prosperity and fair competition due to a lack of uniform laws with consistent standards. High-net-wealth individuals in China have shown a high demand for professional services provided by wealth management institutions.[127] Also, the number of investors reporting

---

on-provision-of-digital-advisory-services; Australian Securities and Investments Commission, Regulatory Guide 255 Providing Digital Financial Product Advice to Retail Clients, 2016, https://asic.gov.au/regulatory-resources/find-a-document/regula tory-guides/rg-255-providing-digital-financial-product-advice-to-retail-clients/.

[125] The basis of discretionary management is trust. Studies on trust influencing mechanisms of Robo-Advisors found that relevant factors influencing clients' trust on Robo-Advisors include investors' attitude towards AI, reputation of the providers, quality of the investment information, service quality and commitment and government regulation. See Xusen Cheng et al, 'Exploring the Trust Influencing Mechanism of Robo-Advisor Service: A Mixed Method Approch, School of Information Technology & Management, University of International Business and Economics' (2010) 11(18) *Sustainability* 4917.

[126] Pam Krueger, 'The 5 Levels of Discretion: How Much Control Should You Give Your Financial Advisor?', IRIS, 2016, www.iris.xyz/viewpoints/the-5-levels-of-discretion-how -much-control-should-you-give-your-financial-advisor/.

[127] In the past, investors tended to rely on a single class of asset for high returns; however, over the years, high-net-wealth individuals have learned lessons from market turmoil

a willingness to seek professional investment advice has increased over the past few years.[128] To encourage fair competition in the robo-advisor market, legislators should establish unified and streamlined asset management power rules that encourage investors to seek robo-advice from both financial and non-financial companies.

7.5.3 Strengthening Fiduciary Duties and KYC Standards

The US law imposes fiduciary duties on robo-advisors as well as human advisors. To protect investors, the Department of Labor has released the Conflict of Interest Rule that create a more stringent fiduciary standard and eliminates conflicts of interest between clients and advisors.[129] China should also elaborate on the fiduciary duties of robo-advisors. Disputes involving robo-advisors and data analysis malfunctions may include three parties: the clients, the financial company providing robo-advisor services, and the designer or programmer of the robo-advisors (the creator of algorithms). Thus, Chinese legislators need to clarify each party's legal obligations and duties, and render the financial company and the designer jointly liable for clients' losses.

Specifically, the Chinese law should provide detailed rules that require financial companies to act with due care, skill and diligence to ensure that all information and data relating to robo-advisor services are correct on its website. The financial company should have a duty to ensure that the online platform providing robo-advisor services is stable and reliable to run the algorithms. The financial company should act with due care, skill and diligence to protect the data of any third party (including the clients and the creator of algorithms). Such algorithms are commercial secrets and should not be disclosed to any other person or firm. The creators of

---

and are now tending to rely on professional asset allocation to accumulate wealth in a long term. See China Merchants Bank and Bain and Company, China Private Wealth Report 2019, 'China's Private Banking Industry: Back to Basics', 2019, pp 14–37, https://wm.cmbi.com.hk/Content/PDF/China_Private_Wealth_Report_2019_en.pdf.

[128] Zhongguo Zhengquan Touzi Jijinye Xihui (中国证券投资基金业协会) [Asset Management Association of China], Jijin Geren Touzizhe Touzi Qingkuang Diaocha Wenjuan Fenxi Baogao Erling Yiba Niandu (基金个人投资者投资情况调查问卷分析报告（2018年度）) [The 2018 Analysis Report of Questionnaires by Individual Fund Investors], 2018, p 18, www.amac.org.cn/researchstatistics/report/tzzbg/202001/P020200106520189708039.pdf.

[129] Dominic Litz, 'Risk, Reward, Robo-Advisers: Are Automated Investment Platforms Acting in Your Best Interest' (2018) 18 *Journal of High Technology Law* 367.

algorithms have a duty to test the robo-advisors and ensure that they are professionally competent and well designed.

The KYC process is crucial for the undertaking of fiduciary duties. To better improve the KYC process, the Chinese law should clarify what kinds of data are disclosable to robo-advisors, which employees of the financial companies, under what circumstances, can have access to such data.[130] Most robo-advisors rely on questionnaires during the KYC process. Two potential issues are detected. (1) The law should ensure that such questionnaires provided to investors are not broad or vague in its wordings.[131] The issue of information sufficiency also applies to the design of such questionnaires. (2) Both US law and Hong Kong law address the issue of clients' inconsistent answers on their questionnaires. The Chinese law should require the robo-advisors or the platform operator to alert clients when inconsistency appears and allow them to reconsider and change their previous responses.[132]

7.5.4   Enhancing Information Disclosure Duties

Hong Kong's SFC states that the focus of the disclosure requirement is that clients are provided with information that enables them to assess whether to use the services of a robo-advisor.[133] The US SEC states that the regulatory purpose is to address potential gaps in a client's understanding of how a robo-advisor provides its investment advice, and thus

---

[130] Scholars have proposed several questions that should be asked: (1) whether the robo-advisors has obtained access to reasonable sources of data that enable them to perform unbiased algorithms that are not disadvantageous to the clients; (2) when there is a gap to data, how the robo-advisor could address reasonably; (3) whether the regulators have any authority to increase the access to data and thereby improve the quality of the advice. See Tom Baker and Benedict G. C. Dellaert, 'Regulating Robo Advice across the Financial Services Industry' (2018) 103 *Iowa Law Review* 713.

[131] For example, when asking questions such as 'to what level of risk you are able to bear', it is not enough for the questionnaires to provide very broad options such as 'high–mid–low'. It must present specific options to the clients, and if necessary, explain each option in detail so that the clients can fully understand the question and respond correctly.

[132] The US Securities and Exchange Commission Division of Investment Management, IM Guidance Update No. 2017-02, 2017, p 7, www.sec.gov/investment/im-guidance-2017-02 .pdf; Hong Kong Securities and Futures Commission, Guidelines on Online Distribution and Advisory Platforms, 2019, p 14, www.sfc.hk/web/EN/assets/components/codes/files-current/web/guidelines/guidelines-on-online-distribution-and-advisory-platforms/guidelines-on-online-distribution-and-advisory-platforms.pdf.

[133] The HK Guidelines Q&A, Q14, www.sfc.hk/web/EN/faqs/intermediaries/supervision/guidelines-on-online-distribution-and-advisory-platforms/guidelines-on-online-distribution-and-advisory-platforms.html#14.

the robo-advisor should provide information regarding its particular business practices and related risks.[134] From a comparative point of view, Mainland China should learn from overseas experiences and require robo-advisors to warn clients about risks inherent in the use of algorithms (e.g. that the algorithms do not consider political risks, that the algorithms may not address long-term market changes, etc).[135]

To promote clients' trust in robo-advisors and address their doubt that robo-advisors are selling products for financial companies, the Chinese law needs to enable clients to understand the investment philosophy of robo-advisors and how they come up with a portfolio customized for clients. Robo-advisors must prepare disclosure documents drafted in plain wording that is suitable for investors with different levels of financial knowledge, highlight important sections and explain difficult or essential concepts in detail. It is also important that disclosure of material facts is made before investors engage in any important conduct such as signing up, opening an account with the company, or making any investment decision.

Specifically, China should learn from the experience of the U.S. by requiring robo-advisor operators to disclose the following crucial information: a statement that robo-advisors are using algorithms to design investment strategies; an explanation of the algorithms (including what are they, how they function, what factors are driving them, the outcome or goals the algorithms intend to achieve etc.); an analysis of the clients' financial status based on information gathered from them, including risk-tolerance levels, income levels, future predictions etc.; an explanation of how the algorithms customize portfolios for clients (e.g. what information gathered from the clients are used and how do they match with customized portfolios); a statement that robo-advisors may not take into account certain factors such as estate planning, retirement planning and debts.[136]

It is noteworthy that there should be a balance between clients' information rights and robo-advisors' commercial secrets. A person may obtain investment advice from the robo-advisor and disseminate the information to his or her friends for free, making the robo-advisor business unsustainable. Hence, the law should allow robo-advisors to

---

[134] The US Securities and Exchange Commission Division of Investment Management, IM Guidance Update No. 2017-02, 2017, p 3, www.sec.gov/investment/im-guidance-2017-02.pdf.

[135] Ibid, p 4.

[136] Ibid, p 3.

make investment decisions on behalf of the clients but not disclose unnecessary details of ongoing transactions such as the timing of executing such transactions.[137]

7.6 Conclusion

Automation in the Chinese financial industry is a fast-growing trend that will increase the capacity and productivity of financial companies and improve customer experiences. Robo-advisors can provide high-quality financial services to customers while allowing employees to focus on more valuable projects. Mainland China is undoubtedly facing a need to facilitate the evolution of robo-advisors while effectively protecting investors in the financial market. However, the essential regulatory rules concerning the fiduciary relationship between robo-advisors and investors have not yet been established completely and enforced properly.

By studying overseas experiences and China's local conditions, this research examines the Chinese regulatory framework of robo-advisors as well as its strengths and weaknesses. It suggests that to promote investors' confidence in robo-advisors and allow robo-advisors to fully perform their full functions, a relaxed and refined entry threshold of the robo-advisory service market should be established. The Chinese law should allow robo-advisors to provide limited discretionary asset management services and encourage fair competition between robo-advisors from both financial and non-financial companies. The robo-advisor companies should undertake more detailed fiduciary duties and KYC standards for clients, otherwise the service provider and the algorism designer should be jointly and severally liable for clients' losses according to their roles in the decision-making process. The information disclosure duties should be enhanced and fulfilled in a manner to balance clients' information rights and robo-advisor companies' commercial secrets.

---

[137] Li Guo, 'Regulating Investment Robo-Advisors in China: Problems and Prospects' (2020) 21 *European Business Organization Law Review* 69.

8

Equity Crowdfunding and Central Bank Digital Currency

8.1 Introduction

Having discussed several selected topics at great length in the previous chapters, this chapter will examine two other topics, including equity crowdfunding and central bank digital currency, namely that being developed by the Chinese central bank, the PBOC.

Unlike its sibling, debt crowdfunding (online P2P lending), equity crowdfunding is not given a full-chapter treatment. This is because, although it was once one of the Fintech sectors that China tried to develop early on, it has never been legalized in China and the recent reform of China's Securities Law has ruled out the possibility of legalizing it in the foreseeable future. However, equity crowdfunding is a popular form of Fintech in many other jurisdictions and thus for the sake of completeness, it is included in this chapter.

The topic of central bank digital currency is undoubtedly of profound theoretical and practical significance. However, it is still in its early stage of development, and many details are yet to be known. The topic has already attracted a lot of attention from the academic community and society at large, and hence this chapter will conduct a preliminary discussion of this important issue.

8.2 Equity Crowdfunding

8.2.1 Overview

Crowdfunding, derived from microfinance and crowdsourcing, generally refers to the practice of raising capital on internet platforms from a large number of investors, each of which typically contributes a small sum.[1] Depending on the context of the transaction and the benefits investors

---

[1] C. Steven Bradford, 'Crowdfunding and the Federal Securities Laws' (2012) 1 *Columbia Business Law Review* 1.

expect to receive in return for their contributions, crowdfunding can be classified into different categories, such as donation crowdfunding where people simply donate money to a project; reward crowdfunding where people receive a non-security benefit such as product or service; debt crowdfunding, also called peer-to-peer (P2P) lending, where people make loans to entrepreneurs and thus become creditors of the firm crowdfunded; and equity crowdfunding (EC) where people receive ownership interests in the firm or the project funded.

Conceptually, crowdfunding is hardly a novel thing in the sense that people like beggars and monks have used it to raise small amounts of money from the general public for thousands of years. Modern crowdfunding is different and innovative, to the extent that it uses the internet to significantly reduce the transaction costs associated with communication and payment between fundraisers and investors. According to some studies, modern crowdfunding is a recent phenomenon, originating in the United Kingdom in 2006 and then spreading to other jurisdictions such as China in 2009.[2] In fact, China's first well-known crowdfunding platform did not appear until 2011 when Demohour (Dian Ming Shi Jian) was set up as a platform for promoting and pre-selling innovative products.[3]

8.2.2 Legal Framework

When equity crowdfunding was introduced into China in around 2009, it was subject to the public offering regime under the 2005 Securities Law. The key provision on public offering is found in Article 10(2) of the 2005 Securities Law, which states:

It shall be deemed as a public issuance under any of the following circumstances:

a. securities are issued to unspecified objects;
b. securities are issued to accumulatively more than 200 specified objects;
c. making a public issuance as prescribed by any law or administrative regulation.

As shown above, there are two main types of public offerings in China: namely offerings made to the general public and offerings to accumulatively

---

[2] Eleanor Kirby and Shane Worner, 'Crowd-funding: An Infant Industry Growing Fast', *IOSCO Research Department Staff Working Paper No. SWP3/2014*.
[3] P2P lending platform first appeared in China in 2007. See Chapter 2.

8.2 EQUITY CROWDFUNDING

no more than 200 specified objects. Equity crowdfunding is, by definition, a fundraising practice under which equity products are offered to a crowd, namely a large number of unspecified investors. Hence, equity crowdfunding usually constitutes public offerings under the Chinese Securities Law.

In China, public offerings of securities are subject to a merits-review-based regulatory regime.[4] In addition to information disclosure, the issuer is required to pass a merit review conducted by the CSRC. For various reasons, it can be very difficult to get approval for public offerings from the CSRC. Even if the issuer is lucky enough to get the approval, there are usually high costs in undertaking public offerings, such as the commission and service fees required from market intermediaries. In general, the costs cannot be justified for equity crowdfunding, which is just meant to raise a small amount of funds.

Therefore, the trend of equity crowdfunding regulation in overseas jurisdictions is to exempt equity crowdfunding from the traditional regulation of securities offerings. Some jurisdictions, such as the United States[5] and the United Kingdom,[6] chose to make a special regulatory regime tailored to equity crowdfunding, while others, such as Hong Kong and Singapore, prefer to rely on the conventional exemption for small-scale offerings under the existing regulatory regime.[7] Some scholars have suggested that China should adopt special regulatory measures for equity crowdfunding in line with the experiences of the United States and the United Kingdom.[8] However, China has shown little interest in doing so, and instead has paid considerable attention to the small-scale exemption approach in Hong Kong and Singapore.

---

[4] Robin Hui Huang, *Securities and Capital Markets Law in China* (Oxford University Press, 2014), section 3.01

[5] Jumpstart Our Business Startups Act, section 302 Title III, issued by US Congress on 27 March 2012.

[6] Regulation (EU) 2017/1129, art. 3, section 2, on the prospectus to be published when securities are offered to the public or admitted to trading on a regulated market, and repealing Directive 2003/71/equity crowdfunding issued by European Parliament and the Council of The European Union on 14 June 2017.

[7] R. Huang (黄辉), 'Zhong guo gu quan zhong chou de gui zhi luo ji he mo shi xuan ze' (中国股权众筹的规制逻辑和模式选择) [The Regulatory Logic and Model of Equity Crowd-funding in China], (2018) 40(4) Xian dai fa xue (现代法学) [Modern Law Science] 94–109.

[8] See e.g. Lin Lin, 'Managing the Risks of Equity Crowdfunding: Lessons from China' (2017) 17(2) *Journal of Corporate Law Studies* 327; D. Yang (杨东), 'Hu lian wang jin rong feng xian gui zhi lu jing' (互联网金融风险规制路径) [The Regulatory Path of Internet Financial Risk], (2016) 03 Zhong guo fa xue (中国法学) [China Legal Science] 80–97.

The small-scale offering exemption approach had been considered by the Standing Committee of the National People's Congress (NPCSC) in the recent overhaul of the Securities Law. Under the First Draft of the Amendment of Securities Law as published on 20 April 2015, it was stipulated that small-scale offerings in the form of equity crowdfunding can be exempted from the traditional regulatory regime for securities offerings.[9] The provision was also seen in the Third Draft.[10]

However, due to various reasons, notably the stock market crisis of 2015 and the rapidly deteriorating situation of the P2P lending market which culminated in a disaster in 2019, the NPCSC reconsidered the exemption provision and eventually deleted it in the final version of the Securities Law which was passed on 28 December 2019 with effect from 1 March 2020 (2019 Securities Law).[11] Hence, there is no special regime nor small-scale exemptions for equity crowdfunding under the new law, which came as a big disappointment for many. While it can be understood on the grounds of risk prevention, the 2019 Securities Law will likely stifle the equity crowdfunding market in China.

8.2.3 The Modes of Equity Crowdfunding

As discussed above, it is practically unfeasible to engage in equity crowdfunding under the public offerings regime, and hence, China's equity crowdfunding platforms have tried to utilize the private offerings regime. Basically, if securities are offered to accumulatively less than 200 specified objects, the offering would be a private offering and thus could avoid the stringent regulatory requirements for public offerings. This type of equity crowdfunding can be called private equity crowdfunding. Hence, equity crowdfunding, according to the type of investors it involves, can be divided into private and public equity crowdfunding. Specifically, private equity crowdfunding refers to the practice of tailoring equity crowdfunding to selected groups of investors, while public equity crowdfunding involves the general public.

---

[9] Zhong hua ren min gong he guo zheng quan fa (xiu ding cao an) (中华人民共和国证券法 (修订草案)) [First Draft of the Amendment of Securities Law of the People's Republic of China] (issued by NPCSC on 20 April 2015), art. 13.

[10] Zhong hua ren min gong he guo zheng quan fa (xiu ding cao an) (san ci sheng yi gao) (中华人民共和国证券法（修订草案）（三次审议稿）) [The Third Reviewed Draft of the Amendment of Securities Law of the People's Republic of China] (issued by NPCSC on 26 April 2019), art. 11.

[11] Zhong hua ren min gong he guo zheng quan fa (中华人民共和国证券法) [Securities Law of the People's Republic of China (2019 Revision)] (issued by NPCSC on 28 December 2019, effective from 1 March 2020).

On 18 December 2014, the SAC issued a consultation paper titled 'Measures for the Administration of Private Equity Crowdfunding (for Trial)'.[12] This is the first time the term 'private equity crowdfunding' (*simu guquan zhongchou*) has been used in a formal document, representing an effort to recognize the legality of private EC. On 29 July 2015, the SAC issued 'Administrative Measures for Record-keeping of Off-exchange Securities Businesses',[13] listing private EC as one of the off-exchange securities businesses which are conducted outside of national exchanges including the Shanghai Stock Exchange, the Shenzhen Stock Exchange, the Beijing-based National Equities Exchange and Quotations, and futures exchanges.

Unfortunately, due to various reasons, notably the worsening situation and increasing risks of crowdfunding businesses, the SAC's consultation paper has not yet been adopted as a formal regulation to legally recognize and facilitate the operation of private equity crowdfunding. There seems to be no hope of the adoption of the consultation paper in the foreseeable future.

Furthermore, the term 'private equity crowdfunding' is actually self-contradictory, in the sense that crowdfunding, by definition, involves a large group of investors, each contributing a small amount. Thus, 'private' seems as though a strange bedfellow of 'crowdfunding'. On 3 August 2015, the CSRC announced a specific campaign to examine the institutions which engage in equity financing activities via the internet, stating that equity crowdfunding has the essential features of 'openness, small amount and large crowd', and without approval from the CSRC, no entities or individuals may carry out equity crowdfunding.[14] Importantly, the CSRC specifically mentioned that the so-called private equity crowdfunding is actually non-public equity fundraising via the internet, and thus does not fall within the scope of equity crowdfunding. Indeed, it would cause confusion if the term crowdfunding were to be used to cover internet-based non-public offerings of equity securities or

---

[12] Si mu gu quan zhong chou rong zi guan li ban fa (shi xing) (zheng qu yi jian gao) (私募股权众筹融资管理办法（试行）（征求意见稿）) [Measures for the Management of Private Equity Crowdfunding (for Trial Implementation) (Consultation Draft)] (issued by Securities Association of China (中国证券业协会) on 18 December 2014).

[13] Chang wai zheng quan ye wu bei an guan li ban fa (场外证券业务备案管理办法) [Over-the-Counter Securities Business] (issued by Securities Association of China (中国证券业协会) on 29 July 2015, effective 1 September 2015).

[14] Guanyu dui tongguo hulianwang kaizhan guquan rongzi huodong de jigou jinxing zhuanxiang jiancha de tongzhi (关于对通过互联网开展股权融资活动的机构进行专项检查的通知) [Notice on the Specific Examination of the Institutions that Engage in Equity Financing Activities via Internet] (issued by the CSRC on 3 August 2015).

262 CROWDFUNDING & CENTRAL BANK DIGITAL CURRENCY

fundraisings by private equity investment funds. On 10 August 2015, the SAC took notice of the position of the CSRC, issuing a specific notice to change the term 'private equity crowdfunding' to 'internet non-public equity financing' (INPEF, 互联网非公开股权融资) in the aforementioned 'Administrative Measures for Record-keeping of Off-exchange Securities Businesses'.[15] Hence, in a strict sense, there is no equity crowdfunding in China, because public equity crowdfunding is practically unfeasible under the current law and private equity crowdfunding is simply a misnomer.

However, for brevity and to facilitate comparisons with ordinary equity crowdfunding, this chapter will still use the term 'private equity crowdfunding' to refer to the way in which China's equity crowdfunding platforms conduct business via the route of private offerings. Indeed, due to the impracticability of the mode of public equity crowdfunding, China's equity crowdfunding platforms has tried to make use of the mode of private equity crowdfunding since the beginning of business.

The case of Meiwei Media represents the first attempt to conduct equity crowdfunding in China.[16] On 5 October 2012, there appeared an online shop selling membership cards for a company called Meiwei Media on Taobao, China's popular online shopping platform. The membership card would entitle the holder to the subscription of an electronic magazine published by Meiwei Media as well as the original shareholder status of the company. In other words, the membership card would serve as a certificate for the shares in the company, and the company planned to offer shares to the general public to raise money for a new business programme. In the first round of offerings, Meiwei Media raised about RMB 400,000, and in January 2013, the second round raised about RMB 816,000, totalling RMB 1,203,700 during the whole exercise with the involvement of up to 1,193 investors. It should be noted that in order to avoid the upper limit of 200 investors, the company used contractual arrangements to allow investors to hold their shares in the name of nominal shareholders, thereby keeping the number of investors below 200 in compliance with the public offering requirement.

---

[15] Guanyu tiaozheng "changwai zhengquan yewu beian guanli banfa" gebie tiaokuan de tongzhi (关于调整《场外证券业务备案管理办法》个别条款的通知) [Notice on the Change of A Provision in the 'Administrative Measures for Record-keeping of Off-exchange Securities Businesses'] (issued by the Securities Association of China on 10 August 2015).

[16] Cui Xi (崔西), 'Meiwei Chuanmei Chouzi bei Jiao Ting Beihou: Zhongchou zai Zhongguo Shifou KeXing' (美微传媒筹资被叫停背后：众筹在中国是否可行) [The Fundraising of Meiwei Media Was Halted: Is Crowdfunding Permitted in China?], 22 March 2013, http://tech.sina.com.cn/i/2013–03–22/09578172527.shtml.

Nevertheless, the fundraising generated a heated public debate on whether it constituted public securities offerings without governmental approval, and also attracted the attention of the CSRC. On 4 March 2013, the CSRC launched an investigation into the case and on 24 May 2013, found that the offering was made to the general public in violation of the public offering regime.[17] In the interest of encouraging innovation and internet finance, however, the CSRC treated the case as a special one and did not impose severe penalties other than making three orders: first, it must not engage in such fundraising anymore; second, it must protect the lawful interests of existing shareholders; and third, it must report to the CSRC about its business conditions on a periodical basis. As the case of Meiwei Media shows, the CSRC strictly applies the public offering regime, which makes it practically impossible to conduct equity crowdfunding with the general public.

Hence, crowdfunding platforms can only make use of the '200 specified objects' exemption which is extremely narrow in scope because the offering must satisfy both the 'specified objects' requirement and the numerical cap of 200. In practice, crowdfunding platforms try to make their offerees 'specified objects' through many ways such as real-name account certification and investment qualification certification. For instance, Angelcrunch (Tian Shi Hui), a crowdfunding platform targeting wealthy elite investors, only accepts 'qualified investors' who must register using their real names and meet one of the highly specified investment qualification thresholds with reference to annual income, financial assets, fixed assets or investment experiences.[18] Similarly, Tian Shi Jie, another well-known crowdfunding platform, divides investors into different categories, but all investors must be registered and satisfy certain requirements in terms of annual income and investment experience.[19] However, as the law is currently silent on what is meant by 'specified', there is a level of legal uncertainty over the various techniques adopted by crowdfunding platforms.

8.2.4   A Case Study: Feidu v Nuomiduo

Feidu v Nuomiduo is the first case brought to the court and thus dubbed 'Crowdfunding Case Number One'.[20] On 21 January 2015, the plaintiff,

---

[17] Ibid.

[18] Official website of Angelcrunch, http://angelcrunch.com/.

[19] Official website of Tian Shi Jie, http://sz.tianshijie.com.cn/.

[20] She Fa (佘法), 'Quan guo shou li zhong chou rong zi an' yi shen xuan pan' (全国首例众筹融资案" 一审宣判) [First Case of Crowdfunding in China: Judgment of First Instance

Beijing Feidu Internet Tech Co (Feidu), which runs the equity crowd-funding platform 'Renren Tou', and the defendant, Beijing Nuomiduo Catering Company, signed a fundraising service contract under which Nuomiduo entrusted Feidu to use its 'Renren Tou' platform to ra se an amount of RMB 880,000 for the purpose of opening a restaurant. After the contract was signed, Nuomiduo prepaid to Feidu a service fee of RMB 176,000, and started relevant work such as house renting and renovation. Feidu posted the restaurant project on the crowd-funding platform 'Renren Tou', and a total of eighty-six investors participated and contributed money. During the period of restaurant renovation, Feidu found that the house rented by Nuomiduo had many problems and Nuomiduo did not make proper disclosures. For instance, the house had a different structure than was indicated in the contract, did not have an official registration certificate, and the rent was significantly higher than the average price in the area. Hence, Feidu refused to transfer the money raised to Nuomiduo. The two parties tried to negotiate a solution to the issue, but eventually failed. On 14 April 2015, Nuomiduo sent a notice to Feidu to rescind the services contract and demand the return of the prepaid service fee as well as the payment of damages. On the same day, Feidu also notified Nuomiduo of the rescission of the services contract and demanded damages. Later in May 2015, Feidu brought a case before the Haidian District Court of Beijing, claiming that Nuomiduo should pay a service fee of RMB 44,000, default fine of RMB 44,000 and damages of RMB 19,712.5. Nuomiduo counter-sued, asking the plaintiff to return the prepaid service fee of RMB 176,000 and interests as well as damages of RMB 50,000.

On 20 August 2015, the Haidian District Court heard the case, looking at two key issues in dispute. The first issue concerns the legality of the fundraising service contract. In this case, the investors were all registered under their real names with the equity crowdfunding plat-form 'Renren Tou' and met the investment qualification requirements set by the platform. Moreover, the number of the investors was less than 200. Hence, the court held that the fundraising should not be treated as public offerings within the definition of Article 10 of the 2005 Securities Law. Furthermore, Feidu was properly licensed to provide information services and thus had the eligibility to enter into the fundraising service

---

Handed Down], 人民法院报 [People's Court Daily], 16 September 2015, http://rmfyb .chinacourt.org/paper/html/2015-09/16/content_102835.htm.

contract. On the above grounds, the court found that the fundraising service contract was duly made in accordance with law.

The second issue was whether there was any breach of contract by the parties. Feidu withheld the fund raised because the commercial premises rented by Nuomiduo were found to be problematic, which may adversely affect the interests of the investors participating in the fundraising. Under the contract, Nuomiduo was obligated to provide true, accurate and complete information while Feidu had a duty to check the adequacy of the information disclosure. Hence, Nuomiduo breached the contract by failing to make proper information disclosed.

On 15 September 2015, the Haidian District Court handed down its judgement, ordering that (1) Nuomiduo pay to Feidu a service fee of RMB 25,200 and a default fine of RMB 15,000; (2) Feidu return the prepaid service fee of RMB 167,200 to Nuomiduo; (3) all other claims from both parties be rejected.

This case has made several important points. First, if the investors are registered, they can be treated as 'specified' for the purposes of the private offerings regime. Second, equity crowdfunding businesses can be contractually based. Third, the crowdfunding platform can play an important role in ensuring the quality of the information disclosed by the clients. These points are of fundamental importance to the business of equity crowdfunding. However, there is still a great need for China to issue a formal regulation to give more guidance on relevant issues.

First, the court does not discuss whether there are any criteria that the registration must comply with, and how the registration process interacts with the general regime for private offerings. Second, it is not clear whether and if so, how the contract can stipulate other powers and functions for the crowdfunding platform, or whether there are any duties for the platform outside of the contract. In a later case, the court further imposed a duty of care on the crowdfunding platform in the form of risk warnings, and a duty of impartiality in protecting unsophisticated investors.[21] Finally, as China is by and large a civil law jurisdiction, the cases do not have binding effects.

---

[21] Wu wen xiao yu bei jing wang xing zhong chou wang luo ke ji you xian gong si deng ju jian he tong jiu fen yi shen ming shi pan jue shi (吴文骁与北京网信众筹网络科技有限公司等居间合同纠纷一审民事判决书（2017）京0105民初1168号) [Judgement of First Instance Regarding the Dispute of Intermediation Contract Wu wen xiao v Bei jing wang xing zhong chou wang luo ke ji you xian gong si and Others] (handed downed by the People's Court of Beijing Chaoyang District (北京市朝阳区人民法院) on 31 December 2018).

8.2.5 The Current Situation

The equity crowdfunding market in China witnessed a strong growth from 2014 to 2015, but has plummeted since then from 2016 onwards. The average financing amount of equity crowdfunding projects decreased from RMB 4.5 million in 2016 to RMB 3.29 million in 2017, and dropped further to RMB 1.5 million in 2018.[22] The number of initiated projects also fell from 1,609 in 2016 to 875 in 2018.[23] Only twenty-one crowdfunding platforms were still in operation in April 2020,[24] representing less than 20 per cent of the peak number of 133 in 2016. In November 2015, the CSRC approved the pilot programme of public equity crowdfunding and selected three platforms to participate in the programme, including Jingdong Dongjia (京东东家), Antsdaq (蚂蚁达客) and Pingan Puhui (平安前海普惠众筹). Up until July 2020, Jingdong Dongjia and Antsdaq have transformed to the mode of private equity crowdfunding, while Pingan Puhui has ceased to operate the platform.

In order to bypass the '200 investors' limit, most private equity crowdfunding platforms adopt the mechanism of 'leader+follower' by using the form of limited partnership. Basically, individual investors and leading/institutional investors form a limited partnership and then use the partnership as the vehicle to invest, so that more than 200 individual investors can participate without breaching the '200 investors' limit. In the limited partnership, leading investors serve as general partners (GP) while individual investors serve as limited partners (LP). The GP makes investment decisions on behalf of the partnership, communicate with the company it invests in, and may even sit on its board of directors. The participation of leading investor is a major attraction for individual investors' involvement, partly because portals invite famous fund managers with qualified experiences or venture capital to serve as leading investors. For example, EC portal 'Zhongtou8' lists Sequoia Capital Goldman Sachs, Blue Ridge Capital etc. on its website to demonstrate

---

[22] Z. D. Liu, G. L. Han and X. Zhao (刘泽东, 韩光林 & 赵星), 'Wo guo gu quan zhong chou xiao e gong kai fa xing huo mian zhi du de gou jian yan jiu' (我国股权众筹小额公开发行豁免制度的构建研究) [Research on the Construction of the Exemption System for Small Public], (2019) 248 Zheng xin (征信) [Credit Reference] 63–69.

[23] Z. D. Liu and G. L. Han (刘泽东 & 韩光林), 'Wo guo gu quan zhong chou he ge tou zi zhe zhi du de gou jian yan jiu' (我国股权众筹合格投资者制度的构建研究) [Research on the Construction of Equity-based Crowdfunding Qualified Investor System], (2019) 09 Jin rong fa zhan yan jiu (金融发展研究) [Journal of Financial Development Research] 42–48.

[24] Zhong Chou Jia (众筹家), '2020 nian 4 yue zhong guo zhong chou hang ye yue bao' (2020年4月中国众筹行业月报) [Monthly Report for Crowdfunding in China April 2020], 2020.

the high quality of potential projects with possible endorsements from famous institutions.[25] The model is widely used by most successful projects. For private EC projects on Jingdong Dongjia up until mid-2016, there are eighty-three successful financing cases and the investment percentage of leading investors can range from 25 per cent to 94 per cent with an average rate of 59 per cent.

However, according to statistical analyses, the 'leader+follower' model is not a positive factor for the scale of financing.[26] In other words, the model does not positively encourage more individual investors to participate in the project. This puts certain reservation on whether leading investors can significantly boost the participation of individual investors. At the same time, though the direct influence of the model on individual investors has not been tested affirmatively, it has been proved that it can serve as a useful mechanism to ease any distrust between individual investors and the issuer.[27]

Apart from the effectiveness of the model, there are also potential legal issues for individual investors in protecting their own right since the LP will not be able to participate in the daily management of the limited partnership.[28] All investment decisions have to be made through GP, and potential conflicts of interest can leave LP with few remedies.

8.2.6 *The Way Forward*

I have argued elsewhere that China should take a gradualist approach to develop the equity crowdfunding market by, namely firstly adopting the private equity crowdfunding model and when the time is ripe, allowing public equity crowdfunding.[29] This suggestion is based on a practical

---

[25] Zhongtou8 (众投邦), 'Tou zi ren' (投资人) [Investment Institutions], 2020, https://zhongtou8.cn/invest-company.

[26] H. F. Peng (彭红枫) and Y. X. Mi (米雁翔), 'Xin xi bu dui cheng, xin hao zhi liang yu gu quan zhong chou rong zi ji xiao' (信息不对称、信号质量与股权众筹融资绩效) [Information Asymmetry, Signals' Quality and Performance of Equity-Based Crowdfunding], (2016) 38(5) *Cai mao jing ji* (财贸经济) [Finance & Trade Economics] 80–95.

[27] E. J. Xia (夏恩君), S. Li (李森) and X. W. Zhao (赵轩维), 'Rong zi xiang mu de bu que ding xing dui gu quan rong zi ji xiao de ying xiang' (融资项目的不确定性对股权众筹融资绩效的影响) [Impact of Uncertainty of Financing Project on Performance of Equity Crowdfunding: Mediating Effect of Lead Amount], (2016) 35(7) Ji shu jing ji (技术经济) [Technology Economics] 38–45.

[28] Zhong hua ren min gong he guo he huo qi ye fa (中华人民共和国合伙企业法) [Partnership Enterprise Law of the People's Republic of China] (issued by NPCSC on 27 August 2006, effective on 1 June 2007), art. 68.

[29] R. Huang (黄辉), 'Zhong guo gu quan zhong chou de gui zhi luo ji he mo shi xuan ze' (中国股权众筹的规制逻辑和模式选择) [The Regulatory Logic and Model of Equity

assessment of the desirability and feasibility of public equity crowdfunding in the context of China. At present, the model of public equity crowdfunding has problems such as information asymmetry, adverse selection and agency costs, which may lead to investor protection concerns. By contrast, private equity crowdfunding can deal with those problems through the expertise and self-protection of qualified investors. This has been borne out from the experiences of advanced economies such as the United States, the United Kingdom and Singapore. It is more so in China where private equity crowd-funding can largely meet the fundraising needs, while public equity crowd-funding may lead to investor protection problems and even systemic financial risks.

Furthermore, depending on the type of companies, different fundraising methods should be used. For instance, public equity crowdfunding may be more suitable for SMEs and start-ups while private equity crowdfunding for more established companies.[30] Indeed, equity crowdfunding can play an important role in meeting the financing needs of SMEs and start-ups which have difficulty in getting funds from traditional means such as banks and stock markets. It was estimated that the financing needs for SMEs in 2018 reached CNY 4.4 trillion, 1.9 trillion of which could not be provided by formal direct finance from banks.[31] In practice, SMEs have to resort to other channels for funding, including underground or black markets, which have a much higher average interest rate of about 17 per cent than the bank loan rate of about 6 per cent. Hence, it is important to provide SMEs and start-ups with more alternative financing tools such as equity crowdfunding.

8.3 Central Bank (Sovereign) Digital Currency

8.3.1 Introduction and Definition: DC/EP

This section will focus on the Digital Currency Electronic Payment project (DC/EP) initiated by the PBOC. In many circumstances, the digital currency is also named as 'cryptoasset', 'cryptocurrency' or 'virtual currency', whereas 'cryptoasset' designates to a wide range of electronic

---

Crowd-funding in China], (2018) 40(4) *Xian dai fa xue* (现代法学) [Modern Law Science], 94–109.

[30] D. Q. Xu and M. Y. Ge, 'Equity-Based Crowdfunding in China: Beginning with the First Crowdfunding Financing Case' (2017) 4(1) *Asian Journal of Law and Society* 81–107.

[31] Z. D. Liu (刘泽东), G. L. Han (韩光林) and X. Zhao (赵星), 'Wo guo gu quan zhong chou xiao e gong kai fa xing huo mian zhi du de gou jian yan jiu' (我国股权众筹小额公开发行豁免制度的构建研究) [Research on the Construction of the Exemption System for Small Public], (2019) 248 *Zheng xin* (征信) [Credit Reference] 63–69.

8.3 CENTRAL BANK (SOVEREIGN) DIGITAL CURRENCY 269

tokens which might not necessarily have the essential function of money.[32] 'Cryptocurrency' mainly refers to the utilization of technology of cryptography for the purposes of settlement and verification, and it sometimes refers more narrowly to Bitcoin and other digital coins that use the technology of distributed ledger (DLT). 'Virtual currency' explains the feature of electronic payment without physical presence. For consistency, this chapter will use 'DC/EP' to describe the electronic sovereign currency initiated by the PBOC and 'digital currency' in a broader sense, including all electronic currencies issued either by central banks or private entities.

According to the Bank of England (2020), the sovereign digital currency can be defined as a form of liability of a central bank to individuals, which embodies many similar functions of physical banknotes and deposits in commercial banks.[33] Similar to a fiat currency, a sovereign digital currency is a store of value, a medium of exchange and a unit of price.

This section will briefly introduce the current developments of DC/EP in China and compare the DC/EP with other popular digital currencies. Potential concerns and suggestions are also discussed in the last section for further considerations.

8.3.2 Development and Main Characteristics

Money is roughly divided into two categories, namely bank deposits in electronic form and physical banknotes (banknotes are also called as Currency in Circulation or M0). Currently, in China, only 3.75 per cent of money is in the form of banknotes,[34] and the DC/EP aims to serve as a powerful supplement to the M0. It is useful to briefly review the development process of DC/EP for a better understanding as to how it could achieve the purpose.

8.3.2.1 Development Progress of DC/EP

The development timeline of DC/EP can be broadly divided into three stages to date. The first stage is research and design, when the PBOC raised

---

[32] Board of the International Organization of Securities Commissions, Global Stablecoin Initiatives Public Report, 2020, www.iosco.org/library/pubdocs/pdf/IOSCOPD650.pdf.

[33] Bank of England, 'Central Bank Digital Currency: Opportunities, Challenges and Design', discussion paper, 2020, www.bankofengland.co.uk/-/media/boe/files/paper/2020/cen tral-bank-digital-currency-opportunities-challenges-and-design.pdf.

[34] People's Bank of China, 'Money Supply of 2020', 2020, www.pbc.gov.cn/diaochatongjisi/ resource/cms/2020/08/2020081718051457867.pdf.

the idea of developing a sovereign digital currency in 2014. A research group was established by the PBOC to conduct preliminary studies. In 2016, the Institute of Digital Currency of the PBOC and its subsidiary, Shenzhen Fintech Institute, were formally established. Their tasks include DC/EP framework design and standard setting. The framework and standard of DC/EP were approved by the State Council in 2017.[35]

Second, after four years of preparation, in 2018, the PBOC announced that the design of DC/EP was completed. More details about technology and operation modes were made available to the public.[36] After this, China has started to issue various policy guidelines and administrative plans to support the development of DC/EP. For example, in August 2019, the PBOC rolled out a plan to put the DLT into application;[37] in the same month, the Chinese central government supported Shenzhen to explore the possible implementation of digital currency and to accelerate research on mobile payment.[38] As of 21 August 2019, the PBOC has applied for seventy-four patents related to the design of digital currency,[39] including account information inquiry, the transferring mechanism between DC/EP and bank deposits, payment mechanisms, nodes management, DC/EP tracing systems etc.[40]

The third stage is the trial of DC/EP in real life. In August 2020, the Ministry of Commerce approved a pilot programme under which four cities (Shenzhen, Chengdu, Suzhou, District of Xiong'an) will implement the DC/EP on a trial basis.[41] Several commercial banks in the four cities

---

[35] People's Bank of China, 'Yang hang jiu "jin rong gai ge yu fa zhan" da ji zhe wen' (央行就'金融改革与发展'答记者问) [PBOC's Response to Journalists about 'Financial Reform and Development'], 2018, www.xinhuanet.com/politics/2018lh/zb/20180309a/index.htm.

[36] Ibid.

[37] Jin rong ke ji (FinTech) fa zhan gui hua (2019–2021) (金融科技（FinTech） 发展规划 (2019–2021年)) [Development plan of FinTech (2019–2021)] (issued by the People's Bank of China in August 2019).

[38] Guan yu zhi chi shen zhen jian she zhong guo te se she hui zhu yi xian xing shi fan qu de yi jian (关于支持深圳建设中国特色社会主义先行示范区的意见) [Opinion of Supporting Shenzhen to Establish the Pilot District of Socialism with Chinese Characteristics] (issued by Central Committee of the Chinese Communist Party and the State Council of the People's Republic of China on 9 August 2019).

[39] Xinhua Net, 'Yang hang 20 tian san ci "fa sheng" tan shu zi huo bi' (央行20天三次'发声 谈数字货币) [PBOC Talked about Digital Currency Three Times within 20 Days], 2019 www.xinhuanet.com/fortune/2019-08/22/c_1210252327.htm.

[40] China National Intellectual Property Administration, 'Zhong guo zhuan li gong bu gong gao' (中国专利公布公告) [Notice of Publication of Patent in China], 2020, http://epub.sipo.gov.cn/patentoutline.action.

[41] 'Quan mian shen hua fu wu mao yi chuang xin fa zhan shi dian zong ti fang an' (全面深化 服务贸易创新发展试点总体方案) [General Plan for Pilot Programme of

published their electronic wallets for DC/EP. For example, China Construction Bank updated its mobile application in August 2020, adding two function modules about digital currency.[42] The modules are currently only available for selected testing targets. Testing targets can choose one out of four degrees of identity authentication: strong verification, relatively strong verification, relatively weak verification, and weak verification. Different degrees of authentication correspond to different transaction limitations where the customer finishing with strong verification can enjoy a much higher transaction amount than the customer who does not want to fulfil personal information requirements (e.g. annual transaction limitation of CNY 300,000 vs CNY 10,000).[43]

8.3.2.2   Major Characteristics of DC/EP

The DC/EP project is specifically designed for the Chinese political and financial systems, and therefore, it possesses several distinguishable characteristics that aim to serve as a safe and efficient supplement to physical banknotes. Through the assessment of the DC/EP framework, it can be argued that the design and characteristics are helpful for achieving such a goal.

Firstly, DC/EP serves as a supplement to physical banknotes and does not serve as a competing existence to the bank deposit. Unlike a bank deposit, which is the liability of a particular commercial bank to individual customers, the digital currency can be treated as the liability of the central bank to individual customers. Customers bear the possible loss of deposits in case of insolvency of the commercial bank. Since the central bank has better repayment abilities, customers have less of a chance to lose the value in digital currency. In most cases, the central bank has the strongest repayment ability in the domestic financial environment. Therefore, the digital currency is the asset with the lowest risk of default.

Comprehensive Innovation and Development of Service and Trading] (issued by Ministry of Commerce on 12 August 2020), www.gov.cn/zhengce/zhengceku/2020-08/14/content_5534759.htm.

[42] 'Shu zi ren min bi zhen de lai le? Jian hang APP shang xian shu zi huo bi qian bao' (数字人民币真的来了？建行APP上线数字货币钱包) [Is Digital RMB Coming? China Construction Bank Put Forward Digital Currency Wallet in Its APP], (2020) Zhong guo zheng quan bao (中国证券报) [China Securities Journal], https://finance.sina.com.cn/stock/relnews/cn/2020-08-29/doc-iivhvpwy3816043.shtml.

[43] 'Kui jian shu zi huo bi, fen xi ren shi: ju you yi yi de bian hua reng xu jia yi shi ri' (窥见数字货币，分析人士：具有意义的变化仍需假以时日) [Peeking the Digital Currency, According to Analyst: Meaning Changes Still Need Further Observation], (2020) Sina News, https://tech.sina.com.cn/roll/2020-08-30/doc-iivhvpwy3923828.shtml.

Some scholars even regard the digital currency issued by the central bank as a risk-free asset.[44] Though DC/EP enjoys a lower risk of repayment than a bank deposit, it is not used to substitute the latter. On the contrary, in order to maintain the stability of commercial banks and monetary system (which is discussed in Section 8.3.1), the PBOC strictly separates DC/EP from bank deposits. Zero (even negative) interest rate is attached to DC/EP such that the customer will be discouraged from converting deposits into DC/EP.[45]

Secondly, the PBOC will adopt a two-tier system in the currency issuance process. The PBOC will issue DC/EP to commercial banks in exchange for full value reserve. Commercial banks will then distribute DC/EP to individual customers directly and collect equivalent amounts in banknotes.[46] Since DC/EP can reach individual customers quicker than traditional currency circulation, scholars are positive that the promotion of digital currency can benefit the effective implementation of monetary policies.[47] In the two-tier system, the PBOC can shift the burdens of customer services and due diligence to commercial banks who have accumulated vast experience in these areas.

Thirdly, the payment of digital currency can be made even without access to the internet. The PBOC has not disclosed technical details about offline payment, but it is possible that the digital currency might use similar technology as near-field communication, which is widely used in credit card transactions and other electronic payments.[48] However, offline credit card payment involves the risk of the payer having insufficient funds, which is borne by the merchant who accepts the transaction.[49] Hence, the PBOC may have to set a maximum limit for offline payment in order to minimize the risk faced by the party accepting the payment.

---

[44] M. Bech and R. Garratt, 'Central Bank Cryptocurrencies' (2017) *BIS Quarterly Review* 55–70.

[45] C. C. Mu, 'Jie kai yang hang shu zi huo bi de mian sha' (揭开央行数字货币的面纱) [Lifting the Veil of DC/EP], 2019, https://weibo.com/ttarticle/p/show?id=2309404404107401101337.

[46] G. M. Guan (管弋铭) and X. C. Wu (伍旭川), 'Shu zi huo bi fa zhan: dian xing te zheng, yan hua lu jing yu jian guan dao xiang' (数字货币发展: 典型特征、演化路径与监管导向) [The Development of Digital Currency: Typical Characteristics, Evolution, and Guidelines for Regulation], (2020) 35(3) Jing rong jing ji xue yan jiu (金融经济学研究) [Financial Economics Research] 130–145.

[47] Ibid.

[48] C. C. Mu, 'Jie kai yang hang shu zi huo bi de mian sha' (揭开央行数字货币的面纱) [Lifting the Veil of DC/EP], 2019, https://weibo.com/ttarticle/p/show?id=2309404404107401101337.

[49] S. H. Liao and L. L. Yang, 'Mobile Payment and Online to Offline Retail Business Models' (2020) 57 *Journal of Retailing and Consumer Services* 102230.

8.3 CENTRAL BANK (SOVEREIGN) DIGITAL CURRENCY 273

Fourthly, the key technology of account management is not predetermined by the PBOC, in other words, DLT or any other technology is not necessarily utilized in DC/EP. According to statistics, the peak number of transactions can be over 90,000 cases per second in China, while Bitcoin's capacity of transaction is seven cases per second.[50] For a country with a large population envisaging a payment system dealing with a large number of transactions in short period of time, it is important for DC/EP to ensure its capacity to process the data. However, the technology of DLT applied in Bitcoin cannot satisfactorily fulfil the requirements, thus, the PBOC adopts the strategy of 'long-term evolution', testing various possible proposals simultaneously and using the most suitable one.

8.3.2.3 Sovereign Digital Currencies in Other Jurisdictions

Many other countries are also exploring the possibility of sovereign digital currencies. Scholars in the United States have proposed the idea of 'Fedcoin', which is issued by the Federal Reserve and can be converted into physical US dollar at face value.[51] However, this idea has not been finalized: the Federal Reserve is still conducting research and testing on the potential usage of Fedcoin. Canada is also embarking on a similar programme to issue the central bank digital currency,[52] but the technologies to be applied remain undetermined. By contrast, Sweden proposed its digital cash in 2017[53] and is now testing the pilot project for technical solutions.[54] The United Kingdom[55] also proposed similar concepts, but it is too early to evaluate their everyday usage and implementation progress.

---

[50] C. C. Mu, 'Jie kai yang hang shu zi huo bi de mian sha' (揭开央行数字货币的面纱) [Lifting the Veil of DC/EP], 2019, https://weibo.com/ttarticle/p/show?id=2309404044107401101337.

[51] R. Garratt and N. Wallace, 'Bitcoin 1, Bitcoin 2, . . . : An Experiment in Privately Issued Outside Monies' (2018) 56(3) *Economic Inquiry* 1887–1897.

[52] The 'CADcoin' proposed by the Bank of Canada. See in R. Garratt, 'CAD-coin versus Fedcoin', *R3 Reports*, June 2016, www.r3.com/wp-content/uploads/2017/06/cadcoin-versus-fedcoin_R3.pdf.

[53] The 'eKrona' proposed by the Central Bank of Sweden, Sveriges Riksbank. See in Sveriges Riksbank, *Riksbankens e-krona Project plan*, 2017, www.riksbank.se/globalassets/media/rapporter/e-krona/2017/projektplan-e-kronan_170314_eng.pdf.

[54] The Riksbank to test technical solution for the e-krona. See in Sveriges Riksbank, 2020, www.riksbank.se/en-gb/press-and-published/notices-and-press-releases/notices/2020/the-riksbank-to-test-technical-solution-for-the-e-krona/.

[55] The Central Bank Digital Currency proposed by the Bank of England. See in Bank of England, 'Central Bank Digital Currency: Opportunities, Challenges and Design', discussion paper, 2020, www.bankofengland.co.uk/-/media/boe/files/paper/2020/central-bank-digital-currency-opportunities-challenges-and-design.pdf.

One of the significant proposals by other developed economies is the partnership with private entities in framework development and daily operations. For example, in the United Kingdom, the Bank of England only provides essential services and regulations while the licensed 'Payment Interface Providers' design services to end-users.[56] In the United Kingdom, the private sector is given more power to interact with customers and personal data would not be exclusively held by the Bank of England.

By briefly reviewing the current proposals of sovereign digital currencies in different jurisdictions, it can be more readily concluded that at the current stage, China is one of the leading pioneers in implementing sovereign digital currency out of most major economies.

8.3.3 Comparison with Bitcoin and Libra

8.3.3.1 Bitcoin: Intrinsic Struggle and External Dilemma

Bitcoin is a successful application of the DLT and one of the best-known cryptocurrencies in the world. The most significant feature that makes it different from the conventional payment is its ability to work in a decentralized manner, enabling payments between strangers to be validated without a clearing agency.[57] Other strengths such as anonymity and security have been fully explored by scholars.[58] However, it is argued that three major inherent shortcomings render Bitcoin being unable to function validly and stably as a payment medium and price unit.

The first shortcoming is Bitcoin's volatile value. It is well recognized that Bitcoin is not linked with any other stable assets. Though the cost of mining process can be accurately calculated, it has no direct link to the Bitcoin generated from the mining process. Therefore, it is better to regard Bitcoin as a high-risk investment product instead of a stable medium of payment.

Secondly, the blockchain is not as secure as one envisages. There are usually massive computations of other miners who are verifying the payments; however, when two or more competing chains containing different information exist, the longest chain prevails over the others and will be treated as the correct record (this is the rule of 'follow the

---

[56] Ibid.
[57] R. Auer, 'Beyond the Doomsday Economics of "Proof-of-Work" in Cryptocurrencies', working paper, Bank for International Settlement, 2019.
[58] Ibid.

longest chain').[59] With enough computing power, fraudsters can firstly use the same Bitcoin to pay different payees (a process called 'double spending'), then create a longer chain containing false information. Consequently, when all payees have accepted payment, the forged chain will be updated to overwrite the correct short chains.

The only method for payees to tackle this problem is to wait a certain amount of time before taking the next action (e.g. shipping goods or providing services). Since the cost of forging blocks accumulates as the chain grows longer, after a certain period of time, it would no longer be economically desirable to forge a chain since the cost is more than the potential benefit from such forgery. According to the calculation of scholars, if the payer is willing to pay 1 per cent of total payment as the transaction fee to other miners for verification, and if an attack would result in a loss of value for one-third, it would take fifty blocks (roughly 500 minutes) to make an attack cost more than its possible benefit.[60] The lower the transaction fee the payer is willing to pay, the longer the time it takes for final confirmation. The issue can be worsened if more miners cease to operate, which allows fraudster to hire more spare computing resources to forge a block. This is the major reason why payees are suggested to prudently wait for a further five to six blocks after its payment record is updated before taking the next action.

Finally, the future development of Bitcoin is uncertain. The maximum amount of Bitcoin that can be found is capped at 21 million. The reward mechanism makes the mining process less profitable. The reward for one block is initially 50 coins, which is halved after every 210,000 coins, and it reduces to zero if the reward is less than 1/100,000,000 of a coin. The high cost of electricity and mining equipment drives miners out of the mining process, which affects Bitcoin's supply and reduces the speed of verification required by paying parties. The only way for parties to accelerate the verification process is to pay increased transaction fees to miners, who will then prioritize such task over those that come with lower fees. As a result, the transaction fee had reached its peak in 2017 at USD 50, which is a rather unacceptable amount for small transactions.

Scholars have proposed solutions for the slow verification process such as one called 'Lightning network', which allows transaction participants to link each other together and sign off each other's payment without updating the transaction to blockchain. However, up until 11 September 2020,

[59] Ibid.
[60] Ibid.

there were just around 1,000 Bitcoins circulated in Lightning Network.[61] Additionally, the 'Lightning Network' can be easily controlled by participants with a large amount of Bitcoin. Other blockchain platforms such as Corda also apply certain degree of centralization, empowering trusted clearing agents to solve the payment issue.[62]

Apart from the internal problems resulting from the design and mechanism, Bitcoin is also facing strong regulations due to its high correlation with illegal activities. Because of the high degree of anonymity, Bitcoin has a close link with illegal activities and is used to avoid regulations.[63] Some scholars estimate that 46 per cent of Bitcoin transactions are aiding illegal activities.[64] Furthermore, 74 per cent of bit exchange are cross-border in 2020,[65] raising more concerns on anti-money laundering and CFT. The amount of money lost in crypto thefts, hacks and frauds in 2020 has reached USD 1.36 billion, raising serious issues of financial safety.[66]

Given the high risk and unstable supply of Bitcoin, which is susceptible to attack and manipulation, on 4 September 2017, the PBOC issued a notice to formally ban all platforms providing Bitcoin transactions or information in China.[67] However, regulators did not explicitly prohibit individual investors from holding or trading Bitcoin through overseas accounts or platforms. Furthermore, the notice did not address issues of miners and the action of mining.[68] Regulations related to blockchain information services providers were promulgated on 10 January 2019,

---

[61] Bitcoin Visuals, 'Network Capacity: Cumulative Bitcoin Capacity across All Channels', 2020, https://bitcoinvisuals.com/lightning.

[62] M. Bech and R. Garratt, 'Central Bank Cryptocurrencies' (2017) BIS Quarterly Review 55–70.

[63] Ciphertrace, 'Spring 2020 Cryptocurrency Crime and Anti-Money Laundering Report, 2020, https://ciphertrace.com/spring-2020-cryptocurrency-anti-money-laundering-report/.

[64] S. Foley, J. R. Karlsen and T. J. Putniņš, T. J., 'Sex, Drugs, and Bitcoin: How Much Illegal Activity Is Financed through Cryptocurrencies?' (2019) 32(5) Review of Financial Studies 1798–1853.

[65] Ciphertrace, 'Spring 2020 Cryptocurrency Crime and Anti-Money Laundering Report', 2020, https://ciphertrace.com/spring-2020-cryptocurrency-anti-money-laundering report/.

[66] Ibid.

[67] Guan yu fang fan dai bi fa xing rong zi feng xian de gong gao (关于防范代币发行融资风险的公告) [Notice on Preventing Risks Associated with ICOs] (issued by the People's Bank of China and others on 4 September 2017).

[68] H. Deng, H. R. Huang and Q. R. Wu, 'The Regulation of Initial Coin Offerings in China: Problems, Prognoses and Prospects' (2018) 19 European Business Organization Law Review 465–502.

which defined blockchain information services as those 'provided to the public through website and applications based on the technology or system of blockchain'. Under this regulation, the regulated targets are 'the main body or node of blockchain information services or organisation providing technic support to the main body or node of blockchain information services'.[69] However, given the tightened regulation scheme, it is uncertain whether Bitcoin will be legally approved in China in the future.

Regarding the same issue of regulation, in response to the increasing financial risk created by cryptocurrency, regulators in other jurisdictions tried to fit Bitcoin into the existing legal frameworks. The US regulators recently approved banks to provide custody service for digital currency.[70] However, they do not specify whether the digital currency can be a medium of exchange for the purpose of banking regulation,[71] which creates uncertainty as to the legal nature of cryptocurrency. In the meantime, the SEC successfully obtained a preliminary injunction against Telegram Inc. from issuing the digital token for breach of the registration requirement under sections 5(a) and 5(c) of the Securities Act.[72] The District Court of Southern District of New York ruled that the sale of token 'Grams' to 171 purchasers for the consideration of USD 1.7 billion fulfils the four criteria laid in *SEC v. W. J. Howey Co.*,[73] so that in the absence of the exemption stipulated in the Securities Act, the public offering of digital currency without registration was held to be illegal.[74] This case raises serious doubts about the legality of the ICO in the United States. It is foreseeable that companies considering ICO or cryptocurrency exchange might have to rethink their business models.

8.3.3.2 Libra: Embraces the Blockchain and Tiptoes around Regulation

Libra is regarded as a type of stablecoin. Though consensus has not been reached about the precise definition of stablecoins, most of the digital

---

[69] Qu kuai lian xin xin fu wu guan li gui ding (区块链信息服务管理规定) [Administration Regulation on Blockchain Information Services] (issued by Cyberspace Administration of China on 10 January 2019, effective 15 February 2019).

[70] Office of the Controller of the Currency, Interpretive Letter No. 1170, 2020, www.occ.gov/topics/charters-and-licensing/interpretations-and-actions/2020/int1170.pdf.

[71] Title 12 of the US Code §24 Seventh.

[72] 15 USC § 77e(a).

[73] 328 US 293 (US Supreme Court).

[74] *Securities and Exchange Commission v. Telegram Group Inc. and TON Issuer Inc.*, 19 Civ. 9439 (PKC).

coins in this category share certain features including price stability. By linking with other assets or redemption mechanisms at par value, stablecoins enjoy more pricing stability.[75]

To enhance public confidence and solve volatility problems faced by Bitcoin, the organizer of Libra (the Libra Association,) uses two forms of assets as reserves to support the value of Libra: for a domestic transaction within selected places (e.g. EU, United States, United Kingdom), the value of Libra will be linked with cash or cash equivalents in local currency, while for an international transaction or a domestic transaction out of selected places, the value of Libra will be backed by a basket of currencies akin to the mechanism of Special Drawing Rights by the IMF. To further strengthen its financial position, the Libra Association set restrictions on redemption in cases of devastating situations similar to bank runs, so that the coin holder will either wait for a longer time or bear the cost of early redemption. If Libra is facing a serious liquidity problem and the asset cannot be disposed of without a significant discount, redemption might be suspended until the condition is relieved.[76]

The Libra Association ambitiously published its first proposal in June 2019, proposing to set the value of Libra only according to the weighted composition of a basket of currencies without linking to a single one. Libra's initial blueprint is to serve as an international medium of exchange applicable to the majority of economies around the world. A basket of currencies is more suitable for such a grand purpose than any single currency. Nevertheless, the uncertainty and great possibility of rapid implementation without comprehensive regulations trigger severe backlash with major regulators.

The US House of Representatives on 2 July 2019 requested Facebook to suspend the implementation of Libra and its electronic wallet Calibra immediately pending full inquiry and comprehensive regulations.[77] Germany and France issued a joint statement in September 2019, rejecting the proposal of Libra and emphasizing the importance of sovereignty

---

[75] Board of the International Organization of Securities Commissions, *Global Stablecoin Initiatives Public Report*, 2020, www.iosco.org/library/pubdocs/pdf/IOSCOPD650.pdf.

[76] Libra, 'Economics and the Libra Reserve', 2020, https://libra.org/en-US/economics-and -the-reserve/#overview.

[77] US House Committee on Financial Services, Committee Democrats Call on Facebook to Halt Cryptocurrency Plans, 2019, https://financialservices.house.gov/news/documentsin gle.aspx?DocumentID=404009#3.

over monetary policy.[78] At the same time, G7 published its own research paper about Libra, strictly requiring that no further operation can be conducted unless the Libra Association clarifies the legal relationship among various parties involved in the transaction and regulators finalize the monitoring framework.[79] The G7 research also questioned the governance ability of the Libra Association in the absence of wide involvement of authorities around the world and raised doubts about the misuse of funds by privatizing financial profits to the association itself while sharing the loss with all coin holders[80] (according to the Libra Association, Libra is interest-free and the association will keep any positive financial return for future developments[81]).

Other international regulatory authorities also expressed supervisory concerns from their particular prospects. For example, the IOSCO recently made a hypothetical case that shared striking similarities with the operation model of Libra and concluded that the target operator of digital currency in the case analysis would be subject to various principles including monetary infrastructure, investment activities, the transaction of coins and customer protection.[82]

Similar concerns are also expressed in China. Since the Chinese currency, renminbi, is not a currency in the basket of currencies used by the Libra Association, transaction parties may prefer Libra over renminbi as the settlement currency in international dealings, causing a decrease of renminbi reserve in other central banks. Furthermore, since the value and interest of Libra are decided by linked currencies and renminbi is not a designated currency, the Chinese government will have effectively little control over the interest rate of Libra. If Libra is widely used in a domestic environment, it might impair the effectiveness of Chinese monetary policies.[83] Some scholars worry that the

---

[78] Federal Ministry of Finance of Germany and Ministry of the Economy and Finance of France, Joint Statement on Libra, 2019, www.bundesfinanzministerium.de/Content/EN/Standardartikel/Topics/Financial_markets/Articles/2019-09-17-Libra-download.pdf.

[79] G7 Working Group on Stablecoins, 'Investigating the Impact of Global Stablecoins', 2019, www.bis.org/cpmi/publ/d187.pdf.

[80] Ibid.

[81] Libra, White Paper v2.0, 2020, https://libra.org/en-US/white-paper/#cover-letter.

[82] Board of the International Organization of Securities Commissions, *Global Stablecoin Initiatives Public Report*, 2020, www.iosco.org/library/pubdocs/pdf/IOSCOPD650.pdf.

[83] Z. Li (李真), M. C. Liu (刘颖格) and Y. C. Dai (戴祎程), 'Libra wen ding bi dui wo guo huo bi zheng ce de ying xiang ji ying dui ce lue' (Libra稳定币对我国货币政策的影响及应对策略) [The Impact of Libra on China's Monetary Police and Its Countermeasure], (2020) 40(3) Xi an jiao tong da xue xue bao (西安交通大学学报（社会科学版）) [Journal of Xi'an Jiaotong University (Social Sciences)] 55–63.

promotion of Libra will frustrate the internationalization of renminbi and raise new challenges for the Belt and Road Initiative.[84]

Many believe that the alternative measurement of local currency in selected places in the 2.0 version is a compromise made by the Libra Association with central banks and a deference to monetary sovereignty.[85] In response to regulators' distrust, the Libra Association has become more reserved and underlined regulation compliance requirements in the 2.0 version.[86] Comparing to the clear expression of the plan with a detailed timeline in the 1.0 version,[87] the Libra Association became more reserved in the 2.0 version which did not indicate any specific milestone. However, the regulatory attitude towards Libra is still uncertain in most developed countries. It is difficult to predict the actual acceptance of the finalized product by major economies.

8.3.3.3   Summary: Advantages of the DC/EP

Compared to Bitcoin and Libra, DC/EP is backed by a more efficient operation framework, and thus has demonstrated several distinct advantages: First, the two-tier system allows the PBOC to concentrate on blueprint design and infrastructure building and allows the commercial banks to work on customer service and due diligence. The system can reduce the competition between the PBOC and commercial banks while encouraging healthy competition amongst the latter and other service providers for better services provided to investors.

On the other hand, the centralized model allows the PBOC to control credit risk of commercial banks. With the full reserve requirement and clear monitoring system, the PBOC can minimize systemic financial risks and implement sound monetary policies accurately.

---

[84] H. Zhao (赵红) and J. W. Fu (付俊文), 'Qian xi Libra dui guo ji huo bi ti xi de ke neng chong ji' (浅析Libra对国际货币体系的可能冲击 – – 基于数字货币视角) [Brief analysis of possible impact by Libra on international monetary system – from prospect of digital currency], (2020) 1 Shi jie jing ji yu zheng zhi lun tan (世界经济与政治论坛) [Forum of World Economics & Politics] 114–127.

[85] G. M. Guan (管弋铭) and X. C. Wu (伍旭川), 'Shu zi huo bi fa zhan: dian xing te zheng, yan hua lu jing yu jian guan dao xiang' (数字货币发展: 典型特征、演化路径与监管导向) [The Development of Digital Currency: Typical Characteristics, Evolution, and Guidelines for Regulation], (2020) 35(3) Jing rong jing ji xue yan jiu (金融经济学研究) [Financial Economics Research] 130–145.

[86] Libra, White Paper v2.0, 2020, https://libra.org/en-US/white-paper/#cover-letter.

[87] Libra, 'An Introduction to Libra', 2019, www.diem.com/en-us/wp-content/uploads/sites/23/2019/06/librawhitepaper_en_us.pdf.

8.3 CENTRAL BANK (SOVEREIGN) DIGITAL CURRENCY   281

The digitalization of fiat currency also benefits the society as a whole, because it reduces the costs of manufacturing and maintaining physical banknotes. The operation of a physical banknote system is costly especially for a country of large territory and huge population.

Furthermore, developing sovereign digital currency has been widely regarded as a symbolic and essential move to maintain monetary sovereignty. It also facilitates the internalization of renminbi[88] and may make cross-border payment more efficient.

8.3.4 Regulatory Issues

8.3.4.1 DC/EP's Influence on Monetary Policy

General concerns about digital currency have been raised in that since the digital currency gives payment parties better access to the settlement process, the intermediary role that was used to be played by commercial banks might fade out. Furthermore, if the digital currency can be interest-bearing, there will be fewer customers depositing money in commercial banks and this would cause the bank to have fewer assets available for loans, which can further squeeze out the revenues of commercial banks.[89] A small conversion from deposit to digital currency by individual customers could result in a significant reduction of banks' size. A bank with a reduced fund cannot fulfil the duty to provide direct financing to the economy. As a result, to tackle the outflow of deposit to digital currency, commercial banks would increase the interest rate attached to such deposits, and borrowers will bear the higher cost eventually. Worse still, commercial banks will increase borrowings from the central bank as an alternative funding source; however, a large number of banks with shrinking assets but increasing credit have significant influence on the stability of a country's economy. In such a case, the central bank might face increasing issues in fund allocation, which might be inappropriately interfered with by political powers.[90]

---

[88] D. W. Arner, R. P. Buckley, D. A. Zetzsche and A. N. Didenko, 'After Libra, Digital Yuan and COVID-19: Central Bank Digital Currencies and the New World of Money and Payment Systems', *European Banking Institute Working Paper 65/2020*, 2020, https://papers.ssrn.com/sol3/papers.cfm?abstract_id=3622311.

[89] Bank of England, 'Central Bank Digital Currency: Opportunities, Challenges and Design', discussion paper, 2020, www.bankofengland.co.uk/-/media/boe/files/paper/2020/central-bank-digital-currency-opportunities-challenges-and-design.pdf.

[90] T. Zhang, 'Deputy Managing Director Tao Zhang's Keynote Address on Central Bank Digital Currency', 2020, www.imf.org/en/News/Articles/2020/03/19/sp031920-deputy-managing-director-tao-zhangs-keynote-address-on-central-bank-digital-currency.

In addition, since there has not been any electronic sovereign currency formally introduced by major economies in the world, the equilibrium between inflow/outflow of deposit from/to digital currency is hard to measure, and the impact of interest rates on such equilibrium is unknown. Therefore, to maintain the stability of the banking system and implement the DC/EP scheme properly, it is foreseeable that the PBOC might set a limitation that every individual can exchange from deposit to the DC/EP (i.e. limited to 'social use' at the first stage[91]) or impose a significant interest difference between the DC/EP and deposit (i.e. based on the current available information, the DC/EP will have zero/negative interest rate[92]). However, given the current low-interest rate and the continuous adoption of quantitative easing by major economies in the near future,[93] it is rather difficult to create a gap to discourage outflow to digital currency. Compulsory limitation of holding amount might be a practical start. In addition, the central bank can modify the monetary infrastructure to control the flow of digital currency. For instance, the central bank can control the exchange between bank deposits and digital currency by separating the digital currency and bank reserves and prohibiting the use of digital currency in inter-bank settlements.[94]

Another issue that the regulator should consider is the improvement of financial inclusion by the DC/EP. According to a report by the PBOC and CBIRC, up until June 2019, every Chinese person on average holds 7.5

[91] M. Gross and C. Siebenbrunner, 'Money Creation in Fiat and Digital Currency Systems', *IMF Working Paper No. 2019285*, 2019, www.imf.org/~/media/Files/Publications/WP/2019/wpiea2019285-print-pdf.ashx.

[92] G. F. Sun (孙国峰) and S. Chen (陈实), 'Mei guo fei zhu quan shu zi huo bi de fa lv jian guan lu jing' (美国非主权数字货币的法律监管路径) [US Regulation Mechanism over Non-sovereign Digital Currency], (2020) 16 Zhong guo jing rong (中国金融) [China Finance], https://mp.weixin.qq.com/s?__biz=MzA4MzA1MjIzOQ==&mid=2650723478&idx=1&sn=b2f062e9c6fdf4a37e7237de10b09e5f&chksm=87f62736b081ae20c0cfeafd01dd40ec6c5ddaef210e73d278f3caabd47c87ca65ec826d375f&mpshare=1&scene=1&srcid=0822K0E3AWItnTuyXTlIFgT5&sharer_sharetime=1598290178062&sharer_shareid=ca96ae51a24b22894e2c90bf84601cd8&exportkey=Adm0nCuItIigGyG2usS%2BACc%3D&pass_ticket=wCoLbLQQJ5EZQsIyRCcau01atT7JoHMOld5VyAgzJDNHhEWpawSSaxD4OTyxnXyl&wx_header=0#rd.

[93] Bank of China, 2020 nian san ji du zhong guo yin hang jing ji jin rong zhan wang bao gao (2020年三季度中国银行经济金融展望报告) [Forecast Report for Economy and Finance in 2020 Q3 by Bank of China], 2020, www.bankofchina.com/fimarkets/summarize/202006/t20200630_18063133.html.

[94] M. Kumhof and C. Noone, 'Central Bank Digital Currencies – Design Principles and Balance Sheet Implications', *Bank of England Staff Working Paper No. 725*, 2018, www.bankofengland.co.uk/-/media/boe/files/working-paper/2018/central-bank-digital-currencies-design-principles-and-balance-sheet-implications.

bank accounts, and more than 82 per cent of adults have used electronic payments.[95] Up until March 2020, 64.5 per cent of the population (904 million) has access to the internet, with internet users in the urban area taking up 71.8 per cent of the total amount of internet users.[96] The less advanced segments of society (i.e. over 50 per cent of the population are in the rural areas[97]) might have limited access to bank accounts and the internet. While utilizing advanced technology is beneficial for the development of society, it is vital to prevent any further widening of the gap between urban and rural areas, which is usually the case when advanced technology is unavailable in less developed areas. It is vital to bridge the gap caused by developments in society instead of widening it by technology utilization.

8.3.4.2 Anonymity Concerns

The benefits of anonymity include less privacy intrusion by commercial advertisements and less criminal activities such as ID fraud. However, anonymity also creates a convenient environment that fosters crimes such as tax evasion, money laundering and terrorist funding.[98]

On the other hand, empirical investigation shows that customers have low awareness of privacy protection when using mobile apps. A significant proportion of users would not bother to check privacy statements or change the default setting, which allows some sensitive personal data to be made available to the public. This is the case even for users with the background of higher education.[99]

Given the tightened and stringent regulatory regime in China, it is predictable that the PBOC will consider more restricted requirements for authenticating users' identities and verifying other relevant information such as employment records and bank statements. The existing requirements for authenticating users' identities in the mobile phone registration

---

[95] People's Bank of the People's Republic of China and China Banking and Insurance Regulatory Commission, 2019 nian zhong guo pu hui jin rong fa zhan bao gao (2019年中国普惠金融发展报告) [2019 Annual Report of Development of Financial Inclusion in China], 2019, www.cbirc.gov.cn/cn/view/pages/ItemDetail.html?docId=847316.

[96] China Internet Network Information Center, *The 45th China Statistical Report on Internet Development*, 2020, www.cac.gov.cn/2020-04/27/c_1589535470378587.htm.

[97] Ibid.

[98] M. Bech and R. Garratt, 'Central Bank Cryptocurrencies', (2017) *BIS Quarterly Review* 55–70.

[99] S. Athey, C. Catalini and C. Tucker, 'The Digital Privacy Paradox: Small Money, Small Costs, Small Talk', (2017) *Stanford University Graduate School of Business Research Papers* 17–24.

process can be integrated into DC/EP scheme. To address concerns about privacy, regulators can set rules so that payers' identity will not be revealed to payees and other users, and the authority can have access to the necessary information under certain circumstances.[100] Such rules should be designed to fulfil the regulatory requirements for anti-money laundering and CFT while maintaining a reasonable degree of privacy. On the other hand, many customizing and value-added services provided by online platforms nowadays are based on customer data collected in the payment process. Being separated from the essential payment information of customers, online platforms may encounter difficulty in relation to data analysis and customer services.[101]

8.3.4.3 Reliability of Infrastructure and Design of Process

Many regulators of oversea jurisdictions are concerned about the necessary construction of infrastructure given the substantial volume of transactions. Building a reliable and safe payment system is not only the key to the success of the DC/EP project but also exerts decisive influence on customers' confidence in electronic payment. For example, if the PBOC applies DLT in its final model, it will inevitably face the problem of resiliency upon crash of database or failure during transmission. Though the distribution of processing and data storage to various nodes can mitigate the risk of a total failure, in order for the whole system to run successfully, it is vital to know how to select trusted nodes and design a consensus process that ensures every copy of ledge is synchronized and contains the same correct information.[102] Currently, four cities in China have been approved as pilot experiment locations for the implementation of DC/EP,[103] and the reliability of infrastructure can be thoroughly tested in this experiment.

---

[100] Bank of England, 'Central Bank Digital Currency: Opportunities, Challenges and Design', discussion paper, 2020, www.bankofengland.co.uk/-/media/boe/files/paper/2020/central-bank-digital-currency-opportunities-challenges-and-design.pdf.

[101] T. H. Zhu (朱太辉) and H. X. Zhang (张皓星), 'Zhong guo yang hang shu zi huo bi de she ji ji zhi ji qian zai ying xiang yan jiu – ji yu yang hang shu zi huo bi zhuan li shen qing de fen xi' (中国央行数字货币的设计机制及潜在影响研究 – 基于央行数字货币专利申请的分析) [Research on the Design Mechanism and Potential Impact of China's Central Bank Digital Currency – Based on the Analysis of PBC's Digital Currency Patents], (2020) 5 Jin rong fa zhan yan jiu (金融发展研究) [Journal of Financial Development Research] 3–9.

[102] Bank of England, 'Central Bank Digital Currency: Opportunities, challenges and design', discussion paper, 2020, www.bankofengland.co.uk/-/media/boe/files/paper/2020/central-bank-digital-currency-opportunities-challenges-and-design.pdf.

[103] Quan mian shen hua fu wu mao yi chuang xin fa zhan shi dian zong ti fang an (全面深化服务贸易创新发展试点总体方案) [General Plan for Pilot Programme of Comprehensive

8.3 CENTRAL BANK (SOVEREIGN) DIGITAL CURRENCY 285

8.3.4.4 Cross-Border Payment Issues

From the available regulation and guidelines, it is clear that using DC/EP as a powerful cross-border payment option is one of the development goals for the PBOC. Statistics show that the average cost of cross-border payment through a chain of commercial banks is 10.6 per cent.[104] Building an efficient and safe inter-bank settlement system can significantly reduce costs and improve the international acceptance of the DC/EP. This also facilitates the renminbi in becoming an international currency.

The two major disadvantages of commonly used correspondent banking models are high cost and low efficiency. The low efficiency is mainly attributed to the limited opening hours of settlement systems in different places, which causes participating banks to pledge large amounts of funds in the system to 'catch' the window time for settlement. The opportunity cost of such pledged money contributes to 34 per cent of the total transaction cost.[105]

Apart from promoting the DC/EP and internationalization of the renminbi, the IMF's concerns about the expansion of digital currency in advanced economies is worthy of attention. There is a need to address the issue of currency substitution in countries facing inflation and exchange rate fluctuation. The goal is to ensure that the DC/EP can help less developed countries to seize opportunities of digitalization, while at the same time, avoiding the effect of undermining the monetary policy of central banks in those places.[106] As the DC/EP project continues to develop, more information will become available and more research is needed in this area.

Innovation and Development of Service and Trading] (issued by Ministry of Commerce on 12 August 2020), www.gov.cn/zhengce/zhengceku/2020-08/14/content_5534759.htm.

[104] World Bank, 'Remittance Prices Worldwide: An Analysis of Trends in Cost of Remittance Services', report, June 2020, https://remittanceprices.worldbank.org/sites/default/files/rpw_report_june_2020.pdf.

[105] Bank of Canada, Bank of England and Monetary Authority of Singapore, 'Cross-Border Interbank Payments and Settlements: Emerging Opportunities for Digital Transformation', 2018, www.mas.gov.sg/-/media/MAS/ProjectUbin/Cross-Border-Interbank-Payments-and-Settlements.pdf.

[106] T. Zhang, Deputy Managing Director Tao Zhang's Keynote Address on Central Bank Digital Currency, 2020, www.imf.org/en/News/Articles/2020/03/19/sp031920-deputy-managing-director-tao-zhangs-keynote-address-on-central-bank-digital-currency.

9

Conclusion

China has put a lot of effort into the development and regulation of Fintech, because Fintech has a particularly important role to play in China. Due to the various problems with its traditional financial system, China hopes to use Fintech to meet the financing needs of disadvantaged groups such as private, small and medium-sized enterprises. Fintech can also generate necessary and healthy competition in the financial markets, so as to break the monopoly collectively enjoyed by a small group of huge, state-controlled financial institutions in China. Jack Ma of Alibaba once famously said that 'if the banks do not change, we will change them'.[1] Indeed, Fintech has forced the traditional financial system to reform and improve their services. It is hoped that Fintech can help achieve the ultimate goal of financial inclusion in China.

However, as this book has shown, China has achieved mixed results, with some Fintech sectors continuing to prosper while others being less successful. How can we explain the rise and fall of those sectors? What lessons are to be learned from them? This book ventured to make some observations and drew a number of conclusions.

Let's start with the online P2P lending market. China's P2P lending market boomed in the early 2010s thanks to its many advantages over the traditional lending market. But there were a lot of problems too. Then, the 2016 Interim Measures on Online Lending and three implementation rules were issued to makeup the so-called 1+3 regulatory framework for P2P lending in China. It was hoped to safeguard and promote the healthy development of China's online lending market. In general, the Chinese regulatory approach is sensible, compared to some major jurisdictions overseas. The central-local cooperative supervisory arrangement is innovative too. However, given the recent fall of the P2P lending market,

---

[1] 'Ma Yun: If the Banks Do Not Change, We Will Change Them' (马云：如果银行不改变，我们就改变银行), www.sohu.com/a/294003144_117373.

it seems that the regulation has not been implemented as effectively as expected, and there is a need for more research on the reasons behind it.

The ban on ICO in China provides a more extreme example of the difficulty with striking a proper balance between market development and investor protection. Undoubtedly, ICOs must be regulated, but it seems drastic to ban it completely. Clearly, a blanket ban on ICO will stifle innovation and is not conducive to the development of Fintech and blockchain technology. As a result of the ban, cryptoassets are placed in a legal limbo in China, which inhibits the development of the market and forces many players to move their business elsewhere such as Hong Kong and Singapore. For certain, China's decision to ban ICOs can be attributed to many factors, such as peculiar local conditions and the self-interest of regulators, but it does not mean that the ban serves China any good. China is advised to learn from the experiences of overseas jurisdictions to establish a regulatory regime which can better balance the needs for investor protection and market development.

Perhaps mobile payment is currently the most successful sector in China's Fintech market. Albeit not the origin of mobile payment, China has become a frontrunner in the global mobile payment market, in terms of market volume, growth rate and innovation capability. This can be explained by several main factors, including technological advancement in China such as the high penetration of smartphones and the wide coverage of internet, mobile payment's competitive advantages over traditional forms of payment in terms of convenience and flexibility, as well as the distinctive local context in China where people are more receptive to mobile payment due to the lack of credit cards and relative insensitivity to data protection issues. Hence, local conditions are an important variable to explain the success story of mobile payment in China.

However, for the long-term healthy development of mobile payment, regulation will still be key. China has made great efforts to gradually establish a regulatory framework for mobile payment. From a comparative perspective, the Chinese regulatory regime has its distinctive features with both strengths and weaknesses. While mobile payment brings great benefits such as convenience, flexibility and efficiency, they are not without risks. Among the risks that consumers face, the data privacy risk is probably one of the most serious, which is in large part caused and exacerbated by the involvement of multiple players and the extensive collection of personal information. At present, China's regulatory regime for mobile payment and data privacy protection has been developed in a piecemeal manner with relevant rules being scattered across different laws and regulations. There is a need to tidy up and consolidate them into a more coherent framework.

Robo-advisory is a promising Fintech business with the advancement of AI. To further develop the market of robo-advisory while effectively protecting investors, China needs to strengthen regulations in relation to market access, the fiduciary duty, the regime for information disclosure and the power for asset management.

Unlike its sibling of debt crowdfunding, namely online P2P lending, equity crowdfunding has never been officially recognized in China. It provides an example of 'much talk but little action'. Several years ago, the regulator issued a consultation paper on equity crowdfunding, but it did not progress to a formal rule. During the recent reform of the Chinese securities law, although there was a provision for equity crowdfunding in previous drafts, it was dropped in the final bill. The calculus of choice for China over different forms of crowdfunding is complicated, and regulation is one of the main factors contributing to it.

The central bank (sovereign) digital currency has recently been a topical issue, and China appears to be at the international front in this sector. The Chinese central bank has been developing its digital currency for years and has started to conduct pilot programmes in several cities (this is functionally similar to the regulatory sandbox approach in other jurisdictions). It remains to be seen how the digital currency will finally look like and how the regulatory regime should be set up to respond to the potential risks. One thing is certain, however, in that the central bank digital currency will have significant impacts on the financial system and pose challenges to the existing regulatory regime.

Although different sectors of the Fintech market have different features and issues, there are some common threads. First and foremost, the regulatory goal is to achieve two main objectives, namely facilitating financial innovation and market development on the one hand, while ensuring risk control and investor protection on the other. These two objectives may usually be consistent with each other, but in some circumstances, they may be diametrically opposed. Hence, the regulatory task is to strike a balance between the two regulatory objectives.

Second, the regulatory balance is a delicate one and needs to be adjusted according to local conditions. As such, the point of balance is static, but dynamic, which means that it is necessary to review and reform the regulatory regime when the market situation evolves. It should also be noted that the importance of local considerations does not mean that it is

CONCLUSION 289

meaningless for jurisdictions to learn from each other. Different jurisdictions may face the same problems and it is always useful to look at them from a comparative perspective. The point is that foreign experiences should not be taken at face value but should rather be considered in light of local conditions.

Third, the regulatory regime for the Fintech markets is a work-in-progress, which is not surprising given the fast-changing pace of the underlying Fintech markets. In China, this is also generally in line with the gradualist approach that China has taken towards its economic reform. Indeed, the current regulatory regimes for most Fintech sectors have evolved in an accretive way in response to problems without any real focus on the overall mission in the long run. As a result, the relevant rules are scattered around many different laws and regulations, which makes the regime very complex with many internal conflicts. Hence, it is advisable to streamline the regulation to reduce discrepancy and improve coherence. At a more fundamental level, given the novel and disruptive nature of Fintech, it is important to consider whether we can still use the traditional regulatory framework for Fintech or we need to think outside the box and introduce a new one specifically for Fintech.

Fourth, as with other areas of law, the efficacy of the Fintech regulation is a function of the substantive rules and enforcement strategies. For many Fintech sectors in China, such as mobile payment, there are multiple enforcement agencies, which has caused confusion and inconsistency in practice. This is essentially an issue of how to design an efficient institutional structure of financial regulation. In fact, there has been a long-standing debate on it in the context of the traditional financial system,[2] and many of the points there apply almost equally to Fintech regulation. For various reasons, such as interest group politics of the regulators, it can be practically difficult to unify the enforcement agency, but it is something worth trying. Importantly, apart from public enforcement which is mainly initiated by the regulators, private enforcement in the form of court litigation should also be strengthened.[3]

Last but not least, the development and regulation of China's Fintech markets have been heavily influenced by the government's policies. As

---

[2] Robin Hui Huang and Dirk Schoenmaker (eds), *Institutional Structure of Financial Regulation: Fundamental Theories and International Experiences* (Routledge, 2015).

[3] For a more detailed discussion of enforcement strategies, see Robin Hui Huang and Nicholas Howson (eds), *Enforcement of Corporate and Securities Law: China and the World* (Cambridge University Press, 2017).

a transition economy, China still makes strong governmental intervention in the market through policies, and thus commentators have attached the label 'policy market' to many submarkets, including the securities market. While the 'policy market' label is not unique to China's Fintech market, its influence seems to be particularly heavy for several reasons. Fintech is a novel thing and there is no mature, ready-made regulatory pattern anywhere for China to follow. Also, China has every incentive to stimulate and support the Fintech market through policies, given the importance of Fintech for China to upgrading its financial system and the economy at large. The incentive can only become stronger in the current background of the United States–China trade war and the possible decoupling of their economies.

However, policy intervention may be a double-edged sword. Indeed, the rise and fall of China's P2P lending market can be in large part attributed to the precarious policies from the governments at both central and local levels. Regardless of the above, China has recently released a Fintech Development Plan (2019–2021) in August 2019, outlining its development goals and supportive measures.[4] It remains to be seen where the policy document will eventually lead China's Fintech market but let's hope for the best.

---

[4] People's Bank of China, 'The Development Program of FinTech (2019–2021)', August 2019, www.nifa.org.cn/nifaen/2955875/2955895/2985405/2019121820304117109.pdf.

INDEX

Airswap, 85
Alder, Ashley, 113–14
Alipay, 141, 143–4, 145–6, 172, 180–1, 216
Allcoin, 61
Altius Management, 89–90
AML. *See* money laundering and anti-money laundering
Angelcrunch, 263
Antsdaq, 266
Anxindai, 22
Apple Pay, 142, 168
asset management business, 234–6, 238. *See also* investment advisors and consultants
Australia
initial coin offerings, 77–80
robo-advisors, 251
Australian Securities & Investment Commission (ASIC), 77–80
automated investment services. *See* robo-advisors

Baidu, 181, 216
Bank for International Settlements (BIS), 131
Bank of England, 269, 274
banking system. *See* Chinese banking system
Beijing Local Financial Supervision and Administration, 11–13
Betterment, 222, 224, 251
big data, 184
Bitcoin
nature of, 100–1, 102, 112, 274
price volatility, 104, 274
regulation, 113, 276–7

security and verification, 274–6
supply and generation, 54, 66, 101, 275
blockchain, 55–6, 63, 64, 98–9, 100–1, 274–6
blockchain information services, 276–7
ByteDance, 216

Cambridge Analytica, 186
Canada
cybersecurity breaches, 107
digital currency, 273
initial coin offerings, 75–7
CBIRC. *See* China Banking and Insurance Regulatory Commission
CBRC. *See* China Banking Regulatory Commission
Centra, 73
central bank digital currency. *See* sovereign digital currency
CFT. *See* terrorism, combatting financing of
CFTC (Commodity Futures Trading Commission, US), 73–5, 127
China Banking and Insurance Regulatory Commission (CBIRC), 8, 9, 232, 235, 282–3
China Banking Regulatory Commission (CBRC), 8, 9, 14, 32–4, 57–8
online lending guidelines, 25, 27, 29
China Construction Bank, 271
China Insurance Regulatory Commission (CIRC), 8, 9
China Securities Regulatory Commission (CSRC)
corporate bond development, 19

291

INDEX

CSRC (cont.)
  regulation of
    equity crowdfunding, 259, 261,
      263, 266
    securities investment consultancy
      and advisory, 230, 232, 233,
      235, 237–8, 243, 249
    responsibilities and powers, 8, 9, 33,
      242–3
Chinese banking system
  custodian services, 31–2
  inefficiency of, 18–19
  interest rates, 16–17
Commodity Futures Trading
    Commission, US (CFTC),
    73–5, 127
Consumer Financial Protection
    Bureau, US (CFPB), 40,
    161
corporate bonds, 19
Creditease, 15, 23
crowdfunding, 93. *See also* equity
    crowdfunding; online P2P
    lending
cryptoassets, 97–136
  benefits, 109–11
  initial coin offerings. *See* initial coin
    offerings
  nature of, 100–4
  overview, 3–5, 97
  regulation in Hong Kong, 111–36
    AML and CFT standards, 128–9
    commercial importance of, 124
    derivatives, 113
    fund distributors, 116–17, 131–2
    initial coin offerings. *See under*
      initial coin offerings
    investor protection, 124–7
    Mainland China, compared,
      122–4
    overview, 4–5, 97–8, 112–14
    platform operators, 117–21
    portfolio managers, 114–16, 131–2
    regulatory sandbox, 84–5, 117–20,
      127–8, 132–3
    remaining concerns, 129–35
  regulatory approach in China, 4,
    122–4

risks, 104–9
types of, 99
use of term, 98–100, 268–9
Cryptoassets Taskforce, UK, 109
cryptocurrency, use of term, 54–5, 103,
    268–9. *See also* cryptoassets
    initial coin offerings;
    sovereign digital currency
cryptojacking, 107
CSRC. *See* China Securities Regulatory
    Commission
Cyberspace Administration of
    China, 200

DAO Report, 70–3
DAO, The, 70, 79
data controllers, 195–6
data privacy in mobile payment,
    178–221
  consumer approach to, 144
  overview and conclusions, 5–6,
    220–1, 287–8
  privacy risks, 180–6
    data harvesting, 184
    data profiling, 184–6
  regulation in China, 186–201
    adoption of current regime,
      189–92
    concept of personal information,
      193–4
    enforcement, 200–1
    entities responsible, 195–6
    fundamental principles, 157–9,
      196–9
    merits, 210–11
    overview, 5–6
    pre-2016 approach, 187–8
    problems and recommendations,
      212–20
      consent and disclosure
        requirements, 212–14
      data minimisation, 214–15
      public and private enforcement,
        216–20
      purpose limitation, 214
      unification of law, 215
      unified enforcement agency,
        215–16

INDEX

regulation in other jurisdictions
  European Union, 204–7
  generally, 209–10
  Hong Kong, 208–9
  Singapore, 207–8
  United Kingdom, 164–5
  United States, 161–2, 175, 196, 201–4
data processors, 195–6
DC/EP. *See* Digital Currency Electronic Payment project
Demohour, 258
Dian Ming Shi Jian, 258
digital currency. *See* cryptoassets; cryptocurrency; Digital Currency Electronic Payment project; initial coin offerings; sovereign digital currency
Digital Currency Electronic Payment project (DC/EP), 268–85
  Bitcoin, compared, 274–7, 280–1
  development progress, 269–71
  financial inclusion, 282–3
  Libra, compared, 277–81
  major characteristics, 271–3
  overview and conclusions, 7, 256, 257, 288
  regulatory issues, 281–5
  terminology and definitions, 268–9
distributed ledger technology (DLT), 98–9. *See also* blockchain

equity crowdfunding, 257–68
  categories, 257–8
  Feidu v. Nuomiduo case, 263–5
  importance, 268
  market size, 266
  Meiwei Media case, 262–3
  origins, 258
  overview and conclusions, 7, 257, 288
  private offerings, 260–3, 266–8
  public offerings, 258–60, 266, 267–8
  regulatory framework
    China, 33, 93–4, 258–60
    Hong Kong, 41, 93
Ethereum, 66, 88–9, 126–7

European Central Bank, 101
European Commission, 137
European Parliament, 149
European Securities and Markets Authority (ESMA), 85–6
European Union
  data privacy, 201–4
  initial coin offerings, 85–6, 87
  robo-advisors, 251
exchange tokens, 99

Facebook, 186, 278
Fair Information Practices (FIPs), 196, 207
FCA. *See* Financial Conduct Authority, UK
Federal Deposit Insurance Corporation (FDIC), 160, 170
Federal Trade Commission, US (FTC), 186, 202–3
Feidu v. Nuomiduo, 263–5
Financial Action Task Force (FATF), 128–9
Financial Conduct Authority, UK (FCA), 38–9, 85–6
Financial Crimes Enforcement Network, US (FinCEN), 101–2, 103, 159, 161
Financial Stability Board (FSB), 108–9, 126, 128
Fintech
  future regulation, 288–90
  importance to China, 286
  regulatory balance, 2, 283–9
  use of term, 1, 2, 7
France, statement on Libra, 278–9
FSB. *See* Financial Stability Board
FTC. *See* Federal Trade Commission, US
fund distributors, 116–17, 131–2
Fundingcircle, 20

G7, research paper on Libra, 279
Germany
  robo-advisors, 251
  statement on Libra, 278–9
governmental regulators, 8–9
Guangdong, 21, 26, 147

Guiding Opinions on Promoting the Healthy Development of Internet Finance (Guiding Opinions), 8–9

Hong Kong
  crowdfunding, 41, 93, 259
  cryptoassets, 111–36
    AML and CFT standards, 128–9
    commercial importance of, 124
    derivatives, 113
    fund distributors, 116–17, 131–2
    improvements in new regime, 125–9
    initial coin offerings, 84–5
    investor protection, 124–7, 133–5
    Mainland China, compared, 122–4
    overview, 4–5, 112–14
    platform operators, 117–21
    portfolio managers, 114–16, 131–2
    regulatory sandbox, 84–5, 117–20, 127–8, 132–3
    remaining concerns, 129–35
  Lehman Brothers Minibond saga, 105
  mobile payment, 167–9, 208–9
  online lending, 40–3
  regulatory structure, 130–1
  robo-advisors, 247, 249, 251, 254
Hong Kong Monetary Authority (HKMA), 112, 168–9
Hong Kong Steering Group on Financial Technologies, 1
Howey test, 70–2, 76–7, 78–9, 94, 126–7, 277
Hunan, 48

initial coin offerings (ICOs), 52–96
  benefits, 62–4, 67–8, 111
  introduction of, 52
  market size, 52, 56
  overview and conclusions, 3–4, 95–6, 287
  regulation in China
    2017 ban, 58–62, 67–8
    background, 56–7
    overview, 4

    pre-2017 ban, 57–8
    suggested reform, 87–94
  regulation in other jurisdictions
    Australia, 77–80
    Canada, 75–7
    European Union, 85–6, 87
    generally, 68–9, 87
    Hong Kong, 84–5
    Singapore, 81–4
    United Kingdom, 85–7
    United States, 69–75
  risks, 56, 64–7
Inland Revenue Service (US) (IRS), 69–70
interest rates, 16–17
International Monetary Fund (IMF), 109, 128, 285
International Organization of Securities Commissions (IOSCO), 21, 104, 279
Internet Finance, use of term, 1
internet, use of, 16
investment advisors and consultants
  entry threshold, 236–7, 241–2, 243
  fiduciary duties, 239–40, 242, 246–7
  information disclosure duties, 240–1, 248
  KYC process, 247
  permitted activities, 229, 234–5, 238, 244–5
  regulatory overview, 230–3

Japan
  cybersecurity breaches, 107
  online lending, 37
JD.com, 144, 243
Jenkins, Patrick, 43–4
Jingdong Dongjia, 266, 267

Kickstarter, 89–90
KYC (know-your-client), 120, 247, 254

LedgerX, 74
Lehman Brothers Minibond saga, 105
Lending Club, 20, 39, 41, 43
Libra, 277–80
Liu Mingkang, 37

local regulators, 11–13, 25–6, 34–6, 48–50
Luxembourg House of Financial Technology, 54

Ma, Jack, 286
MAS. *See* Monetary Authority of Singapore
McKinsey Corporate Banking, 36–7
Meiwei Media, 262–3
Menon, Ravi, 82–3
Ministry of Industry and Information Technology (MIIT), 34, 200
Ministry of Public Security, 34
mobile payment, 137–77
  benefits, 138, 178
  data privacy. *See* data privacy in mobile payment
  market size, 137, 139–40, 143–6, 179–80
  meaning of term, 137–8
  online banking distinguished, 138
  overview and conclusions, 5–6, 176–7, 287–8
  regulation in China, 151–9
    consumer protection, 157–9
    improvement suggestions, 171–5
    licensing scheme, 152–3
    management of client reserves, 153–6
    money laudering and terrorism financing, 156–7
    regulatory environment, 151–2
    strengths and weaknesses, 169–71
  regulation in other jurisdictions
    generally, 169–70
    Hong Kong, 167–9
    Singapore, 165–7, 171, 174
    United Kingdom, 162–5, 174
    United States, 159–62, 174
  risks, 146–51
    data security, 149–50
    mistakes and misconduct, 150–1
    money laundering and terrorist financing, 148
    overview, 178–9
    unauthorized transactions, 146–8
  typology, 140–2

Monetary Authority of Singapore (MAS), 81, 82–3, 134–5, 165–7
money laundering and anti-money laundering (AML)
  cryptoassets, 108, 128–9
  mobile payment, 148–9, 156–7, 160–1, 163–4, 174–5
MoneySQ.com, 42–3

Nakamoto, Satoshi, 54
National Internet Finance Association of China (NIFAC), 9–11, 28–9, 34
Near Field Communications (NFC), 141–2, 149
NEO (Antshares), 68, 90–1
NetsUnion, 154
network operators, 195
New Generation of AI Development Plan, 223, 225
NIFAC. *See* National Internet Finance Association of China

online P2P lending, 14–51
  business models, 21–3
    client segregated account model, 22
    guaranteed return model, 22–3, 24
    notary model, 39
    originate-to-distribute model, 23, 24
    platform lender model, 23, 24
  definitions, 21, 23–4
  interest rates, 17
  market in China
    dispersed nature, 20
    entrepreneurial focus, 20–1
    geographical distribution, 20–1
    growth, 15–19, 29–30
  market worldwide, 14
  overview and conclusions, 2–3, 50–1, 286–7
  problematic platforms, 30, 31, 32, 43–4, 48–9
  regulation in China, 23–51
    'one plus three' framework, 23, 30

online P2P lending (cont.)
central and local regulators,
32–6, 48–9
comparative perspectives, 36–46
custodian requirement, 27, 31–2
implications of, 30–2
information disclosure, 27–9
lending limits, 26–7, 44–6
registration, 25–6
scope of business, 24
Special Rectification Campaign,
46–50
suitability of lenders, 26
regulation in other jurisdictions
Hong Kong, 40–3
United Kingdom, 37–9, 46
United States, 39–40, 43–4

Paipaidai, 22
PayMe, 103
Payment Systems Regulator (PSR), 162
PBOC. *See* People's Bank of China
peer-to-peer lending. *See* online P2P
lending
People's Bank of China (PBOC)
digital currency. *See* Digital
Currency Electronic
Payment project
influence over commercial banks,
16–17
regulatory activities
generally, 8–9, 33, 34
initial coin offerings, 57, 58–60,
61, 123
mobile payment, 151–8, 180, 216
securities investment consultancy
and advisory, 232, 235
Ping an Insurance, 144, 243
Pingan Puhui, 266
Pooler, Judge Teresa Mary, 69
portfolio managers, 114–16,
131–2
Prosper, 20, 39, 41
Public Security Bureau, 200

qualified investors, 235
quick response code (QR code),
142, 143

regional governments. *See* local
regulators
regulatory framework
governmental regulators, 8–9
local regulators, 11–13, 25–6, 34–6,
48–50
self-regulatory organizations,
9–11, 34
regulatory sandboxes
China, 95–6
Hong Kong, 84–5, 117–20, 127–8,
132–3
Singapore, 82–3, 127–8, 134–5
United Kingdom, 86–7, 127–8
robo-advisors, 222–56
benefits, 222–3, 228
categories of, 226–7
characteristics of service users,
227
definitions, 222, 230
development and size of market,
224–5, 228, 251
extent of use, 243–4
human interaction with, 226
investment and management
process, 225–6
legal risks, 244
overview and conclusions, 6–7,
256, 288
regulatory framework, 230–56
enforcement and penalties, 242–3
entry threshold, 236–7, 241–2,
243–4, 249–50
fiduciary duties, 239–40, 242,
246–7, 253–4
information disclosure duties,
240–1, 242, 248–9, 254–6
KYC process, 247, 254
overview, 230–6
permitted activities, 237–8, 243,
244–6, 250–3
reform suggestions, 249–90
rules and regulations
2017 Asset Management
Guidance, 246
2018 Asset Management
Guiding Opinions, 234–6,
237–8, 239–40, 241

INDEX

297

2019 Notice of Standards, 231, 240, 247, 248
2020 Investment Advisor Provisions, 238, 239, 240–1, 242, 248
2020 Stockpicking Software Provisions, 233–4, 237, 239, 240, 241
fiduciary duties, 246–7
risks and concerns, 223, 229

SAC. *See* Securities Association of China
SEC v W. J. Howey Co. See Howey test
Securities and Exchange Commission, US (SEC), 39–40, 70–3, 100, 126–7, 230, 254–5
Securities and Futures Commission, Hong Kong (SFC)
crowdfunding, 41
cryptoassets. *See under* cryptoassets
initial coin offerings, 84–5
robo-advisors, 254
Securities Association of China (SAC)
equity crowdfunding, 261, 262
robo-advisors, 232, 240–1, 243
2019 Notice of Standards, 231, 240, 247, 248
securities investment advisors. *See* investment advisors and consultants
security tokens, 99
self-regulatory organizations, 9–11, 34. *See also* National Internet Finance Association of China; Securities Association of China
SFC. *See* Securities and Futures Commission, Hong Kong
Shenzen, 49, 270
Simple Token, 85
Singapore
cryptoassets, 128, 134–5
equity crowdfunding, 259
initial coin offerings, 81–4, 124, 134
mobile payment, 165–7, 171, 174, 207–8

regulatory sandbox, 82–3, 127–8, 134–5
robo-advisory market, 251
SMS mobile payments, 140
sovereign digital currency, 269, 273–4. *See also* Digital Currency Electronic Payment project
Standing Committee of the National People's Congress (NPCSC), 260
State Administration of Foreign Exchange (SAFE), 232, 235
State Internet Information Office, 34
Stellar Development Foundation, 54
stockpicking software, 233–4, 237
Sweden, digital currency, 273

Tabao, 262
Taiwan, online lending, 37
target advertising, 186, 210, 214
Target Corporation, 185
Tenpay, 141, 143, 144, 172. *See also* WeChat Pay
terrorism, combatting financing of (CFT), 108, 128–9, 148–9, 160–1, 163–4
Tian Shi Hui, 263
Tian Shi Jie, 263
token sales. *See* initial coin offerings
TokenCapital, 61
tokenisation, 110

UnionPay, 154
United Kingdom
digital currency, 273–4
equity crowdfunding, 258, 259
initial coin offerings, 85–7
mobile payment, 162–5, 174
National Risk Assessment, 108
online lending, 15, 20, 21, 37–9, 46
regulatory sandbox, 86–7, 127–8
robo-advisors, 251
United States
digital currency custody services, 277
equity crowdfunding, 259
Fedcoin, 273
initial coin offerings, 69–75, 277
Libra digital currency, 278

298 INDEX

United States (cont.)
    mobile payment, 159–62, 174, 201–4
    nature of cryptoassets, 100
    online lending, 15, 20, 21,
        39–40, 43–4
    robo-advisors, 227, 251, 253, 254–5
        investment advice and consulting,
            223, 244–5, 247, 250–1, 254
utility tokens, 99

virtual asset trading platforms (VATP),
    119–21
virtual assets. *See* cryptoassets
virtual currency. *See* cryptoassets;
    cryptocurrency; Digital
    Currency Electronic
    Payment project; initial coin
    offerings; sovereign digital
    currency

Wealthfront, 224, 251
WeChat Pay, 143, 180. *See also*
    Tenpay
Willett, J. R., 52
window guidance, 17
Wireless Application Protocol (WAP),
    140–1, 149

Zhongtou 8, 266
Zopa, 15, 20, 37–8, 40

CPSIA information can be obtained
at www.ICGtesting.com
Printed in the USA
LVHW080921030821
694401LV00004B/327